ALTERNATIVE DISPUTE RESOLUTION IN BUSINESS

Lucille M. Ponte

Bentley College

Thomas D. Cavenagh

North Central College

WEST **West Educational Publishing Company**

an International Thomson Publishing company I(T)P®

Cincinnati • Albany • Boston • Detroit • Johannesburg • London • Madrid • Melbourne • Mexico City
New York • Pacific Grove • San Francisco • Scottsdale • Singapore • Tokyo • Toronto

Publishing Team Director: Jack W. Calhoun
Senior Acquisitions Editor: Rob Dewey
Acquisitions Editor: Scott D. Person
Developmental Editor: Susanna C. Smart
Production Editors: Amy C. Hanson, Sandra Gangelhoff
Media Production Editor: Mary Hufford
Production House: Litten Editing and Production
Marketing Manager: Michael Worls
Technology Coordinator: Kurt Gerdenich
Manufacturing Coordinator: Georgina Calderon
Cover Design: Sanger and Eby Design
Cover Illustration: M. C. Escher "Doric Columns" ©1998 Cordon Art B. V. —
Baarn—Hollan. All rights reserved.

ISBN: 0-324-00071-5

2 3 4 5 6 7 8 9 D1 6 5 4 3 2 1 0 9 8

Printed in the United States of America

Library of Congress Cataloging-in-Publication Data
Ponte, Lucille M., 1958–
    Alternative dispute resolution in business / Lucille M. Ponte,
    Thomas D. Cavenagh.
        p.   cm.
    Includes bibliographical references and index.
    ISBN 0-324-00071-5
    1. Dispute resolution (Law)—United States.   2. Arbitration and award—
United States.   I. Cavenagh, Thomas D.   II. Title.
KF9084.P66   1998
347.73'9—dc21   98–20396
                                                                CIP

International Thomson Publishing
West Educational Publishing is an ITP Company.
The ITP trademark is used under license.

To the two most important teachers in my life,
my parents, Alice S. and Joseph L. Ponte.

Lucille

For those who challenge and inspire me—
my family, my friends, my colleagues, and my students.

Tom

CONTENTS

Preface   XI

PART I   **INTRODUCTION**   1

1   LITIGATION AND DISPUTE RESOLUTION   3

An Overview of Major Civil Litigation Systems   4

The Stages of the Lawsuit and the Use of ADR   6

The Impact of Litigation on Business   8

Legal Reforms   22

2   THE ADR RESPONSE TO RESOLVING BUSINESS DISPUTES   27

Introduction to ADR   28

The Major Alternative Dispute Resolution Processes   29
Party-Driven Processes   29 / Adjudicative Processes   30

The Advantages of Alternative Dispute Resolution   31
*Timeliness   31 / Cost   31 / Productive Outcomes   32 / Privacy
32 / Flexibility   33 / Internationalization   33*

The Disadvantages of Alternative Dispute Resolution   34
Procedural Concerns   34 / Public Policy Issues   42 / Enforcement Concerns 50

PART II   **ADR SETTLEMENT MECHANISMS**   59

3   NEGOTIATION   61

Defining Negotiation   62

Negotiation Models   63

Effect of Representation in Negotiation   65

Relationship of Negotiation to the Legal Process   66

Negotiation Practice: A Skills-Oriented Overview   70

Negotiating with Uncooperative Parties   74

Evaluating the Outcome   76

Negotiation Ethics   77

International and Cross-Cultural Negotiation   83

ADR Trends in Negotiation   84

$\overline{\underline{4}}$ **MEDIATION**   89

The Historical Development of Mediation   90

Introduction to the Mediation Process   93
Advantages of Mediation   93 / Disadvantages of Mediation   95

Forms of Mediation   96

Overview of the Mediation Process   97

Selecting Cases Appropriate for Mediation   101

Selection of the Mediator   106

Roles and Ethics of the Mediator   110

Mandatory Mediation   117

$\overline{\underline{5}}$ **HYBRID SETTLEMENT PROCESSES: THE SUMMARY JURY TRIAL
AND MINITRIAL**   125

Development of the Summary Jury Trial (SJT)   126

Components of the SJT   127
*Screening Cases for the SJT   127 / Pre-SJT Conference   134 / Selection of SJT Jurors   134 / The
SJT Hearing   134 / Settlement Talks   136*

Advantages of the SJT   136
*Savings in Time and Costs   136 / Confidentiality of SJT Proceedings and Documents   137 / Respect
for the Jury Process   141 / Empowerment of Businesspeople to Resolve Conflicts   141 /
Psychological Benefits   141*

Disadvantages of the SJT   141
*Mixed Results on SJT Time and Cost Benefits   141 / Predictive Value of the SJT   142 / Lack of
Precedential Value   142 / Constitutional Concerns   142*

Overview of the Minitrial   143

Components of the Minitrial   143
*Initiation of Procedure   144 / Limited Discovery   144 / Selection of a Neutral Advisor   144 /
Information Exchange or "Best Case" Presentations   145 / Settlement Discussions with the Neutral
Advisor   145*

Advantages of the Minitrial   147
*Party Control over the Process   147 / Maintenance of Business Relationships   148 / Expertise of the
Neutral Advisor   148*

Disadvantages of the Minitrial   148
*Credibility of Witnesses   149 / Need for Court's Legal Interpretation   149 / Unequal Bargaining
Power Between the Disputants   149*

PART III   **ADR ADJUDICATORY MECHANISMS**   **155**

6   INTRODUCTION TO COMMERCIAL ARBITRATION   157

Defining Arbitration   157
The Historical Development of Arbitration   158

Main Aspects of Voluntary Arbitration   161
Determining Procedures   161 / Agreement to Arbitrate   162 / Selection of an Arbitrator or Arbitral Panel   172 / Pre-Hearing Preparation   177 / The Arbitration Hearing   177 / The Arbitration or Arbitral Award   178 / Post-Award Actions   179

Advantages of Voluntary Arbitration   183

Disadvantages of Voluntary Arbitration   186

Overview of Court-Annexed Arbitration   188

7   LABOR AND EMPLOYMENT ARBITRATION   199

Overview of Labor and Employment Arbitration   200
Labor Arbitration   200 / Employment Arbitration   201

Interest and Grievance Arbitration   212

Overview of Interest Arbitration   213

Overview of Grievance or Rights Arbitration   218

8   INTERNATIONAL COMMERCIAL ARBITRATION   233

National Litigation Versus Arbitration of International Commercial Disputes   234
Concerns about Neutrality in International Disputes   234 / Dealing with Multiple Lawsuits in Various Countries   240 / Enforceability of International Arbitration Clauses and Awards   244

Distinctions Between Domestic and International Commercial Arbitration   253

9   PRIVATE JUDGING   265

An Overview of Private Judging   266

Contract Private Judges   267

Court-Supervised Private Judging   270
Temporary Judges   270

Reference-Mandated Judging   270
Referees or Special Masters   270 / General or Special References   271

Private Judging Versus Commercial Arbitration   275

Constitutional Concerns about Private Judging   280
Due Process   280 / Equal Protection   284 / The First Amendment   289

PART IV   **CREATING THE ADR ENVIRONMENT**   **293**

10   **BUSINESS DISPUTE RESOLUTION SYSTEMS**   **295**

   An Overview of Business Dispute Resolution Systems   296

   Internal Dispute Resolution Policies   298

   External Dispute Resolution Policies   310
   The Role of Outside Counsel   310 / The Role of the Insurer   311 / The Role of Customers   311

   Appendix 10A: Predispute Contract Clauses from the American Arbitration Association   318
   Predispute Contract Clauses Calling for Negotiation   318 / Predispute Contract Clauses Calling for Mediation   319 / Predispute Contract Clauses Calling for Arbitration   319 / Clauses Providing Details Related to Arbitration   319 / Predispute Contract Clause Calling for Final Offer Arbitration   321 / Predispute Contract Clause Calling for Arbitration Within Monetary Limits   321 / Predispute Contract Clause Calling for a Dispute Review Board   321 / Predispute Contract Clause Calling for a Minitrial   321 / Predispute Contract Clause Calling for Mediation-Arbitration   321 / Clauses for Use in International Disputes   322

11   **THE FUTURE OF BUSINESS ADR**   **323**

   Ethical Concerns Arising from the Use of ADR   324

   Institutionalizing Dispute Resolution: Future Trends in ADR   329

   Future Trends in Business ADR   333

   Appendix 11A: Model Standards of Conduct for Mediators   338
   Introductory Note   339 / Preface   339

   Appendix 11B: The Code of Ethics for Arbitrators in Commercial Disputes   344
   Preamble   344 / Canon I   345 / Canon II   346 / Canon III   348 / Canon IV   348 / Canon V   349 / Canon VI   350 / Canon VII   351

APPENDICES

A   UNIFORM ARBITRATION ACT   355
B   THE UNITED STATES ARBITRATION ACT 9 U.S.C. 1-16   363
C   THE CONVENTION ON THE RECOGNITION AND ENFORCEMENT OF FOREIGN ARBITRAL AWARDS 9 U.S.C. 201-208   371
D   AMERICAN ARBITRATION ASSOCIATION COMMERCIAL ARBITRATION RULES   375
E   AMERICAN ARBITRATION ASSOCIATION COMMERCIAL MEDIATION RULES   389

F   AMERICAN ARBITRATION ASSOCIATION RULES FOR THE RESOLUTION OF EMPLOYMENT DISPUTES   393

G   AMERICAN ARBITRATIONN ASSOCIATION INTERNATIONAL ARBITRATION RULES   411

H   CPR INSTITUTE FOR DISPUTE RESOLUTION CORPORATE POLICY STATEMENT ON ALTERNATIVES TO LITIGATION   425

I   CPR LAW FIRM POLICY STATEMENT ON ALTERNATIVES TO LITIGATION   427

PREFACE

There are over 100 colleges and universities that currently list an Alternative Dispute Resolution (ADR) course in their undergraduate catalogs. Graduate schools now are introducing ADR courses in their MBA programs and establishing Master's and specialized certificate programs in ADR. Law schools also are adopting ADR courses for their students. Despite the growth in this field, most textbooks are aimed primarily at practicing lawyers, not business students or even law students.

Alternative Dispute Resolution in Business introduces business students to the important conflict management mechanisms of alternative dispute resolution. Students can explore and analyze established and cutting-edge ADR techniques for dealing with domestic and international business disputes, such as negotiation, mediation, arbitration, summary jury trials, minitrials, and private judging.

Today, about 90 percent of all cases filed are settled without a trial. This number shows that most disputants are resolving their conflicts outside of the formal litigation process, using some method of alternative dispute resolution. ADR provides an extensive menu of options to handle commercial conflicts without resorting to traditional litigation. In an effort to stay competitive in a global marketplace, businesspeople need to become more aware of the alternatives to costly and time-consuming litigation.

Alternative dispute resolution methods put more control over dispute resolution into the hands of businesspersons and emphasizes their empowerment and the preservation of business relationships instead of court mandates and shattered business ties. The premise of this textbook is that ADR works best in some cases, because litigation does not work well in all cases. This approach does not advocate that the trial process is inferior to ADR, but that businesspersons who become familiar with the various alternatives to litigation will be better able to decide whether ADR or litigation will help them to best achieve their desired results.

Alternative Dispute Resolution in Business opens the door to ADR for future managers and businesspersons, providing students with a realistic look at options to trial that can help maintain good business-to-business, community, and international relations. The text begins by introducing dispute resolution, litigation, and the ADR response in Part I. It next covers the major ADR settlement techniques of negotiation, mediation, and the summary jury trial in Part II. Part III covers ADR adjudicatory mechanisms, including labor and employment, and international, arbitration, and private judging. Finally, business dispute resolution systems and the future of business ADR are discussed in Part IV.

FEATURES OF THE TEXT

Each chapter includes specific features to aid student understanding of the field of alternative dispute resolution.

- **Chapter Highlights.** Every chapter includes an overview section with a list of the main learning objectives for each chapter.
- **Relevant Court Decisions.** To help illustrate ADR principles and concepts, each chapter offers several recent and seminal court opinions for student review. Discussion questions follow each case to help generate student analysis and classroom discussion of the court decision. A list of the cases cited in the text is listed alphabetically in a case index at the end of the text.
- **ADR in Action.** Each chapter contains a feature showing the practical use of ADR in a real world situation or business dispute. This component presents a mini-case study or news item on the ADR mechanism relevant to the chapter and its impact on resolving a major business dispute.
- **ADR Web Sites.** Applicable Web sites have been noted in chapter margins to aid on-line research and study.
- **Chapter Conclusion.** A brief summary of the main issues addressed in the chapter and some final perspectives on the chapter topic is provided at the end of each chapter.
- **Best Business Practices.** Following each Chapter Conclusion, this section provides timely tips on the use of ADR. *Best Business Practices* addresses the role of the businessperson in the ADR process and the major issues that businesspeople—or lawyers advising them—should consider when using the various ADR mechanisms.
- **Key Terms.** A list of important terms is included at the end of each chapter along with the page number where the term first appears, to help students locate these terms in the text.
- **Ethical and Legal Review.** To help reinforce chapter concepts, real and hypothetical ADR situations are provided at the end of each chapter. Real cases are followed by an appropriate case citation for further student research.
- **Sample Forms and Appendices.** When appropriate, sample forms have been provided in the text. Major statutes and relevant ADR policies and procedures are included at the end of the book for student reference and review.
- **Suggested Readings.** A brief list of additional readings on the relevant ADR topic is included for further student inquiry or research.

SUPPLEMENTAL MATERIALS

Instructor's Manual. An instructor's supplement provides chapter outlines, teaching tips, role-play examples, answers to chapter questions, and listings of useful videotapes.

West's Business Law Supplements

Ten Complementary Hours of WestLaw. West's computerized legal research gives instructors and students access to U.S. Code, federal regulations, and numerous special libraries.

COURT TV *Trial Stories.* In courtrooms across America, dramatic stories of people in conflict unfold every day. Since 1991, Court TV has covered hundreds of these cases, each one a balance of right and wrong, fact and fiction, truth and lies. Court TV's Trial Story series features highly relevant cases condensed into one-hour programs. Each Trial Story captures the whole story of a trial, including news footage, courtroom testimony and interviews with defendants, plaintiffs, witnesses, lawyers, jurors and judges. Each Trial Story video engages students while presenting important legal concepts.

CNN Legal Issues *Video Update.* You can update your coverage of legal issues, as well as spark lively classroom discussion and deeper understanding, by using the CNN Legal Issues Video Update. This video update is produced by Turner Learning, using the resources of CNN, the world's first 24-hour, all-news network.

ACKNOWLEDGMENTS

We would like to thank the following reviewers, whose ideas and insights have helped to shape the final product:

Richard D. Coffinberger
George Mason University

Lucy Katz
Fairfield University

Clay Hipp
Wake Forest University

Nancy Kubasek
Bowling Green State University

William McCarthy
Western Michigan University

Jack Raisner
St. Johns University

Ann Morales
University of Miami

Professor Ponte would like to acknowledge the research assistance of Margo E. K. Reder, JD, Adjunct Professor of Law and Research Associate, with the international arbitration chapter, and to thank Stephen D. Lichtenstein, JD, Chair and Associate Professor, Law Department, and H. Lee Schlorff, PhD, Vice President of Academic Affairs and Dean of Faculty, for funding support through the Summer Research Grant Program at Bentley College.

We would also like to thank our editors at West Educational Publishing: Rob Dewey, for his foresight and faith in our text on this emerging field; Susanna C. Smart, for her editorial insights on this project; and Amy C. Hanson, for her attention to the details of producing this book.

Finally, this textbook is an important tool for business students who want to know more about managing conflict in a competitive marketplace. We hope you find *Alternative Dispute Resolution in Business* to be useful and challenging as you further your understanding of the legal, ethical and practical issues of the use of ADR.

Lucille M. Ponte
Thomas D. Cavenagh

Part I

INTRODUCTION

Chapter 1: Litigation and Dispute Resolution

Chapter 2: The ADR Response to Resolving Business Disputes

Chapters 1 and 2 begin our discussion of the relationship between business and alternative dispute resolution. Chapter 1 describes and assesses the civil litigation system, the principle method of formally resolving business disputes, both in this country and abroad. Chapter 1 addresses the impact of the litigation system on business as well as several judicial and legislative options for mitigating some of the negative consequences of litigation for business. Chapter 2 describes the nature and sources of business disputes and summarizes some alternative dispute resolution mechanisms that may be used to resolve those disputes. This chapter also lays out the advantages and disadvantages of ADR for business dispute resolution purposes.

1

LITIGATION AND DISPUTE RESOLUTION

CHAPTER HIGHLIGHTS

In this chapter, you will read and learn about the following:

1. The major civil litigation systems of the world.
2. The stages of the lawsuit in the United States and the points at which it is appropriate to consider using ADR to resolve a dispute.
3. The ways in which civil litigation affects business.
4. Several judicial and legislative suggestions for reforming the system to reduce its adverse impact.

A variety of processes exist to resolve disputes arising in the course of commerce. Some of these processes, such as litigation, are familiar to most businesspersons. Others, like the minitrial or mediation, may be less well understood. This chapter lays the groundwork for our comprehensive treatment of alternative dispute resolution (ADR) by describing the impact on business of the process to which all others are an alternative—the civil lawsuit. When one makes a decision to use an ADR process, by default he or she is, in most cases, rejecting litigation. It is important to be aware of the costs of litigation and to acquire a comparative understanding of the systems used around the world before making a decision to use—or not use—ADR.

ADR is any formal or semiformal process (other than litigation) used to resolve a business dispute. The premise of this book is that ADR works best in some cases because litigation does not work well in all cases. The coverage throughout this text does not, however, suggest that the trial process is inferior in any general sense to alternative dispute resolution. This chapter presents an overview of major civil litigation systems and their impact on American business, and addresses judicial and legislative legal reforms intended to reduce that impact.

AN OVERVIEW OF MAJOR CIVIL LITIGATION SYSTEMS

Essentially two models of civil litigation are used throughout the world: the **adversarial, common law model** and the **inquisitorial, civil law model.** The adversarial system is used most prominently in the United States. It involves the introduction of evidence in a process governed by extensive procedural rules following which a jury renders a judgment on the basis of legal instructions given by a judge. The inquisitorial system is used in civil law nations, including Japan and the European Union (excluding England). It too considers evidence, but in different ways and to different ends.

One can draw distinctions between the adversarial and inquisitorial systems on any one of three bases. The first is the sources of law from which the systems draw their direction. The adversarial approach is normally encompassed within a common law system as it is in the United States. As such, it draws from many sources of legal regulation, including: constitutional law, treaties, state and federal statutes, municipal ordinances, administrative regulations, and precedential case law. These various sources of legal authority are interpreted and applied by judges at both the trial and appellate levels.

In inquisitorial jurisdictions such as Japan, which normally use civil law systems, all of the applicable law is drawn from statutes. These statutes attempt to distill all legal authority into an orderly and comprehensive code of law. As a result, while adversarial common law systems develop over time as judges interpret and apply the various authorities to which they are subject, inquisitorial civil law is contemporaneous, with statutes developed on an "as needed" basis. In addition, while judges in common law countries have considerable power, inasmuch as they not only apply the law but develop it by interpreting it, civil law countries relegate virtually all legal authority to the legislative branch. Judges in civil law countries simply apply the law as laid down in the code.

The second basis for distinction is the processes used to resolve conflict. Adversarial law countries rely heavily on the trial because the various sources of law have a common nexus in the judge, who applies the laws to individual litigants. Conversely, civil law countries use a wide variety of processes including many of the negotiated processes described later in this text. Because the law is clear, the processes concentrate less effort on applying the law than on resolving the difficulty between the parties. Civil law countries have other procedural differences as well. For example, while the adversarial system, particularly in the United States,

http://

For a comparison of the inquisitorial and adversarial systems see: http://www. ozemail.com.au/ ~dtebbutt/oj/ ojeurope3.html makes extensive use of pretrial discovery (the exchange of information related to the case), civil law systems permit little, if any, discovery. Curtailing discovery reduces the time and expense of the trial, but it may also diminish the accuracy of the result.

The third basis for distinction is the outcomes available under each system. Common law countries normally use juries to resolve legal disputes; some, like the United States, make access to a jury an almost absolute right. However, civil law countries normally do not provide a jury trial, preferring instead to allow a judge to act within the code to solve a dispute. In common law countries, juries may award punitive damages and a fairly wide range of compensatory damages such as for pain and suffering. In civil law systems damages are much more limited, normally excluding punitive damages and very significantly restricting noneconomic compensatory damages.

Each system has its strengths and weaknesses. The common law system tends to be less consistent, more costly, and more acrimonious than the civil law system because of the multiple sources of legal authority at both the state and federal levels and the difficulty of interpreting and applying them. It does, however, provide

FIGURE 1.1   Summary Comparisons of Major Civil Litigation Systems

Category	United States	European Union	Japan
Nature of system	Win-lose; adversarial	Win-win; primarily inquisitorial	Win-win; primarily inquisitorial
Types of actions	Individual plaintiffs; class actions	Individual plaintiffs; no class actions	Individual plaintiffs; no class actions
Discovery process	Highly detailed process; 80% of legal fees	Civil law—not allowed; common law— very limited	Not allowed
Legal fee arrangements	Hourly rates; contingency fees— % of money recovered	Hourly rates; no contingency fees— loser pays other's legal fees	Commencing fees—up to 8% of attorney fees, court costs and damages, no contingency fees
Right to jury trial	Guaranteed in most civil cases	No guarantee	No guarantee
Damage awards	Usually determined by juries	Determined by judges	Determined by judges
Types of damages	Compensatory, including pain and suffering; punitive	Compensatory, with very limited pain and suffering; no punitive	Compensatory, with very limited pain and suffering; no punitive
Costs of tort system	Totals @ 2.5% of U.S. GNP; about 1.5 million per case	Totals @ 0.5% of EU GNP	Most costs confidential, yet damages seldom exceed 150,000 per case

a wider and therefore more complete range of remedies, a greater degree of flexibility to address the exigencies of a particular case, and the opportunity for plaintiffs to create new causes of action by successfully relying on the novel application of precedent and the broad legal dictates of the common law. The civil law system is relatively consistent, easily accessible, and comparatively expeditious and inexpensive. It does not, however, allow for meaningful variances between cases and parties, and it limits damages in ways that may leave significant gaps between harm done and recompense paid. Furthermore, some case types are simply excluded from consideration altogether. Both systems are costly and time-consuming. Although the American civil law system can be quite expensive, the civil law systems of Europe and Asia, though less costly, are not without many of the same shortcomings.

ADR IN ACTION

Religious Law Systems

Some countries rely on neither the common law system nor the civil law system. These countries exercise a third option, resembling the civil system of law but based on religious doctrine and practice. These **religious law systems** tend to be more monolithic and insular than standard civil law systems. Consider, for example, India. Its system of law is considered a nominally civil law system. Yet the country's law, particularly in the area of family law, is based significantly on Hindu teaching as codified in books of Hindu law called *Smitris*. This law is highly personal and is based on religious faith rather than on public consensus or judicial decision. Similarly, Muslim countries like Saudi Arabia apply Islamic law, called *Sharia,* which is drawn from the *Koran* and related sacred writings. Even some Western European countries weave religion into their law; consider, for example the ban on abortion present in Irish law, which is steeped in Catholic religious belief.

THE STAGES OF THE LAWSUIT AND THE USE OF ADR

The civil justice system in the United States is an adversarial, common law system in which a neutral party, normally a jury, decides both questions of law and fact to reach a conclusion regarding the claims made by the parties. Civil cases, those in which ADR is normally used, are very different from criminal cases. While a criminal trial requires a jury to determine guilt "beyond a reasonable doubt," the jury in a civil trial must determine liability based on a "preponderance of evidence." This means that the claims made by the plaintiff simply must be more likely true than not. It is, consequently, easier to prevail in a civil trial than in a criminal trial. Also, while the criminal case seeks to establish guilt, the civil case seeks to establish liability. Liability means finding that an error was made; guilt entails a finding of intentional culpability. While criminal cases typically end with the imposition of punishment, civil cases are generally resolved through the payment of damages. Jail is not an option for the civil judge or jury. Indeed, money is likely all that a civil tribunal can award. Those money damages may simply compensate a plaintiff or go beyond compensation to deter future conduct in the form of punitive damages. Finally, while the criminal trial is a public matter between the state, the "victim" of a crime, and a defendant, the civil trial is a private matter between two parties.

The American civil lawsuit consists of three stages: pretrial, trial, and appeal. Each of these three stages can entail considerable time and expense. The **pretrial stage** of the lawsuit begins with the preparation of formal documents commencing the lawsuit. After the parties have exchanged these documents and filed them with a court, **discovery** takes place. This is the point at which parties provide extensive information to each other in the form of witness statements and documents; this process can be quite lengthy. Indeed, discovery may account for the bulk of the time spent in litigation and as much as 80 percent of the cost. Finally, during the pretrial stage, additional documents (called motions) prepared as a result of the information gleaned from discovery might be filed by one party or the other seeking a final judgment prior to trial or a ruling on some aspect of the forthcoming trial.

The **trial** consists of the orderly presentation of evidence to a judge or jury with arguments on the meaning and importance of the evidence made by the attorneys trying the case. The presentation of evidence is highly structured and governed by formal rules of procedure. Following the presentation of evidence and the arguments on the meaning of the evidence, the judge will render a decision or prepare the jury with instructions to deliberate and render a decision.

Finally, parties dissatisfied with the ruling at trial usually have the right to **appeal** to a higher court, and many do so. Indeed, litigants who lose at trial may appeal through several levels of state and federal courts seeking a new trial or a reversal of the trial court's ruling. When a party wins an appeal, it may begin the entire trial and appeal process again.

The movement of civil litigation through these three stages can be very costly and time-consuming. Remember, though, that there is no legal obligation to file suit to resolve a dispute—it can be resolved informally. It is also possible to settle a case at any stage of litigation, including during appeal, because there is no obligation to complete the process of litigation once commenced. Indeed, as many as 90 percent of all civil cases filed are settled prior to trial. As a result, disputing parties may initiate ADR at many points during litigation or instead of litigation altogether.

Parties may, for example, try to directly negotiate a resolution to the dispute before filing suit. If they cannot reach a negotiated agreement, they may use mediation to more formally attempt to settle. This may take place prior to filing suit, or after filing suit and on the basis of some discovery. A minitrial or summary jury trial may also be used after filing suit and taking discovery, but in an attempt to settle the matter without an actual trial. Parties may even substitute arbitration for a jury trial or try to negotiate *following* a trial if a lengthy and costly appeal is likely. In short, ADR is possible throughout the life of the dispute and at any stage of formal litigation.

Parties who use ADR prior to, or at some point during, litigation do so for a variety of reasons. Although we cover many of these reasons later in the text, four warrant attention here. First, the cost of litigation, in legal fees and trial expenses, can be prohibitively high. (Later in this chapter we address the formidable economic impact of litigation on business.) In addition, the length of time to reach a judgment through litigation may compel parties to seek resolution outside of the courthouse. The pretrial stage itself is known to take months, even years. The appeals process may be just as lengthy and could start the entire time-consuming process over. Moreover, the longer the process takes, the more expensive it becomes. This is true partly because legal fees accrue throughout the process and partly because the process distracts key people from important business pursuits. For example, instead of devoting undivided attention to managing the business, a CEO may be obligated to give deposition testimony. Or, rather than working on new product development, an engineer may be forced to spend time preparing extensive answers to interrogatories or preparing documents for the opposing party. At every stage of the process is the risk of an adverse ruling that will end the case unfavorably. Litigation is a winner-take-all event. Even when the evidence would seemingly ensure a favorable outcome, a judge or jury may perceive it differently. The result may be an adverse verdict with significant costs incurred. Finally, important business *relationships* may be lost in the acrimony of a trial.

THE IMPACT OF LITIGATION ON BUSINESS

http://

A Study of the U.S. and Illinois tort systems can be found at: http://www.icjl. org/data2/ niu2.htm

The American legal system bears the brunt of blame for the high cost of doing business. Indeed, some people, claim that a **liability crisis** exists. Clearly, the effects of the American legal system on business can be significant, and occasionally businesses find themselves defending against cases that lack merit. However, whether the system is to blame for all the negatives ascribed to it is another question altogether.

Fair-minded people can and do disagree on how extensively the litigation system affects business, on whether its impact is uniformly negative, and on whether there is a need to change the system. There is even debate about whether a lawsuit or liability crisis exists at all. In the case that follows, considering whether a plaintiff has a right to question a jury on its predispositions toward the liability crisis, it becomes clear that very different perspectives on the liability crisis or lack thereof abound. It is also evident that the belief or lack of belief in the liability crisis is perceived to affect jury decision making.

BABCOCK V. NORTHWEST MEMORIAL HOSPITAL
767 S.W.2d 705 (1989)

FACT SUMMARY

Artaruth Babcock broke her pelvis and was hospitalized. During her hospitalization, Mrs. Babcock developed blisters on her heels, which allegedly ultimately resulted in the amputation of both her legs. Mrs. Babcock and her husband sued the hospital and her doctors, alleging negligence in their care of Mrs. Babcock. During voir dire, the trial judge refused to allow the Babcocks' attorney to question the jury panel about the alleged lawsuit crisis, which he believed would bias the jury against the claim.

The trial court granted two pretrial motions. The first motion prohibited "[a]ny mention of the alleged 'liability insurance crisis,' 'medical malpractice crisis,' or any similar mention of or questions to potential jurors regarding the current state of affairs in the liability insurance industry." The second motion prohibited "calling the jury's attention to any advertisements either on radio, television, in newspapers or magazines which speak of malpractice crisis and are paid for by and credited to insurance companies." During voir dire, a member of the jury panel stated that he had read articles and advertisements discussing the alleged liability crisis, and his concern for the effect of jury awards on insurance premiums might impede his ability to be impartial. After that juror was struck for cause, the Babcocks renewed their request for permission to question the entire jury panel about the alleged "lawsuit crisis." The trial court again denied the request. The following exchange took place

before the bench:

Counsel for Babcocks: Your Honor, while everybody is still up here and on the record, I would like to bring—bring out the Court's ruling on my motion—on their Motion in Limine. It's my understanding that the Court has precluded me from asking questions as to whether the jury has heard or read about, not necessarily the insurance crisis, but the liability crisis and the lawsuit crisis. This man obviously is very influenced by it and I think his answer that he was concerned about malpractice, the insurance premiums specifically, I think that that brings forth the need and the necessity for a fair trial that the Plaintiff be allowed to go into this in a little more depth with all the rest of the jurors.

The Court: All right. Let the record show that was made, carefully considered, and the same ruling is in effect. Otherwise, it would open the door completely to both sides to go into that, which would completely prejudice the jury. We couldn't get a fair trial.

After the jury was selected, the Babcocks for the third time objected to the trial court's refusal to allow questions concerning the alleged "lawsuit crisis" and asked for an opportunity later in the day to include the questions they would have asked the jurors on the record. The objection was overruled and the request denied. The Babcocks' motion for a new trial included an affidavit that delineated the questions they would have asked during voir dire about the "lawsuit crisis."

OPINION: *MAUZY, Justice*

At issue in this case is whether the trial court abused its discretion by prohibiting voir dire examination inquiring about the "lawsuit crisis" or "liability insurance crisis."

In Texas, the right to a fair and impartial trial is guaranteed by the Constitution and by statute. It is widely recognized that Texas courts permit a broad range of inquiries on voir dire. At the time of trial, tort reform and the debate concerning the alleged "liability insurance crisis" and "lawsuit crisis" were the subject of much media attention. No one can deny the media blitz spurred by the controversy over tort reform during the 1987 legislative session. Advertisements proclaiming a "lawsuit crisis" asserted that personal injury lawsuits had created an economic crisis and that excessive jury awards resulted in higher premiums. Media coverage of the alleged "lawsuit crisis" has unquestionably created the potential for bias and prejudice on both sides of the personal injury docket.

In a recent opinion, the Second Court of Appeals, when confronted with the same issue, held that the plaintiffs had a right to question the jury to determine if anyone was prejudiced against plaintiffs' rights by such advertising. The defendants [in that case] alleged error by the trial court because the plaintiffs were allowed to question prospective jurors about certain advertisements on tort reform. They contended that such questioning interjected liability insurance into the case. The court of appeals held that such questions were necessary to ask and that the questions in no way indicated the defendants were insured.

Similarly, the respondents in this case contend that allowing such questions would interject insurance into the case.

We are unpersuaded by this argument. The mere mention of insurance is not necessarily grounds for reversal. When the Babcocks requested to ask the prospective jurors questions about the "liability crisis" and the "lawsuit crisis," they specifically stated they did not want to question the jury about insurance. The proposed voir dire questions that were subsequently filed with the trial court avoid any mention of insurance.

Both the Fourteenth Court of Appeals and the Second Court of Appeals have concluded that litigants have a right to question prospective jurors about their exposure to media coverage of the "lawsuit crisis." This right is based on the fundamental right to trial by a fair and impartial jury. We hold that the trial court abused its discretion by refusing to allow the Babcocks to question the jurors about the alleged "lawsuit crisis."

A broad latitude should be allowed to a litigant during voir dire examination. This will enable the litigant to discover any bias or prejudice by the potential jurors so that peremptory challenges may be intelligently exercised. Although we recognize that voir dire examination is largely within the sound discretion of the trial judge, a court abuses its discretion when its denial of the right to ask a proper question prevents determination of whether grounds exist to challenge for cause or denies intelligent use of peremptory challenges.

In the instant case, the Babcocks were denied the opportunity to intelligently exercise challenges. The trial court's refusal to allow questions directed at exposing bias or prejudice resulting from the controversy over tort reform denied the Babcocks the right to trial by a fair and impartial jury.

Respondents contend that the trial court's refusal to allow the questions was harmless error. We disagree. The trial court's action, which resulted in the denial of the Babcocks' constitutional right to trial by a fair and impartial jury, was harmful. Therefore, we hold that the trial court's refusal to allow questions during voir dire addressing the alleged "liability insurance crisis" and "lawsuit crisis" was an abuse of discretion and was reasonably calculated to cause and probably did cause the rendition of an improper judgment.

The judgment of the court of appeals is reversed and the cause is remanded to the trial court.

Discussion Questions

1. Do you believe there is a genuine litigation crisis? Why or why not? Do you believe you possess sufficient information to reach a conclusion?
2. Should jurors be permitted to consider cases based on their personal feelings about the litigation system if doing so would prejudice their decision?
3. Assuming a liability crisis exists, would greater use of ADR alleviate it? How?

One impact of litigation on business is that on world competitiveness. U.S. businesses must operate within a common law system that allows for larger, more frequent, and more easily obtained judgments. Thus, it may be somewhat more difficult for business to be profitable here versus abroad, in systems implementing civil law. Another significant impact of the U.S. legal system is cultural. Harvard law scholar Mary Ann Glendon argues in her book *Rights Talk: The Impoverishment of Political Discourse* that the pervasive use of litigation to resolve claims, particularly those involving questions of individual rights, has decreased our sense of community and increased our feelings of cynicism and indifference. Others besides Glendon think we are a more acrimonious and adversarial society as a result of the ready access to our system of civil justice. UCLA Law Professor Carrie Menkel-Meadow argues, for example, that the adversarial system makes justice less likely in a modern, multicultural society. She criticizes the adversarial system in four ways. First, she asserts that the adversarial system relies on "oppositional thinking" that may leave important information undisclosed and undiscussed. In addition, she asserts that the structure of the adversarial system limits cases unreasonably to two sides, despite the possibility that many sets of interests may be at stake in a case. Third, she contends that the adversarial system is unnecessarily and deleteriously limited in the economic remedies it permits, remedies she describes as "binary" or win-lose. Finally, she, like Glendon, believes that adversarial processes create adversarial cultures.[1]

In all likelihood, however, economic costs top the list of impacts of the civil litigation system on the business world. Proponents of legal reform estimate that the

---

1. Carrie Menkel-Meadow, "The Trouble with the Adversary System in a Post-Modern, Multicultural World," *The Institute for Study of Legal Ethics,* 49, 1996.

annual cost to the American economy of the civil justice system may reach as high as $130 billion. The cost can be measured both in terms of the expenses associated with the process of law and the cost of the outcomes permitted by the law. Because of the tremendously disparate nature of the cases brought, it is difficult to calculate accurately the average cost of trying a civil suit in the United States. It is equally difficult to calculate the average length of time it takes to pursue a case to its legal conclusion, particularly because different jurisdictions at both the state and federal levels have very different docket sizes and waiting times. What can be said is that legal fees are high—reaching as high as $500 an hour for litigation in some cities—and that the litigation process takes years to complete, up to ten years in some jurisdictions.

Another contributor to high economic costs associated with litigation is the **frivolous lawsuit.** Defining a frivolous suit is difficult. The following case considers the question of whether the judgment in a particular lawsuit should be set aside. Consider the analysis of that question in terms of what has been said here regarding the American common law system, because such a suit would likely never be filed or considered in a civil law system.

FERLITO V. JOHNSON & JOHNSON PRODUCTS, INC.
771 F. Supp. 196 (E.D. Michigan 1991)

FACT SUMMARY

Plaintiffs Susan and Frank Ferlito, husband and wife, attended a Halloween party in 1984 dressed as Mary and her little lamb. Mrs. Ferlito had constructed a lamb costume for her husband by gluing cotton batting manufactured by defendant Johnson & Johnson Products (JJP) to a suit of long underwear. She had also used defendant's product to fashion a headpiece, complete with ears. The costume covered Mr. Ferlito from his head to his ankles, except for his face and hands, which were blackened with Halloween paint. At the party Mr. Ferlito attempted to light his cigarette by using a butane lighter. The flame passed close to his left arm, and the cotton batting on his left sleeve ignited. Plaintiffs sued defendant for injuries they suffered from burns which covered approximately one third of Mr. Ferlito's body. Following a jury verdict entered for plaintiffs, the Honorable Ralph M. Freeman entered a judgment for plaintiff Frank Ferlito in the amount of $555,000 and for plaintiff Susan Ferlito in the amount of $70,000.

OPINION: *GADOLA, District Judge*

To recover in a "failure to warn" product liability action, a plaintiff must prove each of the following four elements of negligence: (1) that the defendant owed a duty to the plaintiff, (2) that the defendant violated that duty, (3) that the defendant's breach of that duty was a proximate cause of the damages suffered by the plaintiff, and (4) that the plaintiff suffered damages. To establish a prima facie case that a manufacturer's breach of its duty to warn was a proximate cause of an injury sustained, a plaintiff must present evidence that the product would have been used differently had the proffered warnings been given. In the absence of evidence that a warning would have prevented the harm complained of by altering the plaintiff's conduct, the failure to warn cannot be deemed a proximate cause of the plaintiff's injury as a matter of law. Similarly, a failure to warn cannot be deemed a proximate cause of injury if the plaintiff knew of the danger about which he claims the defendant failed to warn. A manufacturer has a duty "to warn the purchasers or users of its product about dangers associated with intended use." Conversely, a manufacturer has no duty to warn of a danger arising from an unforeseeable misuse of its product. Thus, whether a manufacturer has a duty to warn depends on whether the use of the product and the injury sustained by it are foreseeable. Whether a plaintiff's use of a product is foreseeable is a legal question to be resolved by the court. Whether the resulting injury is foreseeable is a question of fact for the jury.

In the instant action no reasonable jury could find that JJP's failure to warn of the flammability of cotton batting was a proximate cause of plaintiffs' injuries because plaintiffs failed to offer any evidence to establish that a flammability warning on JJP's cotton batting would have dissuaded them from using the product in the manner that they did.

Plaintiffs repeatedly stated in their response brief that plaintiff Susan Ferlito testified that "she would never again use cotton batting to make a costume." However, a review of the trial transcript reveals that plaintiff Susan Ferlito never testified that she would never again use

cotton batting to make a costume. More importantly, the transcript contains no statement by plaintiff Susan Ferlito that a flammability warning on defendant JJP's product would have dissuaded her from using the cotton batting to construct the costume in the first place. At oral argument counsel for plaintiffs conceded that there was no testimony during the trial that either plaintiff Susan Ferlito or her husband, plaintiff Frank J. Ferlito, would have acted any differently if there had been a flammability warning on the product's package. The absence of such testimony is fatal to plaintiffs' case; for without it, plaintiffs have failed to prove proximate cause, one of the essential elements of their negligence claim.

In addition, both plaintiffs testified that they knew that cotton batting burns when it is exposed to flame. Susan Ferlito testified that she knew at the time she purchased the cotton batting that it would burn if exposed to an open flame. Frank Ferlito testified that he knew at the time he appeared at the Halloween party that cotton batting would burn if exposed to an open flame. His additional testimony that he would not have intentionally put a flame to the cotton batting shows that he recognized the risk of injury of which he claims JJP should have warned. Because both plaintiffs were already aware of the danger, a warning by JJP would have been superfluous. Therefore, a reasonable jury could not have found that JJP's failure to provide a warning was a proximate cause of plaintiffs' injuries.

The evidence in this case clearly demonstrated that neither the use to which plaintiffs put JJP's product nor the injuries arising from that use were foreseeable. Susan Ferlito testified that the idea for the costume was hers alone. As described on the product's package, its intended uses are for cleansing, applying medications, and infant care. Plaintiffs' showing that the product may be used on occasion in classrooms for decorative purposes failed to demonstrate the foreseeability of an adult male encapsulating himself from head to toe in cotton batting and then lighting up a cigarette.

ORDER

Defendant's motion for judgment notwithstanding the verdict is GRANTED.

Discussion Questions

1. How, exactly, should a frivolous suit be defined? Under what circumstances should a person be permitted to try to prove a loss? Should the basis for judicial consideration of a suit be whether or not its cost to the system outweighs the benefits of a decision to the litigants?
2. In the present case, can it not be said that the system worked well? In other words, did the court not prevent an unjust judgment?
3. If so, can business bear the expense of defending such suits all the way through to a judgment notwithstanding the verdict or appeal? Is this cost of justice too high?
4. Would more extensive use of ADR lead to an *increase* in frivolous claims by encouraging parties to sue, secure in the knowledge that they could negotiate a settlement without judicial interference?

ADR IN ACTION

The Case of the Scalding Coffee

Perhaps no case has so inflamed the American people against the civil legal system in recent years as the case of *Liebeck v. McDonald's*. The case prompted House and Senate floor debates in Washington and was cited regularly as representative of every excess in the legal system that could be cured with meaningful legal reforms. One congressional representative, Christopher Cox of California, described the tort reform movement this way: "If there is a Robin Hood aspect, it is to take from the lawyers and give to the average working American." The *Liebeck* case presents some interesting facts, very few of which were widely publicized, and all of which present a simple question: Was it really a frivolous suit?

Stella Liebeck spent one full week in the hospital and three weeks recuperating at home after suffering third-degree burns on her thighs, genitalia, and buttocks following a spill of a cup of McDonald's coffee purchased at a drive-through window. She was eighty-one years old at the time of the accident. She spilled the coffee while her car was parked and as she endeavored to remove the cap to add cream and sugar to the coffee. During her recovery, she lost more than 20 pounds and underwent a series of very painful skin grafts. She incurred just over $2,000 in out-of-pocket medical expenses plus the lost wages of her daughter, who stayed home to care for her. The case was litigated to a jury, members of which said later that they began the case insulted to have to hear it at all; they believed, in short, before the testimony even began that this was a truly frivolous case. They later awarded Ms. Liebeck $2.9 million; $200,000 in compensatory damages including pain and suffering, but reduced by 20% for her negligence; and $2.7 million in punitive damages. The damages were later reduced to about $650,000 and reportedly privately settled for still less. Here are some of the facts the jurors heard that may have changed their initial opinions of the suit:

- McDonald's had received more than 700 complaints of burns from coffee spills in the ten years preceding the Liebeck burn but did not lower the temperature of the coffee because, in the words of one of their safety consultants, 700 complaints was "basically trivially different than zero."

- McDonald's coffee in the city in which the burn occurred was served at about 190 degrees—at least 20 degrees hotter than any other venue tested. This is a temperature that causes a third-degree, full-thickness burn to skin, muscle, and fatty tissue in 3.5 seconds. (Following the case, the temperature was reduced to 158 degrees, which causes a similar burn—after 60 seconds.)

- McDonald's own witnesses testified that they believed that consumers were unaware of the risk posed by a liquid of this temperature but that McDonald's was and had been aware of the danger for years.

- McDonald's own witnesses also admitted that McDonald's coffee is "not fit for consumption" as and when sold because it will cause severe burns if spilled *or* ingested.

- Ms. Liebeck offered to settle the case before the trial for her out-of-pocket expenses and a promise to turn down the temperature of the coffee; McDonald's countered with an $800 offer, less than one third of Ms. Liebeck's actual losses.

- McDonald's sells more than one billion cups of coffee each year, with daily coffee profit exceeding $1.3 million; Ms. Liebeck's awarded damages, therefore, equaled roughly two days' coffee profits; after the reduction, she recovered less than one day's profits.

It is not just the public that perceives a problem in the justice system. Courts have become concerned about and responsive to the economic impact of litigation on the participants. The following case illustrates this point. The opinion addresses the right of a third party to intervene in a suit that is subject to an agreement to use private ADR to settle a matter that has been in litigation for several years. The court balances the rights of the proposed intervenor against those of the parties already involved in the suit and engaged in settlement negotiation. In doing so, the court provides some astonishing facts and figures related to the impact of litigation—on both the parties and the judicial system.

HAWORTH, INC. V. STEELCASE, INC.
1992 WL 457284 (1992)

FACT SUMMARY

This matter comes before the Court pursuant to Herman Miller's *Motion to Intervene for the Purpose of Discovery*. Haworth filed suit in this Court, charging Steelcase with infringement of two Haworth Patents. Steelcase's answer denied the validity, infringement, and enforceability of the two patents in suit. In addition, Steelcase counterclaimed for judgment holding the patents invalid, not infringed, and unenforceable. Judge Enslen conducted a bench trial, the parties submitted post-trial briefs to the Court, and Judge Enslen entered judgments in favor of Steelcase on Haworth's infringement claim, in favor of Haworth on its validity claim, and in favor of Haworth on its unenforceability claim. Both parties appealed the judgment. The Federal Circuit reversed the findings of non-infringement but affirmed that the defendant had not proven inequitable conduct on the part of the plaintiff. The case was remanded to this Court for further proceedings. On remand, Judge Enslen scheduled a settlement conference to attempt settlement of this case.

James F. Davis, a former judge in the United States Court of Claims, was appointed to serve as a neutral advisor in the settlement negotiations between the plaintiff and defendant. Thereafter, by consent of the parties and pursuant to the inherent power of this Court, the parties entered into a special ADR agreement to settle the issues presented in the civil actions. Judge Enslen also appointed James F. Davis as a special master "for the purposes of encouraging and facilitating settlement, supervising the orderly progress of discovery, and conducting a trial of and deciding the issues between the parties if trial should become necessary." The ADR agreement allowed the parties to include for resolution all claims of which they were aware.

Subsequent to the creation of the ADR agreement, the plaintiff filed suit against Herman Miller, Inc. In its complaint, the plaintiff alleged Herman Miller had been willfully and deliberately infringing, contributorily infringing, and/or actively inducing infringement of the plaintiff's patents. Herman Miller filed its *Motion to*

Intervene in the instant case. Herman Miller alleges it needs discovery of documents connected with the proceedings before the special master, including documents produced in discovery by Haworth and others, for these reasons: (1) to prevent the plaintiff from taking inconsistent positions before the special master and in the lawsuit against Herman Miller, thereby avoiding collateral estoppel on adverse rulings and (2) to prevent the plaintiff from having witnesses change their testimony depending on the proceeding.

The plaintiff vigorously opposes Herman Miller's *Motion to Intervene.* It argues intervention by Herman Miller is not appropriate in this case, given the private nature of the ADR proceedings it has entered into for the purpose of settling its complaints. Furthermore, the plaintiff asserts that allowing Herman Miller's intervention in this case would have a chilling effect on the usefulness of the ADR proceedings and could jeopardize the existence of the ADR procedure, thereby causing the cases to revert back to the federal court for resolution.

OPINION: *DENSLEN, District Judge*

Central to my decision is the importance of alternative dispute resolution methodologies this Court utilizes to manage its case docket, in particular the alternative dispute resolution methodology set up by both parties in this case.

Following a lengthy trial and appellate process, on July 26, 1989, plaintiff and defendant commenced negotiations for settlement purposes. The two lawsuits pending between these litigants were consolidated for this purpose. On December 13, 1989, their settlement negotiations culminated in the order of reference of the disputes to James F. Davis, as Special Master, for resolution. James F. Davis was invested with the power to encourage and facilitate settlements, to supervise the orderly progress of discovery, to conduct the trial and decide all issues between the parties, if necessary. The alternative dispute resolution procedure covered all patent-based claims between plaintiff and defendant; as well as any other patent related issues arising after December 15, 1989, included by mutual agreement between both parties and the Special Master. Thus, both civil actions pending in the Western District of Michigan were stayed pending the conclusion of the alternative dispute resolution proceedings. Both parties agreed to relinquish any right to appeal to any court any decision by the Special Master, either of discovery or procedural matters or the relief granted in final disposition of the civil actions. All transcripts, documents, and other information produced and testimony given during the alternative dispute resolution proceeding would be kept confidential, and neither party to the agreement could disclose any information concerning the conduct of the proceedings without the express written permission of the other. Both plaintiff and defendant specifically agreed in Paragraph 21 that the purpose of the proceedings was for settling the existing litigation between them.

The explosion of litigation in the federal courts, and the resulting burdens placed on the courts as well as all litigants, is well documented. In 1975, it was estimated that assuming the then present growth of litigation, by the year 2010 the federal court system would experience well over 1,000,000 appellate cases, requiring 5,000 appellate judges to decide them, and 10,000,000 cases initiated each year. Among the reasons noted for the expansion of litigation in the federal court system was the decline of church and family as traditional dispute resolution mechanisms, as well as the increasing complexity of modern society. Typically, it takes from two to six years to get a case to trial. However, business litigation, such as in this case, takes longer. The amount of discovery necessary in business litigation is both extensive and expensive. It is fair to say that most business litigation cases take at least two weeks and not uncommonly months to try. The personnel commitment which is essential for that kind of a trial, and especially the breadth and the depth of the preparation, represents a huge demand and an enormous drain on all the staff and officers of a corporation involved in the trial. But for the litigation they would be using their ingenuity and their capability for business purposes of the corporation and for the benefit of the shareholders. Furthermore, in a case such as this one involving patent disputes, time is of the essence. High technology moves quickly. By the time a complex trial has been completed, the issue may no longer be an issue.

Although approximately 96 percent of all cases are settled prior to judgment, many are settled too late, often after the expenditure of too much effort and money. Accordingly, the exigencies of modern dockets demand the adoption of novel and imaginative means lest the courts, inundated by a tidal wave of cases, fail in their duty to provide a just and speedy disposition of every case. Experimentation with new methods in the judicial system is imperative given growing caseloads, delays, and increasing costs. Federal and state judges throughout the country are trying new approaches to discovery, settlement negotiations, trial and alternatives to trial that deserve commendation and support. The bar should work with judges who are attempting to make practical improvements in the judicial system. Greater efficiency and cost-effectiveness serve both clients and the public.

In order to reduce their caseloads, many federal judges have been utilizing alternative dispute resolution methods. Such methods have served to reduce the time and cost to the litigants. One judge empirically estimated that by utilizing a summary jury trial five times, he had netted a savings in time of about 60 days. Furthermore, use of alternative dispute resolution techniques preserves the trial process for those cases which can be resolved only by trial. In particular, the use of special masters has been endorsed for the facilitation of just, speedy, and inexpensive resolution of complex cases. As the Sixth Circuit has recognized, pursuant to Fed.R.Civ.P. 83, district courts have the authority to enact rules to regulate their practice in matters not inconsistent with the federal rules, including rules requiring the litigants to submit to some variety of alternative dispute resolution. Former Chief Justice Burger referred to those judges who make efforts to formulate alternative dispute resolution mechanisms as "judicial pioneers [who] should be commended for their innovative programs. We need more of them in the future." W. Burger, 1984 Year End Report on the Judiciary.

Aside from relieving the burdens on federal courts' dockets, and saving the litigants time and money, alternative dispute resolution methods produce other favorable results. Summary jury trials allow the litigants to vent their grievances in a forum which does not entail the time and costs of a full-blown trial, and accordingly, they can walk away having had their day in court. Furthermore, the proceeding allows each litigant the opportunity to reassess the strengths and weaknesses of their and their opponent's cases, so that a fresh assessment can be made of the costs and benefits of fully litigating the case. In mediation, the parties can reorient themselves by helping them achieve a new and shared perception of their relationships. Mediation helps the parties to avoid or at least minimize conflicts in the future, and so helps to preserve and enhance relationships between parties which need to be maintained. In virtually all cases, the solution that two parties can work out themselves, voluntarily, will be better than the solution that the most Solomonic court could come up with, as the court is limited in the remedies that it can prescribe.

Reacting to these needs, the Western District of Michigan has promulgated the Local Rules of Practice and Procedure, which includes provisions for various forms of alternative dispute resolution. The judges of this District favor initiation of alternative formulas for resolving disputes, saving costs and time, and permitting the parties to utilize creativity in fashioning non-coercive settlements.

Herman Miller argues it wants to intervene in this case only to conduct discovery. It argues this would expedite the process of discovery in its lawsuit with plaintiff in the pending case in the Northern District of Georgia, thereby producing judicial economy because many of the issues presented to the Special Master may be similar or the same as issues presented to the Court in Georgia. Accordingly, the decisions made by James F. Davis could be asserted as having a collateral estoppel effect on the same issues presented in the Northern District of Georgia. Herman Miller further argues it wants to intervene in order to ascertain what positions plaintiff has taken on issues in the alternative dispute resolution proceedings before the Special Master, because these positions may be inconsistent with the positions plaintiff is taking before the Court in the Northern District of Georgia. Finally, Herman Miller expresses its need to openly discuss its litigation with the attorneys representing Steelcase, and plaintiff is taking its position with respect to intervention to create a "steel curtain" between the attorneys. Herman Miller asserts plaintiff's characterization of the Special Master proceeding as a settlement agreement is wrong, because the Order of Reference incorporates provisions for discovery and trial in addition to settlement conferences. In conclusion, Herman Miller argues it has demonstrated a clear need to intervene to have access to the materials and documents generated in the course of the proceedings before the Special Master. Herman Miller argues plaintiff can show no harm if intervention is allowed, because intervention would not have a chilling effect on plaintiff's and defendant's proceedings before the Special Master. Herman Miller argues that allowing intervention would not constitute a breach of the Order of Reference, because plaintiff must have known it would at a later date sue other parties on the patents in dispute, and therefore the possibility of intervention was something plaintiff could have and should have contemplated.

In response, plaintiff argues its proceedings before the Special Master are part and parcel of its agreement to settle the case with defendant. The preparation of the Order of Reference was the culmination of lengthy negotiations between the parties, and confidentiality was a very important ingredient to the ultimate package. Plaintiff further asserts Herman Miller's argument it needs to ascertain whether plaintiff is taking inconsistent positions in the two proceedings is wrong. Plaintiff asserts its positions regarding both patents involved in the disputes with Herman Miller have been made abundantly clear in the proceedings before Judge Enslen as well as in the appeal to the Federal Circuit. The alternative dispute resolution methodology was carefully constructed in order to resolve all the disputes in litigation as well as additional patent disputes between plaintiff and defendant should they mutually agree to include the disputes in the ADR proceeding. Plaintiff argues the methodology was set up in order to give both parties the unfettered right to compromise with the other in order to resolve their disputes, and such a proceeding is not regular in the course of litigation. Allowing Herman Miller to intervene would place plaintiff in a position to look over its shoulder during the course of negotiations, and if plaintiff did take a position which could be construed to be inconsistent, Herman Miller would then race to the federal court in the Northern District of Georgia with this argument. Plaintiff argues this prospect would have a chilling effect on the possibility of its engaging in the give and take essential to compromising which is necessary to resolve issues, as well as bringing a close to the patent disputes between it and defendant. Plaintiff argues Herman Miller has failed to show the special need to discover inconsistent positions, especially in light of Herman Miller's representation to the Court it has no evidence plaintiff is taking inconsistent positions in the different court proceedings. In fact, Herman Miller presumes that plaintiff's attorneys, as officers of the court, are not being deceitful. Plaintiff

argues that should Herman Miller be able to demonstrate a special need for the material it seeks to obtain through intervention, it can file a second motion. However, in this instance, Herman Miller is only engaging in a giant fishing expedition, based on mere suspicion. Allowing intervention would undermine the confidentiality contemplated by both plaintiff and defendant, essential for facilitating the open exchange of information in order to resolve their disputes, and to be creative in resolving their disputes, without a showing of substantial need on the part of Herman Miller.

Plaintiff further argues that allowing Herman Miller to intervene would potentially destroy the alternative dispute resolution procedure because of Herman Miller's desire to argue the collateral estoppel effects of the Special Master's decision to the Northern District of Georgia. Essential to the alternative dispute resolution proceeding was the provision whereby each party would forego its right to appeal any decision made by the Special Master. If the decisions by the Special Master thus could be given binding effect in other proceedings, neither party would want to continue with having waived its right to appeal because of the prospect of irreparable damage.

Steelcase has informed the Court it opposes Herman Miller's *Motion to Intervene*. Allowing intervention into this proceeding most certainly would result in plaintiff attempting to either undo or significantly alter the ADR methodology. Steelcase represents this would be vigorously opposed. Therefore, allowing intervention would at a minimum produce a dispute between plaintiff and defendant, wholly collateral to their ADR proceeding, and indeed, potentially destructive of all the progress they have made in resolving their many disputes. In either case, the progress which has been made in these cases would be seriously jeopardized, if not delayed for an undetermined length of time for no substantial purpose.

I conclude Herman Miller's *Motion to Intervene* should be denied. Plaintiff has demonstrated a legitimate need to maintain the confidentiality of the documents and materials generated in its alternative dispute resolution proceeding before the Special Master. Allowing Herman Miller to intervene in order to discover these materials cannot be accomplished without harming plaintiff's and defendant's legitimate secrecy interest. Plaintiff would be inhibited from engaging in the give and take essential for compromising disputes if presented with the possibility Herman Miller, Inc., would race to the Northern District of Georgia with the argument plaintiff was taking inconsistent positions in the two proceedings. A scenario such as this cannot reasonably be construed as enhancing judicial economy. Furthermore, the possible use of the Special Master's decisions for collateral estoppel purposes very well may lead to the destruction of the alternative dispute resolution procedure both parties painstakingly constructed, or at a minimum could produce a modification in the Order of Reference, inevitably causing delay in the ultimate resolution of these cases.

Weighed against Herman Miller's need for the information is plaintiff's need to maintain the confidentiality of its proceedings in the alternative dispute resolution methodology. Plaintiff needs the confidentiality to engage in the give and take essential to resolve disputes. Furthermore, the specter of the collateral estoppel effect of the Special Master's decisions in other court proceedings, without the full panoply of appeals from

those decisions, may jeopardize the existence of the entire alternative dispute resolution method designed by the litigants and approved by the Court in this case. This alternative dispute resolution method was painstakingly hammered out over the course of settlement discussions which lasted about six months. Plaintiff and defendant entered into these settlement discussions only after a 23-day bench trial, the following appeal to the federal Circuit, and the denial of a writ of certiorari by the United States Supreme Court. Allowing intervention would jeopardize the settlement of not one but two lawsuits which were filed in the Western District of Michigan and later consolidated, as well as the resolution of other disputes between these parties. Furthermore, it is unlikely future elaborate alternative dispute resolution methods, such as the one fashioned in this case, would be utilized if confidentiality could not be maintained.

My conclusion should not be read to indicate intervention will not be allowed any time two litigants are engaged in alternative dispute resolution. However, in light of the facts of this case, with its extensive procedural history, the importance of encouraging and utilizing alternative dispute resolution methods, the uniqueness and comprehensive nature of the alternative dispute resolution methodology agreed to by plaintiff and defendant, the danger to the viability of the alternative dispute resolution method should intervention be allowed, and the consolidation of the lawsuits in the alternative dispute resolution proceeding before the Special Master, I conclude plaintiff's privacy interests clearly outweigh Herman Miller's needs for the documents and materials generated during the proceedings before the Special Master.

Discussion Questions

1. Do you agree that the circumstances in this case dictate supporting the ADR agreement even if it works to the disadvantage of Herman Miller, Inc.?

2. Should a litigant ever receive different treatment in a case because the overall expenses in the judicial system are so high? Under what circumstances, if any, should a judge decide that "judicial economy" dictates dismissing a claim?

3. Does the use of ADR as a way to reduce judicial dockets mean some litigants receive second-class treatment?

LEGAL REFORMS

http://

The American Tort Reform Association can be found at: http://www. aaabiz.com/ ATRA/Default. html

http://

Visit the Association for California Tort Reform at: http://www.sna. com/actr/

Because of concerns raised by both litigants and courts, legislatures at both the state and the federal levels have begun to consider reforms calculated to reduce the economic impact of litigation. It is difficult to decide whether the impact of law on business is extensive enough to warrant legislative intervention. Nevertheless, legislatures have begun to consider and pass legislation to reform the civil justice system. Some reforms are explicitly designed to increase the use of ADR, perhaps by mandating it in some cases. Others, such as the ones that follow, attempt to reduce the costs and complexities associated with litigation. Some of these reforms have passed judicial scrutiny and stand, while others have been voided by state and federal appellate courts. The Illinois Supreme Court recently voided the complete set of tort reform measures enacted by the Illinois Legislature.[2] Descriptions of a few of the most popular approaches to reforming the civil justice system beyond the increased use of ADR follow.

Legal **reforms addressing the awarding of damages** are popular means of reducing the cost of litigation. One approach is to eliminate punitive damages or cap them to a percentage of the actual loss or the net worth of the defendant. Doing so serves the important public policy of punishing and deterring intentional or reckless legal wrongdoing without forcing a company into bankruptcy. Dow-Corning, rather than face, among other things, the possibility of punitive damages in its breast implant litigation, simply declared bankruptcy. A second approach involves eliminating or capping noneconomic losses like pain and suffering damages by providing compensation for actual, physical harm only. Although capping any sort of damages may mean plaintiffs are not fully compensated for real losses, and defendants are not truly deterred from similar conflict. Statutes of repose, those placing absolute time limits on the bringing of a suit may also help. A final, relatively novel approach to reducing the cost of damages in lawsuits is to make punitive damages payable in some percentage to the government, to reduce the incentive to lawyers and plaintiffs to file suit in the hope of turning small actual losses into large

---

2. *Best v. Taylor Machine Works,* 1997 NL 777822 (Ill. Sup. Ct., 1997).

punitive losses. Alaska is one state using this approach; it hopes to receive some of the five billion dollars in punitive damages assessed against Exxon as a result of the *Valdez* oil spill.

In addition to reforms addressing damages, **reforms addressing attorneys** have been offered. Some suggest limiting attorneys' fees. One way to do this is to eliminate contingency fees, which allow the lawyer to obtain a percentage of any recovery. Some argue that doing so would discourage the filing of frivolous suits. Others suggest reducing the number of attorneys by raising the standards to obtain a law degree and license to practice law. Still others advocate the elimination of the attorney right to share in a punitive damages award.

However, reforms that make it more difficult to obtain legal counsel have significant downsides. It is unlikely, some argue, that eliminating contingency fees would have any measurable curtailing effect on frivolous suits. Indeed, some counter that it would have precisely the opposite effect—compelling lawyers to file suit more often to make up income lost to tort reform. Similarly, reforms reducing the number of attorneys likely run afoul of the law as an impermissible restraint on free trade at the same time they fail to address the real problem—it is not necessarily true that fewer lawyers results in fewer or more meritorious suits.

Reforms addressing party rights have also been proposed. One option is a "loser pays" system that allows the prevailing party to collect from the opposing party costs and fees associated with the case. Requiring a preliminary case evaluation prior to suit, perhaps by a board empowered to certify cases as either meritorious or meritless, also has support in some quarters. The practice of certifying cases for merit has been adopted, though largely ruled unconstitutional, in several states, when the process interferes with a litigant's right to justice. The elimination of joint and several liability, the legal concept that holds the defendant responsible for the entire verdict regardless of the percentages of negligence, has also been attempted, though courts generally have ruled this reform unconstitutional.

The U.S. system of civil law has traditionally been an open one, allowing virtually free access to litigants. Reforms that represent barriers to potential litigants are viewed with suspicion both judicially and legislatively. Those who oppose such reforms note that motions to dispose of cases prior to trial can be made and that such motions suffice to assure parties of the dismissal of a frivolous suit while leaving the doors to the courthouse largely open to all.

Procedural reforms such as more narrowly defined "causation" and "duty" in tort cases would make it more difficult to prevail in civil suits. In addition, raising the civil burden of proof beyond a mere preponderance of evidence has also been suggested. Some have even argued that elimination of comparative negligence in favor of contributory negligence, so that a plaintiff who contributes to an injury receives nothing or vastly reduced compensation, is an appropriate response to the effects of litigation. Establishment of a system of independent, judicially appointed and paid expert witnesses, which would eliminate the need for paid partisan experts, may provide juries with clearer and more easily understood direction. Finally, some have suggested elimination of civil juries in all technical areas, as

http://
An Illinois plaintiff attorney has written articles opposing tort reform that can be found at: http://www. cliffordlaw.com/

http://
The Ohio Tort Reform Act can be found at: http://www. alliancecourtwatch.com/ppts/ ktunn997/index. htm

http://
An audio file of a speech on tort reform is at the Illinois Institute of Continuing Legal Education site: http://www.icle. org/products/ audio/dcooper. htm

they have been in part in the patent area, to ensure competent deliberation in all cases.

Legal reform is a difficult endeavor. The rights and protections offered by the civil justice system are justifiably cherished by most people and guarded carefully by the courts. In addition, the U.S. Constitution, as well as those of most states, provide relatively easy access to the courts and strong presumptions in favor of permitting a jury to decide a case on the merits as presented at trial. The result is that courts have, in many instances, ruled that tort reform measures are unconstitutional. ADR provides a remedy to those parties for whom and in those cases where the system, because of cost, time, risk, or business relationship factors, is not appropriate. Although some of the reforms described above may at some point be adopted and affirmed by courts, for now, ADR stands as the best alternative to civil litigation.

http://

Comments of Senator Tom Harkin on federal tort reform can be read at:
http://www.policy.com/vcongress/tort/tort-harkin.html

CHAPTER CONCLUSION

Litigation in either an adversarial or inquisitorial system is expensive, time-consuming, risky, and sometimes counterproductive. We have reviewed in this chapter the prevailing public, adjudicative systems used to resolve civil disputes involving businesses. We are now ready to examine the range of processes that stand as alternatives to the public courts, representing perhaps the most significant legal reform of all: far wider use, both voluntary and compelled, of alternatives to trial that reduce the risks, expenses, and time lost on judicial proceedings.

BEST BUSINESS PRACTICES

Here are some practical tips for managers on the use of ADR for the resolution of business disputes.

- Perhaps no other matter affects business as completely as law and the legal process. It is virtually impossible to avoid business disputes and almost as difficult to avoid litigation. As a result, a thorough understanding of the avenues available for the resolution of civil disputes is essential to the businessperson.

- A careful pre-suit analysis of the costs, duration, and likely outcomes of litigation is very useful. Although attorneys cannot predict the outcome of a trial with absolute certainty, they can assess the likely costs and disposition of the case before it is litigated.

- The data are mixed on the question of whether a liability crisis exists, and the ways of resolving it, if it does exist, are far from clear. How one responds to the crisis should be dictated by independent research and analysis.

KEY TERMS

Adversarial, common law model, p. 4

Appeal, p. 7

Discovery, p. 7

Frivolous lawsuit, p. 12

Inquisitorial, civil law model, p. 4

Legal reforms: attorneys, p. 23

Legal reforms: damages, p. 22

Legal reforms: party rights, p. 23

Legal reforms: procedure, p. 23

Liability crisis, p. 8

Pretrial stage, p. 7

Religious law systems, p. 6

Trial, p. 7

ETHICAL AND LEGAL REVIEW

1. Unser purchases a new automobile from BMW, Inc. The car, unbeknownst to plaintiff, was damaged in transit to the seller and has been partially repainted. Instead, Unser is told the car is new and perfect. Following the purchase, the defect is uncovered, and the damage is estimated at $4,000. Unser asks for the amount from BMW and is rebuffed. He sues and receives four million dollars, virtually all of which is in punitive damages. Assuming that the conduct of the defendant is willful and that punitive damages in some amount are appropriate, how much is Unser entitled to? On what do you base your amount? [*BMW v. Gore,* 517 U.S. 559, 116 S. Ct. 1589 (1996)]

2. Acme Corporation produces devices known as breast implants. These devices are used in both elective and nonelective reconstructive cosmetic surgery on women. They are filled with a substance known as silicon. Acme is sued by a class of women who allege that ruptured silicon breast implants cause a range of maladies that are permanent and very serious. They offer as proof a study they commissioned and for which they paid. They have no additional evidence beyond the anecdotal stories told by the plaintiffs themselves. Moreover, your medical experts say that no such harm occurs following rupture of the device. Should a judge dismiss the suit for lack of evidence in response to the defendant's motion for summary judgment? When should cases involving conflicting theories be tried? [*In re Dow Corning,* 86 F. 3d 482 (6th Circ. 1996)]

3. You are retained to draft a state tort reform statute. Which elements of tort reform would you include? Which elements of tort reform would you ignore and why? What constitutional hurdles would you expect to face as you drafted your statute? See for assistance, *Best v. Taylor Machine Works,* 1997 WL 777822 (Supreme Court of Illinois, 1997).

SUGGESTED ADDITIONAL READINGS

Abramson, J. *We, the Jury: The Jury System and the Ideal of Democracy.* Basic Books/Harper Collins Publishers, 1994.

Adler, S. *The Jury: Disorder in the Court.* Doubleday/Main Street Books, 1994.

Glendon, M. A. *A Nation under Lawyers: How the Crisis in the Legal Profession Is Transforming American Society.* Harvard Press, 1994.

Glendon, M. A. *Rights Talk*: *The Impoverishment of Political Discourse.* Free Press, 1991.

Harr, J. *A Civil Action.* Random House, 1995.

Howard, P. *The Death of Common Sense: How Law Is Suffocating America.* Random House, 1994.

Kritzer, H. *Let's Make a Deal: Understanding the Negotiation Process in Ordinary Litigation.* University of Wisconsin Press, 1991.

Lebedoff, D. *Cleaning Up: The Story Behind the Biggest Legal Bonanza of Our Time.* Free Press, 1997.

Nader, R., and W. Smith. *No Contest: Corporate Lawyers and the Perversion of Justice in America.* Random House, 1996.

2

THE ADR RESPONSE TO RESOLVING BUSINESS DISPUTES

CHAPTER HIGHLIGHTS
In this chapter, you will read and learn about the following:

1. The general characteristics of alternative dispute resolution.
2. The unique features of business conflict.
3. The major alternative dispute resolution processes.
4. The advantages and disadvantages of alternative dispute resolution for business.

In the preceding chapter, we considered adversarial litigation systems and how they impact business. This chapter provides a general overview of alternative dispute resolution (ADR) while examining the nature of conflict in business. It also briefly describes the various alternative dispute resolution processes covered at length in later chapters. Moreover, it considers the advantages and disadvantages of alternative dispute resolution for resolving business disputes, presenting several cases and scenarios designed to develop an ability to evaluate and choose among the various nonlitigation processes for resolving business disputes.

INTRODUCTION TO ADR

The phrase **alternative dispute resolution** describes a series of processes available to resolve disputes without formal, public litigation. All alternative dispute resolution processes share several features.

- They are typically less formal than litigation.
- They provide a rapid, relatively inexpensive alternative to litigation.
- They usually encourage negotiated settlement rather than adjudicated decisions.
- They are often highly confidential in relation to litigation.
- They are flexible enough to be adapted on a case-by-case basis, because they are not governed by legal rules.
- They are typically provided by private practitioners for a fee, rather than by judges and lawyers.

ADR processes are well suited to the resolving of business disputes because they recognize the unique features of business conflict. First, unlike disputes involving private individuals, business conflicts may involve many constituencies. Even when one business disputes another, these constituencies can range from shareholders to employees to customers and vendors. Many business disputes involve multiple companies, which vastly increases the number of affected constituencies. One type of dispute resolution mechanism is unlikely to address the disparate needs of all constituencies involved. ADR processes can be tailored to satisfy the interests of all parties.

Second, businesses encounter internal and external disputes, while individuals generally do not. **Internal disputes** involve members of the business, such as managers or employees. **External disputes** apply to business members and some outside party, such as customers or vendors. In both instances, businesses desire resolutions that are prompt, amicable, and foster valuable future relationships. ADR achieves this by focusing on party negotiated outcomes, a result of nonadversarial processes.

Third, businesses, unlike individuals, face economic competition. As a result, businesses must recognize the potential competitive disadvantages associated with litigation, which is often a costly, protracted, public affair. Clearly, maximizing profit while solving corporate disputes is the principal competitive business consideration. However, businesses also want to maintain a favorable corporate image by privately resolving matters. Protecting trade secrets and proprietary information is another matter of importance. Alternative dispute resolution processes are generally less expensive, less time consuming, and more private than litigation.

Fourth, businesses are regulated in ways and to an extent that individuals are not and therefore must resolve disputes more frequently. Businesses value processes that amicably resolve claims brought under, for example, the Americans with Disabilities Act, the Age Discrimination in Employment Act, or Title VII.

THE MAJOR ALTERNATIVE DISPUTE RESOLUTION PROCESSES

Though many ways to address conflict in the business world exist, the major dispute resolution processes consist of two main classes: (1) those that reserve authority for resolution to the parties themselves and (2) those in which a third party decides the matter. By **authority** we mean the power to reach and enforce a resolution to a dispute. The first class includes negotiation, mediation, the summary jury trial, and the minitrial. The second applies to arbitration, private judging, and a hybrid mediation process called mediation-arbitration. Often, parties will attempt to resolve a matter through a process that they control before turning over the case to a third party.

Party-Driven Processes

The first four processes we will briefly define are the party-driven processes. We will begin with the least formal process and arrange the others according to their increasing formality.

Negotiation.   **Negotiation** (Chapter 3), the most widely used, is simply the process of refining and agreeing to the issues and establishing a range of compromise options. Negotiation is often done directly, without legal representation. Introducing legal agents entails a much more formal and often acrimonious negotiation process. Negotiation normally does not bring third parties to the case and is therefore the most private of all dispute resolution processes. Since there are no external rules or protection for the parties, it can also be risky.

Mediation.   **Mediation** (Chapter 4) uses a specially trained, neutral third party to help the disputants present their positions and generate and evaluate options to resolve the dispute. Mediation is more formal than negotiation, since it involves a third party and is often conducted pursuant to rules agreed to by the parties. Like negotiation, it may be done either through legal representatives or directly. Mediation is virtually always voluntary and private.

Minitrials.   **Minitrials** (Chapter 5) allow parties to carefully structure a process blending negotiation, mediation, and litigation. "Minitrial" is a somewhat deceptive term to describe a novel approach to structured negotiations first used to resolve a dispute between TRW, Inc., and Telecredit, Inc., in the late 1970s. In the process, attorneys each semiformally present the case to senior management representatives of each party. The parties structure in advance the length, content, and nature of the presentation so what the executives will hear is balanced and useful. Parties are normally permitted to engage in limited discovery prior to the presentation. Following the presentation, the executives may negotiate directly or with the assistance of a mediator, who often will have presided over the presentation. The minitrial process is voluntary and generally private.

Summary Jury Trial.   The **summary jury trial** (Chapter 5) enables parties to litigate in an abbreviated and mock courtroom proceeding designed to demonstrate the strengths and weaknesses of each side's case. Typically, a six-member jury is impaneled to hear the case *without* being advised that it will render a nonbinding and advisory verdict. Prior to the "trial," parties can engage in discovery, often including depositions and document requests. The parties then present an abbreviated version of their respective cases, including witnesses and evidence. Following this, the jury deliberates and presents its verdict from which the parties then endeavor to negotiate an outcome to the dispute. Like the minitrial, the summary jury trial is designed to preface negotiations with an objective review of the evidence.

Adjudicative Processes

Three adjudicative processes that are used widely by parties for resolution of disputes are arbitration, mediation-arbitration, and private judging. All three entail a decision, generally binding, made by an impartial third party.

Arbitration.   **Arbitration** (Chapters 6–8) is a private version of the public courtroom trial and is based on the presentation of evidence, rather than a negotiated understanding of the facts. It results in a third-party judgment by an arbitrator normally experienced in the subject matter of the case.

Because arbitration involves both evidence presentation, sometimes through witnesses and on the record, and third-party decision making, it is less private than other ADR processes. Arbitration is usually governed by either statutory or private rules. In either event, the parties will have agreed on the exact regulations for the procedure prior to the hearing. Due to these preexisting agreements, arbitration is largely a mandatory process. However, parties may, and often do, submit cases for arbitration without any obligation to do so.

Mediation-Arbitration.   **Mediation-arbitration** (Chapter 4), a blend of mediation and arbitration, initially calls upon a mediator to assist parties in reaching an agreement. If unsuccessful, the case is immediately transferred to arbitration for a binding judgment by a neutral party. Normally, the same neutral party works as both mediator and subsequently as arbitrator. Mediation-arbitration offers parties the advantages of a party-driven, informal process, while at the same time assuring them a specific timeframe within which their dispute will be resolved. In addition, this process, developed primarily in the labor context, motivates parties to settle through mediation so that they can avoid bringing in a neutral to render a judgment.

Private Judging.   Numerous states provide litigants with the opportunity to present their case before a privately hired judge, called **private judging.**[1] This retired state or federal court judge will hear testimony, review evidence, and render a decision in a dis-

---

1.   California (Cal. Civ. Proc. Code sec. 638–645), New Hampshire (N.H. Rev. Stat. Ann. sec. 519:9), and New York (N.Y. Civ. Proc. L. & R. 4301–21) are some examples.

pute. The private judging statutes in several states allow for juries to be impaneled and decisions to be appealed, though few parties actually appeal. States that specifically allow private judging hope to benefit from reduced demands on public court dockets. Litigants should also benefit from much quicker resolution of cases, though once commenced there is likely to be little economic savings as the process is essentially identical to public litigation. Litigants also have the advantage of the procedural experience and talents of one who has actually tried cases. Disputants are generally free to "rent a judge" in states that do not have authorizing statutes. However, they do not have the right to appeal the decision to a state court, nor are they assured of the enforceability of the decision reached in the process, as they would be in a conventional legal judgment.

THE ADVANTAGES OF ALTERNATIVE DISPUTE RESOLUTION

While all nonlitigation dispute resolution processes have unique advantages and disadvantages, some general observations can be made about those of alternative dispute resolution. We will discuss the advantages first.

Timeliness

Any alternative dispute resolution process will likely provide closure more rapidly than litigation. Less time is spent between occurrence and resolution due to the avoidance of vastly overcrowded court dockets. ADR processes can begin as soon as parties have prepared their cases, whereas it may take months to go to trial in federal courts and even years for state courts. Timeliness is also achieved because significantly less time is invested throughout the resolution process where such things as motions, witness preparation, and appeal are unnecessary.

Cost

Many alternative dispute resolution processes can be substantially less expensive than litigation. While a complete arbitration proceeding is unlikely to save much, mediation, for example, can significantly reduce the cost of resolving a dispute. ADR reduces expenses in several ways. First, attorney fees are reduced because there is less preparation and completion time. Indeed, companies may in some instances proceed without attorneys. Second, because expert witnesses seldom testify in most ADR processes, the expense incurred by retaining them is limited or avoided. Third, in cases involving potential substantial economic exposure, it is common for litigants to expend considerable sums on jury selection assistance. Virtually all ADR processes deem this expense unnecessary because juries either are not used or are only used in an advisory capacity. Finally, pretrial motion practice and discovery may both be curtailed in these processes, due to the focus on negotiated outcomes over evidentiary decisions.

Productive Outcomes

Many alternative dispute resolution processes provide negotiated outcomes that can enhance business relationships in a fashion not possible in an adversarial trial setting. Most ADR processes are without the level of acrimony and confrontation that the trial is likely to produce. In addition, the substance of negotiated resolutions is more likely to meet the individual needs and interests of the parties than the "one size fits all" approach taken in litigation. Indeed, negotiated settings can address types of compensation unavailable through a trial. Consider the following two examples of nontraditional remedies reached in real cases settled through mediation.

1. Faced with a possible substantial punitive damages judgment in a products liability case, a company agreed in mediation to pay a sizable sum of money to a charity chosen by an injured customer. The remedy was attractive to both parties. The company benefited by avoiding damages that could have been much greater than those calculated to compensate the plaintiff for actual losses. Such damages are among the most vigorously contested at trial. In addition, the company realized a potential tax benefit that would not have accrued through the payment of punitive damages to the plaintiff. Finally, the company had an obvious altruistic advantage in this sort of settlement. The plaintiff benefited as well. Payment of compensatory damages was quick and comparatively generous. The difficulty and risk of a trial was avoided. The deterrence associated with punitive damages was largely accomplished by the additional payment to the charity. The plaintiff also engaged in a sort of philanthropy.

2. After lengthy negotiations, an insurance company opted to cover college expenses of a high school senior injured in a facility covered by the company rather than to pay any direct damages to the plaintiff. Among the agreement's stipulations were the following: (1) payment was to be made only upon successful completion of each full year of education, (2) the education must take place in four successive years, (3) the education must be provided by a college or university agreed upon and listed in the mediation agreement, and (4) no further payment was required if the plaintiff failed out of or voluntarily left the college or university. Again, both sides gained through the use of ADR. The plaintiff recovered, without a trial, in excess of the probable value of the case if the four-year degree is completed. The insurance company was able to earn interest on the money reserved for payment by structuring payments over four years. In addition, the company was freed of any obligation if the plaintiff did not successfully complete each year of college. Finally, opportunity exists for very favorable public relations for the company.

Privacy

ADR processes are often confidential, which allows businesses to resolve disputes without creation of a public record or response. A company concerned about eroding public confidence in its product or services will be attracted to processes that allow it to negotiate an outcome without a public trial. Similarly, companies concerned about revealing trade secrets or proprietary information during litigation will welcome a process that avoids such disclosure. Finally, companies seeking to evade the creation of legal precedent that may later harm them will be eager to avail themselves of a process following which no appeal through which legal precedent could be established and generalized is permitted or possible.

Flexibility

Most alternative dispute resolution processes can be customized by the parties. For example, arbitration can be advisory or binding, by panel or by individual arbitrator, and with limited or unlimited evidence. Mediation can be done in a single session or a series of conferences with one or two mediators. In short, while several broadly defined processes exist, they can be refined to meet the needs of the participants. Conversely, the trial is governed in all state and federal courts by inflexible rules of procedure, providing parties with a high level of certainty relative to process but virtually no flexibility.

Internationalization

Businesses are competing on an international level with increasing regularity. As a result, they are often involved in disputes with companies from foreign countries. These sorts of disputes are among the most difficult and expensive to resolve because of jurisdiction issues. Jurisdiction is the law regarding which court has power to hear the case and render a judgment. In addition, companies in other countries often have negative perceptions of the American court system and regard defending a suit in the courts as a profoundly unpleasant experience. Moreover, the individuals managing foreign companies may have cultural orientations that suggest that negotiation, rather than litigation, is not simply the preferable fashion for resolving business disputes, but the only way, if a business relationship is to be continued. In resolving international disputes, ADR offers many of the same advantages listed above: speed, economy, flexibility, etc. It also enables American businesses to resolve disputes in a manner consistent with the cultural expectations of many foreign business managers.

ADR IN ACTION

The National Association of Manufacturers Builds a Dispute Resolution Problem

The National Association of Manufacturers (NAM) offers its members the opportunity to mediate business disputes through a joint project with the CPR Institute for Dispute Resolution. NAM is the old-

http://
For further information on the NAM, see this site: http://www.nam. org

http://

For further information on The CPR Institute for Dispute Resolution, see this site: http://www. cpradr.org/ welcome.htm

ADR IN ACTION (continued)

est industrial trade association in the United States. With fourteen thousand member companies and subsidiaries responsible for 85 percent of all domestically manufactured goods, it is also the largest. The CPR Institute for Dispute Resolution is an international, not-for-profit confederation of corporations, law firms, and academics with a panel of approximately six hundred lawyers, judges, and legally trained executives and scholars to serve as mediators and in other neutral roles.

The new program allows NAM members to submit for mediation any claim involving another NAM member. In addition, nonmembers may participate when one or more parties to the dispute are NAM members. Parties choose from the program roster a neutral to mediate the dispute. The program mediates disputes involving amounts in excess of fifty thousand dollars. Parties may be represented by counsel during the mediation conference, and the process

follows a set of rules developed by CPR.

In a recent press release, Jerry Jasinowski, president of NAM, stated that "[t]he Mediation Center for Business Disputes is an excellent way to reduce the problem manufacturers have been fighting for years: excessive litigation." He continued, "[I]f the business community can take the lead in resolving problems without relying on the courts and lawsuits, we will set an example for the rest of the country that there are more productive ways of settling disputes."

The CPR Institute reports an 85 percent settlement rate in mediation. It also finds that companies save an average of three hundred thousand dollars annually by using mediation. Finally, CPR President James Henry believes that "[i]n many cases, [companies] will be able to preserve important business relationships" by using the process.

http://

See the text of the Fifth Amendment as well as annotations at: http://www. findlaw.com/data /Constitution/ amendment05/

THE DISADVANTAGES OF ALTERNATIVE DISPUTE RESOLUTION

Procedural Concerns

Although we have discussed many advantages of ADR processes, there are also some drawbacks. Among the most significant are three constitutional concerns: due process, public access, and equal protection. The civil and criminal court systems at both the state and federal levels are governed by due process requirements rooted in the Fifth and Fourteenth Amendments to the U.S. Constitution. **Due process** is essentially the obligation to create laws and the procedures by which they are applied, including the trial, that are fair and reasonable. To ensure that parties receive due process at trial, carefully constructed rules of civil and criminal procedure have been developed. These rules provide parties with trials that are procedurally fair and consistent. For example, due process prohibits courts in criminal proceedings from requiring self-incriminating statements from a defendant. It provides the right to present evidence, to confront one's adversaries, and to cross-examine hostile witnesses. In short, this bedrock American legal principle assures litigants of consistent and equitable treatment under the law.

It should be noted, however, that due process requirements create longer and more difficult proceedings. In addition, due process, as we know it in the United States, is based upon the adversarial system of evidentiary justice. As a result, parties seeking amicable resolutions to disputes rarely find them through the trial.

Equal protection rights, based on the Fourteenth Amendment of the U.S. Constitution, assure all individuals and businesses of similar, if not identical, treatment at law. Equal protection prohibits governments from closing the courts to the indigent, while allowing access to the wealthy. Likewise, it guarantees the same level of consideration to all litigants once in court. In short, it provides a day in court for all who have a justiciable issue for resolution, irrespective of their social or economic status.

Because alternative dispute resolution processes are informal and private, they are not governed by due process principles in any meaningful way. Parties normally either draft rules of procedure for themselves on a case-by-case basis or rely voluntarily on model rules promulgated by professional associations. As a result, by pursuing an alternative dispute resolution process, parties waive certain due process rights and protections they may have had at trial. Furthermore, because certain claims of minimal economic consequence have become subject to mandatory ADR, the courthouse has been effectively closed to some disputants.

The following two cases consider the variety of constitutional rights affected by alternative dispute resolution. The *State Farm* case, including a dissenting opinion, considers both due process and equal protection rights as they relate to mandatory arbitration of insurance claims. The *Rhea* case explores a right closely associated with due process, the potential violation of the Seventh Amendment right to a jury adjudication of a dispute when mandatory mediation is required prior to a jury trial. These issues are also important in the NLO case, which addresses mandatory participation in a summary jury trial, and which is considered in Chapter 5.

http://

See the text of the Fourteenth Amendment as well as annotations at: http://www. findlaw.com/data /Constitution/ amendment14/

STATE FARM MUTUAL AUTOMOBILE INSURANCE COMPANY V. BROADNAX, ET. AL.

827 P.2d 531 (1992)

FACT SUMMARY

State Farm issued an automobile insurance policy to Earle Broadnax. After being involved in two car accidents, Broadnax submitted claims to State Farm for personal injury benefits under his policy. A dispute regarding payment ensued, and Broadnax served State Farm with a Demand for Arbitration. State Farm filed a Petition to Stay Arbitration and sought a declaration that the No Fault Act requiring mandatory arbitration was unconstitutional. Insurers are obligated under the No Fault Act to provide direct benefits to insureds. When an insured is liable for benefits paid by another insurer, the No Fault Act requires insurers to resolve reimbursement issues through mandatory, binding arbitration.

OPINION: *VOLLACK, Justice*

State Farm contends that the No Fault Act requiring mandatory arbitration of certain claims extinguishes its right of access to courts because the section removes State Farm's statutory cause of action for disputes arising under the No Fault Act from a trial to jury before a district court, without providing a right of review by a district court following an adverse arbitration award. After careful consideration of the constitutional guarantee, we find no violation of State Farm's right of access to courts. State Farm's contention posits that the right of access to courts guarantees Colorado litigants a trial to jury before a district court for disputes arising under the No Fault Act.

The United States Constitution does not expressly provide for a right of access to courts. Rather, the federal right of access to courts has been located in the Due Process Clause of the Fourteenth Amendment, in the First Amendment's provision securing the right to petition the government for redress of grievances, and in the Privileges and Immunities Clause of the Fourteenth Amendment.

The United States Supreme Court has noted that the right of access to courts and the guarantees of due process have developed in response to challenges by defendants involuntarily haled into the formal judicial process. Thus, whether litigants are afforded adequate constitutional access to courts often sounds in due process under federal analysis.

Colorado, however, is one of thirty-seven states which diverged from the federal constitutional model by creating an express right of access to courts independent of constitutional due process guarantees.

In evaluating the right of access under the Alabama Constitution, Justice Shores has noted that the origins of the right can be traced back to the Magna Carta. Although its language is broad enough to be subject to varying interpretations, it can generally be said to incorporate into our constitution a fundamental principle of fairness, a perhaps vaguely conceived but important notion of limitation on the power of government to infringe upon individual rights, and to act arbitrarily. What those rights are, what degree of infringement is permitted, and with how much justification, are inquiries which have been the subject of long-standing debate.

Under the Louisiana constitutional guarantee, for example, the legislature is free to allocate access to the formal judicial system using any system or classification which is not totally arbitrary so long as access to the system is not essential to the exercise of a fundamental constitutional right.

The Utah access to courts provision "guarantees access to the courts and a judicial procedure that is based on fairness and equality." Utah courts construe the constitutional right of access to courts by examining its history and plain language, in addition to its functional relationship to other constitutional provisions. The Utah Supreme Court has accordingly noted that the right of access provision and the due process clause "are related both in their historical origins and to some extent in their constitutional functions." The two provisions are thus "complementary and even overlap, but they are not wholly duplicative. Both act to restrict the powers of both the courts and the legislature."

In Colorado, the access to courts provision guarantees that courts will be available to effectuate rights that accrue under law. This court has stated that "generally, a burden on a party's right of access to the courts will be upheld so long as it is reasonable." We have recently observed that the right of access under the Colorado Constitution "protects initial access to the courts."

In the present case, State Farm calls on this court to evaluate its access to the judicial process as set out in the No Fault Act. Disputes arising under the No Fault Act proceed to binding arbitration before resorting to courts. Each party to the arbitration selects an arbitrator, and these two arbitrators select a third. The arbitrators then set a time and place for a hearing, with the mutual consent of the parties. Arbitrators may issue subpoenas for witnesses and compel production of evidence. Arbitrators must file an order with the insurance commissioner within ten days of the hearing. Such orders may be vacated, modified, or corrected pursuant to the Uniform Arbitration Act.

The Uniform Arbitration Act in turn confers jurisdiction on Colorado courts to enforce and enter judgments on arbitration awards. Parties may apply to courts to confirm arbitration. Parties may also apply to courts to vacate awards where the arbitrators exceeded their powers or where an award was procured by fraud, corruption, or other undue means. Parties may also apply to courts to modify or correct arbitration awards where there was an evident mistake or where the award was premised on a matter not submitted to the arbitrators. Finally, parties may appeal such court orders "in the manner and to the same extent as from orders or judgments in civil actions."

In determining whether this dispute resolution scheme secures State Farm's right of access to the judicial process, we are guided by the requirements of due process. The United States Supreme Court has consistently held that due process requires some form of hearing—the opportunity to be heard at a meaningful time, and in a meaningful manner.

Under the statutory scheme, State Farm clearly has the right to a hearing in which State Farm can present all the evidence, and raise all the defenses available to it. State Farm also has the right to resort to the formal judicial system should it find an arbitrator's order adverse to its interest. We thus conclude that State Farm is not

http://

The American Arbitration Association has placed the Uniform Arbitration Act text on-line at this site: http://www.adr. org/uniform.html #intro deprived of its access to the judicial process under the Colorado Constitution.

We are not alone in our determination. The Court of Appeals for the Fourth Circuit has observed that "it is too late in the day to argue that compulsory arbitration, per se, denies due process of law . . . Congress may require arbitration so long as fair procedures are provided and ultimate judicial review is available." Where a party "may come to the district court to enforce, vacate or modify an arbitrator's award, [the party] is not denied meaningful access to the Courts."

We similarly have noted that the No Fault Insurance Act seeks to reduce tort litigation, and that arbitration serves that end. We conclude that State Farm has not been deprived of its right of access.

We have observed that "arbitration provides an efficient, convenient alternative to litigation." We again note that one of the General Assembly's primary purposes in passing the No Fault Act was "to reduce the amount of tort litigation arising out of automobile accidents," and to provide prompt resolution of disputed payments. Were we to adopt State Farm's position, we would be required to overlook both the current demands on the Colorado judicial system and the need for prompt payment of personal injury protection benefits that we have acknowledged when encouraging the use of arbitration as a method of dispute resolution. We decline to take that approach.

State Farm contends that [the No Fault Act] violates its right to equal protection of the laws because the section imposes a restriction on the fundamental right of access to courts.

We have already recognized the state's interest in reducing tort litigation arising out of automobile accidents and in prompt payment of personal injury

protection benefits. This state prefers arbitration as a method for resolving disputes because it "promotes quicker resolution of disputes by providing an expedited opportunity for the parties to present their cases before an unbiased third party." By promoting quicker resolution of disputes, arbitration thus reduces the parties' costs. Colorado's dispute resolution scheme is rationally related to legitimate interests in expediting dispute resolution, reducing parties' costs, and securing prompt payment of benefits. We reject State Farm's equal protection challenge.

KIRSHBAUM, Justice dissenting

Because the United States Constitution contains no express right of access guarantee, federal courts have by necessity addressed issues with respect to access to state courts in the framework of due process analysis. The right itself, however, is firmly rooted in the right of petition guaranteed by the First Amendment to the United States Constitution. The right has also been defined as one of the privileges and immunities guaranteed to all citizens by article 4 of the United States Constitution. The right is "one of the fundamental rights protected by the Constitution."

State courts assessing the significance of particular right to access provisions contained in their state constitutions have predictably described the characteristics of the right itself in various ways. Some have emphasized its historical roots in sections of the Magna Carta. In a thorough and thoughtful opinion declaring a portion of a statute of repose for products liability cases to be violative of state constitutional open access guarantees, the Utah Supreme Court articulated a two-part test seeking to balance the legislative authority to alter rights and remedies with the fundamental guarantee of access to courts contained in Utah's constitution.

I find persuasive those decisions that conclude that right to access guarantees must be considered in relationship to the significance of the right advanced by the party seeking such access. If the underlying right is a fundamental right, the right of access itself must be fundamental. Such analysis requires careful evaluation of issues and facts on a case-by-case basis. However, it rejects the conclusion that the right of access guarantee is merely a due process guarantee—a conclusion that in this jurisdiction ignores the separate due process guarantee provided by our constitution and tends to reduce the language of article II, section 6, to a mere statement of principle. That analytical framework also avoids many of the problems perceived to result from a conclusion that the right of access is in all contexts fundamental.

In the context of this case, the interest advanced by State Farm—the right to protect its property interests under particular contracts—must be deemed a fundamental right. We have recently noted that at least some of the inalienable rights enumerated in that section are fundamental in nature. Surely the right to protect one's property interests from conduct by private parties allegedly appropriating those interests is fundamental to our concept of ordered liberty.

Application of strict scrutiny analysis to the circumstances of this case requires the conclusion that the compulsory arbitration provisions violate State Farm's fundamental right of access to the courts for the protection of its property interests. The primary justification advanced for the adoption of these compulsory arbitration provisions is the legislative goal of reducing tort litigation. That policy is not furthered through legislation prohibiting a person alleging a deprivation of property interests by conduct of private parties from pursuing appropriate judicial remedies. No other justification appearing of record, the provisions cannot stand.

Even if the right to protect property interests by access to courts secured by our constitution is not accorded fundamental status, application of due process requires the conclusion that the judicial review provisions contained therein are constitutionally inadequate.

Because the General Assembly has authority to alter established rights and remedies, arguments premised on access to courts provisions are unpersuasive to the extent they are based on a vested rights analysis. This legislative authority is not absolute, however; it must be exercised within constitutional constraints, including the limitations established by article II, section 6. Assuming that the minimal rational relationship standard of due process analysis is applicable, the determination of whether a particular statutory scheme limiting access to the courts is rationally related to a legitimate legislative purpose requires examination of the government interests involved and the procedural alternatives provided, as well as the significance of the affected private interests. At a minimum, the legislation must provide the litigant with a meaningful opportunity to obtain independent judicial analysis of those interests at a meaningful stage of the dispute resolving process.

The right to participate in an arbitration proceeding is not a right to participate in a judicial proceeding. At a minimum, due process analysis requires that abolition of the traditional judicial forum be justified on a quid pro quo basis. As has been noted, the General Assembly did not abolish common law contract remedies by [the No Fault Act.] It rather directed disputes about the availability of such remedy to arbitration processes, thus prohibiting determination of those traditional common-law claims by trial. To the extent the reciprocal benefit is the elimination of tort claims, there is no quid pro quo at all. To the extent the reciprocal benefit is a reduction in delay of payments to insureds, it is far from clear that the procedures established will substantially achieve such results.

Assuming the constitutional validity of the General Assembly's decision to require submission of common-law contract claims to compulsory arbitration, thus insulating such claims from adversarial examination of testimony, exhibits and witness credibility under the procedural and evidentiary rules associated with the trial process, such assumption does not answer the serious questions raised by the legislative decision to restrict judicial review of such proceedings to the narrow standards established by the Uniform Arbitration Act. Those provisions are wholly inadequate to protect the important, if not fundamental, right here involved.

The Uniform Act contains stringent limitations on the scope of judicial review of initial arbitration awards. A reviewing court has authority to vacate an arbitration award only if the award was procured by "corruption, fraud, or other undue means . . . ; if there is evidence that a party's rights were prejudiced because of corruption or misconduct or lack of impartiality by one or more arbitrators; if the arbitrators or one of them acted in excess of the powers granted by the Uniform Act; if the arbitrators failed to postpone a hearing or to hear relevant evidence, to the prejudice

of parties; or, in specified circumstances, if there was no arbitration agreement." A reviewing court may modify or correct an award only if the award contains miscalculations of figures or mistakes in descriptions; if it was made upon a matter not submitted to arbitration and the award may be corrected without affecting the merits of the decision appropriately rendered; or if the award is "imperfect in a matter of form, not affecting the merits of the controversy."

The Uniform Act thus does not permit the reviewing court to review the sufficiency of the evidence or the propriety of procedural rulings. Furthermore, the reviewing court is for all practical purposes precluded from reviewing evidentiary rulings, and in the absence of specific contractual directions may not vacate an arbitration award even if the arbitrator misapplied applicable rules of law. In view of the absence of initial judicial evaluation of evidence and issues and the presence of the inalienable, if not fundamental, right to have meaningful access to the judicial process to resolve contractual disputes involving private property interests, this extraordinarily limited right to judicial review is neither meaningful nor reasonable.

At the very least, the right of access provisions of the Colorado Constitution require the availability of meaningful judicial review of non-judicial determinations of private disputes over property interests. In my view, [the No Fault Act] does not provide such meaningful review of State Farm's property interests.

For the foregoing reasons, I find the compulsory arbitration provisions violative of the Colorado Constitution. I therefore respectfully dissent from the contrary conclusion reached by the majority.

http://

For a more in-depth look at dispute resolution in Colorado, see the site of the state office of dispute resolution: http://www.courts.state.co.us/odr/odrcol.htm

RHEA V. MASSEY-FERGUSON, INC.
767 F.2d 266 (6th Cir., 1985)

FACT SUMMARY

Rhea was injured when he inadvertently shifted a Massey-Ferguson 245 tractor into gear while he stood beside it. The tractor began moving forward, although no one had depressed the clutch lever. The tractor's right rear wheel first rolled over Rhea's leg, forcing him under the machine, before it rolled over his shoulder and chest. Rhea suffered numerous fractures and lost part of one ear in the accident. Rhea filed this action in state court alleging that Massey-Ferguson was liable for negligent design and breach of implied warranty. Massey-Ferguson transferred the action to federal district court. The case was then sent to mediation prior to trial, but no settlement was reached.

OPINION: *Per Curiam Decision*

Massey-Ferguson challenges the district court's referral of this case to mediation under the Eastern District of Michigan's Local Rule 32, which provides that a diversity case involving only monetary damages may be referred to mediation before trial. Massey-Ferguson rejected and Rhea accepted the resulting $100,000 proposed award. Therefore, Massey-Ferguson was liable for costs unless the verdict at trial was more than ten percent below the evaluation. The jury returned a verdict that was more than twice the mediation evaluation and the district court awarded $5,400 in actual costs to Rhea.

Massey-Ferguson contends that this procedure violates its Seventh Amendment right to a jury. The Seventh Amendment "was designed to preserve the basic institution of jury trial in only its most fundamental elements, not the great mass of procedural forms and details." At the core of these fundamental elements is the right to have a "jury ultimately determine the issues of fact if they cannot be settled by the parties or determined as a matter of law." Federal courts have repeatedly upheld mandatory arbitration procedures in the face of challenges based on the right to a jury trial. In keeping with the Seventh Amendment's requirements Massey-Ferguson received the jury's determination of the disputed facts in the present action.

Massey-Ferguson also characterizes [the referral to mediation and imposition of costs] as violating numerous Federal Rules of Civil Procedure. Federal Rule of Civil Procedure 83 authorizes district courts to "regulate their practice in any manner not inconsistent with these rules." The challenged local rule is not inconsistent merely because it interposes an additional step between the jury demand and trial. The mediation panel merely issues a settlement evaluation that has no force unless accepted by the parties. In sum, no flaw requiring this Court to intervene in the district court's practice under Local Rule 32 has been raised in the present suit.

http://

See the text of the Seventh Amendment as well as annotations at:
http://www.findlaw.com/data/Constitution/amendment07/

Discussion Questions

1. Does imposing mandatory participation in an alternative dispute resolution process prior to jury adjudication unfairly inflate the cost of resolution for a party unable or unwilling to settle?
2. Is the right to jury adjudication diminished in situations where parties have been given exposure to the case an opponent is prepared to present in litigation?
3. Is a trial a fundamental right? If not, should it be?

Public Policy Issues

See the text of the First Amendment as well as annotations at: http://www.findlaw.com/data/Constitution/amendment01/

Public access and First Amendment questions are often raised by the use of alternative dispute resolution processes. Because virtually all ADR processes are conducted off the record, in private settings, and with no public access, the public and the press have expressed reservations about the processes. The following case addresses the public's right to gain access to information presented during litigation leading to settlement. The case relies on a long-standing, common-law right of access to court proceedings. The dissent is included because it carefully conveys the public policy reasons for supporting settlement by upholding the secrecy of materials used to reach settlement.

BANK OF AMERICA NATIONAL V. HOTEL RITTENHOUSE
800 F.2d 339 (3rd Cir., 1986)

FACT SUMMARY

The dispute that forms the basis for this case arose out of the construction of the Hotel Rittenhouse. In 1981, the Bank of America contracted with Hotel Rittenhouse Associates and other developers to finance the construction of the hotel. FAB III was the concrete contractor on the project. In June 1983, the Bank filed suit against Hotel Rittenhouse Associates, its partners, and some involved individuals, referred to collectively as HRA, in the U.S. District Court in order to foreclose on the Hotel Rittenhouse property and to collect on a loan. HRA counterclaimed on numerous state and federal law grounds. In April 1984, FAB III filed suit in federal court against the Bank, but not against HRA. FAB III was seeking over $800,000 on the basis of an alleged assurance by the Bank of direct payment for FAB III's HRA work. The Bank-HRA action proceeded to trial in January 1985. Before the case could be sent to the jury, the parties reached a settlement, and the jury was discharged. At the parties' request, the settlement agreement was filed under seal. Prior to this, all proceedings in the litigation had been open to the public. Shortly thereafter, the Bank of America and HRA disagreed about the settlement. Release of the documents filed to enforce the settlement would reveal the contents of the settlement agreement.

At this time, FAB III attempted to obtain the settlement agreement and the documents filed in federal court to enforce the settlement. In April 1985, FAB III and other creditors of HRA met with the district court and requested it to unseal the documents. This request was denied. Shortly thereafter, FAB III filed a formal motion with the district court to unseal the settlement documents. Following what FAB III's brief characterizes as "an informal conference in chambers," the court denied the motion to unseal. The court stated that it had weighed "the public interest in access to judicial records," as well as FAB III's interest in access to the settlement, against "the public and private interests in settling disputes" and had found that the latter interest was paramount.

OPINION: *SLOVITER, Circuit Judge*

In this appeal, we are faced with an issue that this court has confronted with increasing frequency in recent years, under what circumstances documents filed in the district court may be sealed from public access.

FAB III bases its claim for access to the documents filed in the district court on the common law right of access, rather than on the First Amendment. The right of the public to inspect and copy judicial records antedates the Constitution. The Supreme Court reaffirmed the common law right of access to judicial records and proceedings in *Nixon v. Warner Communications, Inc.* [435 U.S. 589, 55 L. Ed. 2d 570, 98 S. Ct. 1306 (1978)], where it held that there was a presumption in favor of access to "public records and documents, including judicial records and documents."

This court first considered that right of access in Criden I, where we held that there was a "strong presumption" that the public and the media were entitled to access to tapes played during the criminal trial of two of the Abscam defendants. We have also held that the common law presumption of access encompasses as well all "civil trials and records." More recently, we held that "the common law right of access to judicial records is fully applicable to transcripts of sidebar or chambers conferences in criminal cases at which evidentiary or other substantive rulings have been made."

Other opinions in this court have grounded access to court hearings on the First Amendment. In *United States v. Criden* [675 F.2d 550 (3d Cir. 1982) (Criden II)], we held that there is a First Amendment right of access to pretrial criminal proceedings. We explicitly based our holding that the press and the public could have access to a hearing in a civil proceeding and the transcript thereof on the First Amendment right of access as well as the common law.

Just as the right of access is firmly entrenched, so also is the correlative principle that the right of access, whether grounded on the common law or the First Amendment, is not absolute. Our opinions may be read to suggest that there are somewhat different standards, depending on whether access is sought under the common law presumption or under the First Amendment. In Publicker, we required the party opposing access to show "'an overriding interest based on findings that closure is narrowly tailored to serve that interest'" [733 F.2d at 1073]. In Criden I, we held the strong common law presumption of access must be balanced against the factors militating against access [648 F.2d at 818]. The burden is on the party who seeks to overcome the presumption of access to show that the interest in secrecy outweighs the presumption.

The district court was cognizant that its decision required it to balance the factors favoring secrecy against the common law presumption of access. In denying FAB III's motion for access to the settlement documents, the court held that the "public and private interests in settling disputes" outweighed the "public interest in access to judicial records" and FAB III's private interest in knowing the terms of the settlement.

The balancing of the factors for and against access is a decision committed to the discretion of the district court. Thus, the issue before us is whether the district court abused its discretion in holding that the judicial policy of promoting the settlement of litigation justifies the denial of public access to records and proceedings to enforce such settlements.

We acknowledge the strong public interest in encouraging settlement of private litigation. Settlements save the parties the substantial cost of litigation and conserve the limited resources of the judiciary. In order to encourage the compromise and settlement of disputes, evidence of settlements or offers of settlement are ordinarily not admissible in federal proceedings. See Fed. R. Evid. 408 and advisory committee note thereto.

http://

A complete version of the Federal Rules of Evidence is provided at: http://www.law.cornell.edu/rules/fre/overview.html

Judge Garth [who authored the dissenting opinion that follows] has written an interesting and vigorous essay about the importance of settlement to the overburdened court systems of this country. Since the proposition is self-evident, it is intended to, and undoubtedly will, touch a sympathetic chord in the hearts of all judges who, after all, bear much of the burden of the litigation explosion to which Judge Garth refers.

Noteworthy, however, is the fact that Judge Garth practically ignores the relevant posture of the case before us. This is not like *FDIC v. Ernst & Ernst* [677 F.2d 230 (2d Cir. 1982)], which he relies on, where there was an effort to unseal a settlement agreement made two years earlier. Here, there were motions filed and orders entered that were kept secret, in direct contravention of the open access to judicial records that the common law protects. FAB III began its efforts to unseal the court papers almost immediately after these court documents were filed and sealed.

In the name of encouraging settlements, Judge Garth would have us countenance what are essentially secret judicial proceedings. We cannot permit the expediency of the moment to overturn centuries of tradition of open access to court documents and orders.

Having undertaken to utilize the judicial process to interpret the settlement and enforce it, the parties are no longer entitled to invoke the confidentiality ordinarily accorded settlement agreements. Once a settlement is filed in the district court, it becomes a judicial record, and subject to the access accorded such records.

Such public access serves several of the important interests we identified in our earlier cases. First, it promotes "informed discussion of governmental affairs by providing the public with [a] more complete understanding of the judicial system" and the "public perception of fairness which can be achieved only by permitting full public view of the proceedings." Disclosure of settlement documents serves as a check on the integrity of the judicial process. Although FAB III does not allege that the district court engaged in any impropriety, as a general proposition access assures "that the courts are fairly run and judges are honest." [*Crystal Grower's Corp. v. Dennis,* 616 F.2d 458, 461 (10th Cir. 1980)] The applicability and importance of these interests are not lessened because they are asserted by a private party to advance its own interests in pursuing its lawsuits against the Bank and HRA.

We conclude that the district court abused its discretion in denying FAB III's motion to unseal the motions and settlement agreement papers.

GARTH, J., Dissenting

The majority today, totally disregarding the difference between the sealing and the unsealing of an agreement, in an unprecedented decision, holds that the interest in settlement may not outweigh the public's right of access even in private litigation. I cannot agree, and therefore, I dissent.

I believe that the majority misconstrues the issue now before the court. The majority claims the issue before us to be: "under what circumstances [may] documents filed in the district court . . . be sealed from public access." However, that is not the issue this case presents. The question is not whether material which is already public should now be sealed; the question is whether a privately negotiated settlement agreement, agreed to and entered into a court record only on condi-

tion that it remain secret, should now be unsealed because of the district court's supposed abuse of discretion in permitting it to be filed under seal.

The resolution of the correct issue raised here dictates an approach that would protect the reliance interests of the parties absent exceptional circumstances. Moreover, in reviewing the district court's denial of FAB's motion to unseal the Bank-HRA agreement, the majority adopts, for all practical purposes, a per se rule that the interest in settling cases can never outweigh the public's right of access and thereby justify a court in sealing the terms of a voluntary settlement. The majority opinion holds that the generalized interest in encouraging settlements does not rise to the level of interests that we have recognized may outweigh the public's common law right of access. The majority's holding on this point is not compelled by any precedent, and it utterly ignores the importance of, and the practical realities surrounding, the process of settling lawsuits.

Because I believe that the public and private interest in encouraging settlement is entitled to significant weight, and because the majority's analysis and holding cannot help but impair seriously the efficacy of judicial efforts to encourage settlement of many cases, I cannot join in this result.

As the majority recognizes, in deciding whether the common law right of access compels the disclosure of materials before the court, the district court must "weigh the interests advanced by the parties in light of the public interest and duty of the courts." [*Nixon v. Warner Communications,* 435 U.S. 589, 602, 55 L. Ed. 2d 570, 98 S. Ct. 1306 (1978)] This court has held that the common law right of access creates a presumption of access to all judicial records and documents. I therefore agree that, as a general matter, the common law right of access applies to settlement agreements when such agreements are filed with the court and become a part of the public record.

However, a settlement agreement that has never been disclosed to the public, but which was only entered into the record by the parties with the understanding that it would remain secret, presents a situation different from any situation that this court has addressed before. Although a presumption of access certainly arises when a court seals the transcript of a sidebar conference that has already taken place on the record in open court, or when a party seeks access to material already entered into evidence and provided to the jury, this case involves material and information that was never public, giving rise to a new and different factor: the reliance of the parties on the initial and continuing secrecy of the settlement agreement.

Although this court has not apparently addressed this precise situation, the Second Circuit has held that, "once a confidentiality order has been entered and relied upon, it can only be modified if an 'extraordinary circumstance' or 'compelling need' warrants the requested modification." [*FDIC v. Ernst & Ernst,* 677 F.2d 230, 232 (2d Cir. 1982)] The Second Circuit therefore affirmed the denial of a motion to lift a protective order sealing a settlement agreement.

The *Ernst & Ernst* case presents what I regard as a sensible standard and a sensible result. Although the common law right of access must be given due regard, a court cannot operate in a vacuum. To apply mechanistically the same test no matter what the factual circumstances, is to risk doing injustice to parties before the court. Therefore, I agree that when a doc-

ument or item of evidence has been entered into the public record without any reliance on secrecy, the interests of the parties seeking to seal or unseal such material must be weighed in light of a presumption of openness. However, when a document has only been entered into the record in reliance on an order keeping it under seal, and when time has passed and the parties have acted in reliance on the terms of that settlement remaining under seal, I would hold with the Second Circuit that the presumption must shift. While the public interest in openness of court records must nevertheless be factored into the balance, I think it is appropriate that a protective order or seal order which itself induced the production or entry of the contested material be presumed to remain in effect, absent a showing of an "extraordinary circumstance" or "compelling need" by a third party seeking to unseal that information.

Even if I were to accept (which I do not) the majority's holding that the presumption in favor of access to judicial records still applies when a third party seeks to unseal a settlement agreement entered under seal and in reliance upon secrecy, I still could not agree to the majority's rule of law that the interest in settling cases cannot serve to rebut the presumption of access and therefore cannot justify the sealing of a settlement agreement. I believe that such a rule is completely out of touch with the reality of running a trial court docket—a reality with which our district court judges must wrestle every day—and if permitted to remain as the law of our circuit will wreak havoc with judicial efforts to encourage settlement of appropriate cases.

Although I believe the matter to be self-evident, the majority's out-of-hand rejection of the encouragement of settlement as a relevant factor in the decision to seal a settlement agreement requires me to explain both why I believe that fostering voluntary settlements of civil disputes is desirable and necessary, and why this goal will be unavoidably subverted by the majority's holding in this case.

It is impossible to gainsay that we have experienced a litigation explosion in the United States during the last twenty years and that developing techniques for managing the increased caseloads and for otherwise stemming the burgeoning tide of litigation costs has become a subject of intense interest and debate. Between 1973 and 1983, new filings of civil cases in the federal district courts rose from 98,560 to 241,842, an increase of 145 percent. Perhaps more importantly, the number of long, complex, and difficult-to-try cases has also increased dramatically. The federal courts held 213 trials lasting 20 days or more in 1973. The figure doubled to 426 by 1983.

To cope with the increasing volume of litigation, many commentators have advocated an active, "managerial" role for judges in supervising the course of litigation—a role that includes the encouragement of a variety of alternate means of resolving disputes short of full-dress trials.

Although arbitration, mediation, minitrials, and other forms of alternative dispute resolution have gained prominence in recent years as potent weapons in the war against litigation glut, the key component of every rational approach to reducing the burden on our clogged court dockets has been and remains settlement. With very rare exceptions, commentators and judges who may concur on little else, agree on the value and necessity of a vigorous policy of encouraging fair and reasonable settlement of civil claims whenever possible. Indeed, the literature

on the settlement of civil suits focuses not on whether settlement is desirable, but on how best to achieve it and how far a judge should go to encourage it.

This court, too, has recognized the overwhelming importance of settling civil suits and avoiding the wasted resources and institutional burden of trying every case.

> Voluntary settlement of civil controversies is in high judicial favor. Judges and lawyers alike strive assiduously to promote amicable adjustments of matters in dispute, as for the most wholesome of reasons they certainly should. When the effort is successful, the parties avoid the expense and delay incidental to litigation of the issues; the court is spared the burdens of a trial and the preparation and proceedings that must forerun it. [*Pennwalt Corp. v. Plough, Inc.,* 676 F.2d 77, 80 (3d Cir. 1982)]

Indeed, recognition of the desirability of settlement has even found its way into the Federal Rules of Civil Procedure. Rule 16 was amended in 1983 to include the pursuit of settlement as an express goal of the pretrial conference. Thus, an activist role for judges in managing cases—and encouraging their settlement—has expressly been provided for under the federal rules.

As any trial judge knows, the settlement of civil cases is not just a permissible and desirable goal, but a practical necessity. In one study of cases filed in ten courts, fully 88 percent were settled; only 9 percent went to trial.

While the importance of settlement would seem to be self-evident, I believe it is equally obvious that confidentiality is often a key ingredient in a settlement agreement—and that many settlements would not be reached if the secrecy of their terms could not be safeguarded.

Both courts and commentators have recognized the crucial role of confidentiality in facilitating settlement of civil cases. In addition, the need to keep secret the terms of a settlement has been recognized as a justification for imposing a protective order guaranteeing confidentiality of certain discovery material exchanged prior to settlement.

While few cases address the question of the sealing of settlement agreements, I suspect that this is because many trial judges regard it as self-evident that secrecy is often necessary, and they therefore order settlement agreements filed under seal as a matter of course. This conclusion is supported by the frequent references to such sealings made without comment or challenge in reported cases.

Parties may have many reasons for desiring secrecy for the terms of their settlements. Settlement agreements may include trade secrets or information that threaten the privacy of the parties. While this kind of information would itself justify a seal order, parties may in good faith be concerned about releasing a far wider range of information, including information which would not itself entitle the parties to a protective order, but which might stand in the way of settlement if required to be disclosed.

The necessity for confidentiality may be particularly acute in the mass tort area, where a defendant must look beyond the parameters of a settlement with a single plaintiff and anticipate the impact of its settlement on innumerable future cases. As Edward A. Dauer, Associate Dean of Yale Law School, explained in a Second Circuit Judicial Conference discussion on alternative dispute resolution.

> There are legitimate, good faith reasons for the parties who are trying to work out a solution to something like this toxic tort case to want their discussions to be private, immune both from later admission and immune from discovery by other potential plaintiffs' lawyers later down the road, maybe even from competitors, and I think there are good faith reasons for wanting that privacy. That confidentiality is a very large advantage that will, if it can be guaranteed, make these kinds of [alternative] procedures even more useful as adjuncts to the judicial process than they already are.

For example, if a defendant facing multiple plaintiffs seeks to settle a meritorious claim for a certain sum of money, it may be deterred from doing so if it knows that the terms of such a settlement would have to be made public. The defendant may reasonably assume that disclosure of the comparatively favorable settlement terms would interfere with its ability to settle other cases for smaller amounts. I have no doubt that if all such settlement details were by rule of law always public, many settlements would never take place at all. Many defendants would almost certainly proceed to trial rather than broadcast to all potential plaintiffs how much they might be willing to pay.

Moreover, it is precisely in the context of mass torts with multiple plaintiffs—such matters as air disasters, toxic injuries, and product liability claims—that the interest in settlement is particularly strong. Such cases are characteristically long, complex, and costly to try, and the savings in public and private resources achieved by settling them are immense. As one judge familiar with the trial of mass tort cases noted:

> Even saving one week of judicial time per case would, as most trial judges know, be substantial. For example, in the Dalkon Shield litigation, the record disclosed that, if the usual percentage (90) of the 1000 members statewide class settled their cases, the savings of judicial resources in the trial of the remaining 100 would amount to

400 weeks, or, roughly eight years of trial time. In addition, there would be an estimated savings of $26 million in litigation expense to the parties and $7 million of court expenses.

The rule announced today by the majority flies in the face of this reality. By holding that settlement agreements may not be sealed to serve the interest of encouraging settlements, I believe the majority has removed from the discretion of our district courts an important technique for encouraging settlement. It is my belief that district court judges in this circuit will read the majority's opinion to the same effect.

Under the majority's rule, a district court judge faced with the prospect of a six month, 12 month or longer trial, who is told by the parties that they would settle the case if the terms of settlement could be filed with the court under seal, would have only one choice—to reject the settlement and proceed to trial. The judge would have no discretion to accept the settlement under seal even if the proposed settlement contained little information of public interest and the interests of both sides of the dispute would be furthered by the settlement.

With all due respect to my colleagues in the majority, theirs is an illogical and impractical result. We are dealing here not with a constitutional right, but with a flexible common-law rule that has historically been applied subject to the discretion of the district court. Moreover, decisions regarding the management of its docket and the expediting of case resolutions would seem to lie at the core of the district court's discretionary powers. Therefore, assuming that a district court judge correctly weighs the public and private interests involved in deciding whether to order a settlement admitted under seal, I can see no reason why the interest in encouraging settlement should not be entitled to due weight. Indeed, any other rule would improperly abridge the traditional discretion of the district judge and seriously impair the ability of judges to expedite settlement.

In this case, the district court acknowledged the correct standards and concluded in its order that "FAB III's asserted interest in access to the sealed information does not outweigh the public and private interests in favor of settling disputes." Although I believe that the district court thereby satisfied its duty to weigh the relevant factors, I could nevertheless understand how others might prefer a more detailed and particularized discussion of how the various asserted interests were, and were not, served on the facts before the court. In such a situation, however, the indicated resolution would have involved no more than a remand to the district court for a fuller statement of its reasons in denying FAB's motion to unseal. Unfortunately, the majority holds instead that the interest in settling cases cannot justify sealing a settlement agreement. Consistent with that holding the majority reverses the district court's order.

I believe the adoption of such a rule can only be counterproductive and must necessarily have the effect of discouraging settlement in many cases that would otherwise be routinely ended by the parties' agreement. This, in turn, will undoubtedly force costly and ultimately unnecessary trials. Accordingly, I respectfully dissent from the majority's judgment, and, rather than reverse, I would affirm the district court's order which refused to unseal the Bank-HRA settlement agreement.

Discussion Questions

1. What interest does the public have regarding "access to judicial records," and why is it a foundational legal concept?

2. Could the district court have found a middle ground that supported access and settlement not only by unsealing the records for FAB III but also by retaining the seal as to other parties and the public?

3. The dissent essentially makes an economic argument: more settlement results from more secrecy, which equals dramatic savings in court resources. Is this argument persuasive? Is it a dangerous way to assess public rights relative to the court system?

4. Without public access to judicial records, what safeguards exist against settlements that violate public interest?

Enforcement Concerns

In addition to constitutional concerns, parties in an alternative dispute resolution process are often justifiably troubled by questions regarding an agreement's finality and enforceability. While arbitration decisions normally are accorded great judicial deference, other processes do not have so well-defined a sense of certainty. Generally, the agreements reached in negotiated processes are treated as contracts. They are therefore subject to defenses and subsequent judicial scrutiny for deficiencies. Parties may demand contract performance, but the agreements they reach in ADR do not have the effect of a rapidly enforceable legal judgment. The following case illustrates the sort of analysis possible in such circumstances.

D.R., BY HIS PARENTS AND V. EAST BRUNSWICK BD. OF EDUCATION

109 F.3d 896 (3rd. Cir., 1996)

FACT SUMMARY

D.R. is a multiple-handicapped individual classified by the New Jersey Board of Education as in need of special education. He was diagnosed at age two with athetoid ataxic cerebral palsy and moderate retardation. D.R. is now twenty-one years old, but his adaptive behavior is considered to be at the preschool level. The parties agree that D.R. has difficulty performing simple daily tasks by himself. He has trouble walking, dressing, and toileting without assistance. In the classroom, he often regresses into a hypnotic rocking behavior and must be constantly monitored by an assistant in order to engage him in classroom activity.

At age four, D.R. began attending day school at the Cerebral Palsy Center (CPC) in New Jersey, where he remained until January 1992. While at CPC, D.R. resided with his parents in East Brunswick, New Jersey. During the first semester of the 1991–92 school year, D.R.'s parents became convinced that he was not progressing at CPC and should be enrolled in a residential program. In December 1991, D.R.'s parents filed a petition with the New Jersey Department of Education requesting a due process hearing under the IDEA. The petition alleged that the CPC program was not appropriate for D.R. and that he would benefit from a transfer to the Benedictine School, an out-of-state residential school in Ridgely, Maryland.

The Board, however, disagreed that residential placement was necessary for D.R. His parents proceeded in early January 1992 to unilaterally place him at the Benedictine School. The Benedictine School subsequently informed D.R.'s parents that their son's acceptance in the program would be on a five-week "trial basis." They were told that the proposed program might be modified depending on D.R.'s adaptation to his new circumstances. The Board now complains that it was never informed of the "trial" nature of D.R.'s acceptance at Benedictine, nor that the program in which he was placed was subject to modification.

Before D.R.'s trial period was complete, his parents and the Board met at a mediation conference and entered a settlement agreement. The parties agreed to these three conditions.

1. The East Brunswick Board of Education will compensate placement costs for D.R. at the Benedictine School at an annual rate of $27,500, prorated for the balance of the 1991–92 school year including the summer of 1992 and beginning January 1, 1992.
2. For the 1992–93 school year, the Board will contribute 90 percent of any increase over the 1991–92 rate.
3. The Board will be absolved of any further costs based upon this placement, related service, or transportation in connection therewith.

During D.R.'s first semester at Benedictine, the school "practically" provided one-to-one assistance. Classes were small in size, with a high ratio of assistants and teachers to students; weekend and residential staff were able to provide the personal help that D.R. needed with daily functions. Later in the adaptation process, however, the school felt that it could not continue to expend such resources on D.R. without neglecting its other students. The school informed D.R.'s parents that D.R. would not be allowed to re-enroll for the 1992–93 school year unless personal aides were provided.

In April 1992, the Board received a cost estimate from the Benedictine School for the 1992–93 school year. The tuition totaled $62,487—more than double the amount provided by the settlement agreement. In addition to the amount that the Board had agreed to pay in 1992–93, the estimate charged the Board for the services of a special classroom aide and a special residential aide, each at a cost of $16,640.

The Board refused to pay any portion of the cost of the personal aides. It asserted that, under paragraph 3 of the settlement agreement, the cost of the aides was a "related service" for which the Board was not liable. D.R.'s parents disagreed and requested a hearing before a New Jersey administrative law judge. They sought an order that D.R. was in need of residential placement, that personal aides were necessary, that the current placement at Benedictine was appropriate, and that the Board was required to pay for the cost of the placement and the necessary aides.

At the hearing, the Board moved for dismissal on grounds that the settlement agreement was binding and that under the agreement the Board was not liable for the cost of the aides. The administrative law judge (ALJ) agreed. She dismissed D.R.'s petition, finding the settlement agreement to be binding and determinative.

On the basis of the pleadings and briefs submitted, the court concluded that the settlement agreement was binding. It found that the language of the agreement was unambiguous and required only that the Board pay for 90 percent of any increase in the cost of an array of services provided the previous year. Because personal aides were not within the array of services previously provided, the district court held that the Board would not be liable for the cost of the aides under the terms of the settlement agreement, unless D.R.'s personal circumstances had changed since the parties entered the agreement.

The district court therefore remanded the case to an ALJ to determine whether D.R.'s personal circumstances changed following the closing of the agreement. If the ALJ found that D.R.'s circumstances had changed such that the services provided by the agreement no longer satisfied the requirements of the IDEA, the court instructed that the agreement could not bind the parties and should be invalidated. The Board would then be liable, under the IDEA, for the cost of the personal aides for the 1992–93 school year.

On remand, the ALJ first concluded that during the 1992–93 school year, one-to-one assistance was effectively provided by Benedictine and was "educationally necessary and consistent with the IDEA." She then found that because D.R.'s disability had not changed, his "personal circumstances" had not changed. As a result, the ALJ again ruled in favor of the Board, holding that the settlement agreement was binding and that the Board was not liable for the cost of the additional aides.

D.R.'s parents appealed this decision to the district court, seeking reversal of the ALJ's order. Again, both parties moved for summary judgment. The district court concluded that the record supported the ALJ's finding that a one-to-one aide was "educationally necessary and consistent with the IDEA." It held that this finding dictated the outcome of the case. Applying the Supreme Court's interpretation of the IDEA, the district court concluded that states receiving federal funds under the Act must provide services that are "necessary to permit the child 'to benefit' from the instruction." The district court thus concluded that New Jersey could not refuse to provide educationally necessary services. Such essential services are the right of the disabled individual and cannot be waived by a contract to provide something less.

As a result, the district court held the Board liable for the cost of the personal aides for the 1992–93 school year, which amount was to be established by agreement between the parties. Following the judgment, D.R.'s parents moved for an award of attorneys' fees and related costs as "prevailing parties" in the litigation. A few days later, the Board filed a notice of appeal. The Board then moved to stay the motion for attorneys' fees filed by D.R.'s parents, pending the outcome of this appeal. D.R.'s parents did not oppose the Board's motion, and the court granted a stay on the matter of attorneys' fees and related costs.

The district court set aside the settlement agreement based on its finding that D.R.'s circumstances had changed since the parties entered the agreement. In finding changed circumstances, the district court rejected the conclusions of the state administrative law judge. The court held that, because D.R.'s circumstances had changed, the personal aides had become "educationally necessary" for him to obtain an appropriate education as guaranteed by the IDEA. The court found that the settlement agreement improperly excused the Board from its duty to provide educationally necessary services, and it therefore concluded that the agreement did not meet the IDEA's mandatory standards. As a result, the district court invalidated the agreement and placed liability for the cost of the personal aides on the Board.

OPINION: *ROTH, Circuit Judge*

This action was brought before the United States District Court for the District of New Jersey pursuant to the Individuals with Disabilities Education Act ("the IDEA" or "the Act") [20 U.S.C. Section(s) 1401 et seq]. It raises an important question regarding the enforceability of settlement agreements made between parents and school boards with the intent of enforcing the IDEA. We conclude that the settlement agreement was improperly

voided by the district court. On the facts of this particular case, the settlement agreement was voluntarily and willingly entered by the parties. It is therefore a binding contract between the parties and should have been enforced as written.

We believe that the district court erred when it found that D.R.'s circumstances changed following settlement. Instead, we find that the only change that occurred in this case appeared on the bill sent by the Benedictine School to the Board. There was no change in D.R.'s individual circumstances; he continued to need individual assistance in toileting, dressing, grooming, and eating. The only circumstance that changed was that Benedictine decided that its staff could not maintain the level of individualized attention that D.R. was receiving at the negotiated price. The School decided that additional help was needed to deal with D.R.'s unchanged condition, increasing the total cost of services provided by the School.

Once a school board and the parents of a disabled child finalize a settlement agreement and the board agrees to pay a certain portion of the school fees, the parents should not be allowed to void the agreement merely because the total cost of the program subsequently increases. A party enters a settlement agreement, at least in part, to avoid unpredictable costs of litigation in favor of agreeing to known costs. Government entities have additional interests in settling disputes in order to increase the predictability of costs for budgetary purposes.

We are concerned that a decision that would allow parents to void settlement agreements when they become unpalatable would work a significant deterrence contrary to the federal policy of encouraging settlement agreements. Settlement agreements are encouraged as a matter of public policy because they promote the amicable resolution of disputes and lighten the increasing load of litigation faced by courts. In this case, public policy plainly favors upholding the settlement agreement entered between D.R.'s parents and the Board.

We agree that reaching a settlement agreement during mediation, rather than during litigation, does not lessen the binding nature of the agreement on the parties. When the parties entered the settlement agreement at issue in this case, they entered a contract. [*Columbia Gas System, Inc.,* 50 F.3d 233, 238 (3d Cir. 1995)] We will therefore enforce the agreement as a binding contract voluntarily entered by both parties.

When D.R.'s parents appealed the ALJ's decision to dismiss on grounds of res judicata, the district court noted that, if D.R.'s circumstances had not changed since settlement, the settlement agreement was binding on the parties. It also held that, if the contract was to be enforced as

binding, the terms of the agreement were "clear and unambiguous." Under the agreement and as a matter of law, for the 1992–93 school year, the Board was responsible for 90 percent of any increase in the cost of services provided during the 1991–92 school year. The additional services of personal aides were not provided during the 1991–92 term. Nor was the cost of personal aides contemplated by the parties in negotiating the agreement. Thus, the district court held that, if enforced, the contract clearly required that D.R.'s parents pay the cost of the aides' services provided during the 1992–93 school year.

We agree that this is the proper reading of the settlement. Because we conclude that D.R.'s circumstances have not changed and that the settlement agreement is therefore binding on the parties, we hold that the district court reading of the "clear and unambiguous" terms of the agreement applies.

Discussion Questions

1. Does the rule enunciated in this case seem overly harsh? Should parties be permitted to revisit agreements previously concluded in an ADR process?

2. Under what circumstances, if any, should a court substitute its judgment for that of the parties where a settlement agreement is at issue?

CHAPTER CONCLUSION

Alternative dispute resolution processes offer businesses a range of settlement and private adjudication options that provide rapid, inexpensive, private, and customized methods for resolution. While not appropriate in all cases and subject to constitutional and practical limitations, ADR processes can be used advantageously in many disputes. Courts welcome the considerable reduction to docket size these processes offer. Business managers should be thoroughly schooled in their application.

BEST BUSINESS PRACTICES

Here are some practical tips for managers on using alternative dispute resolution.

- Strongly consider using alternative dispute resolution to resolve business cases unless your attorney feels the specifics of your case don't warrant it. Attorneys resist use of alternative dispute resolution for many reasons, some appropriate, some not. If an ADR process can be beneficial in solving your business dispute, pursue it.

- Implement alternative dispute resolution in your company policies to resolve disputes before they become legal matters. Consider employee handbook provisions and managerial training in dispute resolution as a way to increase the bottom line by preemptively addressing conflict.

- Carefully draft settlement agreements reached through alternative dispute resolution, with input from counsel to avoid subsequent enforcement difficulties. Thoughtful parties will provide for payment of legal expenses incurred if enforcement actions become necessary.

- While accounting for the statute of limitations, parties desiring complete confidentiality should consider submitting their case to a private practitioner before filing with a court. Such a decision avoids the possibility of mandated participation in a court-annexed, and therefore less private, setting.

- Because participation in ADR may be mandated, companies should establish relationships with law firms conversant in the various ADR processes before their legal services become a necessity.

http://

The Rand Institute for Civil Justice provides research data on the use of ADR. Their home page is at: http://www.rand.org

http://

The American Arbitration Association provides a site devoted to forms and rules at: http://www.adr.org/rules/rules.html

KEY TERMS

Alternative dispute resolution, p. 28
Arbitration, p. 30
Authority, p. 29
Due process, p. 35
Equal protection, p. 35
External disputes, p. 28
Internal disputes, p. 28

Mediation, p. 29
Mediation-arbitration, p. 30
Minitrial, p. 29
Negotiation, p. 29
Private judging, p. 30
Public access, p. 42
Summary jury trial, p. 30

ETHICAL AND LEGAL REVIEW

Consider the following questions as you analyze the cases provided: Is alternative dispute resolution appropriate in this matter? If so, is it preferable to litigation? Why? Finally, which ADR process is best suited to the dispute, if one is to be used?

1. Acme Inc. faces a breach of contract case brought by its principal supplier, Imperial Corp. The case involves an ambiguity in their long-term sales contract relating to delivery of component parts by Imperial to Acme. The highly successful parts are integral elements of Acme's product line and are potentially highly profitable. Loss of Imperial as a supplier would be devastating to Acme as the nature and quality of the parts make them difficult to find elsewhere. However, Acme believes that it represents a sizable portion of Imperial's business and, therefore, is unwilling to simply capitulate.

2. Hightech, Ltd., a software design company, is involved in a copyright infringement matter with a competitor, Megasoft Inc. The case involves several highly complex legal and technical questions that a jury is unlikely to fully understand. Moreover, the companies both possess what they regard to be trade secrets which they are reluctant to reveal to one another or the rest of the industry through a public trial.

3. Empire Corporation has been sued by a male employee for sexual harassment by a male supervisor. This is a question of first impression in the jurisdiction where the case has been filed. Empire is reluctant to admit responsibility for the conduct of its manager, but is also concerned about losing a trial and thereby creating new laws that may disadvantage them in future litigation. The conduct of the supervisor was reprehensible but, under the current law, probably not illegal.

4. A class action suit has been filed against the manufacturer of a prosthetic device used by thousands of consumers internationally. While the injuries on an individual basis are fairly minimal, even if taken at face value, the company is deeply concerned about how such a case could impact consumer confidence in its new version of the same device. Moreover, the opposing lawyers are absolutely intractable, insisting that the facts and law are clear and unarguably supportive of their claim. They have tendered what the company regards as an outrageous settlement demand and have refused to negotiate because they believe that their case is airtight.

SUGGESTED ADDITIONAL READINGS

Goldberg, S., E. Green, and F. Sander. *Dispute Resolution.* Little, Brown & Company, 1992.

Harr, J. *A Civil Action.* Random House, 1996.

Kanowitz, L. *Alternative Dispute Resolution: Cases and Materials.* West, 1986.

Lebedoff, D. *Cleaning Up: The Story Behind the Biggest Legal Bonanza of Our Time.* Free Press, 1997.

Murray, J., A. Rau, and E. Sherman. *Processes of Dispute Resolution: The Role of Lawyers.* The Foundation Press, 1989.

Nolan-Haley, J. *Alternative Dispute Resolution in a Nutshell.* West Publishing Company, 1992.

Riskin, L., and J. Westbrook. *Dispute Resolution and Lawyers.* American Casebook Series, West, 1988.

Trachte-Huber, E., and S. Huber. *Alternative Dispute Resolution: Strategies for Law and Business.* Anderson Publishing Company, 1996.

Ury, W., J. Brett, and S. Goldberg. *Getting Disputes Resolved: Designing Systems to Cut the Costs of Conflict.* Jossey-Bass, 1988.

Part II

ADR SETTLEMENT MECHANISMS

Chapter 3: Negotiation

Chapter 4: Mediation

Chapter 5: Summary Jury Trial

The ADR processes described in Part II of this text are facilitative settlement processes. By this we mean processes that are structured to create negotiated outcomes and in which the role of the third party, if one is present, is to assist in those negotiations. Chapter 3 describes the process of negotiation from both theoretical and skills perspectives—teaching the reader to negotiate well and exploring the legal and ethical issues attendant to negotiation as a method of conflict resolution. Chapter 4 describes mediation, likely the fastest growing form of alternative dispute resolution. In Chapter 4 the reader is introduced to the stages and timing of the process as well as the legal and ethical questions associated with mediating business disputes. Finally, in Chapter 5, we describe the minitrial and summary jury trial—two semiformal, evidentiary processes still built around settlement negotiation.

3

NEGOTIATION

CHAPTER HIGHLIGHTS

In this chapter, you will read and learn about the following:

1. The two major dispute resolution negotiation paradigms.
2. The principal skills required for effective negotiation in either paradigm.
3. The relationship of private negotiation to the public legal process.
4. Several significant ethical issues involved in negotiation.
5. International and cross-cultural negotiation.

Negotiation is the most flexible approach to the resolution of business disputes and thus the most common. Most experts agree that approximately 90 percent of all cases filed in state and federal courts are settled through some form of negotiation or alternative dispute resolution. This estimate may be on the low side, when one considers that many disputes are resolved without filing a lawsuit or formal action.

This chapter considers both the theories and the skills associated with the process of negotiation. We will define and assess the prevailing models for negotiation and give an overview of crucial skills employed by effective negotiators. The ethics of negotiation will be addressed as well as international and cross-cultural negotiation.

Perhaps more than any other area of alternative dispute resolution, negotiation is represented in a body of literature from a wide variety of perspectives. This chapter draws from these resources to provide a general primer on effective negotiation. While this chapter emphasizes the negotiation of business disputes, these ideas may also apply when no conflict is involved, such as in the creation of a business contract.

http://

Information about the Harvard Negotiation Project is at: http://www.law. harvard.edu/ Programs/PON

DEFINING NEGOTIATION

Negotiation is a process of balancing one's own needs against the competing needs of another and arriving at an agreement that is mutually satisfying. Because negotiation involves asserting one's needs while accounting for another's, it can lead to very unproductive responses to conflict. Some people are unable or unwilling to assert their own needs and are unwilling to satisfy those of their counterpart; they *avoid* negotiating altogether. Others vigorously assert their own needs and ignore those of the opponent; they see negotiation as a setting in which to *compete*. Still others capitulate to the demands of the opponent without asserting their own needs; in short, they *accommodate*.

Two common models of negotiation balance the needs of all parties against one another. They are competitive-compromise and interest-based collaboration. The competitive-compromise model normally allocates a fixed set of resources in a way that either produces a winner who receives more than the other or a draw in which an equal division is made. Conversely, the interest-based collaborative model seeks to enlarge the pool of resources, to satisfy to a realistic degree all party interests, and to create a result from which all involved draw maximum results.

Negotiation can be a challenging and daunting process for many people, since it is often done without representation and for significant stakes. It is unlike the wide range of dispute resolution processes that involve negotiation, but normally also involve third parties as either decision makers or facilitators. While negotiation is a fundamental skill in business dispute resolution, those uncomfortable with or unskilled in direct negotiation will find attractive negotiation-based alternatives in mediation, the minitrial, and the summary jury trial (Chapters 4 and 5).

Negotiation is the basis for much of what follows in this text. For example, mediation is a process built entirely upon cooperative and effective negotiation facilitated by a third party. However, direct negotiation differs in several significant ways from the processes described in the following chapters. For example, it is less formal, excludes third-party intervention, and can be more confidential. Finally, it likely involves a less adversarial exchange of information, rather than structured presentation of evidence as may be the case in many negotiation-oriented, as well as all of the adjudicative ADR processes.

TABLE 3.1 Direct Negotiation v. Other ADR

Direct Negotiation	**Other Forms of ADR**
Unrepresented	Represented
Unstructured	Structured
No neutral third party	Neutral third party
Information exchange	Evidence presentation

Negotiation can be defined as a three-step process.

1. *It establishes the parameters of the dispute* by identifying party interests and needs through the exchange of information. In other words, it clarifies the facts and issues that bring the parties to the table and the results they seek.
2. *It creates a variety of options to resolve the dispute* by considering all of the resources and alternatives available to the parties.
3. *It refines and secures agreement to those options* by specifying the terms of the agreement.

NEGOTIATION MODELS

As stated previously, there are two general models of dispute resolution negotiation. These models have been widely discussed in both teaching materials and research, and though they represent two very different approaches, each has proponents.

The first model is commonly called distributive or competitive negotiation, but we will refer to it as the **competitive-compromise model.** We do so because this model normally places the parties in opposition to one another so that outcomes are measured comparatively or in a win-lose fashion. It emphasizes maximizing gains in a way that may, concomitantly, maximize the opponent's losses. Parties using this adversarial model may engage in puffery, deception, or coercion to achieve these often unilaterally satisfactory outcomes. Even when practiced in a principled, honest manner, this model stresses the assertion of one's own needs and the diminishment of the opponent's needs. It is a model based in substantial part on negotiating power, rights, and ability.

The second model is variously known as *interest-based, principled, cooperative, integrative,* or *collaborative negotiation,* but we will refer to it as the **collaborative model.** This approach stresses a process that leads to mutually satisfactory outcomes resulting from a nonadversarial, problem-solving approach. It seeks to establish—through truthful and reasonably complete disclosure from each party—a set of genuine interests and needs and to create settlement options to address these needs. Collaborative negotiation requires the parties to negotiate objectively and cooperatively and seeks to maximize the outcomes achieved for both parties. It is a model that strives to *avoid* win-lose outcomes.

Both models have strengths and weaknesses. The competitive approach allows the skillful advocate to achieve maximum advantage in a negotiation setting irrespective of the needs and interests of the other side. It can therefore result in sizable and highly advantageous recoveries. When involving negotiators of equal skill, it may result in agreements consistent with the relative merits of the case. In other words, the competitive model works toward settlements that are consistent with the strengths and weaknesses of a case, assuming the advocates are effective representatives of their respective positions.

However, the competitive model has at least three significant drawbacks. First, the model stresses achieving maximum advantage through power and bargaining tactics and often results in one party or the other perceiving the outcome to be less than desirable. Therefore, it is not a model upon which amicable long-term business relationships are regularly built. Second, it is a model in which unethical conduct may be more common, if not expected. It can be a process in which the end justifies the means. Lawyers, for example, speak of zealously representing clients in negotiation, while being less than forthcoming with information that is not specifically requested. In addition, they may rely on threats of litigation and discovery abuse to achieve high-dollar value agreements. Whether it is ethical to prevail under these circumstances is a difficult question, and one far more likely to be raised by competitive-compromise negotiation than in collaborative negotiation. Finally, if the negotiators are not of equal ability, competitive negotiation may result in agreements that are unfair and inconsistent with the merits of the underlying case. In short, a very good negotiator may obtain an agreement that exceeds the value of the case if the opposing negotiator is less skilled or less well-prepared.

ADR IN ACTION

Competitive Negotiation Training

The competitive-compromise model is the approach taught at many business negotiation seminars and workshops, because of the ease in developing tactics to be employed at different stages of a negotiation or against various opponents. In addition, this model is popular because most people expect to excel in it when they negotiate. But outrageous claims and suggestions can result. Consider the following scenario from an actual seminar delivered by a well-known negotiation training firm.

After concluding a seminar on negotiation that focused on a "winner's approach," the trainer offered the following advice to a group of men who inquired about tips and skills to effectively employ when negotiating with women. "The key is to be tough. So, try the following: First, because women have larger personal space needs than men, get close, lean in, invade her space. Doing so will put her on the defensive and distract her from thinking about the case. Second, women do not gesticulate, so you should slap the table, point fingers, do something to intimidate that doesn't cross any legal lines. Also, women are threatened by vulgarity, so sprinkle some into your delivery. I'm not talking about sexual words, but I am suggesting the use of words that continue your strategy of focusing her attention on something other than the

The advantages and disadvantages of the collaborative model are opposite those of the competitive model. One pitfall of this approach is that highly effective negotiators may forfeit the opportunity to win in favor of pursuing bilateral satisfaction and hence dilute what would otherwise be very strong cases. However the collaborative model is very successful in developing, preserving, or rehabilitating important long-term business relationships. Where losers are not an inevitable result of the process, parties are far more comfortable both in the process and with an ongoing business relationship, perhaps a relationship structured through the collaborative negotiation process. Finally, the process is less susceptible to ethical lapses, since it stresses mutually satisfying interests rather than maximum gains. Table 3.2 summarizes the characteristics of each model.

EFFECT OF REPRESENTATION IN NEGOTIATION

Representation in negotiation dramatically changes the tone and content of the process. **Representation** means turning over a matter to an attorney or other third-party advocate for the purpose of having the advocate participate on a party's behalf

TABLE 3.2   Comparing Negotiation Models

Competitive-Compromise Negotiation	Collaborative Negotiation
Win-lose	Win-win
Deceptive	Legitimate
Power	Interests
Rights	Needs
Evidence	Information
Partisan viewpoints	Agreed perceptions
Process	Outcome
Inauthentic style	Genuine style

in the negotiation process. It is unlikely for formal representation to be sought unless the parties are unsuccessful at negotiations. Also, if the case goes to suit, a lawyer will become involved, or if the matter is extremely complicated, a substantive expert may become involved. Representation has the advantage of allowing one to provide input indirectly yet without any face-to-face negotiations. In addition, representation protects unknown interests by bringing expertise to the case. Finally, the representative is in some ways responsible for the outcome of the case. Should a mistake or miscalculation be made, there is someone to blame.

Using a representative to negotiate changes the process in at least three critical ways. First, the process becomes more formal and, as a result, more expensive and time-consuming. The lawyer, for example, will attempt to settle the case in a way that is consistent with the law and, perhaps, the attorney's need to benefit from the transaction or the management of the transaction. Second, the representative's interests may start taking priority, thereby making it difficult to bargain on the basis of real party interests and needs. When a lawyer becomes involved, the tangible issue of maximizing recovery to support fees or an hourly bill may become important. Intangible concerns, like preserving the representative's ego, may also be introduced into the process. It is possible that some or all of these external concerns will be unrelated or even antithetical to the party interests in the case. For example, an attorney confident of the client's case may be more interested in winning than in settling and may encourage a client to take the case to trial. While the trial might be won, the business relationship with the opponent may be lost. Finally, when representatives are used, settlement becomes more difficult. The more interests involved, the less the likelihood of settling.

Several factors should be considered before relinquishing a case to a representative. First, the nature of the relationship that one has or wishes to have with the other party should be addressed. Negotiating through a representative depersonalizes the process and may eliminate the opportunity to build a relationship with the other side. Second, it should be determined whether the case is complicated in legal or substantive ways. Complicated patent claims involving sophisticated science may, for example, be best negotiated by an expert in the field or science at the heart of the claim. Finally, it would be unwise to negotiate directly with the legal or expert representative on the other side unless one possesses both legal and substantive knowledge. As we shall see later in the chapter, courts enforce settlement agreements fairly rigorously. A party should not expect to void an agreement on the grounds that they were unrepresented and faced a lawyer as an opponent, even if doing so deprived them of an important right.

RELATIONSHIP OF NEGOTIATION TO THE LEGAL PROCESS

Negotiation of a legal dispute is generally a legally protected activity in which the judicial rules of evidence may be applicable. The federal rules of evidence, as well as those of most state courts, provide important protection to the party who endeavors to negotiate a resolution to a legal claim. As a general rule, an offer to compromise a claim is not admissible in court as an acknowledgment of the validity or invalidity of the claim. The same applies for a statement made in support of that offer which is not available from other sources and is made in the course of a settlement negotiation. Consequently, an opponent in a failed settlement negotiation will not likely be permitted to argue that willingness to settle should be interpreted by the finder of fact as evidence of liability. Indeed, evidence of such discussions probably never will reach the the trier of fact. The rule applies to both offers of settlement and completed settlements. This latter situation ordinarily will not occur unless a party to the present litigation has also settled through third-person negotiation.

This evidentiary exclusion is based on two arguments. First, evidence of settlement negotiations is arguably irrelevant, since an offer to settle may be motivated by a desire for peace or by purely economic considerations rather than from any concession of weakness. The validity of this argument will depend on how much the offer varies in relation to the size of the claim, and it may also be influenced by the timing of the proposal. Second, public policy favoring compromise and settlement of disputes is supported by protecting efforts to do so in later litigation. In short, the rules of evidence support settlement discussions, whether direct or indirect, as confidential.

ADR IN ACTION

Federal Rule of Evidence 408

Evidence of (1) furnishing or offering or promising to furnish, or (2) accepting or offering or promising to accept, a valuable consideration in compromising or attempting to compromise a claim which was disputed as to either validity or amount, is not admissible to prove liability for or invalidity of the claim or its amount. Evidence of conduct or statements made in compromise negotiations is likewise not admissible. This rule does not require the exclusion of any evidence otherwise discoverable merely because it is presented in the course of compromise negotiations. This rule also does not require exclusion when the evidence is offered for another purpose, such as proving bias or prejudice of a witness, negating a contention of undue delay, or proving an effort to obstruct a criminal investigation or prosecution.

http://

A complete version of the Federal Rules of Evidence is provided at this site: http://www.law.cornell.edu/rules/fre/overview.html

The following case illustrates another important relationship between the negotiation process and the law: judges are willing to enforce settlement agreements even when they appear to violate principles of fairness. Participants in settlement discussions are generally bound by the results of those discussions when the existence of a contract can be demonstrated. The case presents an interesting discussion of mistakes made in negotiating an employment discrimination lawsuit.

SHENG V. STARKEY LABORATORIES, INC.
117 F.3d 1081 (8th Cir., 1997)

FACT SUMMARY

The parties to this lawsuit attended a settlement conference without knowing that the district court had handed down a summary judgment decision. This appeal addresses what effect, if any, should be given to the agreement they reached before discovering the court's action.

Sheng sued her former employer, Starkey Laboratories, Inc., alleging it violated Title VII. Starkey moved for summary judgment, and after a hearing, the motion was submitted to the district court. While the request was pending, the district court ordered the parties to attend a mediated settlement conference, scheduled for Monday, December 20, 1993. On Friday, December 17, the district court signed an order granting Starkey's motion for summary judgment. Although copies of the order were mailed to each counsel, it was not immediately entered in the official docket, and the clerk of court did not enter judgment. On Monday morning, not yet aware of the district court's decision, the parties met in the chambers of a U.S. magistrate judge. At this conference, the parties agreed that Sheng would dismiss all claims in exchange for Starkey's payment of $73,500. At the conclusion of the meeting, the attorneys shook hands and began discussing the appropriate tax treatment for the payment.

After the conference, the magistrate judge informed the district court of the agreement. The district court then rescinded its summary judgment order,

directing the clerk of court to enter neither the order nor the judgment in the case docket. That afternoon, counsel for both parties received copies of the December 17 order granting summary judgment and the December 20 order vacating the first order. The next day, the district court dismissed the action on the ground that it had been settled.

Starkey filed a Rule 60(b) motion seeking to vacate the court's orders rescinding the summary judgment and dismissing the case. Starkey argues that there was no settlement, because the parties did not agree on all material terms of the contract. Furthermore, Starkey maintains that the agreement is unenforceable because it was based on mutual mistakes.

OPINION: *BEAM, Circuit Judge*

An enforceable settlement requires the parties to reach agreement on the essential terms of the deal. Settlement agreements that do not expressly resolve ancillary issues can, nevertheless, be enforceable . . . [for example a] binding settlement existed when parties had agreed on payment of damages, but failed to resolve property owners' demand for additional drainage. The fact that the parties left some details for counsel to work out during later negotiations cannot be used to abrogate an otherwise valid agreement.

Here, the district court concluded that the parties had an agreement on all material issues. The court specifically found that the deal hinged neither on the tax treatment of the payment nor on other particulars, such as the wording of clauses regarding confidentiality, disclaimers, and the release of liability.

Starkey argues that even if the parties formed a contract, the agreement was based on a mutual mistake. A mistake is a belief that is not in accord with the facts. Restatement (Second) of Contracts Section(s) 151 (1981). "Mutual mistake" consists of a clear showing that both contracting parties misunderstood the fundamental subject matter or terms of the contract.

The district court first held that both parties assumed that Starkey's summary judgment motion was still pending, and then concluded that this misconception rendered the contract voidable as mutual mistake. The intent of contracting parties is an issue of fact, reviewed only for clear error. However, the effect of a mistaken belief is a legal conclusion, reviewed de novo on appeal.

As an initial matter, we are not convinced that the parties' erroneous assumption regarding the disposition of the summary judgment motion would warrant recision. Before a misconception will render a contract voidable, it must be more than an error about the monetary value of the consideration; it must go to the very nature of the deal. In this case, while entry of summary judgment may have affected how much value Starkey was willing to give in exchange for Sheng's release, both parties would have had reason to bargain had they known of the ruling. Litigants who win summary judgment routinely settle with their opponents to avoid the costs of an appeal, to assure confidentiality, or for a wide range of other reasons.

Even if misapprehension about the pendency of Starkey's motion was a fundamental mistake, however, we hold that Starkey assumed the risk of that error. A party may not avoid a contract on the grounds of mutual mistake when it assumed the risk of that mistake. The Restatement instructs courts to examine the purposes of the parties and its own general knowledge of human behavior in bargain transactions to allocate risk in these situations. Here, Starkey knew it had a dispositive motion pending, and yet chose the certainty of settlement rather than the gamble of a ruling on its motion. Practically every settlement involves the element of chance as to future consequences and developments. There are usually unknown and unknowable conditions that may affect the ultimate recovery or failure of recovery. Mutual ignorance of their existence cannot constitute mutual mistake. Consequently, Starkey cannot avoid the deal it struck with Sheng.

The decision of the district court is affirmed in part and reversed in part.

Discussion Questions

1. Under what circumstances is a binding settlement agreement reached? What potential pitfalls should an effective negotiator avoid?

2. What role does intent play in forming an agreement? It would appear that the parties to the Sheng negotiations disagreed about the presence or absence of intent to settle. Should intent to contract be clearly present? How would you determine whether the parties intended to be bound?

3. Is the Sheng court improperly ignoring the rights of the parties in order to support private, out-of-court settlements?

NEGOTIATION PRACTICE: A SKILLS-ORIENTED OVERVIEW

Successful negotiation requires careful preparation, skillful delivery, and thoughtful planning for implementation following negotiation (see Figure 3.1). Let us review four key thinking skills related to negotiation.

- *Effective negotiators think broadly.* The best negotiators can view a case in the broadest sense so that they can develop outcomes that may be novel yet remain consistent with the needs of the business. As they generate options for settlement, they are able to think beyond the normally established boundaries with a view toward understanding the case and all of its implications.
- *Effective negotiators think creatively.* Most cases involve many elements that can be settled in a variety of ways. The best negotiators are artistic thinkers and are capable of seeing noneconomic and other unconventional options for settlement.
- *Effective negotiators think adaptively.* Successful negotiators are often able to make the offer of a counterpart consistent with their own. They modify, manipulate, and reconfigure the issues and settlement options until agreement on each can be reached.
- *Effective negotiators think critically.* Good negotiators recognize negotiation as a process involving problem solving and not merely resource acquisition. The best negotiators can assess a wide range of options and issues in disinterested but careful and thorough ways.

FIGURE 3.1   Stages of the Negotiation Process

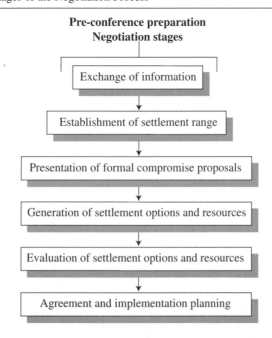

Pre-conference preparation
Negotiation stages

Exchange of information

Establishment of settlement range

Presentation of formal compromise proposals

Generation of settlement options and resources

Evaluation of settlement options and resources

Agreement and implementation planning

Thorough preparation is essential to effective negotiation. You should perform the following important tasks when *preparing to negotiate*.

- Carefully gather *information* about the matter to be negotiated. Consider all of the necessary parties to the process and all of the facts likely to be addressed at the negotiation so that a final agreement can be reached on all issues. Form a set of broadly framed desired outcomes. In short, effective negotiators begin the process with a clear understanding of the factual background of the case and a set of clear goals and objectives.
- Establish a case value and devise specific settlement options consistent with that value. All aspects of the case must be considered in terms of worth and their resolution possibilities.
- Anticipate the offers and strategies likely to be used by the opposing party, including possible counteroffers and assertions of fact.

Opening the negotiation normally involves exchanging information and making preliminary offers. Fundamental facts should be determined first. While parties need not decide who is responsible for an event, they do need to concur on the basic outline of facts. Without some agreement on what took place, it will be difficult to reach agreement on outcomes. Next, parties should begin to establish the boundaries of the disagreement by disclosing preliminary offers. For example, a plaintiff may initially demand $100,000 and receive a defense counteroffer of $35,000, creating an initial settlement range of $65,000.

Formal initial proposals follow the exchange of information and establishment of a settlement range. Parties often have considered their initial proposal before the negotiation begins and will come armed with a compromise offer or demand. However, it is difficult to persuade an opponent to make the first concession or to decide to concede oneself. Here are several tips for getting first compromise offers on the table for discussion.

- *Start with the old, bring in the new.* Settlement discussion is made easier if there is some history upon which to rely. Parties often make an initial offer by referring to where they left off in previous discussions and where they are now willing to go.
- *Consider convention and expectation.* Parties normally expect the aggrieved party, the one seeking a remedy, to make an initial demand. Otherwise, the nonaggrieved party is required to bargain against him or herself.
- *Allow adequate information exchange.* Because of the difficulty in making an initial offer in negotiation, parties should spend sufficient time agreeing on the facts. Doing so allows each party to become familiar and comfortable with the other and to anticipate their opponent's receptiveness of the offer or demand they plan to make. It is easier to negotiate facts than outcomes, so it is wise to start with the factual matters and move to the more difficult outcome-oriented matters only after some momentum and trust has been established.

- *First proposals are lasting proposals.* Generally, in a competitive negotiation, an inflated initial proposal is likely, while in a cooperative negotiation, a more reasonable initial proposal is expected. Whatever the proposal type, parties work from and stay cognizant of the first set of proposals. Therefore, proposals should not be made until the parties have agreed to the basic facts and are ready to consider outcomes. The party who makes the first offer is likely to set the tone for the remainder of the negotiation.

- *Always seek justification for offers or demands.* Parties are wise to request a complete explanation of the demand or offer that has been made. This minimizes the likelihood of mistake and allows time for consideration of the offer or demand. In addition, it permits time for the opposing party to make the case for the offer. Unexplained demands are far too easily dismissed.

- *Preconditions on negotiation may be problematic.* One dubious technique used in negotiation is the demand for a concession from the other side in exchange for participating in the negotiation. Essentially, the party doing so is negotiating already, only surreptitiously, by asking for a substantive concession outside the negotiation process itself.

ADR IN ACTION

The Israeli-Palestinian Peace Process

http://

The Israeli-Egyptian Peace Agreement is at this address: http://www.jcrc. org/main/ isregypt.htm

One of the most intractable international conflicts is the one involving Israel and the Palestinian people. The settlement negotiations between these parties have become highly structured and indirect. An initial obstacle to direct settlement negotiations was an Israeli precondition on participation in the peace negotiations. The Palestinian constitution contains a pledge to abolish Israel as a statement of formal state policy. The Israeli government demanded that this language be stricken from the document and the intention that it embodied be renounced before Israel would begin any form of direct settlement negotiation.

While the language of the Palestinian constitution seems offensive, Israel's demand may be difficult to justify from the standpoint of effective negotiation. The Israelis requested a concession without negotiation and as a precursor to their participation. Parties who make non-negotiable, pre-meeting demands often complicate negotiations, as the subsequent Israeli-Palestinian talks may have demonstrated. In addition, if the pre-conference concession is made, the demanding party may have achieved an advantage that is difficult for the opponent to overcome in later negotiations.

Generating options is the next phase of the negotiation. During this stage, parties move from initial proposals and consideration of the facts toward settlement through modification of party offers and demands. As a preliminary matter, parties must establish a *real* settlement range, which accounts for both the initial and second offer made by each party. Few parties begin a negotiation without an initial offer or demand calculated to set the tone *and* a compromise offer meant to move toward settlement. This second set of offers and demands represents the real settlement range of the case. For example, a plaintiff in a personal injury case may demand $100,000 initially, though this demand is just to set a serious tone in the negotiation, to establish the extent of the injuries, and to appear to be a strong negotiator. While this initial demand will require a response, the plaintiff likely has prepared a compromise position to be made at an appropriate time.

Generating options through negotiation is a difficult process. It requires thoughtful response to offers made, careful reconfiguring of one's own offer, and consistent reference to the facts guiding the negotiation. There are several useful approaches to creating settlement options.

- *Expect incremental movement toward agreement.* Most negotiations move toward compromise in steps. Good negotiators break cases down into small, discrete issues requiring resolution, rather than looking for a complete settlement on the basis of any single offer or demand. Doing so comports with the expectations and the psychological needs of the parties.

- *Expand the resources.* Cases can be settled through structured settlements, annuities, and noneconomic resources as well as lump-sum money payments. Effective negotiators seek to create the largest possible pool of resources and options from which settlements can be crafted. Indeed, in addition to offering more tangible settlement value, they will likely stress the value of the agreement itself to both parties because it ends the cost and distraction presented by the dispute. Parties who think creatively can find settlement options beyond money, and they will settle cases more frequently as a result.

- *Use objective criteria.* Fisher and Ury advocate seeking objective criteria in determining case value and in preparing reasonable offers and demands. There is value in doing so, but only to the extent that additional barriers to settlement are avoided. Objective criteria become detrimental when they are used to defend intransigence. For example, it is not helpful to use the criteria dispositively when it causes a party to refuse to compromise because in a similar case a plaintiff received a certain amount. Instead, effective negotiators use objective criteria late in the negotiation to confirm and solicit agreement to offers, not simply to create them.

- *Prevent early final offer.* The most harmful kind of demand is a "take it or leave it" demand made very early in the negotiation. Such a demand stifles further discussion, creates an artificial settlement range, and unrealistically and unproductively pressures the opposing party. These sorts of offers are rarely legitimate and often force the other party to engage in similar brinkmanship. In addition, because they are usually not true ultimatums, they diminish the credibility of the party who uses them regularly yet has no intention of enforcing them. The response to such final offers should suggest that discussions have not reached the point where such a demand is appropriate or useful.

Evaluating options and reaching agreement is the final phase of negotiation. Parties have substantially narrowed the settlement range and have created pending offers that could successfully conclude the negotiations. It is a point in the process where **impression management** becomes important. Good negotiators realize that allowing the other party to leave with a sense of accomplishment is critical if a long-term relationship is to be established or continued. As a result, agreements should be fully achievable and should give all parties a measure of satisfaction. Negotiators should also carefully consider questions of implementation. Here are some tips for reaching final agreement.

- *Make a grand summary.* Parties respond well to a complete statement of all agreement elements. Even where the parties have summarized discrete issues as they have progressed, it is a good idea to include this summary and the final dispositive elements in the final offer. Doing so takes advantage of the momentum created in the earlier agreements and gives the opponent a sense that the process is nearing conclusion.
- *Articulate the benefits to the parties.* In addition to summarizing all of the elements of the agreement, describing the benefits that each party receives in the deal is a way of enhancing the offer to conclude.
- *Reinforce finality.* Requests for final agreement should include a statement describing and confirming the finality of the agreement. Parties weary of the dispute may compromise considerably just to be finished with it. A concluding summary with a statement of benefits that declares the dispute as fully and finally settled makes for an enticing closing offer.

NEGOTIATING WITH UNCOOPERATIVE PARTIES

Those who negotiate regularly are familiar with the uncooperative party, who agrees to bargain but makes no effort to compromise. Often, they make no substantive offers or demands at all. Because this type of negotiator is rather common, particularly in competitive-compromise negotiation settings, managing the negotiation process with such a difficult party is a crucial skill. Several factors might cause a party to decline to move toward settlement. Competitive irrationality, or the inability to set aside the desire to win, is one possible explanation. Another possibility is that the uncooperative negotiator expected a better initial offer and is hostile at being presented with something less. A third possibility is that the uncooperative party is responding to what they perceive as shoddy treatment in the past. The belligerent party might also be on a "fishing expedition"—doing discovery or considering an opponent's tactics under the guise of negotiation. Finally, some negotiators are simply unwilling to let go. They have a sort of pre-"buyer's remorse" that prohibits them from concluding the dispute.

The effective negotiator should summarize the progress made thus far to remind the aggressive opponent that a settlement is possible. The possibility of a *final* settlement to the dispute can also be presented. A deadline after which no further negotiation will be entertained might also be established. Finally, the overbearing party will likely be asked to reconsider his or her alternatives to agreement, specifically, the time it will take to resolve the dispute in another forum, the cost of doing so, and the risk of an adverse finding.

Here are several additional tips to make the collaborative model work.

- *Create a relationship.* Good negotiators find ways to establish even short-term relationships with the opposing party, because people are far more inclined to agree with someone with whom they have some sort of a favorable connection.

- *Question issues, not people.* Fisher and Ury suggest separating the analysis of the problem from any criticism of the parties. In doing so, placement of blame is avoided. For both legal and personal reasons, parties will rarely agree to settle when one condition of doing so is acceptance of blame. Parties may apologize or otherwise convey feelings of remorse, but they will rarely do so on paper or in response to an unreasonable demand.

- *Make multiple offers simultaneously.* The negotiator who offers multiple options provides an opponent the opportunity to compromise comfortably, to select portions of each offer, and to satisfy a broader set of interests.

- *Encourage parties to respond to their own offers.* Expecting parties to respond to their own offers encourages them to provide a rationale for the offer. It is far easier to agree with an opponent who has rationally supported their offer and "turned the table" to respond to their own offer.

- *Learn to be comfortable with disagreement.* Negotiation is intimidating to many people, partly because it forces them to face disagreement directly. Learning to be comfortable in disagreements allows clear thinking on the issues at hand.

- *Pre-negotiate.* Lay some ground rules and establish the broad issues to be addressed before the negotiating session. Parties who find negotiation awkward might even do some of this preliminary work in written form, so that their actual meeting is a more comfortable and predictable process.

- *Be likable.* It is a myth that the most successful negotiators are the most aggressive and relentless. In fact, functioning in such a way often diminishes the success of a negotiator. It is possible to assert one's needs and appeal to the other side at the same time.

ADR IN ACTION

Decision Analysis Overview: How Much Should You Bet?

http://

To find research at the Harvard Program on Negotiation on Decision Analysis, visit: http://www.hbs .edu/dor/research /SummVG.html

Decision analysis is a sophisticated analytic approach to evaluating the options available to a party and the likelihood of achieving them. It allows complicated cases to be valued objectively and therefore negotiated and settled. It can also assist a party in determining whether a settlement exceeds the possible value of the case at trial. In most cases, the options are manifold and the probabilities variable, so that preparing a "decision tree" is fairly complicated. Here is a very simple example of decision analysis.

Assume you have the following wagering opportunity. On a coin flip,

you will win $5 if the result is heads and lose $1 if the result is tails. How do you decide on an appropriate bet given those potential outcomes? Decision analysis multiplies possibilities by probabilities and adds the results for a final value. In this case you have two possibilities—heads or tails—the odds of each being 50 percent. Therefore,

$$50\% \times \$5.00 = \$2.50$$
$$50\% \times (\$1.00) = (\$0.50)$$

Your bet: $2.00

EVALUATING THE OUTCOME

Negotiators should be judged by the results of their work. Fisher and Ury have suggested that in evaluating a negotiation outcome, one needs to consider whether the result is better than the best non-negotiated alternative to the negotiated agreement. They suggest that the negotiation is a success when parties achieve more by bargaining than by refusing to negotiate, by allowing the dispute to remain unresolved, or by allowing it to be adjudicated. This is an important point because it recommends litigation or another form of dispute resolution in some cases. This position is consistent with that taken throughout this text, namely that ADR is appropriate in some cases but not in others. For example, Chapter 4, on mediation, outlines a number of cases inappropriate for privately negotiated outcomes.

Several other indicia can also be considered in measuring negotiation success.

- An agreement that reflects **legitimacy,** one based on truthful and reasonably complete disclosure of material facts in the negotiation process, is successful.

- Agreements should satisfy to a reasonable degree all party interests.

- An agreement that continues or builds good relationships and contains realistic, well-planned commitments is desirable.

- The agreement ought to be **final,** requiring no further negotiation or approval from third parties wherever possible.

- It should be **noncontingent** upon the conduct or decision of an uninvolved party.

- It should be complete and specific, covering all issues addressed by the parties and in ways that are easily interpreted and understood.

- It should be legally enforceable and ethically defensible.

NEGOTIATION ETHICS

Perhaps no other area of ADR offers the number and complexity of ethical difficulties as negotiation. This is a result of the unstructured, unsupervised, and informal nature of the process. Some participants will have professional responsibility codes governing their participation, while others will be bound only by whatever personal moral code they bring to the process. For example, when representing a client, attorneys are bound to a code of professional responsibility. While these codes are created on a state-by-state basis, they generally require the lawyer to balance zealous representation of the client with an obligation to avoid fraud. To most lawyers, this means not making a material affirmative **misrepresentation** to the other party. It may not, however, preclude them from taking advantage of the other party's misunderstanding of the facts if the misunderstanding is not due to any statement made by the attorney or the client. Attorneys are also prohibited from disclosing any fact not made public by the client without the express permission of the client.

    Deception is perhaps the most common ethical conundrum faced by negotiators. In the absence of either supervision or regulation, some negotiators view their actions as only being governed by legal requirements, such as avoiding fraud. The following case describes the analysis of a fraud claim in which negotiators deceived buyers in the course of property sale negotiations. It lays out the elements of the fraud case—likely the only recourse available to a party who settles on the basis of deception—and addresses the arguments of the party who engaged in the fraud to achieve the sale. These arguments are very similar to those that are made in any case where one party has taken advantage of another in negotiation through misrepresentation.

DAMON V. SUN COMPANY, INC.
87 F.3d 1467 (1st U.S. Cir., 1996)

FACT SUMMARY

Plaintiffs brought suit in this case claiming misrepresentation. Defendant Sun Oil Company, Inc., built a gasoline station with underground storage tanks on the property in question. An underground pipe leading from the tanks to the pumps leaked roughly 2,000 gallons of gasoline. The spill, caused by a rupture of an elbow joint in the pipe, forced the station to close for approximately six weeks. The plaintiffs, Roy and Eleanor Damon, purchased the property from Sun on the basis of representations from Sun that the property was in good condition. Prior to purchasing the property, Damon inquired of Sun the age of the building and whether Sun had experienced any problems with the station, particularly with the underground tanks. Sun knew of the spill but did not reveal it. Rather, Sun answered that it was a "good station" that just needed to be run by a good operator to be successful. One Sun agent stated, "No, we've had no problems with [the underground storage tank system.] It's all good."

On January 31, 1991, the Damons leased the property to K. Rooney, Inc. In November 1991, Rooney began upgrading the station by installing new pumps and Stage II of a vapor recovery system. As digging commenced, the Abington Fire Department, upon observing petroleum product pooling in the surface excavations, shut down the construction and notified the Massachusetts Department of Environmental Protection, who sent a Notice of Responsibility to the plaintiffs and Rooney. Monitoring wells were installed, and samples of groundwater were taken and analyzed. As a result of the pollution discovery, Rooney refused to pay rent from November 1991 to March 1992. The Damons brought suit against Sun alleging common-law misrepresentation. The district court, after a four-day bench trial, found for the Damons, awarding them $245,000 plus reasonable attorneys' fees and costs.

OPINION: *TORRUELLA, Chief Judge*

The Damons charged Sun with the tort of misrepresentation, also referred to as fraud or deceit. The elements of misrepresentation are well established: in order to recover, plaintiff must allege and prove that the defendant made a false representation of a material fact with knowledge of its falsity for the purpose of inducing the plaintiff to act thereon, and that the plaintiff relied upon the representation as true and acted upon it to his or her damage. The party making the representation need not know that the statement is false if the fact represented is susceptible of actual knowledge. Here, the alleged false representations are the statements made by Sun's representatives that it was a "good" station, upon which Damon relied in his purchasing decision. The alleged harm suffered was that the Damons bought a gas station in 1979 that would have been worth more in 1992 if what the defendant's representatives stated had in fact been true. The damages were measured by the difference between the value of the property if it had been uncontaminated, as the defendant represented, and the actual value of the property as contaminated.

Appellant questions the district court's findings related to two of these elements: causation and damages. The causation element requires that the misrepresentation be a substantial factor in the plaintiff's actions, such that it tends along with other factors to produce the plaintiff's harm. The defendant's conduct need not be the sole cause of the injury: It is enough that plaintiffs introduce evidence from which reasonable men and women may conclude that it is more probable that the event was caused by the defendant than that it was not.

Sun first alleges that the alleged representations were opinions and not statements of fact. The distinction is a crucial one, as it is well established that the latter can ordinarily be the basis of a claim of fraud, but the former cannot. The district court held that it should have been clear from Damon's questions to Sun's agents that he was concerned about the past and future integrity of the entire underground gas delivery system; as Damon testified at trial, "the only thing you've got in a gas station is tanks and pumps and the lines. I mean, what else is there?"

Our review of the record leads us to affirm the district court's finding that the statements were factual in nature. The court found that Damon asked if Sun had had any problems with the underground storage tanks, to which Sun responded that it had had "no problems with it. It's all good." Sun further responded to Damon's questions about whether it had any problems with the station, particularly with the underground tanks, by stating "that it was a 'good station' which just needed to be run by a good operator to be successful."

In that context, reading the record in the light most favorable to the Damons, we do not find that the district court erred in finding that the Sun representatives' statements that it was a "good station" were factual. Indeed, we are hard put to see how, where there has been a spill of 2,000 gallons in 1974, which Sun knew of, statements five years later that it was a "good station" and that Sun had had "no problems with it" in reply to a question regarding the underground tanks are not misrepresentations of fact.

Sun's second contention is that the record contains no evidence of the key elements needed to prove fraud. First, Sun asserts that the statements were not misrepresentations of material facts, and thus the first element of the tort has not been shown. We disagree. There can be no doubt that the statements were misrepresentations in terms of the past history of the property: stating that it is a "good station" ignores the fact that there was a 2,000 gallon spill. It may have been a "good station" in 1979, from Sun's perspective: the spill had been cleaned up in accordance with the requirements of the time, and there is no evidence of other problems. Nonetheless, there had been a problem in the past, and to omit that was to misrepresent the situation. The district court found that the fact was material, and it gave credence to Damon's testimony that his affiliation with a car dealership which sold gasoline gave him a general awareness of the growing importance of environmental issues, and that he would not have bought the station had he been aware of the spill. Thus, the statements by the Sun representatives were certainly one of the principal grounds, though not necessarily the sole ground, that caused the plaintiffs to take the particular action that the wrongdoer intended he would take as a result of such representations. Finally, we have already established that these were factual statements. Thus, the statements were misrep-

resentations of material facts.

Affirm the decision of the district court on all points.

Discussion Questions

1. At what point does puffery, exaggeration, or misrepresentation in negotiation become deception or fraud?
2. When made in defense of a misrep-

resentation, how much weight should the assertion hold that parties have an independent duty to confirm facts represented at a negotiation?

The use of **coercion** is a second ethical dilemma in negotiation. It is rare, of course, to find circumstances in which an agreement is forced from a party under genuine duress. Coercion can, however, take many forms. A superior position, such as employer relative to employee,

can result in tacit coercion in a negotiation. In the interesting case that follows, an employer with dominant bargaining power may have coerced employees into settlement agreements that precluded assertion of their rights under a federal statute.

RONALD H. HOWLETT V. HOLIDAY INNS, INC.
120 F.3d 598 (6th U.S. Cir., 1997)

FACT SUMMARY

Plaintiffs are former upper-level management employees of Holiday Inns, Inc. In 1991, Holiday Inns was acquired by a British corporation, and after a corporate restructuring, plaintiffs lost their jobs. Each plaintiff signed an individual separation and release agreement in exchange for an unspecified sum of money. The agreement provides, in pertinent part:

Employee forever and unconditionally releases the Released Parties from any and all claims related in any way to anything occurring up to and including

the date hereof. Without limiting the generality of the foregoing, this Agreement applies to any and all claims which in any way result from, arise out of, or relate to Employee's employment, termination or resignation from employment with the Company or any of the Released Parties, including but not limited to, any and all claims which could have been asserted under any fair employment, contract or tort laws, ordinance [sic], including Title VII of the Civil Rights Act of 1964, the Tennessee Anti-Discrimination Act, the Employee Retirement Income Security

Act, or under any of the Company's employee benefit, compensation, bonus, performance, award, severance, or vacation pay plans.

Each plaintiff was instructed that he or she had 72 hours to sign and return the agreement in order to be eligible for the incentive. Nowhere does the agreement explicitly refer to ADEA claims.

Under the Older Workers Benefit Protection Act (OWBPA) amendment to the ADEA, there are eight minimum requirements an ADEA release must meet before it can be considered "knowing and voluntary." 29 U.S.C. § 626(f). Paraphrasing, they are:

1. The release must be written in a manner calculated to be understood by the employee signing the release, or the average individual eligible to participate.
2. The release must specifically refer to the ADEA.
3. The release must not purport to encompass claims that may arise after the date of signing.
4. The employer must provide consideration for the ADEA claim above and beyond that to which the employee would otherwise already be entitled.
5. The employee must be advised in writing to consult with an attorney.
6. The employee must be given at least 21 or 45 days to consider signing, depending on whether the incentive is offered to a group.
7. The release must allow the employee to rescind the agreement up to seven days after signing.
8. If the release is offered in connection with an exit incentive or group termination program, the employer must provide information relating to the job titles and ages of those selected (or eligible) for the program, and the corresponding information relating to employees in the same job titles for those who were not selected (or not eligible) for the program.

OPINION: *RYAN, Circuit Judge*

Holiday Inns acknowledges that none of the foregoing requirements were met with respect to the release in question, save possibly the first. Thus, under the terms of the ADEA, the release signed by the plaintiffs was not knowing and voluntary; therefore, it was not valid.

The congressional committee that proposed the OWBPA amendment to the ADEA discussed several of the common-law instances in which a voidable contract could be ratified, such as instances in which the original contract was procured through fraud, duress, coercion, or mistake, thus suggesting that Congress viewed noncompliance with the OWBPA requirements in the same light.

Thus, it is clear from the statute that a former employee could no more assent to the waiver of his or her ADEA claims after having signed the defective release than he or she could at the time of signing it. Although Congress utilized the familiar language of the common law when it deemed that no waiver would be "knowing and voluntary" unless the eight OWBPA requirements were met, it did not stop there; it also provided that an individual may not waive an ADEA claim unless the waiver is knowing and voluntary. 29 U.S.C. § 626(f)(1). Allowing an employee to ratify a release which violates the OWBPA would directly contradict this language.

Congress has purposely interposed an obstacle to application of the traditional ratification doctrine by requiring that a knowing and voluntary waiver of an ADEA claim cannot occur except in cases in which, at a minimum, the eight OWBPA factors are met. The common law would invalidate a contract as not being knowing or voluntary if it were secured through fraud, duress, coercion, or mistake. But, under the common law, such an invalid contract could be ratified by the retention of the consideration once the fraud, duress, coercion, or mistake was uncovered. The rationale for this rule is that, by keeping the consideration after the voidability of the contract is discovered, the promisor makes a new contract, this time knowing all the facts and circumstances. He renews his promise and keeps the consideration, forming a new contract, because the element which made the original contract invalid is no longer present.

But, in this case, the invalidating flaw has not been eliminated. The OWBPA information still has not been supplied. It is as if, under a common-law analysis, the fraud, duress, coercion, or mistake infected the new, supposedly ratified contract as well. Thus, even under this analysis, the employee cannot validate the noncomplying release simply by retaining the consideration.

The overarching purpose of the OWBPA amendment is to provide employees with information giving them the ability to assess the value of the right to sue for a possibly valid discrimination claim. These plaintiffs are in no better position now to make this assessment than they were when they signed the releases.

As a practical matter, we note that the eight OWBPA requirements should not be difficult for an employer to meet. Although questions may arise as to whether the information provided by the employer can be understood by the average individual eligible to participate in the severance program, or as to what constitutes a "job title," courts should read these requirements in a common-sense manner and not dogmatically. When the provided information reasonably assists the employee in determining whether he or she wishes to waive a potential ADEA claim, then summary judgment may be appropriate in favor of the employer. Thus, Holiday Inns can hardly complain about the inequity of losing the benefit of its bargain, when it did not even attempt to comply with the minimal requirements of the OWBPA.

For the foregoing reasons, the district court's order is affirmed.

Discussion Questions

1. How extreme should coercion be before a court orders the recision of a resulting agreement? For what external indicia of coercion should a court look?
2. In the present case, it seems very likely from the relationship of the parties as well as the violation of law that coercion was present. Could coercion be proved in a negotiation between parties of apparently equal status?
3. How might coercion be prevented in a negotiation session? Would representation solve the problem of coercion? If so, how should it be employed in cases like the present one?

A **conflict of interest** poses a third area of ethical uncertainty particularly when representatives are introduced to the negotiation process. The representatives have a fiduciary obligation to those they represent. Consequently, they must scrupulously avoid any conflict of interest, whether real or apparent. In addition, the *duty to bargain in good faith* has been addressed by a number of courts, primarily in the area of labor relations. In short, the negotiator is compelled by duty to put forth a good-faith effort to settle in a way that comports with the interests of the client.

INTERNATIONAL AND CROSS-CULTURAL NEGOTIATION

A **culture,** at its simplest definition, is a group of people who live and work together. More specifically, cultures are based on shared values, laws, and language. As the economy and business have become increasingly global, negotiating across cultures has become a far more important topic. Most businesses receive supplies from a foreign company or depend on foreign consumption of their product. Consequently, understanding the unique aspects presented by cross-cultural negotiation is critical. This text provides only a brief overview of this topic.

Negotiating in cross-cultural settings does not require substantial change to the negotiation models. However, a careful *choice between the models* needs made, consistent with the likely orientation of the opponent. Obviously, it would be detrimental to pursue a competive negotiation model with a negotiator from another culture that values cooperation. Doing so would magnify any weaknesses of the process. Additionally, negotiating across cultures suggests the need to become *conversant in the norms and expectations* of the other culture in terms of both personal comportment and communication. Finally, cross-cultural negotiations present *technical difficulties* beyond language that must be addressed thoroughly during the preparation phase and prior to actual negotiation. For example, a negotiator facing a foreign opponent must understand the economic currency and rate of exchange for that nation before any meaningful monetary settlement can be reached.

The preceding ethical considerations are just as important in this setting as in conventional negotiation. However, cross-cultural negotiation presents an additional important ethical consideration. Much of the popular literature on cross-cultural negotiation stresses the importance of imitating the behaviors of the person with whom one negotiates. This may involve bowing when in Asia, not shaking hands in certain parts of the world, and negotiating over a meal in others. It seems clear that one ought to balance in these contexts authenticity, at both personal and cultural levels, with accommodation of the person and culture with whom one is negotiating. Doing so conveys respect for oneself and one's counterpart in the process, while avoiding manipulation based on fairly superficial criteria.

Finally, cross-cultural negotiation is often successfully done with the aid of a mediator. Such a third-party neutral (not necessarily acting in the same formal role that is discussed later in Chapter 4) acting in an informal, facilitative role can function in several important ways. First, the mediator can act as a buffer, filtering lan-

http://

See The Latin Business Exchange for an example of services available to support cross-cultural negotiation at: http://www .latinbiz.org/ contract.html guage and conduct so that each side is heard clearly and without distractions related to cultural differences. Second, the mediator may act as an interpreter of culture, providing both sides with insight into one another. Finally, the mediator can be a scapegoat of sorts. When cultural issues become an obstacle, the mediator can take or be given the blame, rather than one of the parties, so that negotiations can continue productively. Use of a mediator in this specialized context can be a very productive approach.

ADR TRENDS IN NEGOTIATION

http://

An example of the training resources available in negotiation can be found at these sites:
http://www.negotiationskills.com/speaking.html
http://www.negotiation.com/
http://www.smartbiz.com/sbs/cats/buysell.htm

The trend in ADR is toward the development of processes that integrate negotiation into dispute resolution. These nonadjudicative, negotiation-oriented ADR processes include the minitrial, the summary jury trial, and mediation. At least three reasons exist for the emergence and likely continued viability of such processes. First, such processes empower business executives who seek control over their cases to participate personally and meaningfully in the process. Even when representatives are used, the input into a negotiated process is fairly direct and current. Adjudicative processes rely far more heavily on experts to cover the unfamiliar terrain of the courtroom. Second, negotiation-oriented processes allow parties to retain control over the outcome in their case, rather than relinquishing control to a judge, jury, or arbitrator. This helps preserve the ability to shape a resolution consistent with one's own needs. Finally, negotiated processes are normally cheaper and less time consuming than adjudicative processes.

The trend certainly seems to be toward integrating voluntary, private negotiation into dispute resolution in all areas. Business benefits from such a direction. There also appears to be an inclination, one that will emerge as a central theme in many of the cases covered throughout this text, toward fairly significant judicial deference to and protection of outcomes reached in private ADR settings, including negotiation. Nonadjudicative processes are normally good public policy, so courts fairly consistently honor commitments to use them and commitments made through them.

CHAPTER CONCLUSION

Negotiation forms the basis for all effective nonadjudicative dispute resolution and therefore is a key business skill. The business professional must become comfortable with the process and the many ways in which it is practiced. The business professional should also learn to negotiate in both the competitive and cooperative models and should understand that a crucial test of negotiator effectiveness is the long-term viability of the commercial relationship between the opposing parties following negotiation. Finally, complete preparation is essential to avoiding fraud and coercion and succeeding when negotiating across cultures.

BEST BUSINESS PRACTICES

Here are some practical tips for managers on using alternative dispute resolution.

- Because negotiation is the single ADR process in which the manager may directly resolve a business dispute, it should serve as the preferred method in most cases.
- The cooperative model of negotiation may not maximize the results in any individual case because it stresses compromise and mutual satisfaction; it may, however, create long-term business relationships that more than compensate for the incremental losses it potentially involves.
- Negotiation becomes a completely different process when representatives engage in it; one should carefully consider whether to include them and should have a good substantive or procedural reason to support that decision.
- The most effective way of eliminating the pitfalls presented by an unscrupulous negotiator is to thoroughly understand one's own case. It is very difficult to coerce or deceive a party who understands the facts and law that underpin a case as well as the likely outcomes.
- The best negotiators know that not everything can be settled nor everyone settled with; be prepared to walk away if the deal or the opponent presents sufficiently negative consequences.
- When negotiating across cultures, an informal mediator can bridge some cultural differences; one should consider using an interpreter who has skills as a mediator.

KEY TERMS

Coercion, p. 80
Collaborative model, p. 63
Competitive-compromise model, p. 63
Conflict of interest, p. 82
Culture, p. 83
Deception, p. 77
Final, p. 77

Impression management, p. 74
Legitimacy, p. 76
Misrepresentation, p. 77
Negotiation, p. 62
Noncontingent, p. 77
Representation, p. 65

ETHICAL AND LEGAL REVIEW

1. During the course of a difficult negotiation session involving a commercial dispute, you realize that the other party does not fully understand the facts. More specifically, the other party believes that your losses are greater than they

actually are. You did not create the misapprehension, nor did you obscure facts or evidence in such a way as to encourage it. Moreover, you could greatly benefit from it. Should you correct the mistake and potentially reduce your recovery or settle the case without disclosing the truth and achieve a more significant recovery than is due? Does your answer change if you believe that something you actually said contributed to the other party's misunderstanding? Does your answer change if you represent someone else in the negotiation?

2. Your counterpart in a contract renegotiation is a relatively inexperienced negotiator from a small supplier and is obviously intimidated by you because you represent a large company with considerable resources. You believe that a very aggressive, even threatening approach may allow you to maximize your position by creating contract terms more favorable to your company. Should you assert your case in ways calculated to subdue and defeat your opponent? What are the consequences of doing so? Is it appropriate in this setting to threaten to seek another supplier in order to obtain concessions?

3. You are aware that a competitor is negotiating to purchase a company that would give it a strategic advantage over you. Indeed, as you learn more about the negotiations, you realize that in principle a deal has already been reached. Formal documents have not yet been drafted, but the parties appear to have successfully concluded the negotiation. Hoping to prevent such an alliance, you contact the target company and make them an offer above and beyond that of your rival. In the process of making that proposal, you make some disparaging comments about your competitor. As a result of your offer, the target company declines to complete the negotiated deal and seeks to enter talks with you. Have your actions been illegal or unethical?

4. You are preparing to send a valued colleague to a foreign country to consummate a highly technical deal. She has spent weeks preparing for the negotiation and has mastered several difficult areas of technical expertise. In addition, she has supervised the "number crunching" and is more familiar with the costs of the project than anyone else in the company. During a brief phone call from an employee of the company with whom you are negotiating, you accidentally learn that a male negotiator is expected and that the presence of a woman as the principal negotiator will adversely affect the process and may delay the deal. The employee tells you that as a cultural matter, his company is simply not ready to embrace the more liberal American attitude toward women. Should you send your female colleague anyway, as both a statement of your trust in her and your ethics, or should you delay the process to master the material yourself?

SUGGESTED ADDITIONAL READINGS

Bazerman, M., and M. Neale. *Negotiating Rationally.* The Free Press, 1992.

Cohen, R. *Negotiating Across Cultures.* United States Institute of Peace Press, 1991.

Craver, C. *Effective Legal Negotiation and Settlement.* The Michie Company, 1993.

Fisher, R., and W. Ury. *Getting to Yes: Negotiating Agreement Without Giving In.* 2d ed. Penguin, 1991.

Guernsey, T. *A Practical Guide to Negotiation.* National Institute for Trial Advocacy, 1996.

Kritek, P. *Negotiating at an Uneven Table: Developing Moral Courage in Resolving Our Conflicts.* Jossey-Bass Publishers, 1994.

Lewicki, R., et. al. *Negotiation: Readings, Exercises and Cases.* Richard D. Irwin, Inc., 1993.

Lindley, D. *Making Decisions.* 2d ed. Wiley, 1985.

Thompson, L. *The Mind and Heart of the Negotiator.* Prentice-Hall, Inc., 1998.

Ury, W. *Getting Past No: Negotiating With Difficult People.* Bantam Books, 1991.

Williams, G. *Legal Negotiation and Settlement.* West Publishing Company, 1983.

Zartman, I., ed. *International Multilateral Negotiation.* Jossey-Bass Publishers, 1994.

4

MEDIATION

CHAPTER HIGHLIGHTS

In this chapter, you will read and learn about the following:

1. The development of mediation as an alternative to adversarial dispute resolution models like arbitration and trial.
2. The advantages and disadvantages of voluntary facilitative mediation as a method of ADR.
3. The specific mediation models, including facilitative mediation as well as hybrid mediation processes, such as evaluative mediation and mediation-arbitration.
4. The steps in a typical facilitative mediation conference.
5. The evaluation of cases' suitability for mediation.
6. The selection of the proper mediator and the roles, tasks, and ethical responsibilities of the mediator.

Mediation is perhaps the fastest growing form of alternative dispute resolution (ADR) in business today. Lawyers and clients seeking rapid, economical, and private dispute resolution are using mediation in court-annexed and private, for-fee settings. Mediation allows parties to negotiate outcomes to disputes themselves, rather than relinquish control of the case to a judge, jury, or arbitrator.

THE HISTORICAL DEVELOPMENT OF MEDIATION

Although mediation is a much newer process than trial or arbitration, it has been used to resolve labor and commercial disputes for decades. It is also used successfully in community disputes and divorce cases. It is a process that can be adapted to many different types of cases and parties.

Arbitration has always been the primary means of formally resolving labor difficulties under collective bargaining agreements. Attempts to settle labor disputes through mediation occurred as early as the nineteenth century in both the United States and England. The U.S. government first sponsored labor mediation in 1913, when the Department of Labor made a "commission of conciliators" available to parties involved in labor disputes that were often profoundly contentious, sometimes violent disputes.

In 1947, the commission of conciliators was renamed and rechartered as the **Federal Mediation and Conciliation Service.** The **Labor Management Relations Act of 1947** provided a broad mandate to the Service, allowing it to "proffer its services in any labor dispute in any industry affecting commerce . . . whenever in its judgment such dispute threatens to cause substantial interruption in commerce."[1] Federal Mediation and Conciliation Service mediators have participated in virtually every major labor-management confrontation in recent history, including those involving Caterpillar throughout the 1990s and the Major League Baseball strike that ended the 1994 season. Many states maintain similar agencies.

For at least fifty years mediation has also been used to resolve commercial disputes. Although arbitration is probably the most common ADR mechanism used outside of the courtroom, due to the relatively recent proliferation of arbitration contract clauses, mediation is being used with increasing frequency. Commercial disputes often arise between parties who, out of necessity, must be able to maintain an amicable working relationship. Mediation's nonadversarial approach to dispute resolution is an attractive option. For example, Ford Motor Company provides a dispute resolution process resembling mediation to some customers unsatisfied with Ford products in the hope of avoiding litigation and preserving customer goodwill.

Private commercial mediation is far less well defined than labor mediation, which is normally conducted according to fairly formal rules of procedure. A small number of states have relatively minimal mediator qualification and/or privilege statutes, but the mediation process remains largely unregulated and undefined in most states. As a result, mediation is less widely used in commercial matters than in labor disputes. Nonetheless, it is a viable and growing alternative as both state and federal court dockets become increasingly congested. Further contributing to the use of mediation in commercial cases has been the formulation of model rules for commercial mediation by the American Arbitration Association, the most widely recognized of the national commercial dispute resolution process providers.

http://
Find information on the DOL's Dispute Resolution Program at:
http://www.dol.gov/dol/asp/public/programs/adr/main.htm

http://
A complete text of the model rules for the American Arbitration Association is available at:
http://www.adr.org/rules/medrules.html

---

1.   29 U.S.C. 171 (a)(b).

Mediation has been used for decades to resolve domestic relations disputes, particularly asset allocation and child custody issues resulting from divorce. Because of the need for the parties involved to be able to maintain an amicable long-term relationship, and because of the emotional costs of an adversarial resolution, mediation can be an ideal mechanism for settlement of these often intractable cases.

The successful use of mediation in labor, commercial, and domestic relations cases has led to the broader use of private mediation to resolve business disputes. Mediation is mandated for certain types of disputes. While parties may not be required to settle, they are occasionally required to participate in a mediation conference. Some jurisdictions, for example, require mediation for entire categories of cases, such as contested divorce cases where child custody is at issue.[2] Certain labor disputes must also be taken to mediation before arbitration or litigation can begin.[3]

Courtroom rules of procedure have also contributed to the development of mediation. The **Federal Rules of Civil Procedure** mandate use of a settlement conference, often presided over by a judge, magistrate, or special master.[4] Because the conference resembles mediation in many significant ways, private mediation is accepted more readily by attorneys as a mechanism for conflict resolution. In fact, attorneys often prefer to use a skilled mediator to resolve the case, rather than the judge who may later be called upon to try the case. Mediation prevents the parties from biasing the judge's impression of the case through his or her participation as a neutral advisor during the pretrial settlement conference. Finally, the rules empower a judge to consider the "possibility of the use of extrajudicial procedures to resolve the dispute."[5]

Another factor contributing to the increased popularity of mediation is Federal Rule of Evidence 408. This rule allows parties to offer compromises and disclosures in a mediation conference that will not be admissible in court should their case go to trial.[6] The federal rule is limited in scope and subject to differing interpretations. Therefore, parties are still somewhat cautious about the disclosures they make at a mediation conference. Most states have similar rules covering the admissibility of the contents of settlement negotiations in state courts. All of the rules have the intent and effect of encouraging parties to consider settlement prior to commencing a more formal proceeding.

Finally, attorneys are being called on by courts and state licensing bodies to explore the use of nonlitigation alternatives, like mediation, to resolve disputes. The following case illustrates the need for mediation. It concerns a complicated patent infringement matter, and the court addresses the obligation of the attorney to discuss the costs attendant to litigation and the alternatives available to the client to reduce those costs. The decision is rooted in the **Civil Justice Reform Act,** a

http://
The text of Rule 408 is at:
http://www.law. cornell.edu/rules/ fre/408.html

http://
A searchable database containing the U.S. Code and the Civil Justice Reform Act is at: http://www.gpo. ucop.edu

2. See, for example, the Cook County Rules of the Circuit Court, Section 13.4(g)(C).
3. 29 U.S.C. 173 allows a Federal Mediation and Conciliation Service mediator to intervene even without party consent.
4. F.R.C.P. 16.
5. F.R.C.P. 16 (c)(7).
6. F.R.E. 408.

federal law designed to reduce federal court dockets. Under this act all federal courts must adopt measures that incorporate ADR mechanisms.[7] Pursuant to the Act, trial court judges may require counsel to educate their clients as to the costs and time of litigation and alternatives to it.

7.   23 U.S.C. sec. 471 ff.

SCHWARZKOPF TECHNOLOGIES CORPORATION V. INGERSOLL CUTTING TOOL COMPANY
142 F.R.D. 420 (D. Del., 1992)

FACT SUMMARY

Schwarzkopf brought this patent infringement action against Ingersoll. The patents in suit concern a coating designed to improve certain industrial tools. Ingersoll's Answer contains eleven affirmative defenses relating to patent unenforceability and invalidity.

OPINION: *FARNAN, District Judge*

C. The Civil Justice Reform Act

Section 471 of the Civil Justice Reform Act (CJRA) requires that each United States district court implement a civil justice expense and delay reduction plan:

> to facilitate deliberate adjudication of civil cases on the merits, monitor discovery, improve litigation management, and ensure just, speedy, and inexpensive resolutions of civil disputes. 28 U.S.C. § 471.

The mandate of the CJRA is clear. Federal trial courts are now required, by statute, to implement techniques and strategies designed to dispose of cases in an efficient and inexpensive manner. District courts may employ various methods to achieve the goal of delay and

expense reduction, depending on the character of the court's caseload, geography, volume and a myriad of other factors. In this district, patent cases represent a statistically significant portion of the caseload and a significant challenge with regard to delay and expense reduction methods. The judges of the district have adopted a Plan under the CJRA, which incorporates measures to foster a reduction in the disposition time of all cases filed in the district.

Although the Plan relies principally upon the reduction in time delays as the catalyst for cost reduction, the Court is convinced that additional efforts are necessary to accomplish the CJRA's goal of expense reduction. In this regard, the Court is persuaded that courts must entrust the task of expense reduction to attorneys and their clients with courts acting in a supportive role.

In particular, courts should facilitate dialogue between an attorney and client regarding the cost of litigation. A meaningful discussion on the subject of litigation expense should include, at a minimum, the attorney's estimation of costs and fees vis-á-vis the anticipated result, as well as consideration of the alternative means available to the client for dispute resolution. With these principles in mind, the Court will require counsel to certify to the Court that they have discussed with their clients the estimated costs of this litigation, the anticipated result, and alternative means of dispute resolution. The certification shall be signed by counsel and the client.

The Court will require counsel to certify to the Court that they have discussed with their respective clients the anticipated costs and fees of this litigation and the alternatives to litigation. An appropriate Order will be entered.

Discussion Questions

1. Is there any way to accurately determine whether attorneys have meaningfully advised their clients on the costs and expected outcomes of litigation?
2. Can an attorney or client be reasonably expected to predict with any certainty the results of a trial by jury?
3. Will rulings like this one deter litigants with meritorious claims from requesting a trial? Should this decision have a prohibitive effect on litigants?

INTRODUCTION TO THE MEDIATION PROCESS

Mediation is defined as a private, voluntary negotiation process using a trained neutral third party to facilitate a final, contractually binding settlement between parties involved in a dispute. Unlike litigation and arbitration, which consist of a formal evidentiary hearing, mediation is a semiformal negotiation between the parties without the use of evidence or witnesses. While litigation and arbitration are presided over by a judge who renders a decision in the case, mediation is facilitated by a specially trained neutral advisor who is not empowered to decide the case, only to assist the parties in negotiating effectively. Mediation is also unlike litigation in that it is non-adversarial. Indeed, the most effective mediators build a process in which parties understand their role as active participants and collaborate to resolve the dispute. Unlike a trial or arbitration, mediation often results in a mutually agreeable outcome.

http://

Information on the Federal Mediation and Conciliation Service's efforts is at:
http://www.fmcs.gov

Advantages of Mediation

Mediation, now readily available throughout the United States, has several advantages over traditional adversarial forms of dispute resolution. First, it is less costly than evidentiary processes. Mediation is normally completed in a matter of hours through a series of one to three conferences. It may occur much earlier and with much less preparation in a dispute than in a trial or an arbitration. Furthermore, mediation is not a formal evidentiary process requiring extensive use of expert witnesses or demonstrative proof. Indeed, the process is most effectively accomplished without introduction of evidence or witnesses, relying instead on the parties to negotiate in good faith. As a result, the costs associated with the use of expert witnesses, trial counsel, and case preparation are substantially reduced or even eliminated. Costs are further controlled because parties traditionally share the comparatively minimal fees of hiring a mediator.

Second, the process is more efficient than most evidentiary processes. One of the principle attractions of mediation is the speed with which parties can resolve their disputes. Because mediators are present to manage negotiation, not to represent a party or render a legal decision, they need not prepare extensively to conduct the conference. As a result, one can retain a mediator on relatively short notice. In addition, mediation requires less preparation by the parties than formal processes, so they are able to participate sooner. Finally, overcrowded court dockets throughout the United States often delay trials for years. Private mediation can be accomplished virtually on demand.

Third, the process offers a range of settlement options limited only by the creativity of the parties and the mediator. Judicial processes and arbitration are largely tailored to create economic outcomes. Although certain forms of injunctive relief are possible through litigation, most judges and juries think of the resolution of a civil case in dollar terms. Conversely, mediation allows parties to consider a far wider range of remedies. Long-term structured payment schedules and annuities allow parties to treat economic outcomes more creatively. In addition, noneconomic remedies like provisions for service, public statements of apology, and charitable gifts or gifts in kind are possible. In short, parties can create outcomes custom designed for their particular situation. Parties can also craft outcomes likely to sustain important business relationships by avoiding the confrontation and acrimony associated with a trial.

Fourth, the process does not preclude the use of further, more formal dispute resolution mechanisms such as arbitration or litigation. Parties are therefore free to strive for a settlement without jeopardizing their chances for or in a trial if mediation is unsuccessful. Parties do not formally waive their right to litigate or arbitrate in the event they cannot settle, nor are they bound to legal arguments made in mediation. Indeed, mediation is often a process of weighing the costs and benefits of a formal process against those of a settlement. Parties can, and sometimes do, decline to settle, and will move on to more formal proceedings. For those parties able to settle, the time and expense saved can be substantial. For those who cannot settle, the cost of mediation has likely been minimal relative to the total costs associated with the continuing litigation. They may even settle some portion of the case, reducing the issues remaining for trial or arbitration.

Fifth, as noted earlier, the parties control the outcome of the case. Mediation does not create the risk of outright loss associated with trial, because the parties do not transfer the power to decide the case to someone else. This is invaluable to those who are able to negotiate, want to be involved in the resolution of the dispute, and seek outcomes tailored to their particular case.

Disadvantages of Mediation

Mediation is not without its disadvantages. Principal among them is the absence of due process protections for the participants. The formalized procedural and evidentiary rules of due process designed to protect parties and associated with the trial or arbitration of a lawsuit are lacking in mediation. This lack of formality is a disadvantage in the eyes of those who believe it may permit mediator bias, coercion, or party bad-faith. For others, it affirms the need for an attorney to assist in preparation before mediating and to participate during the process to ensure that important legal rights are not being waived without informed consent and that the agreement reached is legally enforceable. It also underscores the need for a mediator who is neutral and experienced in creating and managing a process that is fundamentally fair.

A second concern for some parties and attorneys is the absence of an appeal process in the event that the privately negotiated agreement is later determined by one of the parties to be flawed in some way. Because mediation is a highly confidential process, it is never performed on the record or recorded by a court reporter. In addition, it precedes trial and does not involve an official legal judgment by a third party. Thus, unlike arbitration, mediation agreements are virtually impossible to appeal. As a result, parties are generally bound by the agreements they reach in mediation. It is possible to argue that an agreement was tainted by fraud, duress, or some other legal defense to a contract, but this is much different from formally appealing a court's judgment or an arbitrator's decision.

Finally, the lack of standardized rules and the tremendous flexibility of the process sometimes make it inconsistent, haphazard, unpredictable, or unreliable. In fact, the process is entirely within the discretion of the individual mediator, though parties unsatisfied with the proceedings may withdraw from them at any time. Parties should therefore ask mediators specific questions on how they intend to conduct the process.

ADR IN ACTION

Delaware's ADR Program

Delaware, a state where a substantial number of major American businesses are incorporated, recently adopted an innovative state ADR law. Entitled the Delaware Voluntary Alternative Dispute Resolution Act, the law encourages individuals and businesses to voluntarily file with the state a certificate of agreement to submit disputes to ADR.[8] An entity that files this certificate is bound to participate in an ADR procedure in all cases in which it becomes involved, and which a court

8.   77 Delaware Laws sec. 7701 ff.

ADR IN ACTION Continued

designates as suitable for such a process. The entity may later file a certificate of revocation and pay an additional fee to be released from this agreement.

The Delaware program is noteworthy for at least three reasons. First, it binds parties to participate in an ADR process in all disputes in which they are involved, rather than encouraging parties to select some of the cases they may have pending for an alternative dispute resolution process. Although the cases are designated for ADR by a judge with party input, the law is designed to move cases out of the courthouse. In fact, a party involved in a dispute with an opponent who has not filed the certificate of agreement is permitted to request that the other party submit to ADR. Enabling parties to agree to ADR before they are actually involved in a dispute results in more reasoned and prudent consideration of the value of ADR procedures.

Second, the official Delaware ADR process to which these cases are subjected is a form of mediation provided by a trained ADR practitioner rather than arbitration. Many states have adopted mandatory arbitration provisions to alleviate court overcrowding. These provisions send parties to a panel of arbitrators for an abbreviated evidentiary hearing that resembles a trial in both procedure and outcome, rather than to a courtroom for a genuine trial. Such programs generally arbitrate cases with relatively minimal dollar values. Delaware has elected instead to employ a negotiated process to resolve all suitable disputes regardless of dollar value. The state will allow a trial if the case cannot be settled amicably or if the case is determined to be unsuitable for mediation at the outset.

Third, the Delaware provision carefully describes the qualifications of the ADR professionals permitted to resolve cases under the statute. The law permits either currently licensed and experienced attorneys or nonattorneys with state-approved mediation training to provide the services. In addition, because the statute provides those practitioners with a clear and complete testimonial privilege with respect to all matters introduced at the mediation conference, confidentiality is guaranteed. The statute even includes a fee provision allowing mediators to charge prevailing rates for the services provided.

FORMS OF MEDIATION

Mediation is normally an informal process to which the parties voluntarily submit their cases. As a result, they are free to tailor the process, with input from the mediator selected, to meet their needs. Three major forms of mediation exist: facilitative mediation, evaluative mediation, and mediation-arbitration. In the first and most prominent, **facilitative mediation,** the mediator manages the process by which the parties negotiate their case. The mediator rarely offers direct assessment of the merits of the cases, nor appraises the outcomes the parties suggest. Instead, he or she constructs a process that allows the parties to negotiate effectively, offering procedural assistance and nonbinding substantive input.

Evaluative mediation or mediation-recommendation is a hybrid form of facilitative mediation. Here, the role of the mediator changes significantly. Unlike facilitative mediation, in which the mediator provides few, if any, judgments on the case, the evaluative mediator is often an expert in the area of law or controversy confronting the parties and is called on to provide input from that perspective after hearing the case from both parties. The mediator does not provide legal counsel, as the attorneys representing the parties do, but does provide a neutral and informed evaluation of the merits and demerits of the positions and options offered to and by each party. The object of such mediation is to move the parties toward an objectively defensible resolution of the case based on the estimate provided by the mediator.

In **mediation-arbitration,** a less common, hybrid form of mediation, the initial step is conventional facilitative mediation. However, in this process, the mediator assumes the role of arbitrator in the event that the parties cannot negotiate a resolution to all aspects of the case. In that capacity, the mediator renders a final and legally enforceable judgment for the parties. Parties must, of course, consent to this process before it begins at the first stage.

Mediation-arbitration blends elements of negotiation, mediation, and arbitration by strongly encouraging parties to create their own best settlement because of the threat of the binding settlement the mediator will otherwise impose. This process has the advantage of being highly efficient because it guarantees a final resolution of the case during the conference. However, it may reduce the level of disclosure from the parties during the mediation phase because they will be aware that the mediator may later use this statement to their disadvantage in the arbitration phase. In response to these concerns, occasionally parties will substitute a different neutral to act as arbitrator in the event that a mediated settlement is not reached.

OVERVIEW OF THE MEDIATION PROCESS

Mediation is most frequently initiated when one party contacts a mediator and requests the mediator to solicit the participation of other parties to the dispute in a mediation conference. When such a request is made, the mediator will typically begin by confirming that no conflicts of interest exist between him or herself and the parties. **Conflicts of interest** exist when the mediator has a personal stake in the outcome of the case or appears to have such a stake. If no conflicts exist, the mediator will contact the remaining parties and explain the process of mediation in an effort to secure their agreement to participate.

Fees will likely be arranged at this point as well. Private mediators typically charge on an hourly or flat conference fee basis, which includes minimal preparation time. Some mediators levy an additional payment if they settle the case. Parties normally are expected to share the expenses of the mediator. Although some mediators will allow one party to pay the entire fee, this may create the appearance of partiality toward that party. In addition, the nonpaying party arguably has a diminished incentive to participate actively in the settlement of the case.

In the event that both parties agree to mediate, the mediator has several additional preconference responsibilities beyond scheduling duties. The mediator will send and explain a formal document entitled the **agreement to mediate,** which lays out the expectations of the parties and the mediator when the conference begins. The agreement is normally in contractual form and contains, among other things, guarantees regarding the confidentiality of the process, the finality of any agreement reached, and the authority to settle. The parties will be expected to sign the document at the mediation conference. In addition, the mediator will ask the parties to consider who must be present to settle the case so that a final agreement may be reached. Finally, the mediator will confirm that all parties participating agree to do so with full authority to settle the case. **Authority to settle** does not mean that a party agrees to settle but that it agrees to participate with intent to settle if a satisfactory offer is made. Authority to settle also implies that a lawyer or agent representing the party at the mediation is authorized to resolve disputed issues in a binding fashion for the principal.

Mediators often do not familiarize themselves with the details of the dispute before commencing the conference. For a variety of reasons, they may avoid reviewing pleadings and discovery documents as well as discussing the facts of the case with the parties. First, discussions of the case outside of the mediation conference may bias the mediator or create the appearance of bias. Second, mediation is not an adversarial or evidentiary process. Therefore, reviewing the documents used in litigation sends an inappropriate signal to the parties that the mediator seeks or expects argument of the case, rather than negotiation leading to settlement. Third, parties often find that at the heart of their dispute is a miscommunication. When a mediator forces the parties to completely describe the case at the start of the mediation conference, he or she allows for the possibility that parties may view the case differently than they did while discussing it in the context of litigation.

The mediation process itself consists of several stages. The mediation conference begins with a brief, relatively informal **mediator opening statement.** The mediator's statement has at least three objectives. The opening statement describes the process and the role of the mediator. The opening statement also establishes the tone of the proceedings. The mediator will want the parties to understand that, unlike an adversarial process, mediation is a process that seeks cooperative approaches and mutually satisfactory resolutions. Both the tone and the language of the mediator opening statement are important in setting the stage for this to happen. Finally, the mediator seeks to establish his or her credibility, as well as that of the process, by describing both thoughtfully and professionally.

Following the mediator opening statement, the **party opening statements** will be delivered. Typically, each party's opening statement is directed to the mediator and summarizes all of the facts, issues, and desired outcomes. Most mediators ask that the party opening statements be uninterrupted and provide a complete description of the facts that lead to the dispute as well as the outcomes each party seeks. The party opening statements allow the mediator to assess the negotiation skills and approaches of the parties and to understand the facts of the case so that negotiations may proceed in a productive manner. The party statements offer the mediator a chance to establish a settlement range for the case, acclimate the parties to the process, and set the stage for the parties to begin to negotiate effectively.

The heart of the mediation process is the **facilitated negotiation** that takes place next. During this period, the mediator will assist the parties in articulating their respective cases to one another in more productive ways than they may have used previously. The mediator will summarize positions, ask questions calculated to elicit additional information, and suggest approaches not yet considered by the parties.

Throughout the negotiation period, the mediator will attempt to facilitate incremental compromise from both parties toward settlement. This is accomplished most significantly by helping the parties to expand the resources by identifying assets not previously described by the parties, by redefining or reconfiguring certain assets, or by looking for noneconomic assets that may be of some value to the parties.

Most mediators understand the value of allowing parties to speak fully on their case, perhaps to vent frustration and emotion and to foster an environment that permits such free expression. Often mediators will use objective criteria to change the perceptions of the parties with respect to the offers and demands on the table. The mediator will always structure the process carefully by selecting useful issues and addressing them in a productive order, by moderating the tempo and tone of the negotiations, and by allowing the parties time to think through the options presented to them.

At some point in virtually all mediation conferences, the mediator will caucus with each party. The **caucus** is a private meeting taken separately with each party to allow the parties to address issues not suitable for open session coverage, such as strengths and weaknesses of a particular aspect of the case. Caucuses, when used, are always taken with each party involved and are always strictly confidential. Many mediators will hold several sets of caucuses during the mediation conference. In addition to allowing the mediator to address and be addressed by the parties more candidly, the caucus can serve to overcome a negotiating impasse, a point at which the parties refuse or are unable to bargain. The caucus is also a useful mechanism for addressing an emotional outburst by a party who interrupts the process. Finally, it is a point in the process at which the mediator may assist a party struggling to negotiate effectively.

The caucus fulfills several additional objectives from the mediator's standpoint. It provides an opportunity to confirm his or her understanding of the information and settlement options offered by each party. It allows him or her to collect any additional information the parties are willing to provide in a more private setting. Finally, it serves as an opening for parties to create and evaluate new settlement options in a less threatening forum than directly in front of the opposing party.

When the parties have negotiated to a point of agreement, the mediator will assist them with **closure.** At this point, the mediator will assume two roles. First, the mediator will function as a catalyst, helping the parties to reach a point of final, formal acceptance of the settlement. For example, the mediator may set a deadline for agreement, effectively signaling to the parties that they have reached a point at which the mediator deems settlement advisable. The mediator may ask the parties to consider the costs saved through settlement compared with the costs associated with moving to a more formal process. In addition, the mediator will likely remind the parties of the finality of any agreement reached, in an effort to make settlement appear more attractive. Finally, the mediator will summarize the positions and offers of the parties in such a way as to elicit an unequivocally favorable response.

As the mediator works to move the parties to agreement, he or she will also likely assist the parties in evaluating and clarifying the agreement they have crafted. The most successful mediation conference results in an agreement that is final, permanent, and immediate. It should be, as well, noncontingent. This means it does not depend on the approval of an absent and uninformed third party. It should, of course, also be complete in the sense that all issues described during the party opening statements as essential to settlement are fully resolved. In addition, it should be realistic and specific. Finally, most mediators would argue that they must avoid illegal or unethical agreements.

Once the agreement is reached, the mediator may assist the parties in implementation planning. As a final measure, in some cases, though far less often when lawyers are involved, the mediator will write a settlement agreement for the parties. In all cases, the mediator will seek to gain the parties' agreement that they will return to mediation in the event that the settlement agreement becomes impossible to perform. Parties are often asked to evaluate both the process and the mediator prior to leaving the conference. See Figure 4.1 for a summary of the steps involved in a typical mediation conference.

Evaluating the success of mediation as an ADR mechanism in business is difficult. The most obvious indicator of success is the total number of cases settled and therefore moved out of the litigation system. A second, perhaps more meaningful measure for business is dollars saved by mediating versus litigating or arbitrating. An accurate measure of dollar savings is difficult to obtain, but certainly would include not only legal expenses but also any potential judgment rendered against a company.

Participant satisfaction with the process, notwithstanding dollars saved, is another way to measure success. It is likely that in some cases parties will be principally interested in whether, regardless of cost, they achieve an outcome consistent with their mutual needs. One might also consider the fairness of the outcome, as well as the rate of compliance with agreements reached in mediation.

FIGURE 4.1 Steps in the Typical Facilitative Mediation Conference

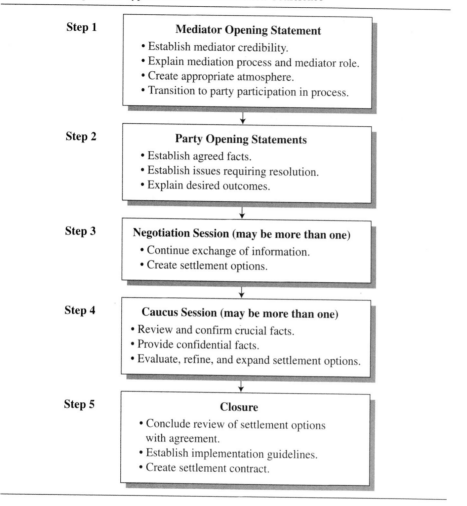

Step 1

Mediator Opening Statement
- Establish mediator credibility.
- Explain mediation process and mediator role.
- Create appropriate atmosphere.
- Transition to party participation in process.

Step 2

Party Opening Statements
- Establish agreed facts.
- Establish issues requiring resolution.
- Explain desired outcomes.

Step 3

Negotiation Session (may be more than one)
- Continue exchange of information.
- Create settlement options.

Step 4

Caucus Session (may be more than one)
- Review and confirm crucial facts.
- Provide confidential facts.
- Evaluate, refine, and expand settlement options.

Step 5

Closure
- Conclude review of settlement options with agreement.
- Establish implementation guidelines.
- Create settlement contract.

SELECTING CASES APPROPRIATE FOR MEDIATION

Virtually all disputes can be resolved through some form of mediation as both a legal and a practical matter. Some cases, however, are particularly well suited to the mediation process. Perhaps the most significant indicator of appropriateness for mediation is the presence of an important ongoing or potential business relationship. Mediation is, arguably, the only ADR process that offers parties the opportunity to resolve their dispute without disrupting their relationship, and in a way that may in fact strengthen it over time.

Cases involving parties who desire but fail to reach settlement are also well suited for mediation. The addition of the third-party neutral advisor, trained to move intransigent or incapable parties to a point of compromise, may remove impediments to a desirable settlement. A mediator may serve as an intermediary, allowing the parties to talk to one another through the mediator in cases where they are reluctant to meet with one another directly. An example of this would be a case involving sexual harassment allegations.

Cases that involve highly confidential or proprietary information are well addressed in mediation as the parties will likely be attracted to the complete privacy afforded them. Cases that involve trade secrets or that involve conduct that may not reflect well on an individual or company may also be addressed best through mediation.

When the economics of a case require a rapid resolution to avoid further harm to one or both parties, mediation can provide a forum for an expeditious settlement. Companies that are dependent on one another for economic viability, and unable to wait for a trial to address their disputes, may find mediation to be an advantageous process.

The proper selection of a case for mediation is, therefore, less a matter of determining whether a case is suitable for mediation than of determining whether it has factors indicating that mediation is inappropriate. One case type that is arguably better litigated than mediated is that which should receive significant due process protections. When information important for meaningful negotiation is being withheld, but could be obtained through a judicial process, or when a party has consistently acted in bad faith, the due process protections available in court may be necessary to achieve a suitable outcome. In addition, when it is important, either for a legal or a personal reason, to place blame on a party, such as a criminal or intentional tort case, litigation may be a more effective process than mediation because it results in a finding of liability or guilt.

Similarly, cases in which the establishment of important legal rights or responsibilities is a central issue are often best managed by formal litigation. Consider the case of a creditor who forgoes participation in a bankruptcy proceeding and reaches agreement with a debtor through mediation. Such a course of action may prevent the creditor from establishing formal creditor status and therefore deny him or her the right to recover later from the bankruptcy estate.

Cases likely to create important legal precedent may be better resolved through a legal judgment. For example, the Americans with Disabilities Act continues to present courts with cases involving unique facts subject to judicial interpretation, including whether certain conditions should be classified as disabilities and, if so, what accommodations must made for those afflicted. In addition, many aspects of sexual harassment law continue to require judicial interpretation. Without it, the parties themselves and the broader business community are deprived of any clarifying law on the novel questions presented.

It is important to note that there is no legal obligation to litigate a **case of first impression,** one that may set legal precedent. In consultation with their attorneys, parties must decide if there is some substantial benefit in such litigation that outweighs the costs and risks associated with that course of action. Although a case may present new and interesting legal questions, it is not necessarily a case that may be litigated to the best interests of the parties involved. Indeed, some parties may wish to avoid the creation of a new legal precedent.

Finally, judges may decide that particular cases present such costs and difficulties to the court that mediation is warranted. The following case describes such a decision and the factors that might lead a judge to refer a case on this basis.

SAUK COUNTY V. GREDE FOUNDRIES, INC. AND TEEL PLASTICS, INC. V. WILLIAM BEARD, ET AL.
145 F.R.D. 88 (E.D. Wis., 1992)

FACT SUMMARY

The complaint in this case regarding alleged or threatened release of hazardous substances from a landfill was filed on December 18, 1990. When the case arrived in court, the names of 48 parties appeared on the varied and numerous pleadings, and the docket sheet contained 311 entries. Of immediate concern to the court was the pending motion of the defendant, Teel Plastics, Inc., to refer the matter to a special mediator for settlement discussions. To facilitate this procedure, Teel Plastics and Sauk County jointly submitted a discovery agreement which would provide for a standstill on discovery.

OPINION: *GOODSTEIN, United States Magistrate Judge*

By letter dated October 16, 1992, this court sent a questionnaire to each party requesting that it identify its status in the case and list all parties who have filed a claim against the responding party. More importantly for purposes of the pending motion, the questionnaire asked the party whether it would be willing to participate in mediation at this time, and whether it would consent to a limited further extension of the discovery stay and a modification of the scheduling order so as to facilitate settlement proceedings. Although the court recognizes that it does not need the consent of the parties in order to initiate and compel their attendance at settlement proceedings . . . it is preferable to proceed on the basis of a consensus when exploring settlement.

The questionnaires have been returned and the results have been tabulated. Ninety-two percent of those responding indicate a willingness to participate in mediation. The other respondents simply rejected mediation out of hand. An identical percentage responded affirmatively to staying discovery and modifying the scheduling order, but here certain qualifications were voiced based upon the length of any extension; the concern was that any extension not be unduly long and that the present trial dates remain. Questions were also raised regarding depositions now scheduled for November and discovery responses due during November.

This court concurs with the overwhelming majority that this case is a prime candidate for mediation proceedings. This is a civil action brought under the Comprehensive Environmental Response, Compensation and Liability Act (CERCLA) in regard to the alleged release or threatened release of hazardous substances from a property known as the Sauk County landfill. It is alleged that during a ten-year period, the defendants deposited hazardous substances at this site which has since been closed. As stated earlier, numerous parties have been brought into this action and based upon some of the questionnaire responses, more parties may be on the way. The factual and legal issues are complex. With the plethora of parties and attorneys, the logistics alone of conducting discovery and holding a trial are extremely cumbersome. It is estimated that a trial to the court would last at least two weeks. This has been, and will continue to be, a very costly and time-consuming case.

This district's local rule 7.12, which was enacted as part of the Civil Justice Expense and Delay Reduction Plan, adopted pursuant to the Civil Justice Reform Act, authorizes a judicial officer to invoke one of several settlement options when appropriate. Section 7.12(3) authorizes the court to refer the case "for neutral evaluation, mediation, arbitration, or some other form of alternate dispute resolution." The section goes on to provide that a referral is to be made to persons who have the requisite abilities and skills, and that the reasonable fees and expenses of such person shall be borne by the parties as directed by the court.

This court will enter an order referring the case for mediation. This order will be entered as soon as possible, but the court is still in the process of considering an appropriate person to act as a mediator and the terms and conditions under which such person shall act.

In order that the parties are able to devote their full efforts to mediation, and in order to prevent discovery costs from escalating at an exponential rate as a result of the number of claims, counterclaims and cross-claims, the entry of a discovery order along the lines jointly proposed by Sauk County and Teel Plastics is warranted. Accordingly, the motion of Teel Plastics, Inc. to refer this case to a special mediator for purposes of settlement is GRANTED.

Discussion Questions

1. Is a party forced to participate in mediation likely to participate in good faith?
2. What factors should be considered by a judge prior to referring a case for an ADR process?
3. If the parties fail to settle, is it likely that the referring judge will be prejudiced against them during a subsequent trial?

ADR IN ACTION

What Do Lawyers Think of ADR?

The litigation services group of the accounting firm of Deloitte and Touche conducts surveys to determine whether corporate and outside counsel prefer mediation or arbitration to resolve company disputes. (See Table 4.1 for a comparison of mediation and arbitration.) The 1997 survey was completed by 62 corporate in-house counsel and 77 private law firms. The survey results show for the first time that in-house corporate counsel prefer mediation to arbitration, and by a sizable percentage. Indeed, the number of in-house attorneys who prefer mediation has increased substantially, while those opting for arbitration has declined dramatically since the same data were collected in a 1993 survey.

The 1997 survey found that 65% of in-house counsel prefer mediation, while only 28% prefer arbitration. By way of comparison, in a 1993 survey, 51% of in-house counsel preferred arbitration with only 41% listing mediation as their process of choice. The preferences of outside counsel changed very little from one survey to the next; in 1993, 57% pre-ferred mediation and in 1997, a slight decline to 54% was revealed. There was 34% of outside counsel who preferred arbitration in 1993, and 38% preferred it in 1997. Perhaps most significantly, 71% of all respondents indicated that they believe that ADR processes, whether mediation or arbitration, make solving disputes easier than trial.

In-house counsel indicated that they preferred mediation for many reasons, including cost or time savings, better potential results, and superior qualifications of the neutral advisor. However, respondents indicated concern with the enforcement of ADR solutions, the absence of an appropriate court-annexed process, and the opposing party's lack of commitment to ADR processes as reasons to avoid mediation and arbitration. Despite these concerns, the survey results show that ADR is used most often in cases with dollar values over $500,000 (46% of all cases) and by some very large companies (35% with $1 billion–$4 billion in revenue and 22% with $4 billion–$9 billion in revenue).

TABLE 4.1   Comparison of Mediation and Arbitration

	Mediation	**Arbitration**

Nature of process	Facilitative
	Negotiated
	Informal
	Flexible procedures
		Adjudicative
		Evidentiary
		Formal
		Set by parties or
		  administering agency
		  chosen by parties

Witnesses	Rarely	Usually
Documentary evidence	Rarely	Usually
Nature of third party intervenor	Expert in process Unregulated Individual Neutral	Expert in subject matter of dispute Unregulated to semiregulated Individual or panel Neutral or representative

Nature of participation	Virtually always voluntary	Voluntary or mandatory
		  • By contract term/party
		    agreement
		  • Court-annexed
		  • Applicable statute

	Direct with legal assistance
	  permitted
		Through legal representative
		  or pro se

Cost	Low to moderate	Moderate to high
Timing	Presuit to post-discovery Virtually always single session	After limited discovery Single or multi-session
Party preparation	Minimal to moderate	Moderate to extensive
Nature of decision	Party controlled Uncertain Binding	Third-party controlled Certain Advisory or binding
Nature of remedies	Broad range Economic and noneconomic	Narrower range Limited primarily to economic

Nature of enforcement	Contract	Valid arbitral agreements
		  enforceable as court
		  judgment

Confidentiality	Complete (by agreement)	Proceedings and awards may be confidential
Right of appeal	None	Limited

http://

The Mediation Information and Resource Center, including a full national mediator directory, can be found at: http://www.mediate.com/resolution.cfm

SELECTION OF THE MEDIATOR

Mediators are often attorneys possessing training and expertise in the mediation process. In addition to legally trained mediators, a wide range of nonattorney mediators is available. This group comprises professionals typically possessing social science or business backgrounds. Parties seeking to retain a mediator consider many factors when doing so. The most significant, of course, is the training and experience of the mediator, as well as any related professional training. Another important factor in mediator selection is the role the mediator is to assume in the process. All mediators do not provide all types of mediation services. Consequently, parties seeking conventional facilitative mediation, for example, should look for mediators trained in that type of mediation.

Parties often look for a mediator with substantive expertise in the area of dispute. This approach often yields mixed results, particularly in facilitative mediation in which process, rather than substantive expertise, is important. The mediator with substantive expertise can help parties grasp the facts of the case quickly, understand the points that need resolution efficiently and accurately, and explore useful settlement options. However, such a mediator may appear biased toward one side or another, or appear to work toward a settlement that is consistent with his or her own views. Although the best choice for evaluative mediation is a person whose expertise is primarily within the scope of the dispute, the best choice for facilitative mediation is a person whose expertise is primarily in the procedural aspects of assisted negotiation.

In either situation, it is helpful to use a mediator experienced in the resolution of the type of case under dispute, whether environmental, product liability, or contractual. This sort of mediator may not be a technical expert in the area of law but will have developed a sense of the approaches taken by other parties to similar problems and of options available that the parties may not have considered.

In addition, parties are often interested in the professional affiliations of the mediators they consider. Membership in the Society of Professionals in Dispute Resolution or the Academy of Family Mediators is an indicator of meaningful professional development in mediation practice.

Finally, when selecting a mediator, parties should be aware that there are circumstances under which they may surrender their right to sue the mediator for malpractice. The following case presents the question of whether a court-appointed mediator or neutral case evaluator, performing tasks within the scope of his or her official duties, is entitled to absolute immunity from damages in a suit brought by a disappointed litigant.

http://

The home page for The Society of Professionals in Dispute Resolution is at: http://www.igc. apc.org/spidr

http://

Find The Academy of Family Mediators home page at: http://www.igc. apc.org/afm

JEROME S. WAGSHAL V. MARK W. FOSTER

28 F. 3d 1249 (D.C. Cir., 1994)

FACT SUMMARY

Jerome S. Wagshal filed suit against Charles E. Sheetz, the manager of real property owned by Wagshal. The assigned judge, Judge Richard A. Levie, referred the case to alternative dispute resolution pursuant to Superior Court Civil Rule 16 and the Superior Court's alternative dispute resolution (ADR) program. Although the program does not bind the parties (except when they agree to binding arbitration), participation is mandatory.

Judge Levie chose "neutral case

evaluation" from among the available ADR options and appointed Mark W. Foster as case evaluator. Pursuant to the order of appointment, the parties signed a "statement of understanding" providing (among other things) that the proceedings would be confidential and privileged, and that the evaluator would serve as a "neutral party." Moreover, the parties were not allowed to subpoena the evaluator or any documents submitted in the course of evaluation, and "[i]n no event [could the] mediator or evaluator voluntarily testify on behalf of a party." Wagshal signed in January 1992 (under protest, he alleges).

After Foster held his first session with the parties, Wagshal questioned his neutrality. Foster then asked that Wagshal either waive his objection or pursue it: If Wagshal made no response to waiving the objection, Foster would treat it as a definite objection. Receiving no response by the deadline set, and later receiving a communication that he regarded as equivocal, Foster wrote to Judge Levie in February 1992 with copies to counsel, recusing himself. The letter also reported to the judge on his efforts in the case and recommended continuation of ADR proceedings. In particular, Foster said that the case was one "that can and should be settled if the parties are willing to act reasonably," and urged the court to order Wagshal, "as a precondition to any further proceedings in his case,. to engage in a good-faith attempt at mediation." He also urged Judge Levie to "consider who should bear the defendant's costs in participating" in the mediation to date.

Judge Levie then conducted a telephone conference call hearing in which he excused Foster from the case. Wagshal's counsel voiced the claim that underlies this suit—that he thought Foster's withdrawal letter "indicates that he had certain feelings about the case. Now, I'm not

familiar with the mediation process but as I understood, the mediator is not supposed to say, give his opinion as to where the merits are." On that subject, Judge Levie said, "I don't know what his opinions are, and I'm not going to ask him because that's part of the confidentiality of the process." Neither Wagshal nor his counsel made any objection or motion for Judge Levie's own recusal.

Judge Levie soon after appointed another case evaluator, and Wagshal and the other parties settled the *Sheetz* case in June 1992. In September 1992, however, Wagshal sued Foster and sixteen others (whom he identified as members of Foster's law firm) in federal district court. Wagshal claimed that Foster's behavior as mediator had violated his rights to due process and to a jury trial under the Fifth and Seventh Amendments and sought injunctive relief and damages under 42 U.S.C. § 1983. Besides the federal claims, Wagshal added a variety of local law theories such as defamation, invasion of privacy, and intentional infliction of emotional distress. His theory is that Foster's conduct as case evaluator forced him to settle the case against his will, resulting in a far lower recovery than if he had pursued the claim.

OPINION: *WILLIAMS, Judge*

Foster's first line of defense against the damages claim was the assertion of **quasi-judicial immunity**. The immunity will block the suit if it extends to case evaluators and mediators, so long as Foster's alleged actions were taken within the scope of his duties as a case evaluator.

Courts have extended absolute immunity to a wide range of persons playing a role in the judicial process. These have included prosecutors, law clerks, . . . probation officers, . . . a court-appointed committee monitoring the unauthorized practice of law, . . . a psychiatrist who interviewed a criminal defendant to assist a trial judge, . . . persons performing binding arbitration, . . . and a psychologist performing dispute resolution services in connection with a lawsuit over custody and visitation rights. On the other hand, the Supreme Court has rejected absolute immunity for judges acting in an administrative capacity, . . . court reporters charged with creating a verbatim transcript of trial proceedings, . . . and prosecutors in relation to legal advice they may give state police. The official claiming the immunity "bears the burden of showing that such immunity is justified for the function in question."

We have distilled the Supreme Court's approach to quasi-judicial immunity into a consideration of three main factors: (1) whether the functions of the official in question are comparable to those of a judge; (2) whether the nature of the controversy is intense enough that future harassment or intimidation by litigants is a realistic prospect; and (3) whether the system contains safeguards which are adequate to justify dispensing with private damage suits to control unconstitutional conduct.

In certain respects it seems plain that a case evaluator in the Superior Court's system performs judicial functions. Foster's assigned tasks included identifying factual and legal issues, scheduling discovery and motions with the parties, and coordinating settlement efforts. These obviously involve substantial discretion, a key feature of the tasks sheltered by judicial immunity. . . . Further, viewed as mental activities, the tasks appear precisely the same as those judges perform [when] going about the business of adjudication and case management.

Wagshal protests, however, that mediation is altogether different from authorita-tive adjudication, citing observations to that effect in radically dissimilar contexts. However true his point may be as an abstract matter, the general process of encouraging settlement is a natural, almost inevitable, concomitant of adjudication. Rule 16 of the Federal Rules of Civil Procedure, for example, institutionalizes the relation, designating as subjects for pretrial conferences a series of issues that appear to encompass all the tasks of a case evaluator in the Superior Court system: "formulation and simplification of the issues," "the possibility of obtaining admissions of fact and of documents," "the control and scheduling of discovery," and a catch-all, "such other matters as facilitate the just, speedy, and inexpensive disposition of the action." Fed.R.Civ.P. 16(c) Wagshal points to nothing in Foster's role that a Superior Court judge might not have performed under Superior Court Rule 16(c), which substantially tracks the federal model. Although practice appears to vary widely, and some variations raise very serious issues, it is quite apparent that intensive involvement in settlement is now by no means uncommon among federal district judges.

Wagshal does not assert that a case evaluator is performing a purely administrative task, such as the personnel decisions—demotion and discharge of a probation officer—at issue in *Forrester v. White*. Because the sort of pretrial tasks performed by a case evaluator are so integrally related to adjudication proper, we do not think that their somewhat managerial character renders them administrative for these purposes.

Conduct of pretrial case evaluation and mediation also seems likely to inspire efforts by disappointed litigants to recoup their losses, or at any rate harass the mediator, in a second forum. . . . Although a mediator or case evaluator makes no final adjudication, he must often be the bearer of unpleasant news—that a claim or defense may be far weaker than the party supposed. Especially as the losing party will be blocked by judicial immunity from suing the judge, there may be great temptation to sue the messenger whose words foreshadowed the final loss.

The third of the Supreme Court's criteria, the existence of adequate safeguards to control unconstitutional conduct where absolute immunity is granted, is also present. Here, Wagshal was free to seek relief from any misconduct by Foster by applying to Judge Levie. Alternatively, if he thought Foster's communications might prejudice Judge Levie, he could have sought Levie's recusal under Superior Court R.Civ.P. 63-I, Bias or Prejudice of a Judge. The avenues of relief institutionalized in the ADR program and its judicial context provide adequate safeguards.

Wagshal claims that even if mediators may be generally entitled to absolute immunity, Foster may not invoke the immunity because his action was not taken in a judicial capacity, . . . and because he acted in complete absence of jurisdiction. . . . Neither exception applies.

Wagshal's argument that the acts for which he has sued Foster are not judicial (apart from the claim against mediators generally) rests simply on his claim that Foster's letter to Judge Levie, stating that he felt he "must recuse" himself and giving his thoughts on possible further mediation efforts and allocation of costs, breached Foster's obligations of neutrality and confidentiality. We assume such a breach for purposes of analysis. But "if judicial immunity means anything, it means that a judge will not be deprived of immunity because the action he took was in error . . . or was in excess of his authority." . . . Accordingly "we look to the particular act's relation to a general function normally performed by a judge." Applying the same principle to case evaluators, we have no doubt that Foster's announcing his recusal, reporting in a general way on the past course of mediation, and making suggestions for future mediation were the sort of things that case evaluators would properly do.

We hold that absolute quasi-judicial immunity extends to mediators and case evaluators in the Superior Court's ADR process, and that Foster's actions were taken within the scope of his official duties.

Discussion Questions

1. Should a private mediator retained by parties *without* judicial assistance be immune from suit?
2. Under what circumstances should a party be permitted to recover from a private, nonjudicially appointed mediator?
3. If parties participate in mediation and settle voluntarily, should the mediator be immune from suit if the parties later regret the terms of the agreement?

ROLES AND ETHICS OF THE MEDIATOR

The mediator plays several roles during the mediation process. It is important to note again that the mediator does not have the authority to force the parties to settle, or to decide the case for the parties in matters not addressed in mediation-arbitration. Consequently, parties are free to speak candidly and completely about their cases, describing both strengths and weaknesses to the mediator who will try to satisfy the following roles and tasks.

The paramount mediator role is that of **facilitator** of party communications. To that end, mediators structure a process that permits all parties to fully recount the facts of the dispute and to describe completely the outcomes they seek. In doing so, the mediator will assist the parties in uncovering or clarifying their real needs and interests. The mediator will also frequently summarize the positions and offers of the parties, providing new, more productive language for them. Good facilitators also set a careful agenda for the settlement discussions. To do so, they will break down the issues to be resolved into discrete and manageable units and arrange them in a way likely to build momentum toward settlement. Throughout all of this, they will address emotions and allow parties to express them, but only in ways and to the extent that doing so increases the possibility of settlement.

The mediator also controls the process by moving the parties deliberately toward agreement. Without forcing the parties to settle, the mediator intervenes in the negotiations with the intention of securing an agreement. This can be done by asking questions of the parties calculated to clarify issues or to elicit potential settlement options. It can also be done by altering the format of the mediation, by separating the parties, or by suspending mediation pending further preparation by one or both parties.

In addition, the mediator is a resource for the parties, offering settlement options, assessing the options offered by the parties, and perhaps linking the parties with outside experts to assist in the evaluation and resolution of the case. The most capable mediators are skilled at crafting settlement options that include ideas generated by the parties as well as by the mediator into a package that advances the interests of all parties. In addition to generating settlement options for the parties to consider, the mediator should assist the parties in assessing the settlement options they have generated and comparing the outcomes available through negotiation with the outcomes likely at trial or through arbitration. Finally, the mediator will guide the parties in a discussion of implementation of the settlement agreement and draft a written memorandum of agreement if requested.

Mediators have ethical responsibilities as they carry out these tasks. They are obliged to maintain the **confidences** of the participants involved in the mediation and to maintain **impartiality.** Although some states certify mediators and establish minimal rules governing the practice, no uniform set of ethical rules or responsibilities exists. Furthermore, disciplinary actions against mediators are virtually unknown, largely because no formal bodies are empowered to move against mediators who act unethically. In addition, because the process of mediation is one in which the outcomes are controlled by the parties, they, not the mediator, normally are considered responsible for the settlements they reach voluntarily. The following case describes the application of the ethical obligations of a lawyer acting as a mediator.

POLY SOFTWARE INTERNATIONAL, INC., ET AL. V. YU SU, DATAMOST CORPORATION, ET. AL.

880 F. Supp. 1487 (D. Utah, 1995)

FACT SUMMARY

Su was employed as a software engineer by Micromath, Inc., a company specializing in the development and marketing of mathematical software. Wang later joined him in the same capacity. They left Micromath, formed Polysoft Partnership, and began producing their own line of mathematical software. Micromath subsequently sued Polysoft Partnership for copyright infringement. The focus of the litigation was a Polysoft Partnership product entitled "Techplot," later renamed "PS-Plot," and then "PSI-Plot." Micromath claimed that Wang and Su had obtained user's handbooks and computer source codes while working for Micromath, and had illegally used that information in their development of Techplot.

Soon after the complaint was filed, the parties agreed to submit their dispute to mediation and chose Berne S. Broadbent to serve as mediator. Broadbent conducted a series of intensive meetings, conferring with the parties both individually and together. During Broadbent's private caucuses with the Polysoft Partnership, both Wang and Su were present and openly discussed confidential aspects of their case, including a detailed analysis of their source codes and handbook comparisons. At the conclusion of the mediation process, Micromath and the Polysoft Partnership successfully negotiated a settlement of their dispute.

Subsequent to the settlement of the Micromath litigation, Polysoft Partnership continued to market PSI-Plot, and began developing new programs. Two of these were "PSI-Stat" and "PSI-Math." However, in December 1993, Wang and Su dissolved the partnership. Under the terms of the dissolution, Su surrendered his ownership interest in Polysoft Partnership to Wang, and received the rights to the PSI-Stat software. Wang retained the rights to the PSI-Plot and PSI-Math programs. Subsequently, Wang restructured the business as Poly Software International, Inc., and Su formed Datamost Corporation.

The present litigation was commenced when Poly Software filed an action asserting copyright infringement and other related claims against Su and Datamost. These claims asserted that "Statmost for DOS," Datamost's version of the program PSI-Stat (the rights to which had passed to Su upon dissolution of the Polysoft Partnership), illegally duplicated significant portions of the PSI-Plot user's handbook and incorporated source codes unique to PSI-Plot. Prior to commencing suit, Wang interviewed a number of attorneys for the purpose of finding a law firm to pursue his claim against Su and Datamost. Wang ultimately retained Broadbent to represent him and his company. Su and Datamost brought a motion to disqualify Broadbent.

OPINION: *WINDER, Chief Judge*

" 'The control of attorneys' conduct in trial litigation is within the supervisory powers of the trial judge,' and is thus a matter of judicial discretion." . . . When a federal district court is presented with a motion to disqualify, it relies on two sources of authority to guide the exercise of its discretion. The first source is "the local rules of the court in which [attorneys] appear." . . . Additionally, "because motions to disqualify counsel in federal proceedings are substantive motions affecting the rights of the parties, they are decided by applying standards developed under federal law [and are thus] governed by the ethical rules announced by the national profession and considered in light of the public interest and the litigants' rights."

That motion is based on Broadbent's previous role as a mediator in the Micromath litigation. With respect to the appropriate rule governing mediators, this case is one of first impression. In making their arguments on this issue, both parties have cited to the *Utah Prof. Conduct Rules,* Rule 1.12(a). That provision states that "a lawyer shall not represent anyone in connection with a matter in which the lawyer participated personally and substantially as a judge or other adjudicative officer, arbitrator or law clerk to such a person, unless all parties to the proceeding consent after disclosure." Su also cites Nancy H. Rogers & Craig A. McEwen, *Mediation: Law, Policy Practice* (2d Ed., 1994), and its proposed code of ethics for mediators, which provides that "[w]ithout the consent of all parties, a mediator shall not subsequently establish a professional relationship with one of the parties in a related matter." . . . In substance, this proposal is analogous to Model Rule 1.9's proscription of subsequent employment on a "substantially related matter."

Thus, Rules 1.9 and 1.12 promulgate a significant distinction in the scope of prohibited subsequent representation. This distinction becomes important in this case

because the Micromath litigation mediated by Broadbent and the present lawsuit possess a common actual nexus but are distinct legal disputes. With respect to "matter" as that term is employed by Rule 1.12, there is virtually no case law or other comments. Commentary has observed that the same lawsuit or litigation is the same matter. The same issue of fact involving the same parties and the same situation or conduct is the same matter. The same matter is not involved when there is lacking the discrete identifiable transaction of conduct involving a particular situation and specific parties.

A substantially related matter on the other hand is not defined by any particular, discrete legal proceeding. By its terms, it includes aspects of past controversies which are similar, but not necessarily identical to those encompassed within a present dispute. So long as there are substantial factual threads connecting the two matters, the criteria of Rule 1.9 are met.

In this case the lawsuit between Su and Wang is legally distinct from the earlier Micromath litigation because it involves a separate dispute between differing parties, and thereby "lack[s] the discrete, identifiable transaction of conduct involving a particular situation and specific parties." Thus, it is not the same "matter" as that term is understood in Rule 1.12 or 1.11.

The present litigation is, however, "substantially factually related" to the Micromath litigation. Poly Software accuses Su and Datamost of impermissibly copying source code and handbook information from the PSI-Plot program. Micromath accused Wang and Su of pirating source code and handbook information to formulate an earlier version of the very same program. The complaints filed in the two cases are virtually identical in many respects, at times employing precisely the same phrasing. Moreover, as a mediator in the Micromath litigation, Broadbent examined in detail the disputed source code and elicited frank discussions in private caucus with Wang and Su as to which of them might be responsible for alleged illegal copying. Therefore, the determinative question on the issue of the ethical status of Broadbent's current representation of Poly Software is whether mediators should be governed by a same "matter" standard similar to that enunciated in Rule 1.12 and 1.11, or by a "substantially factually related" standard similar to that employed by Rule 1.9.

Preliminary to answering that question a brief discussion of the definition of "mediator" is necessary. For the purposes of this opinion, a mediator is an attorney who agrees to assist parties in settling a legal dispute, and in the course of assisting those parties undertakes a confidential relationship with them. Such mediation may often occur in the context of a court-supervised Alternative Dispute Resolution ("ADR") program. Mediator in this particular context does not apply to circumstances already covered by the *Utah Prof. Conduct Rules,* Rule 2.2, where attorneys take on the role of intermediary between two or more clients with potentially conflicting interests. Rather, it applies to situations where litigation has already commenced, the parties subsequently agree to suspend their litigation, and also agree to the appointment of an attorney to facilitate settlement. The attorney who thus serves as mediator is a neutral individual who confers with each party in private caucus, learning what results are acceptable to each of them and assessing in confidence the strengths and weaknesses of their cases. The mediator also meets with all parties together to facilitate settlement of the case. In this regard,

mediation may well be the most valuable ADR option. "Unlike the litigation and arbitration processes, mediation does not necessarily cast the parties in an adversarial relationship. Nor do parties emerge from the mediation process as clearly defined winners and losers." *Utah District Court ADR Manual.*

These characteristics of mediation demonstrate that it differs significantly from more formal adversarial proceedings at which an adjudicative officer presides. Most importantly, the mediator is not merely charged with being impartial, but with receiving and preserving confidences in much the same manner as the client's attorney. In fact, the success of mediation depends largely on the willingness of the parties to freely disclose their intentions, desires, and the strengths and weaknesses of their case; and upon the ability of the mediator to maintain a neutral position while carefully preserving the confidences that have been revealed. The *Utah District Court ADR Manual,* for instance, encourages the parties to disclose to the mediator (in strict confidence) "[a]ll critical information, whether favorable or unfavorable to the party's position," and recommends that mediators "advise the parties and their attorneys that it is neither helpful nor productive to withhold information with the intent of gaining some tactical advantage."

Adversarial proceedings, on the other hand, are characterized by vigorous attempts to maintain confidences. Attorneys who have received such confidential information are under a strict duty to avoid, without consent of the client, any disclosures of that information. Because adjudicators do not occupy a relationship of confidence and trust with the parties akin to that occupied by the attorneys, they do not, for the most part, have access to those confidences. Thus, although mediators function in some ways as neutral coordinators of dispute resolution, they also assume the role of a confidant, and it is that aspect of their role that distinguishes them from adjudicators.

As a result, the appropriate ethical rule for mediators differs somewhat from the text of the *Utah Prof. Conduct Rules,* Rule 1.12. Where a mediator has received confidential information in the course of mediation, that mediator should not thereafter represent anyone in connection with the same or a substantially factually related matter unless all parties to the mediation proceeding consent after disclosure. This rule also takes into account some important policy considerations. If parties to mediation know that their mediator could someday be an attorney on the opposing side in a substantially related matter, they will be discouraged from freely disclosing their position in the mediation, which may severely diminish the opportunity for settlement. If, on the other hand, the disqualification net is thrown too wide, attorneys will be discouraged from becoming mediators. The "substantially factually related" standard best balances those two interests. It encourages parties to freely disclose their positions during mediation by assuring them that the specific information disclosed will not be used against them at a later time. It also limits disqualification to subsequent situations where there is a substantial factual nexus with the previously mediated dispute. Applying the "substantially factually related" standard to the present motion, it is evident that Broadbent received confidential information in the course of the Micromath dispute. It is also undisputed that Su and Datamost did not consent to his subsequent representation of Wang in a sub-

stantially factually related lawsuit. Therefore, his current representation constitutes a violation of the rule established by this opinion.

Nevertheless, because this is a case of first impression, the court wishes to make clear that in one respect this violation assumes a dramatically different posture than an infraction of a more clearly established rule. Given the paucity of literature on the issue and the tendency of many commentators to lump all ADR methods under the same ethical rubric, an attorney could have understandably selected the "same matter" standard . . . , and thereby reasonably assumed that no violation would occur. Thus, imposition of sanctions or criticism of Mr. Broadbent's professional reputation is unwarranted in this case.

In any event, a finding that a violation has occurred does not necessarily end the inquiry. "The sanction of disqualification of counsel in litigation situations should be measured by the facts of each particular case as they bear upon the impact of counsel's conduct upon the trial. . . . The essential issue to be determined in the context of litigation is whether the alleged misconduct taints the lawsuit." . . . Broadbent received a significant amount of confidential information during the mediation of the Micromath litigation. In particular, he was present while Wang and Su conducted heated conversations on the topic of which of them might be responsible for the copying alleged by Micromath. Poly Software argues that, because Wang was present whenever Su revealed anything to Broadbent, Poly Software does not gain access by employing Broadbent in the present litigation to any confidential information that it does not already possess. However, this argument ignores the fact that Broadbent's professional expertise afforded him a perspective on the legal significance of the confidences that Wang himself could not possibly obtain or communicate to new counsel. In short, his role as a mediator with experience in intellectual property litigation gives him an unfair advantage as an attorney in the present case.

Discussion Questions

1. Should mediators refrain from representing those with whom they have mediated in any subsequent matter, regardless of its relationship to the previously mediated matter?

2. Does the case suggest that courts should prohibit parties from requesting, and mediators from offering, to testify in related litigation?

ADR IN ACTION

Environmental ADR Anticipated by CEOs

JAMS/Endispute, a private ADR services provider, is at: http://www. jams-endispute. com

This site contains information on environmental mediation: http://www. virginia.edu/ ~envneg/links. html

A 1995 joint survey by Coopers & Lybrand and JAMS/Endispute found that a significant percentage of corporate executives, including both chief executive officers and general counsel, expect the use of ADR in environmental matters to increase. The survey, mailed to 2,000 officers at Fortune 1000 companies, was designed to gather data on current and projected ADR use in environmental matters as well as cost information related to environmental litigation. The survey revealed that 74% of those who responded predict increased use of environmental ADR. Respondents particularly favor use of ADR in Superfund matters in which allocation of environmental cleanup costs is an issue.

In addition, 86% of the respondents cited cost savings as the leading reason for using ADR in environmental matters, describing ADR as either "considerably" or "somewhat less" costly than tradi-

tional litigation. Approximately 65% of the respondents indicated that costs, primarily legal fees, associated with environmental matters have increased. Indeed, 58% of respondents for those companies with $5 billion or more in revenue stated that costs related to litigating environmental matters exceed $500,000 annually.

Citing a lack of experience and training in ADR, respondents reported fairly sparse use of ADR in the past. A mere 19% of those responding had used ADR in more than 10% of previous environmental matters. In addition, a fairly low percentage of respondents believe that ADR has been or will be used to resolve matters involving local, state, or federal government. Respondents indicated that as they, their counsel, and their opponents become more familiar with the processes, they expect significant increases in use.

MANDATORY MEDIATION

Opinion is divided on whether, and when, mediation should be made **mandatory**. There is, however, pressure from many sources to make mediation mandatory in a wider variety of cases. Judges typically support any opportunity to resolve matters before trial and thereby reduce their dockets. Similarly, legislators faced with mounting public pressure to reform the judicial system are calling more regularly for broader use of mediation and arbitration. However, although most mediators favor wider use of the process, they often disagree on whether mandating mediation is the answer.

When mediation is mandated, parties should be concerned with several factors. First, mandated mediation should be nonbinding; it should not require a party to settle. What distinguishes mediation from other dispute resolution processes is that the parties are free to choose the settlement conditions. Without this freedom, parties would likely resist mediation. Second, the pressure to settle should not be overwhelming. Judges, for example, should be prohibited from penalizing parties who decline to settle with accelerated trial dates or abbreviated discovery periods. Third, meaningful confidentiality guarantees should be given and enforced to assure the parties that their participation in mandatory mediation will not jeopardize them in subsequent proceedings. Referral guidelines and authority should be made clear to parties. When a case is sent to, rather than volunteered for mediation, parties should understand why the case was sent and on whose authority. Finally, a right to review the outcome should be provided. When cases are forced into the process, parties should have the right to independent judicial review of the outcome if they believe the case was inappropriately referred or improperly mediated.

The following case illustrates the power a federal court has to compel parties to participate in settlement discussions and the reasons for that power.

G. HEILEMAN BREWING COMPANY V. JOSEPH OAT CORPORATION
871 F. 2d 648 (7th Cir., 1989)

FACT SUMMARY

A federal magistrate ordered Joseph Oat Corporation to send a "corporate representative with authority to settle" to a pretrial conference to discuss disputed factual and legal issues and the possibility of settlement. Although counsel for Oat Corporation appeared with another attorney who was authorized to speak on behalf of the principals of the corporation, no principal or corporate representative personally attended the conference. The court determined that Oat Corporation's failure to send a principal of the corporation to the pretrial conference violated its order. Consequently, the district court imposed a sanction of $5,860.01 on Oat Corporation pursuant to *Federal Rule of Civil Procedure* 16(f). This amount

http://

The text of Rule 16 can be found at:
http://www.law.cornell.edu/rules/frcp/rule16.htm

represented the costs and attorneys' fees of the opposing parties attending the conference. Oat Corporation appealed the sanction, claiming that the district court did not have the authority to order litigants represented by counsel to appear at the pretrial settlement conference.

OPINION: *KANNE, Circuit Judge*

In this case, we are required to determine whether a court's power to order the pretrial appearance of litigants who are represented by counsel is inconsistent with, or in derogation of, Rule 16. We must remember that Rule 1 states, with unmistakable clarity, that the Federal Rules of Civil Procedure "shall be construed to secure the just, speedy, and inexpensive determination of every action." This language explicitly indicates that the federal rules are to be liberally construed. . . . There is no place [in] the federal civil procedural system for the proposition that rules having the force of statute, though in derogation of the common law, are to be strictly construed.

"[The] spirit, intent, and purpose [of Rule 16] is . . . broadly remedial, allowing courts to actively manage the preparation of cases for trial." *In re Baker.* 744 F. 2d 1438, 1440 (10th Cir., 1984). Rule 16 is not designed as a device to restrict or limit the authority of the district judge in the conduct of pretrial conferences. As the Tenth Circuit Court of Appeals sitting en banc stated, "the spirit and purpose of the amendments to Rule 16 always have been within the inherent power of the courts to manage their affairs as an independent constitutional branch of government."

We agree with this interpretation of Rule 16. The wording of the rule and the accompanying commentary make plain that the entire thrust of the amendment to Rule 16 was to urge judges to make wider use of their powers and to manage actively their dockets from an early stage. We therefore conclude that our interpretation of Rule 16 to allow district courts to order represented parties to appear at pretrial settlement conferences merely represents another application of a district judge's inherent authority to preserve the efficiency, and more importantly the integrity, of the judicial process.

To summarize, we simply hold that the action taken by the district court in this case constituted the proper use of inherent authority to aid in accomplishing the purpose and intent of Rule 16. We reaffirm the notion that the inherent power of a district judge—derived from the very nature and existence of his judicial office—is the broad field over which the Federal Rules of Civil Procedure are applied. Inherent authority remains the means by which district judges deal with circumstances not proscribed or specifically addressed by rule or statute, but which must be addressed to promote the just, speedy, and inexpensive determination of every action.

Having determined that the district court possessed the power and authority to order the represented litigants to appear at the pretrial settlement conference, we now must examine whether the court abused its discretion to issue such an order.

At the outset, it is important to note that a district court cannot coerce settlement. *Kothe v. Smith,* 771 F. 2d 667, 669 (2d Cir., 1985). In this case, considerable concern has been generated because the court ordered "corporate representatives with authority to settle" to attend the conference. In our view, "authority to settle," when used in the context of this case, means that the "corporate representative" attending the pretrial conference was required to hold a position within the corporate entity allowing him to speak definitively and to commit the corporation to a particular position in the litigation. We do not view "authority to settle" as a requirement that corporate representatives must come to court willing to settle on someone else's terms, but only that they come to court in order to consider the possibility of settlement.

As Chief Judge Crabb set forth in her decision which we now review: "There is no indication . . . that the magistrate's order contemplated requiring Joseph Oat . . . to agree to any particular form of settlement or even to agree to settlement at all. The only requirement imposed by the magistrate was that the representative [of Oat Corporation] be present with full authority to settle, should terms for settlement be proposed that were acceptable to [Oat Corporation]." *G. Heileman Brewing Co., Inc. v. Joseph Oat Corporation,* 107 F.R.D. 275, 276-77 (1985).

If this case represented a situation where Oat Corporation had sent a corporate representative and was sanctioned because that person refused to make an offer to pay money—that is, refused to submit to settlement coercion—we would be faced with a decidedly different issue—a situation we would not countenance.

The Advisory Committee Notes to Rule 16 state that "[a]lthough it is not the purpose of Rule 16(b)(7) to impose settlement negotiations on unwilling litigants, it is believed that providing a neutral forum for discussing [settlement] might foster it." Fed.R.Civ.P. 16 advisory committee's note, subdivision (c) (1983). These Notes clearly draw a distinction between being required to attend a settlement conference and being required to participate in settlement negotiations. Thus, under the scheme of pretrial settlement conferences, the corporate representative remains free, on behalf of the

corporate entity, to propose terms of settlement independently—but he may be required to state those terms in a pretrial conference before a judge or magistrate.

As an alternative position, Oat Corporation argues that the court abused its discretion to order corporate representatives of the litigants to attend the pretrial settlement conference. . . . Oat Corporation determined that because its business was a "going concern." Consequently, Oat Corporation believes that the district court abused its authority. We recognize, as did the district court, that circumstances could arise in which requiring a corporate representative (or any litigant) to appear at a pretrial settlement conference would be so onerous, so clearly unproductive, or so expensive in relation to the size, value, and complexity of the case that it might be an abuse of discretion. Moreover, "[b]ecause inherent powers are shielded from direct democratic controls, they must be exercised with restraint and discretion." *Roadway Express, Inc. v. Piper,* 447 U.S. 752, 764, 100 S.Ct. 2455, 2463, 65 L.Ed. 2d 488 (1980) (citation omitted). However, the facts and circumstances of this case clearly support the court's actions to require the corporate representatives of the litigants to attend the pretrial conference personally.

This litigation involved a claim for $4 million—a claim which turned upon the resolution of complex factual and legal issues. The litigants expected the trial to last from one to three months and all parties stood to incur substantial legal fees and trial expenses. This trial also would have preempted a large segment of judicial time—not an insignificant factor. Thus, because the stakes were high, we do not believe that the burden of requiring a corporate representative to attend a pretrial settlement conference was out of proportion to the benefits to be gained, not only by the litigants but also by the court.

Additionally, the corporation did send an attorney, Mr. Fitzpatrick, from Philadelphia, Pennsylvania to Madison, Wisconsin to "speak for" the principals of the corporation. It is difficult to see how the expenses involved in sending Mr. Fitzpatrick from Philadelphia to Madison would have greatly exceeded the expenses involved in sending a corporate representative from Camden to Madison. Consequently, we do not think the expenses and distance to be traveled are unreasonable in this case.

Furthermore, no objection to the magistrate's order was made prior to the date the pretrial conference resumed. Oat Corporation contacted the magistrate's office concerning the order's requirements and was advised of the requirements now at issue. However, Oat Corporation never objected to its terms, either when it was issued or when Oat Corporation sought clarification. Consequently, Oat Corporation was left with only one course of action: it had to comply fully with the letter and intent of the order and argue about its reasonableness later. We thus conclude that the court did not abuse its authority and discretion to order a representative of the Oat Corporation to appear for the pretrial settlement conference on December 19.

POSNER, *Circuit Judge, dissenting*

Rule 16(a) of the Federal Rules of Civil Procedure authorizes a district court to "direct the attorneys for the parties and any unrepresented parties to appear before it for a [pretrial] conference."

The main purpose of the pretrial conference is to get ready for trial. For that purpose, only the attorneys need be present, unless a party is acting as his own attorney. The only possible reason for wanting a represented party to be present is to enable the judge or magistrate to explore settlement with the principals rather than with just their agents. Some district judges and magistrates distrust the willingness or ability of attorneys to convey to their clients adequate information bearing on the desirability and terms of settling a case in lieu of pressing forward to trial. The distrust is warranted in some cases, I am sure; but warranted or not, it is what lies behind the concern that the panel opinion had stripped the district courts of a valuable settlement tool—and this at a time of heavy, and growing, federal judicial caseloads. The concern may well be exaggerated, however. The panel opinion may have had little practical significance; it is the rare attorney who will invite a district judge's displeasure by defying a request to produce the client for a pretrial conference.

The question of the district court's power to summon a represented party to a settlement conference is a difficult one. On the one hand, nothing in Rule 16 or in any other rule or statute confers such a power, and there are obvious dangers in too broad an interpretation of the federal courts' inherent power to regulate their procedure. One danger is that it encourages judicial high–handedness ("power corrupts"); several years ago one of the district judges in this circuit ordered Acting Secretary of Labor Brock to appear before him for settlement discussions on the very day Brock was scheduled to appear before the Senate for his confirmation hearing. The broader concern illustrated by the Brock episode is that in their zeal to settle cases judges may ignore the value of other people's time. One reason people hire lawyers is to economize on their own investment of time in resolving disputes. It is pertinent to note in this connection that Oat is a defendant in this case; it didn't want its executives' time occupied with this litigation.

On the other hand, "die Not bricht Eisen" ["necessity breaks iron"]. Attorneys often are imperfect agents of their clients, and the workload of our district courts is so heavy that we should hesitate to deprive them of a potentially useful tool for effecting settlement, even if there is some difficulty in finding a legal basis for the tool. Although few attorneys will defy a district court's request to produce the client, those few cases may be the very ones where the client's presence would be most conducive to settlement. If I am right that Rule 16(a) empowers a district court to summon unrepresented parties to a pretrial conference only because their presence may be necessary to get ready for trial, we need not infer that the draftsmen meant to forbid the summoning of represented parties for purposes of exploring settlement. The draftsmen may have been unaware that district courts were asserting a power to command the presence of a represented party to explore settlement. We should hesitate to infer inadvertent prohibitions.

The narrowly "legal" considerations bearing on the question whether district courts have the power asserted by the magistrate in this case are sufficiently equivocal to authorize—indeed compel— us to consider the practical consequences for settlement before deciding what the answer should be. Unfortunately, we have insufficient information about those con-

sequences to be able to give a confident answer, but fortunately we need not answer the question in this case—so clear is it that the magistrate abused his discretion, which is to say, acted unreasonably, in demanding that Oat Corporation send an executive having full settlement authority to the pretrial conference. This demand, which is different from a demand that a party who has not closed the door to settlement send an executive to discuss possible terms, would be defensible only if litigants had a duty to bargain in good faith over settlement before resorting to trial, and neither Rule 16 nor any other rule, statute, or doctrine imposes such a duty on federal litigants. There is no federal judicial power to coerce settlement. Oat had made clear that it was not prepared to settle the case on any terms that required it to pay money. That was its prerogative, which once exercised made the magistrate's continued insistence on Oat's sending an executive to Madison arbitrary, unreasonable, willful, and indeed petulant. This is apart from the fact that since no one officer of Oat may have had authority to settle the case, compliance with the demand might have required Oat to ship its entire board of directors to Madison. Ultimately Oat did make a money settlement, but there is no indication that it would have settled sooner if only it had complied with the magistrate's demand for the dispatch of an executive possessing "full settlement authority."

Discussion Questions

1. Does mandatory mediation deprive a party of a constitutional right to jury adjudication of a dispute?
2. Is there any adequate safeguard against improper judicial pressure to settle in mandatory mediation settings?
3. On what basis should judges select and refer cases for mandatory mediation?

CHAPTER CONCLUSION

Mediation, in all its available forms, offers parties in certain cases an opportunity to resolve disputes quickly, cheaply, privately, and in a fashion consistent with their real needs and interests. The ready availability of mediators, combined with the finality of agreements reached in mediation, further enhances its use in resolving business disputes. Mediation does not prejudice parties in future litigation or arbitration if they cannot settle, but does allow parties to preserve important business relationships if they can.

BEST BUSINESS PRACTICES

Here are some practical tips for managers on the use of mediation for the resolution of business disputes.

- Consider including in all contracts and employee handbooks a pre-suit dispute resolution clause mandating a good-faith attempt to use mediation in all disputes between parties to the contract. Such a clause does not preclude subsequent arbitration or litigation, but it does force the parties to attempt to formally negotiate the case with the assistance of a mediator prior to using an adversarial process. Such clauses are generally enforceable.

- In cases where maintaining a long-term continuing relationship is important, mediation is clearly the dispute resolution process of choice. No other process allows so completely for mutually satisfactory outcomes to be created by the parties in a setting that does not diminish the possibility of future commerce.

- Fully prepare your case before mediating. Although mediation is an informal process, with party-controlled outcomes, good settlements are the result of thorough preparation before the conference on both factual and liability issues.

- Select your mediator carefully. Remember that the practice of mediation is largely unregulated, and the competence and training of mediators vary widely. Although confidentiality will prohibit many mediators from giving client references, one should inquire about membership in professional organizations, specialized training, and professional background before hiring a mediator.

- Retain a lawyer and have him or her present for the mediation. Mediation agreements are generally enforceable by courts when properly drafted. Because the agreement is final and binding, you should solicit legal advice during the process of negotiating and drafting it.

- A written and signed **Memorandum of Agreement** created by the parties before they leave the mediation conference will considerably strengthen a later claim that contractual agreement was reached in the mediation. A handshake deal is rather difficult to prove in the absence of testimony from the mediator, who has agreed not to testify under any circumstances. Therefore, being able to show proof of the agreement independent of the mediator is very important.

KEY TERMS

agreement to mediate, p. 98
authority to settle, p. 98
case of first impression, p. 102
caucus, p. 99
Civil Justice Reform Act, p. 91
closure, p. 100
confidences, p. 111
conflicts of interest, p. 97
evaluative mediation, p. 97
facilitated negotiation, p. 99
facilitative mediation, p. 97
facilitator, p. 111

Federal Mediation and Conciliation
   Service, p. 90
Federal Rules of Civil Procedure, p. 91
impartiality, p. 111
Labor Management Relations Act of
   1947, p. 90
mandatory mediation, p. 117
mediation-arbitration, p. 97
mediator opening statement, p. 98
Memorandum of Agreement, p. 122
party opening statements, p. 99
quasi-judicial immunity, p. 108

ETHICAL AND LEGAL REVIEW

1. Following the alleged settlement of a matter through mediation, plaintiff engages new attorneys and insists that no agreement was consummated as a result of lengthy and difficult negotiations in mediation. During the mediation session, plaintiff stated that her attorneys would speak for her and that she would not make any statements on her own behalf. Plaintiff approved a settlement offer related to her privately by her attorney, who in turn related plaintiff's agreement to the defendant's counsel. Plaintiff represented to her family members that the case had been settled. Plaintiff did not speak directly to the defendant or the defendant's attorney on the matter. Was an agreement reached and can it be enforced by a court? [*Snyder-Falkingham v. Stockburger,* 457 S.E. 2d 36 (1995); see also *Crain v. Dore,* 578 So. 2d 555 (1991)]

2. In an enforcement proceeding before the National Labor Relations Board, company requests that the Board subpoena the testimony of the Federal Mediation and Conciliation Service mediator who assisted the parties in negotiating the case. Testimony from the mediator was requested on the question of whether an agreement had been reached at the series of mediation conferences over which the mediator presided; company believed no agreement had been reached, while union asserted that one had. Should the Board require the testimony of the mediator? [*NLRB v. Macaluso, Inc.,* 618 F. 2d 51 (1980)]

3. A defendant asbestos manufacturer moved to disqualify a special master appointed by the court to assist the parties in resolving a mass tort litigation case involving asbestos exposure. The company alleged that the appointed special master was not neutral regarding the instant case because he had acted on behalf of another asbestos defendant in a case related to public education and legislative efforts aimed at promoting alternative compensation systems to mass tort

litigation. Should the court disqualify the special master? [*In re Joint Eastern and Southern Districts Asbestos Litigation,* 737 F. Supp. 735 (1990)]

4. Plaintiff in a banking case, in which mediation is being used, discloses to a local newspaper that a settlement offer has been made by the defendant in mediation. Plaintiff's attorney is quoted by the paper as saying the defendant made the settlement offer because the defendant regarded the case as "shaky." All parties had signed a mediation agreement promising confidentiality unless all participants waived it. The defendant bank did not waive confidentiality prior to the plaintiff's statements to the newspaper. How should the trial judge respond to this matter? Is dismissal of the plaintiff's case an appropriate solution? [*Paranzino v. Barnett Bank,* 690 So. 2d 725 (1997)]

SUGGESTED ADDITIONAL READINGS

Bush, R., and J. Folger. *The Promise of Mediation: Responding to Conflict Through Empowerment and Recognition.* Jossey-Bass, 1994.

Cooley, J. *Mediation Advocacy: N.I.T.A. Practical Guide Series,* National Institute for Trial Advocacy, 1996.

Folberg, J., and A. Taylor. *Mediation: A Comprehensive Guide to Resolving Conflicts Without Litigation.* Jossey-Bass, 1984.

Golann, D. *Mediating Legal Disputes: Effective Strategies for Lawyers and Mediators,* Little, Brown, 1996.

Kressel, K., and D. Pruitt, et. al. *Mediation Research: The Process and Effectiveness of Third Party Intervention.* Jossey-Bass, 1989.

Lovenheim, P. *How to Mediate Your Dispute.* Nolo Press, 1996.

Marcus, L., et. al. *Renegotiating Health Care: Resolving Conflict to Build Collaboration.* Jossey-Bass, 1995.

Moore, C. *The Mediation Process: Practical Strategies for Resolving Conflict.* Jossey-Bass, 1986.

Rogers, N., and C. McEwen. *Mediation: Law, Policy & Practice.* Lawyers Co-Operative, 1989.

Rothman, J. *Resolving Identity Based Conflict in Nations, Organizations and Communities.* Jossey-Bass, 1997.

Yarbrough, E., and W. Wilmot. *Artful Mediation: Constructive Conflict at Work.* Cairns, 1995.

5

HYBRID SETTLEMENT PROCESSES: THE SUMMARY JURY TRIAL AND MINITRIAL

CHAPTER HIGHLIGHTS

In this chapter, you will read and learn about the following:

1. The judicial development and main components of the SJT.
2. The primary objectives of the SJT process.
3. The roles of the judge and advisory jury in the SJT settlement process.
4. Controversies over public access to and mandatory use of the SJT.
5. The private development and major components of the minitrial.
6. Use of a neutral advisor in minitrial proceedings.
7. The empowerment of business executives in the SJT and minitrial processes.
8. The advantages and disadvantages of the SJT and minitrial for resolving business disputes.

In recent years, a number of hybrid processes have been developed that draw on different elements of standard litigation and alternative dispute resolution (ADR). This chapter will focus on two hybrid mechanisms: the **summary jury trial (SJT)** and the **minitrial.** Both nonbinding methods incorporate facets of adversarial litigation, negotiation, and mediation previously discussed in Chapters 1–4. The SJT is primarily a court-supervised hybrid process, while the minitrial is largely overseen by private organizations. Although the term *trial* appears in the name of both methods, the focus of each is to encourage parties to settle their business disputes rather than to adjudicate them in court. The SJT uses the perspectives of a mock jury to guide the disputants in their settlement talks, while the minitrial relies on the business expertise of a neutral advisor and business executives to aid settlement negotiations.

DEVELOPMENT OF THE SUMMARY JURY TRIAL (SJT)

Under most state and federal rules of civil procedure, the judiciary has the authority to fashion methods for the rapid and equitable resolution of disputes. In addition, the Supreme Court has recognized that judges, as part of their inherent judicial authority to manage their dockets, may introduce procedural revisions to aid in swift and fair resolution. Federal court judge Thomas Lambros took an active approach to judicial innovation through his creation and refinement of the summary jury trial process.

Judge Lambros envisioned the SJT process while presiding over two personal injury cases, both of which he thought should have been settled but instead ended up being scheduled for two separate, full trials. In some instances, Judge Lambros believed that parties took a weak case to trial in hopes of winning before a jury. The litigants may have failed to objectively realize the strengths and weaknesses of their respective cases or had a psychological need for their day in court. A plaintiff's attorney might turn down a reasonable settlement offer from a defendant in a products liability case in the hope that juror sympathy for the plaintiff might result in a more lucrative award than the strictly legal aspects of the case truly warranted. Judge Lambros believed that more parties could settle their cases without the cost and time of a complete trial if they had an opportunity to state their case, listen to each other's perspective, and receive a jury's view of the evidence.

Judge Lambros developed the SJT as a nonbinding, confidential method to provide litigants with a realistic sense of a potential jury's view of liability and damages, thereby encouraging parties to settle their dispute without a full-blown trial. Drawing on several provisions of the Federal Rules of Civil Procedure and the inherent authority of judges to manage their case dockets, Judge Lambros initially implemented the SJT in 1980 in his courtroom in an effort to balance the need to reduce the number of cases on the court docket with the litigants' desire for their day in court. Judge Lambros sought to restrict the SJT hearing to a half-day session to maximize the savings in time and costs for both the litigants and the court. Since its implementation in the 1980s, a number of federal district courts and state courts have incorporated the SJT into their court-annexed programs to complement other forms of court-sponsored ADR.

Judge Lambros set forth his views on the inherent and rule-based authority of judges to create and use innovative methods of conflict resolution in his 1984 Report to the Judicial Conference of the United States, *The Summary Jury Trial and*

Other Alternative Methods of Dispute Resolution [103 F.R.D. 461 (1984)]. In this report, Judge Lambros provided a detailed discussion of his SJT innovation, an overview of the goals and objectives of the SJT process, the main steps in the SJT process, its successful use in Ohio and other jurisdictions, and samples of SJT court orders and memoranda. A debate still rages over the breadth of authority judges possess in using extrajudicial procedures such as the SJT and other ADR processes.

COMPONENTS OF THE SJT

The SJT is normally a court-initiated, court-supervised settlement process. The SJT involves **summary presentations** of proof before a judge and an **advisory or mock jury.** Borrowing from traditional litigation, this process is the only form of ADR that uses a jury to aid settlement. Unlike other ADR settlement procedures, the SJT recognizes the value of the real world opinions of jurors in the settlement of cases.

Typically, judicial officials will select cases in which settlement is hampered primarily by the differing views a jury has toward evaluating evidence and awarding damages to the litigants in the dispute. These differing views may encompass juror perceptions of party documents and expert witness testimony or the impact of emotions on a case award.

Screening Cases for the SJT

Under the SJT, the parties undergo the initial phases of standard litigation. Litigants file a standard complaint and answer and go through the discovery process. A judge or magistrate normally will consider a case for a SJT only after the parties have completed the discovery process and the judge has ruled on any pending motions. The court will then issue a judicial order that sets forth the basic aspects of SJT. (See Figure 5.1.) In some instances, the judge will seek agreement from both parties to use the SJT, but a judge may also mandate the use of the SJT without the parties' consent. Judges requiring SJT use, prior to trial, assert that they have the authority to do so under the Federal Rules of Civil Procedure or as part of their inherent judicial authority to regulate their court dockets.

In addition, these judges hold that because the SJT is nonbinding, its mandatory use does not strip the parties of any of their substantive or procedural rights, or determine the outcome of the case. Critics of the SJT argue that judges do not have the authority under either the Rules or their inherent judicial authority to mandate the use of the SJT.

The following two cases illustrate the debate over a judge's power to innovate and to mandate the use of the SJT without party assent. In both cases, the courts take opposite views on mandating a SJT. When reading the cases, consider the different reasons used by each court to defend its decision. In this first case, the court supports the use of the SJT without requiring party consent by focusing on the numerous benefits for both the court and the litigants.

FIGURE 5.1   Judicial Orders for a Summary Jury Trial

SUMMARY JURY TRIAL
Cite as 103 F.R.D. 461

UNITED STATES DISTRICT COURT
NORTHERN DISTRICT OF OHIO
EASTERN DIVISION

IN RE:	)	
	)	
RULES OF PROCEDURE	)	ORDER
FOR SUMMARY JURY TRIAL	)	
PRETRIAL PROCEDURE	)	
(As Amended January 1983)	)	
	)	

LAMROS, DISTRICT JUDGE

1. This order is entered pursuant to Rule 16 of the Federal Rules of Civil Procedure and Local Civil Rule 17.02.

2. This action is designated as one for summary jury trial proceedings to be conducted by the Court or a Magistrate of this District upon assignment from the Court. If assigned to a Magistrate, the Magistrate is authorized to exercise the same authority which the Court may exercise.

3. The action shall be in trial readiness when called for summary jury trial, with an expectation of trial on the merits within 30–60 days thereafter if not otherwise disposed of.

4. This action shall be heard before a six-member jury. Counsel will be permitted two challenges a piece to the venire, and will be assisted in the exercise of such challenges by a brief voir dire examination to be conducted by the presiding judicial officer and by juror profile forms. There will be no alternate jurors.

5. Unless excused by order of court, no later than three working days before the date set for hearing counsel shall submit proposed jury instructions and briefs on any novel issues of law presented.

6. Unless excused by order of court, clients or client representatives shall be in attendance at the summary jury trial.

7. All evidence shall be presented through the attorneys for the parties. The attorneys may summarize and comment on the evidence and may summarize or quote directly from depositions, interrogatories, requests for admissions, documentary evidence and sworn statements of potential witnesses. However, no witness' testimony may be referred to unless the reference is based upon one of the products of the various discovery procedures, or upon a written, sworn statement of the witness, or upon sworn affidavit of counsel that the witness would be called at trial and will not sign an affidavit, and that counsel has been told the substance of the witness' proposed testimony by the witness.

8. Prior to trial counsel shall confer with regard to physical exhibits, including documents and reports, and reach such agreement as is possible as to the use of such exhibits.

9. Objections will be received if in the course of a presentation counsel goes beyond the limits of propriety in presenting statements as to evidence or argument thereon.

10. After counsels' presentations the jury will be given an abbreviated charge on the applicable law.

11. The jury may return either a consensus verdict or a special verdict consisting of an anonymous statement of each juror's findings on liability and/or damages (each known as the jury's advisory opinion). The jury will be encouraged to return a consensus verdict.

12. Unless specifically ordered by the Court, the proceedings will not be recorded. Counsel may, if so desired, arrange for a court reporter.

13. Counsel may stipulate that a consensus verdict by the jury will be deemed a final determination on the merits and that judgment be entered thereon by the Court, or may stipulate to any other use of the verdict that will aid in the resolution of the case.

14. These rules shall be construed to secure the just, speedy and inexpensive conclusion of the summary jury trial procedure.

IT IS SO ORDERED.

Thomas D. Lambros
United States District Judge

FEDERAL RESERVE BANK OF MINNEAPOLIS V. CAREY-CANADA, INC.
123 F.R.D. 603 (D. Minn. 1988)

FACT SUMMARY

The plaintiff, Federal Reserve Bank of Minneapolis, claimed that the defendant, Carey-Canada, Inc., had damaged its commercial property and endangered the health of its employees by fireproofing the bank with products containing asbestos. The plaintiff sought $48 million in compensatory and punitive damages. The district court judge ordered the parties to participate in a three-day summary jury trial. Both parties objected to the mandated process. They claimed that the summary jury trial would be too costly and would waste about $50,000 in costs. In addition, the parties argued that the summary jury trial would not be a true synopsis of an actual trial, as major evidentiary rulings still needed to be made by the trial judge. Furthermore, the parties asserted that there was little chance of settling the dispute and that the summary jury trial would not significantly contribute to defining issues or preparing attorney presentations for trial.

OPINION: *JANICE M. SYMCHYCH, United States Magistrate*

This court is called upon to decide whether the court may compel attendance and participation in a non-binding summary jury trial absent consent of the parties. . . .

The Supreme Court has long acknowledged the power of the court to control its docket. In *Link v. Wabash*, 370 U.S. 626, 82 S. Ct. 1386, 8 L. Ed. 2d 734 (1962), the Court made clear that this power is inherent, and not dependent upon any express statute or rule confronting such power. The ability of a court to use its discretion to manage its crowded docket must be protected. . . . Parties and attorneys are often reluctant to accept and participate in procedures outside the traditional norm. It is often difficult to focus the attention of counsel and litigants on settlement as an alternative means of resolving a case. The need to compel the parties to address settlement, is an integral aspect of the docket management function of the court in this era of complex, protracted litigation. . . .

. . . . [I]t is clear that settlement of cases prior to litigation provides a major cost saving for the parties as well as conservation of judicial resources. There may be a variety of reasons why cases do not settle. Parties may refuse to accept settlement as they feel that they are entitled to and need their day in court. Parties may believe that the only way to prevail on a weak case is to get a case before a jury. Parties may be unable to objectively recognize or assess the strengths and weaknesses of their position without submission of the issues to a finder of fact. These reasons, among others, act as impediments to settlement of cases which should otherwise be resolved without trial.

The SJT provides a means by which to eliminate these barriers to settlement. SJT is the only dispute resolution technique which uses the input of a jury of laymen as fact finders. It is this facet of SJT which permits the parties, not the attorneys, to believe that their story has been told, and a decision reached by an objective body. The decision resulting from the SJT inevitably results in both sides re-examining and re-evaluating their positions and demands.

. . . . Even in cases where SJT does not result in settlement, it provides clarification of the issues, and results in superior preparation for trial. The SJT does not abolish any substantive rights of the parties; they are still entitled to a binding trial, if the summary proceedings do not lead to settlement of the case. The SJT represents one alternative which courts are employing in an effort to secure to civil litigants just, speedy, and inexpensive determination of their claims of which litigants may be otherwise deprived because of the overwhelming and over-burdening caseloads in many federal courts.

Learn more about the Federal Rules of Civil Procedure at: http://www.cornell.edu/rules/frcp/htm

. . . .

The SJT process recognizes the importance our judicial system places on decisions rendered by jurors. This is consistent with Fed. R. Civ. P. 39(c), which provides for an advisory jury in cases not triable to a jury as of right. Additionally, the use of SJT is consistent with Fed. R. Civ. P. 83 which provides in part, "in all cases not provided for by rule, the district courts may regulate their practice in any manner not consistent with these rules."

The Federal Rules of Civil Procedure were amended in 1983. The Advisory Committee Notes articulate that the obvious goal of the amendments was the promotion of case management of which settlement is a valuable tool. Fed. R. Civ. P. 16 Advisory Committee Note to 1983 Amendments. Therefore, it is difficult to reconcile the argument that Rule 16 does not permit courts to order the parties to participate in summary jury trials with the goals of that rule. It is hard to imagine that the drafters of the 1983 Amendments actually intended to strengthen courts' ability to manage their caseloads while at the same time intended to deny the court the power to compel participation by the parties to the litigation.

. . . .

. . . The parties argue that the investment of attorney time and money would be wasted on the SJT proceeding. However, an investment of three days for the SJT when compared to a potential real jury trial lasting four-to-six courtroom weeks is reasonably proportionate. The court further believes that the SJT procedure, even if it does not lead to settlement, will be of substantial benefit in this case by clarifying issues for trial, both for the parties and the court.

The parties complain also that the SJT procedure would not be a representative synopsis of the actual trial . . . due to the pending evidentiary motions before Judge Devitt. This court finds the complaint to be without merit. Because of the nonbinding nature of the SJT procedure, evidentiary rules are more flexible than in an actual trial. Furthermore, in order to more adequately reflect the outcome of the actual trial, this court can decide evidentiary issues for the purpose of the SJT proceeding.

For the foregoing reasons, this matter is deemed appropriate for SJT, as a step in consideration of settlement in this case. The court finds it likely that the procedure will be of benefit to both the parties and the court both in the event of settlement or nonsettlement.

Discussion Questions

1. How does the court use the Federal Rules of Civil Procedure to support its decision on compulsory SJT?
2. Do you agree with the court's reasoning that judges should be able to mandate the use of the SJT without the parties' prior consent?
3. Why does the court assert that the SJT can reduce obstacles to settlement prior to trial?

In this second case, the court decides that parties cannot be forced to use the SJT without prior consent. The court voices its concern that a compulsory SJT is too coercive and impedes the effectiveness of ADR methods.

IN RE NLO, INC.
5 F. 3d 154 (6th Cir. 1993)

FACT SUMMARY

The plaintiffs (employees and subcontractors) sued the defendant, owners of a uranium-processing facility, for claimed intentional or negligent exposure to radioactive and hazardous materials. The plaintiffs alleged that the exposure to hazardous levels of radioactivity increased their risk of cancer and caused emotional distress. The plaintiffs sought compensatory and punitive damages, and costs for a court-supervised medical monitoring program, along with attorneys' fees and interest. The district court ordered the parties to participate in a SJT and took the unusual step of mandating that the process be open to the public. The defendant moved for reconsideration, but the district court denied that request. The district court supported its order under Rule 16 of the Federal Rules of Civil Procedure. There was no local rule in effect to allow for SJT use. The defendant then filed a petition for mandamus. An emergency stay was granted and oral argument scheduled before the Sixth Circuit Court of Appeals.

OPINION: *MERRITT, Chief Judge*

. . . .

We turn first to the order of the district court concerning the summary jury trial. . . . [W]e find the district court's order compelling participation in a summary jury trial under threat of sanctions to be clearly erroneous as a matter of law.

. . . .

The district court held that compulsory summary jury trials are permitted in this circuit under *Cincinnati Gas and Electric Company v. General Electric Company,* 854 F. 2d 900 (6th Cir. 1988), *cert. denied,* 489 U.S. 1033, 109 S. Ct. 1171, 103 L. Ed. 2d 229 (1989). In *Cincinnati Gas,* a panel of this court upheld the district court's decision to exclude the press from a summary jury trial. We indicated that a summary jury trial was a permissible tool for a district court to use in promoting resolution of cases before it. . . . The district court expressly stated that the proceeding was undertaken with the *cooperation* of the parties. . . .

. . . .

District courts unquestionably have substantial inherent power to manage their dockets. . . . That power, however, must be exercised in a manner that is in harmony with the Federal Rules of Civil Procedure. . . .

. . . .

[Federal Rule of Civil Procedure] 16(a) gives district courts the power to compel attendance at pretrial conferences. Rule 16(c) gives guidance concerning "subjects to be discussed" at those conferences:

The participants at any conference under this rule *may consider* and take action with respect to . . . (7) the possibility of settlement or the use of extrajudicial procedures to resolve their dispute; . . . (10) the need for adopting special procedures for managing potentially difficult or protracted actions that may involve complex issues, multiple parties, difficult legal questions, or unusual problems of proof . . .

(emphasis supplied). The Advisory Committee notes to Rule 16(c)(7) indicate that no compulsory authority exists:

[I]t is not the purpose of Rule 16(c)(7) to impose settlement negotiations on unwilling litigants. . . . The rule does not make settlement conferences mandatory. . . . In addition to settlement, Rule 16(c)(7) refers to *exploring* the use of procedures other than litigation to resolve the dispute. This includes *urging* the litigants to employ adjudicatory techniques outside the courthouse.

(emphasis supplied). The Supreme Court has established that "in ascertaining [the] meaning [of the Rules] the construction given to them by the Committee is of weight. . . . We hold that the provisions of Rule 16, as amplified by the Commentary of the Committee, do not permit compulsory participation in settlement proceedings such as summary jury trials."

District courts struggle to deal effectively with caseloads expanding at a precipitous rate. The utilization of procedures designed to facilitate settlement whenever possible is expressly encouraged by Rule 16, for a case that settles obviously consumes much less of the court's scarce resources than a case that proceeds to a full trial on the merits. Although judges should encourage and aid early settlement, however, they should not attempt to coerce that settlement (citation omitted). . . . Requiring participation in a summary jury trial, where such compulsion is not permitted by the Federal Rules, is an unwarranted extension of the judicial power. (footnote omitted)

. . . .

We do not question the proposition that summary jury trials may be valuable tools in expediting cases. However, the voluntary cooperation of the parties is required to maximize the effectiveness of such proceedings. Indeed, if such proceedings truly are valuable, voluntary cooperation will be forthcoming.

. . . . A jury trial, even one of a summary nature, however, requires at minimum the time-consuming process of assembling a panel and (one would hope) thorough preparation for argument by counsel, no matter how brief the actual proceeding. Compelling an unwilling litigant to undergo this process improperly interposes the tribunal into the normal adversarial course of litigation. It is error.

. . . .

Accordingly, we . . . VACATE that portion of the district court's order . . . ordering a summary jury trial.

Discussion Questions

1. What authority does the court indicate that judges have to use the SJT and other ADR processes to resolve party conflicts?
2. Do you agree with the court's interpretation of Rule 16?
3. Why is voluntary participation in the SJT and other ADR mechanisms viewed as important?

Recent revisions to the Advisory Committee's notes to Rule 16 of the Federal Rules of Civil Procedure now indicate that judges can require parties to use non-binding ADR procedures as a precondition to trial, with or without party consent. Statutory changes in the 1990s illustrate the growing public and legislative demands for the judiciary to take a more active role in court reform. Congress recently enacted **The Judicial Improvements Act of 1990.** Under the Act, federal courts are directed to develop **civil justice expense and delay reduction plans.** These plans require each district court to collaborate with an advisory group of lawyers and major litigants to draw up programs and policies aimed at better management of case dockets and reducing court costs and delays. The Act anticipates that these plans will include the use of appropriate ADR methods, including the SJT.

The pertinent section of the Act states that:

http://

The U.S. Code can be accessed at:
http://law.house.gov/use.html

(a) In formulating the provisions of its civil justice expense and delay reduction plan, each United States district court, in consultation with an advisory group . . . shall consider and may include the following principles and guidelines of litigation management and cost and delay reduction:

(6) authorization to refer appropriate cases to alternative dispute resolution programs that:

(A) have been designated for use in a district court; or

(B) the court may make available, including mediation, minitrial, and the summary jury trial.

28 U.S.C. § 473 (1993).

The passage of the Act and the revisions to the Advisory Committee notes to Rule 16 illustrate growing legal support for judicial authority to create innovative ADR programs, which may include the SJT. However, the Supreme Court has yet to render a definitive interpretation on whether these updates mean that a compulsory SJT is a valid exercise of judicial authority.

Pre-SJT Conference

After a case is assigned to a SJT, each party prepares and submits trial briefs addressing legal issues and requested jury instructions. The presiding judge will often convene a pre-SJT conference in an attempt to narrow the issues of law and fact to be presented to the mock jury. Because formal objections are discouraged during the SJT, this conference enables the judge to deal with party objections to anticipated evidence.

Selection of SJT Jurors

Six or twelve jurors make up the SJT jury, with six being the norm. Potential SJT jurors are drawn from the standard jury pool. Like regular jurors, each potential mock juror completes a written questionnaire designed to ferret out potential bias. (See Figure 5.2.) Along with party counsel, the court conducts a brief voir dire with each side allowed a strictly limited number of preemptory challenges. Once an SJT jury has been seated, some judges will inform jurors of their advisory role, while others do not until after the verdict is rendered. Critics of the SJT argue that it is unethical not to inform SJT jurors in advance that they are only giving an **advisory verdict.** Their concern is that word will spread that some trials are real and some are merely advisory, thereby eroding juror participation and attention in all court cases. Other experts assert that jurors should not be informed of their mock roles until after they have rendered their verdict, fearing that some jurors will be less likely to take their roles seriously if told their verdict was not binding.

The SJT Hearing

The SJT hearing itself begins with each party's attorney making an opening statement. Summary presentations of proof, rather than lengthy live testimony from parties and witnesses or detailed introductions of documentary or demonstrative evidence, yield the primary savings in time and money. Normally, party counsel will summarize the anticipated testimony and present exhibits to the jury. In some instances, parties may augment summary presentations with relevant videotape clips of party and expert witness testimony. Attorney summaries are limited to evidence admissible at trial with any representations to be supported by evidence

FIGURE 5.2   Sample Juror Questionnaire

APPENDIX C
<u>JUROR PROFILE FORM</u>
Cite as 103 F.R.D. 461

TO THE JUROR

You have been selected to take part in a "summary jury trial." Briefly, it is a summarized presentation of a case upon which you will be expected to decide the issues within one day.

To assist the Court in empaneling a summary jury, you are requested to answer the following questions. Your responses to these questions and such additional questions which may be asked of you by the Court will be helpful in the selection of an impartial summary jury.

<u>QUESTIONS:</u>   (Please Print)

1. Name:——————————————————————————————————

2. Occupation and place of employment. (If retired, add your former occupation and place of employment.)——————————————————————

3. Are you married or single?——————————————————————
4. Your spouse's name?——————————————————————————
5. Spouse's occupation and place of employment. (If retired, add the former occupation and place of employment.)——————————————————

6. Your children's names and ages?——————————————————————

This case involves:
    The parties in this case are:

——————————————   ——————————————
——————————————   ——————————————
——————————————   ——————————————
——————————————   ——————————————

Plaintiff(s)   Defendant(s)
The attorneys appearing today will be:

——————————————   ——————————————
——————————————   ——————————————
——————————————   ——————————————

For Plaintiff(s)   For Defendant(s)

7. Do you know any of the parties or their counsel? If so, specifically state who.——

8. Are you in any way personally connected with the facts of this case or do you have personal knowledge of this case? If so, state how.————————————

9. Is there anything you can think of that would bias your opinion so that you would be unable to give a fair and just consideration to the merits of this case? If so, state what.————————————————————————————

Your signature

derived from the discovery process. There is no cross-examination, and evidentiary objections are discouraged. Parties or company representatives with authority to settle the dispute must be present during these summary presentations to maximize the chances for settlement.

Following the attorney summaries, the judge provides the mock jury with an abbreviated set of jury instructions on the relevant law. The jury then begins its deliberations, returning with either consensus or separate advisory verdicts on party liability and damages. (See Figure 5.3.) In rendering its advisory verdict, the jury uses the standard civil litigation burden of proof of preponderance of the evidence.

One of the most critical aspects of the SJT occurs after the verdict has been announced. Instead of leaving the courtroom, the jurors remain for a **question-and-answer session** with the parties and their lawyers. In this session, similar to those used for marketing focus groups, each party probes the jurors' perceptions to determine the strengths and weaknesses of their case. By doing so, the parties can realistically reassess their cases and perhaps move toward productive **settlement talks** in lieu of going to trial.

Settlement Talks

The initial phases of the SJT rely heavily on the legal and advocacy skills of the parties' attorneys and the perspectives of lay jurors. However, the real work of the SJT does not begin until the process moves into the critical negotiation phase, at which point the conflicting parties have the opportunity to fashion more creative business solutions than a court could award. The SJT judge will often serve as a mediator, helping the parties to find common ground and generate options for mutual gain. If the parties reach an agreement, the terms of the settlement will become the subject of a court decree. Because the SJT is not binding, however, the parties may seek a new full trial on the merits if negotiations are unsuccessful.

ADVANTAGES OF THE SJT

The SJT is a unique, court-supervised process that draws on elements of litigation, negotiation, and mediation. It has many of the same advantages of other ADR mechanisms.

Savings in Time and Costs

At the trial stage, the SJT provides savings in time and money for both the litigants and the judicial system through reductions in party attorneys' fees and the time and costs for judges and juries in actual trials. With a SJT, a four- to six-week trial might shrink to as little as a half day. If successful, substantial savings can result for both the parties and the court. Even with no settlement, the SJT clarifies trial issues and

FIGURE 5.3   Sample Jury Verdict Form

APPENDIX D
<u>JURORS' ADVISORY OPINION</u>
Case No. _____
Cite as 103 F.R.D. 461
WE, THE JURY, HAVE REACHED THE FOLLOWING CONSENSUS:
   We, the Jury, find defendant
   _____ not liable.
   _____ liable, in the amount of _____ .
   _____ liable, but not able to reach a unanimous decision as to the amount.
   We, the Jury, being unable to reach a unanimous decision, submit our
anonymous, individual findings as follows:
1.   _____ not liable.
     _____ liable, in the amount of _____ .
2.   _____ not liable.
     _____ liable, in the amount of _____ .
3.   _____ not liable.
     _____ liable, in the amount of _____ .
4.   _____ not liable.
     _____ liable, in the amount of _____ .
5.   _____ not liable.
     _____ liable, in the amount of _____ .
6.   _____ not liable.
     _____ liable, in the amount of _____ .

                _____
                Foreperson

<u>JURORS' ADVISORY OPINION</u>
WE, THE JURY, HAVE REACHED THE FOLLOWING CONSENSUS:
   The issue of liability having already been determined in favor of plaintiff(s)
against defendant(s), we, the Jury, find that defendant(s) is/are liable in the amount
of $ _____ .
   We, the Jury, being unable to arrive at a unanimous decision on the amount of
liability, make the following anonymous, individual findings:
1. Defendant is liable in the amount of $ _____ .
2. Defendant is liable in the amount of $ _____ .
3. Defendant is liable in the amount of $ _____ .
4. Defendant is liable in the amount of $ _____ .
5. Defendant is liable in the amount of $ _____ .
6. Defendant is liable in the amount of $ _____ .

                _____
                Foreperson

---

improves attorney preparation and trial performance, thus resulting in savings in
time and money should the case go to trial.

Confidentiality of SJT Proceedings and Documents

The SJT is a confidential process that is not accessible to the general public and the
media. As with other settlement discussions in traditional litigation, Judge Lambros
intended SJT proceedings to be confidential to encourage fruitful negotiations

between the disputing parties. Confidential proceedings can encourage frank discussions of settlement without the fear of negative publicity or outside pressure. In addition, the SJT allows business litigants access to input from an actual jury without the damaging publicity or open access associated with a standard jury trial.

However, some opponents of confidential ADR processes like the SJT fear that disputes with public interest aspects will be resolved behind closed doors without public access to the proceedings or documents. The following seminal case concerns the media's First Amendment right of access to the SJT proceedings and documents.

CINCINNATI GAS AND ELECTRIC COMPANY V. GENERAL ELECTRIC COMPANY

854 F. 2d 900 (6th Cir. 1988), cert. denied, 489 U.S. 1033 (1989)

FACT SUMMARY

The plaintiffs, Cincinnati Gas and Electric Company and two other power companies, brought an action for breach of contract duties and common law, fraud, and RICO violations against defendants, General Electric Company and Sargent & Lundy Engineers, regarding the design and construction of the William H. Zimmer Nuclear Power Plant. Due to the sensitive information needed to process the lawsuit, a complex protective order was worked out with the parties to provide for confidentiality of discovery documents. The district court ordered the parties to participate in a SJT with the proceedings closed to the press and public and to keep any documents generated during the SJT confidential. The *Cincinnati Post* and other newspapers challenged both orders.

OPINION: *KEITH, Circuit Judge*

The precise issue before us is whether the first amendment right of access attaches to the summary jury trial proceeding in

this case. Appellants argue that the district court erred in refusing to allow them to intervene for the purpose of attending the summary jury trial proceeding. Appellants specifically argue that: (1) the summary jury proceeding is analogous in form and function to a civil or criminal trial on the merits, and therefore, the First Amendment right of access which civil and criminal trial and pretrial proceedings also encompasses the summary jury proceedings; and (2) public access would play a significant positive role in the functioning of the judicial system and summary jury trials. (citations omitted). . . .

Appellees contend that the First Amendment right of access does not apply to summary jury proceedings. Appellees argue that settlement proceedings are totally lacking in any tradition of public access, and that appellants exalt form over function in arguing that a summary jury trial is no different from a trial on the merits. *Palmieri v. New York*, 779 F. 2d 861, 865 (2d Cir. 1985)(citation omitted) ("[s]ecrecy of settlement terms . . . is a well-established American litigation practice . . ."). Appellees further argue that public access would not play a significant positive role in the functioning of summary jury trials. We agree with appellees' arguments and hold that the First Amendment right of access does not attach to summary jury trial proceedings. (footnote omitted).

. . . .

In *Press Enterprise II* the [Supreme] Court held that a qualified right of access applied in criminal proceedings to a preliminary hearing which was conducted before a magistrate in the absence of a jury. The Court held that the analysis of a First Amendment claim of access involves two "complimentary considerations." First, the proceeding must be one for which there has been a "tradition of accessibility." *Press Enterprise II,* 106 S. Ct. at 2740 (citation omitted). This inquiry requires a court to determine "whether the place and process [to which access is sought] has historically been open to the press and general public." *Id.* (citation omitted). Moreover, even if these elements are satisfied, the right of access is a qualified one and must be outweighed by a strong countervailing interest in maintaining the confidentiality of the proceedings. *Id.* at 2740 (citation omitted).

With regard to the first part of the test, we concur with the district court that "there is no historically recognized right of access to summary jury trials in that this mechanism has been in existence for less than a decade." (citation omitted). The summary jury trial is a device that is designed to settle disputes. (footnote and citation omitted). Settlement techniques have historically been closed to the press and public. *See, Palmieri,* 779 F. 2d at 865. Thus, we find that "while the history of the summary jury trial is limited, there is a general agreement that historical settlement techniques are closed rather than open." (citation omitted).

Appellants argue that summary jury trials are structurally similar to ordinary civil jury trials, which have historically been open to the public. However, it is clear that while the summary jury trial is a highly reliable predictor of the likely trial outcome, there are manifold differences between it and a real trial. . . .

At every turn the summary jury trial is designed to facilitate pretrial settlement of the litigation, much like a settlement conference. It is important to note that the summary jury trial does not present any matter for adjudication by the court. (footnote omitted). Thus, we find appellants' argument to be unpersuasive and therefore hold that the "tradition of accessibility" element has not been met.

The second criterion in the Court's public access analysis is whether access "plays a significant positive role in the functioning of the particular process in question." *Press Enterprise II,* 106 S. Ct. at 2740. Appellants contend that public access would have community therapeutic value because of the importance of the nuclear power and utility rate issues raised. We disagree.

"[I]t is necessary to consider whether the 'practice in question [furthers] an important or substantial governmental interest unrelated to the suppression of expression' and whether 'the limitation of First Amendment freedoms [is] no greater than is necessary or essential to the protection of the particular government interest involved.'" *Seattle Times Co. v. Rhinehart,* 467 U.S. 20, 32, 104 S. Ct. 2199, 2207, 81 L. Ed. 2d 17 (1984). The summary jury trial can play a particularly useful role in facilitating the settlement of complex cases and is typically employed in cases that either will consume significant judicial resources if they proceed to trial, or that are not amenable to settlement through other techniques. However, where a party has a legitimate interest in confidentiality, public access would be detrimental to the effectiveness of the summary jury trial in facilitating settlement. Thus, public access to summary jury trials over the parties' objections would have significant adverse effects on the utility of the procedure as a settlement device. Therefore, allowing access would undermine the substantial government interest in promoting settlements, and would not play a "significant positive role in the functioning of the particular process in question." *Press Enterprise II,* 106 S. Ct. at 2740. (footnote omitted).

Appellants' claim of a public "right to know" has no validity with regard to summary jury trials. As the lower court correctly noted, the public would have no entitlement to observe any negotiations leading to traditional settlement of the case, (citation omitted), and the parties would be under no constitutional obligation to reveal the content of the negotiations. Thus, the public has no First Amendment right to access to the summary jury trial.

Appellants also argue that the summary jury trial should be open to the public because of the facilitation of a settlement between the parties has a final and decisive effect on the outcome of the litigation. . . .

. . . . Summary jury trials do not present any matters of adjudication by the court. (footnote omitted). Thus, it is the presence of the exercise of a court's coercive powers that is the touchstone of the recognized right to access, not the presence of a procedure that might lead the parties to voluntarily terminate the litigation. Therefore, we find appellants' arguments to be meritless. . . .

OPINION: *EDWARDS,*
Senior Circuit Judge,
concurring in part and dissenting in part

The proceeding conducted in this case resulted in a settlement and a court decree. It resembled both settlement negotiations and a bench trial. While I join the majority in holding that the negotiations which led to the settlement of this case could properly be conducted in camera, I do not agree that the record can appropriately continue to be sealed after a settlement has been effected. I recognize that the view expressed above might impede some settlements, but I cannot reconcile complete suppression of this record with the First Amendment which our forefathers placed as the first condition for the founding of our nation.

Discussion Questions

1. Under the *Press Enterprise II* standard, how does the court evaluate media access to SJT proceedings and documents?
2. What substantial government interest is promoted by the confidentiality of the SJT?
3. Do you agree with Judge Edwards that the press and public should have access to the SJT documents?

Respect for the Jury Process

The SJT is the only ADR mechanism that uses a jury in the resolution of a dispute. The mechanism recognizes the value of the jury's input in clarifying for disputants and their attorneys potential juror perceptions of party evidence and likely awards. This process encourages the litigants to reassess objectively their cases and reach a meaningful settlement. In addition, jurors can participate in the process without sacrificing as much time away from their personal and professional responsibilities.

Empowerment of Businesspeople to Resolve Conflicts

The success of the SJT relies heavily on the empowerment and creativity of business executives to resolve their own disputes. Although summary presentations and mock juror perceptions are important elements of the SJT, the main aspect of the dispute resolution process is the settlement talks between the disputants. The SJT judge can assist the business litigants by acting as a mediator, but the process can only conclude successfully if the businesspeople can objectively evaluate their cases and creatively negotiate the outcome. Drawing from principles of negotiation and mediation, the SJT assigns businesspeople a primary role in determining the resolution of their dispute. As 90 to 95% of all cases end in settlement, businesses can reduce their trial time and costs through the SJT.

Psychological Benefits

One obstacle to settlement of a business dispute may be hostility between the parties. Business disputants may have pent-up anger, which may be blinding them to options for reasonable settlement. With the SJT's courtroom aura, parties may feel that they have been given their day in court, along with a meaningful chance to air their side before objective parties. This venting process may reduce party hostility, leading to consideration of each other's perspective and a possible settlement.

DISADVANTAGES OF THE SJT

Though judges, lawyers, and scholars initially applauded Judge Lambros's creativity in inventing the SJT, criticisms began to surface a few years later. Seventh Circuit Judge Posner voiced serious doubts about both the usefulness and ethics of the SJT. Other legal commentators soon followed with a barrage of criticisms.

Mixed Results on SJT Time and Cost Benefits

Eighty percent of all legal costs arise in the discovery phase of trial. Yet, because the SJT is used only *after* discovery, it has no impact on this time-consuming and costly aspect of traditional litigation. Savings are derived only from reduced trial costs and time. Another concern is the lack of serious research confirming the claims of savings in time and money. Aside from anecdotal judicial experiences, there are no clear data to substantiate the notion that the SJT increases judicial efficiency and reduces litigation costs. This lack of empirical research, Judge Posner believed, has led to sweeping, unsupported conclusions being made about the SJT.

The results of the limited empirical studies of SJT use have been mixed, further clouding the debate on the effectiveness of the SJT. Some studies indicated that, in a majority of cases, the SJT process resulted in fewer billable hours and the preservation of party and court resources through half-day sessions. Yet in another study, a majority of the lawyers asserted that they expended more billable hours and seldom completed their SJT session within Judge Lambros's half-day goal. Therefore, until more comprehensive research studies are undertaken, parties and their attorneys must individually assess the time and cost savings of the SJT.

Predictive Value of the SJT

In addition to questioning SJT time and cost benefits, critics assert that the SJT may not accurately predict actual trial jury outcomes, thereby limiting the value of party evaluations of their cases. The SJT's use of summary presentations with no live witness testimony may skew juror impressions and hamper meaningful juror assessments of witness credibility. Moreover, the rules of evidence are relaxed in SJT summary presentations, placing too much emphasis on each attorney's advocacy style and personality. In this context, the SJT may encourage party attempts to present inadmissible evidence, to gather information that should have been requested during discovery, or to learn about opposing counsel's trial strategy. These problems may detract from the predictive value of SJT.

For example, *Stites v. Sundstrand Heat Transfer, Inc.*, 660 F. Supp. 1516 (W.D. Mich. 1987), concerned a company's liability for a chemical spill. The parties agreed to a SJT. To test the predictive value of the SJT, the judge divided the mock jury into two separate groups. Each group deliberated separately after hearing the same SJT presentations. They came back with completely opposite verdicts despite hearing the exact same presentations. Such divergent results call into question the predictive value of SJT.

Lack of Precedential Value

Although the SJT is a court-supervised process, the court does not adjudicate the dispute. The outcome results from party negotiations, and the proceedings and outcome remain confidential, unless the parties agree otherwise. Thus, the SJT may not be useful in a business conflict in which the parties desire a clear precedent that establishes their rights and deters future claimants.

Constitutional Concerns

Unlike private ADR mechanisms, the SJT is a court-supervised process. However, despite the fact that most court processes are open to public and media scrutiny, this is not the case with the SJT. Certain business disputes involving important public policy matters can raise critical First Amendment concerns. Yet in *Cincinnati Gas,* the court determined that the public and media are not entitled access to a SJT under the First Amendment. Keep in mind, however, that no Supreme Court decision has definitively determined the issue of First Amendment access to a SJT.

OVERVIEW OF THE MINITRIAL

Similar to a SJT, the **minitrial** is derived from various facets of litigation, negotiation, and mediation. The minitrial is a carefully structured, nonbinding settlement process that, like SJT, seeks to convert legal disputes into business decisions. This voluntary, confidential settlement tool involves abbreviated, trial-like presentations of each party's perspective on a dispute before management executives of each party. The parties may also request the assistance of a neutral advisor with expertise in any area of industry or law under dispute.

The minitrial can be particularly useful in highly technical cases which may be more difficult for judges or laypersons without industry experience to understand. For example, the first minitrial in 1977 involved a patent infringement dispute between Telecredit, Inc., and TRW, Inc. The conflict focused on ownership of patents on computerized credit card and check-authorization devices. By using savvy business executives and a neutral advisor with relevant expertise, the minitrial served as an effective vehicle for resolving this technically and legally complex controversy. (See the *ADR in Action* feature in this chapter.)

Like the SJT, the minitrial empowers businesspeople to make sound but creative business decisions in resolving business disputes. Used in both the private and public sectors, the minitrial has helped resolve disputes between private businesses and between private industry and government agencies. Businesspersons assume a primary role in negotiating the settlement, while the attorneys mainly act as advocates during the information exchange.

Unlike the SJT, minitrials were originally pioneered by organizations outside of the court system. The CPR (Center for Public Resources) Institute for Dispute Resolution, an international nonprofit ADR organization in New York, has been a strong advocate of the minitrial for resolving domestic and international disputes and is a solid resource for minitrial procedures and forms. International organizations, such as the Zurich Chamber of Commerce, have also recommended the minitrial to resolve international business disputes. In recent years, some judges have begun to experiment with the hybrid **court-annexed minitrial** sometimes referred to as the **conditional summary jury trial.**

http://
Find the Center for Public Resources Institute for Dispute Resolution at: http://www. cpradr.org

COMPONENTS OF THE MINITRIAL

As the minitrial is largely a private process, there is no established set of procedures for it. Certain administering organizations have established model procedures, but it is primarily left up to the parties to determine the appropriate steps in the process. The following discussion presents some of the typical components of the minitrial.

Initiation of Procedure

In both private and court settings, minitrials are based on consent of both parties. In a privately administered minitrial, the parties enter into a written agreement to resolve their dispute through a minitrial, with or without the assistance of an administering entity such as the CPR Institute for Dispute Resolution. The parties then determine the ground rules for the process, including the length of discovery, the composition and role of the minitrial panel, the outline of the minitrial hearing or information exchange, and the nature of the settlement talks. The parties can create their own process or follow the established procedures of administering organizations.

In court-supervised minitrials, the parties follow a similar approach. In agreeing to use the minitrial, the parties stipulate to the terms of a procedural order. The court order spells out the elements of the process. Some courts have model procedural orders on minitrials that parties can modify to meet their needs.

Limited Discovery

Once the parties have agreed to use the minitrial, they typically will establish a limited discovery period to maximize the benefits of the minitrial. For example, TRW and Telecredit set up a rigorous six-week discovery schedule that involved a limited information exchange and included briefs and position papers to help narrow the legal and factual issues in the case.

Selection of a Neutral Advisor

In the minitrial, the parties often hire an expert to hear the minitrial presentations and to facilitate settlement talks. The **neutral advisor** must be agreeable to both parties. Businesspeople often play a major role in the selection process. The parties may select an advisor from a panel of experts from an administering agency or an individual whom both parties believe has the legal or business expertise necessary to comprehend the dispute. Parties in private minitrials may elect not to use the services of a neutral advisor.

The neutral advisor moderates the minitrial sessions and moves the process forward in a timely manner. In some instances, parties will ask the neutral advisor for a confidential opinion of the strengths and weaknesses of each party's case. That opinion, either written or oral, is not binding and serves primarily to aid settlement of the dispute. The neutral advisor may also act as mediator during the settlement talks to help the parties avoid an impasse.

In court-supervised minitrials, the court normally requires that the parties select a neutral advisor, typically a judicial officer or special master. Alternatively, the parties may elect to have the trial judge serve as the neutral advisor. Selecting the trial judge can provide parties with a clear sense of how a court may rule on the factual and legal issues. If settlement is not reached, however, participation of the trial judge raises troubling issues of judicial prejudice or bias and may result in calls for recusal at trial.

Information Exchange or "Best Case" Presentations

At the **information exchange,** the neutral advisor, along with a key business executive with settlement authority from each side, make up the minitrial panel. Similar to the SJT, lawyers for each party present an abbreviated **"best case" presentation** of their side within reasonable time limits. Unlike the SJT, the "best case" presentations are made before the minitrial panel, rather than a mock jury.

Attorneys for each side may call on a limited number of witnesses for live testimony and may bring in experts to support their contentions. However, attorneys often will merely summarize pertinent testimony and provide an overview of demonstrative evidence, after which the parties may agree to allow each side a brief rebuttal. With the limited presentation time and knowledgeable businesspeople involved in the process, the information exchange requires attorneys to condense their side's case down to its main components. Weeks of trial time can be reduced to days or even hours. In some court-supervised minitrials, parties may be required to introduce all claims and defenses that they plan to litigate in the dispute. Failure to raise these points at the minitrial information exchange may prohibit raising them at trial.

Throughout the information exchange, the panel plays a participatory rather than a passive role. The neutral advisor, as well as the businesspeople, may ask questions of either attorney. These questions can help clarify essential factual or legal issues in dispute.

Settlement Discussions with the Neutral Advisor

After hearing each side's "best case," executives for each party evaluate their positions and initiate negotiations on settlement. Like the SJT, the minitrial assigns primary responsibility for resolving the dispute to the businesspeople, who have greater freedom than a court in determining the outcome. Throughout negotiations, the neutral advisor assists the parties in their efforts to reach settlement. At the parties' request, the neutral advisor may also issue a nonbinding opinion. If settlement is reached, the neutral advisor works with the parties to outline the terms of agreement.

For example, in the TRW and Telecredit dispute, the parties reached a working agreement within thirty minutes of negotiations between the business executives. That working draft was then translated into formal legal language over the course of the next few weeks. By using the minitrial, the parties estimated that they saved about $1 million in lawyers' fees alone. If no agreement had been made, the matter would have been processed in the courts or possibly referred to another ADR method for appropriate resolution. (See the *ADR in Action* feature in this chapter.)

In some court-annexed minitrials, the **procedural order** may set an express time limit for negotiations. If the parties reach an agreement within the time limit, the judge must review and approve the negotiated result, called the **judgment of acquiescence.** This judicial review process ensures a fair outcome and protects against inequitable settlements based on uneven bargaining power. If the parties fail to reach an agreement within the time limit, the presiding officer may make a proposed ruling in the case. That ruling may be based on the presiding officer's independent evaluation or may involve selecting one of the final negotiated offers of the disputants. The ruling becomes an order of the court, unless one of the parties makes a timely objection. An objecting party may be required to post a bond before litigating the matter or may be penalized if unable to substantially improve on the proposed ruling at time of trial.

ADR IN ACTION

The Birth of the Minitrial—Telecredit and TRW

Telecredit, Inc., and TRW, Inc., had competed fiercely against each other for the lucrative computerized credit and check-authorization devices market. Telecredit, though smaller than multinational TRW, held several patents for these devices, which had not yet been tested for their validity through litigation. In 1974, Telecredit sued TRW for $6 million in damages for patent infringement and obtained an injunction to block further infringement. TRW denied any wrongdoing and countered that Telecredit's patents were invalid.

With the filing of the lawsuit, the competitors had now become locked into a bitter court battle, both costly and lengthy. Both companies spent nearly three years and hundreds of thousands of dollars in expensive discovery efforts. Much time was spent exchanging more than 100,000

documents, responding to numerous interrogatories, and attending seemingly endless depositions. As hostilities between the parties escalated, attempts at settlement seemed futile.

Although the parties originally considered arbitration, they ultimately began to negotiate the minitrial option. The parties agreed to determine the conduct of the process, as well as keep it confidential. Each party committed to complete the discovery process and to exchange briefs and case position papers within a six-week time period. Initial "best case" presentations, moderated by a neutral advisor, were limited to four hours for each party. Following the presentations and rebuttals, senior managers, along with the neutral advisor, but without their attorneys, met privately to negotiate. To aid settlement, the neutral advisor was given the authority to render a nonbinding opinion of each party's strengths and weaknesses, after which the parties would attempt to settle.

On July 20, 1977, Telecredit and TRW conducted the first minitrial at a conference room in the Century Plaza Hotel in Los Angeles. Telecredit CEO Lee A. Ault III and TRW Vice President Richard A. Campbell attended the minitrial, both possessing settlement authority for their respective companies. Former U.S. Court of Claims Judge James F. Davis, who had extensive patent law experience, participated as the neutral advisor. At the information exchange, each party made its "best case" presentation and rebuttal case, using expert witnesses to bolster their claims. Each had the opportunity to hear the other side's view of the dispute and gained new insights into the legal and technical issues in

dispute. At the end of the information exchange, the neutral advisor gave an informal oral opinion of his view of the dispute. The information exchange was completed in two days; an actual trial would have gobbled up weeks.

CEO Ault and Vice President Campbell then met privately to discuss how to best resolve the conflict that had beset their companies. Within thirty minutes, the two executives had outlined the basic terms of the settlement agreement. Attorneys for each company then took several weeks to convert their ideas into a legally binding agreement. The entire minitrial process, from initial negotiations to final settlement, took ninety days. Telecredit estimated that the process saved about $1 million in attorneys' fees alone. What had started as a bitter patent infringement battle ended up giving birth to a new form of ADR—the minitrial.

ADVANTAGES OF THE MINITRIAL

Many of the same advantages of the SJT characterize the minitrial: the savings of time and money, the benefits of confidentiality, and the empowerment of business-people to resolve a dispute. The minitrial has some unique advantages as well.

Party Control over the Process

Unlike standard litigation, there are no set procedures for a minitrial. The parties maintain much control over the nature of the process. In private minitrials, the disputants can create their own minitrial process or select established procedures that best meet their needs. Also, in private minitrials, the parties can decide whether or not they wish to employ a neutral advisor to aid in their settlement talks. Regardless of the presence of a neutral advisor, the parties have the opportunity to resolve the conflict by creatively fashioning mutually beneficial results. In court-annexed minitrials, parties can work with the judge to tailor a procedural order that reflects the concerns of the parties.

Maintenance of Business Relationships

Often, conflicting parties may still wish to maintain ongoing business relationships. For example, two companies may have entered into a joint oil drilling and distribution venture. A conflict may arise between these parties over production schedules and payment issues. In the confidential setting of the minitrial, these parties can learn about each other's view of the conflict, express their concerns to each other, and resolve their conflict in a collaborative environment. Without the hostility of an adversarial court battle, these parties are more likely to retain their business relationship.

Expertise of the Neutral Advisor

In standard litigation, judges are normally assigned randomly to cases. Thus, a judge without expertise in the energy field may be asked to rule on highly technical factual and legal issues between two power companies. Parties will have to expend time and effort trying to explain complicated technical matters to the judge and possibly a jury.

Parties opting for a neutral advisor with relevant industry or legal expertise may improve their chances of successfully resolving their dispute. A neutral advisor can ask important questions during the summary presentations that may clarify issues and expose weaknesses in each party's case. The neutral advisor can also mediate the settlement talks based on a greater understanding of the legal or business issues involved. Finally, a neutral advisor can render a credible advisory opinion that may avoid an impasse in negotiations and aid the rapid settlement of a dispute.

DISADVANTAGES OF THE MINITRIAL

The minitrial has many of the same disadvantages as other ADR mechanisms: lack of precedential value, lack of party consent due to the absence of trust or party unfamiliarity with the process, or the strategic use of litigation by an opponent to embarrass a competitor or to defer liability. However, the unusual nature of the minitrial also gives rise to the following specific disadvantages.

Credibility of Witnesses

In some instances, the success or failure of a case may hinge on the credibility of lay and expert witnesses. With limited discovery and summary presentations, a persuasive attorney outlining witness testimony can disguise problems with witness credibility that might arise in either direct or cross-examination of a witness. For example, a panel composed of an experienced neutral advisor and several savvy business executives might be able to assess realistically the testimony of an engineer who may be trying to cover up some construction errors. However, a lawyer in a minitrial may decide merely to summarize the engineer's testimony, making it difficult for the panel to recognize deficiencies in the testimony or to determine fully and accurately the facts.

Need for Court's Legal Interpretation

In some cases, the parties may not disagree about the facts, only about the application of the law to these facts. The dispute might even focus on some novel issue of law that has yet to be addressed by any court. In these cases, the disputants may need a judge to determine these purely legal issues, to deal with past conduct, and to guide future business behavior. In such private minitrials, settlement discussions cannot go forward without a definitive ruling on how the law affects the dispute. For example, Company A may have entered into a marketing strategy for the distribution of its computer software. A competitor, Company B, claims that Company A's conduct violates antitrust law. Company A disagrees but does not deny the facts of its marketing scheme. Here, persuasive attorney presentations or the expertise of a neutral advisor are no substitute for a judicial interpretation of the law.

Unequal Bargaining Power Between the Disputants

Some critics of the minitrial express concern that the problem of unequal bargaining power could be heightened in minitrials in which the parties do not employ a neutral advisor. In standard litigation or court-annexed minitrials, judicial review and approval of a settlement provides some safeguards for the parties. However, there is no judicial protection in private minitrials. Because large companies need to retain good working relationships with other smaller entities, this potential risk should be evaluated before electing the minitrial. Smaller companies may want to consider carefully the selection of a respected, experienced neutral advisor who can reduce this risk through careful mediation of the settlement talks.

CHAPTER CONCLUSION

Both the SJT and the minitrial are important settlement mechanisms that draw on elements of traditional litigation, negotiation, and mediation to successfully resolve

TABLE 5.1   Comparison of Summary Jury Trial and Minitrial Processes

	Summary Jury Trial	**Minitrial**
Party Consent	May be by party consent or court order.	Parties must consent.
Discovery	Normally used after full discovery process completed.	Normally used after limited discovery process.
Administering Entity	Primarily court-supervised.	May be private or court-supervised.
Third-Party Participation	Involves judge and advisory jury. Jury renders advisory verdict and participates in question-and-answer session with parties and their attorneys.	May involve assistance of neutral advisor who may be asked to offer nonbinding opinion of case.
Hearing	Summary presentations before judge and advisory jury. Executives with settlement authority present.	Summary presentations before executives with settlement authority and possibly neutral advisor. Executives and neutral advisor may ask questions during presentations.
Settlement Talks	Judge helps mediate settlement talks after advisory verdict and question-and-answer session with jury.	Neutral advisor will mediate negotiations between parties at completion of presentations.
Binding or Nonbinding	Not binding unless parties agree on settlement terms.	Not binding unless parties agree on settlement terms.

business conflicts. The SJT is primarily a court-annexed process, while the mini-trial is usually handled through private channels. Despite their differences, both methods strive to provide the disputing businesspeople with the opportunity to learn about each other's viewpoint and to make a summary presentation of their view of the conflict. Each mechanism empowers the businesspeople to negotiate creative solutions to their business disputes. The SJT uses the perceptions of lay jurors to encourage settlement talks, while the minitrial relies on the business insight and expertise of company executives and a neutral advisor to help bring about a negotiated result. (See Table 5.1 for an overall comparison of these two processes.)

Business disputants should evaluate the nature of their conflict to determine which method best serves their needs. Cases most appropriate for SJT focus primarily on differing views of how a jury will evaluate evidence or how much a jury will award in the dispute. The litigants may be reluctant to settle their dispute because of their uncertainty surrounding juror perceptions of party documents and testimony or the impact of emotions on a case award. Although the minitrial can be used in a wide range of business disputes, the process is particularly useful in highly technical cases which may be more difficult for judges or lay jurors without industry experience to comprehend.

BEST BUSINESS PRACTICES

Here are some practical tips on how businesspeople can effectively use the SJT and the minitrial to resolve business disputes.

- Participate in negotiation training to maximize the benefits of settlement talks in the SJT and the minitrial.
- Consult with local, state, and federal courts on the availability of SJT programs for resolving business disputes.
- Contact the CPR Institute for Dispute Resolution to garner more information as well as model procedures and forms on the use of the minitrial.
- Provide input to counsel and administering agencies on the desired credentials and industry or legal experience of neutral advisors.
- Establish a checklist or other evaluation tool for determining whether the SJT or minitrial process is appropriate for a particular business dispute.

KEY TERMS

advisory or mock jury, p. 127
advisory verdict, p. 134
"best case" presentations, p. 145
civil justice expense and delay reduction plan, p. 133
conditional summary jury trial, p. 143
court-annexed minitrial, p. 143
information exchange, p. 145
judgment of acquiescence, p. 146

minitrial, p. 143
neutral advisor, p. 144
procedural order, p. 146
question-and-answer session, p. 136
settlement talks, p. 136
summary jury trial (SJT), p. 125
summary presentations, p. 127
The Judicial Improvements Act of
   1990, p. 133

ETHICAL AND LEGAL REVIEW

1. A civil rights action was brought against Jackson County, Illinois arising from the alleged arrest, strip search, imprisonment, and suicide death of Michael Strandell. The parents of Michael Strandell brought the action, seeking $500,000 in damages. After the close of discovery, the defendants filed a motion

to compel the plaintiffs to produce copies of witness statements they had obtained. Plaintiffs argued that these materials were privileged attorney work-product that the defendants should have requested during, not after, the discovery phase. The court denied the defendants' motion. The trial court suggested that, in light of the court's crowded docket, the parties use a SJT to resolve the matter. Citing attorney work-product concerns, the plaintiffs rebuffed the court's recommendation and indicated their readiness for trial. The district court ordered a SJT as authorized under Rule 16 as there was no local rule permitting its use. The plaintiffs again refused, and the district court found the plaintiffs in criminal contempt. Will the appeals court uphold the contempt citation based on the plaintiffs' refusal to use a SJT? [*Strandell v. Jackson County, Ill.,* 838 F. 2d 884 (7th Cir. 1987)]

2. Plaintiffs McKay and Williams, former employees and officers of defendant Ashland Oil Corporation, brought a wrongful discharge action. Both alleged that the defendant had bribed government officials in Middle Eastern countries in violation of the Foreign Corrupt Practices Act. The plaintiffs alleged that claimed investments in a chrome mine were faked to hide these illegal bribes. The plaintiffs further asserted that they were fired for refusing to aid in cover-ups of these illegal activities. A six-week trial was scheduled. Over the objections of the plaintiffs, the district court ordered the parties to participate in a five-day SJT in an effort to settle the case without a trial. The plaintiffs filed a motion for reconsideration with the district court. Will the plaintiffs be required by the appeals court to participate in the SJT? [*McKay v. Ashland Oil, Inc.,* 120 F.R.D. 43 (E.D. Ky. 1988)]

3. American Can Company brought a lawsuit against Wisconsin Electric claiming breach of contract concerning industrial waste sold to the power company for boiler fuel. American Can Company sought $40 million in damages, and Wisconsin Electric countersued for $20 million. The case involved complex, technical information, and a trial was estimated to take as long as seventy-five days. After seven grueling months of discovery, the parties decided to use the minitrial to help resolve their conflict. The parties selected former federal district judge Henry R. Tyler, Jr. to serve as their neutral advisor. The minitrial's information exchange lasted three days. Were American Can Company and Wisconsin Electric able to successfully resolve their dispute through the minitrial? [James F. Henry and Jethro K. Lieberman, *The Manager's Guide to Resolving Legal Disputes.* "Seven Advantages of a Minitrial," pp. 37–39, 1985]

4. Plaintiff Cynthia Hume brought a fair housing case against the defendant, M & C Management. After failing to resolve the conflict, the parties requested a SJT. The district court refused the parties' request for a SJT. In this case, the court determined that it lacked the statutory authority to impanel jurors for a SJT. The judge indicated that under federal law, jurors can only be called to participate in certain types of jury panels; the law does not specifically state their attendance on SJT panels. What are the court's policy reasons for refusing to call jurors to

serve on a SJT panel in this case? Do you agree with the court's decision? [*Hume v. M & C Management,* 129 F.R.D. 506 (N.D. Ohio 1990)]

5. In 1980, Borden filed a $200 million antitrust lawsuit against Texaco regarding a Louisiana natural gas contract. The legal and factual issues were quite complicated. The parties spent thousands of hours in the discovery process, with Texaco alone producing some 300,000 documents. Hoping to limit the ever-increasing demands of discovery, the trial judge scheduled a preliminary jury trial for two and one half years later in hopes of determining the basic terms of the contract. Just a few weeks before the start of trial, the parties agreed to use the minitrial and to present their best cases before an executive from each company. After the "best case" presentations, negotiations started and then broke off. A few days later, the parties began telephone negotiations. Ultimately, the case was resolved without any money changing hands. Instead of awarding monetary damages, the parties renegotiated key terms of the gas supply contract. What five lessons did Texaco's associate general counsel, Charles F. Kazlauskas, indicate that the parties learned from the minitrial? [James F. Henry and Jethro K. Lieberman, *The Manager's Guide to Resolving Legal Disputes.* "Seven Advantages of a Minitrial," pp. 40–42, 1985]

SUGGESTED ADDITIONAL READINGS

Alfini, James J. *Summary Jury Trials in State and Federal Courts: A Comparative Analysis of the Perceptions of Participating Lawyers.* 4 Ohio St. J. on Disp. Resol. 213, 1989.

CPR Practice Guide, The Minitrial. pp. A102-106, A107-109, C22-25, Fall 1988.

Henry, James F., and Jethro K. Lieberman. *The Manager's Guide to Resolving Legal Disputes.* pp. 19–25, 36–47, 48–56, 1985.

Metzloff, Thomas B. *Reconfiguring the Summary Jury Trial.* 41 Duke L. J. 806, 1992.

Ponte, Lucille M. *Putting Mandatory Summary Jury Trial Back on the Docket: Recommendations on the Exercise of Judicial Authority.* 63 Fordham L. Rev. 1069, March 1995.

Part III

ADR ADJUDICATORY MECHANISMS

Chapter 6: Introduction to Commercial Arbitration

Chapter 7: Labor and Employment Arbitration

Chapter 8: International Commercial Arbitration

Chapter 9: Private Judging

In Part II, our primary focus was on the use of alternative dispute resolution (ADR) methods that encourage parties to settle their disputes through various forms of negotiation and mediation. These settlement processes keep the primary responsibility for resolving conflicts in the hands of the disputing parties. However, in Part III, we will examine **ADR adjudicatory mechanisms** that use third-party decision makers, such as arbitrators or private judges who decide the outcome of the conflict for the parties. Although businesspeople play an important role in these dispute mechanisms, their ability to shape the outcome is much more limited. There is also a greater emphasis on the use of lawyers, as these methods reflect many aspects of our adversarial litigation process. Part III will provide an overview of the main ADR adjudicatory mechanisms. Chapter 6 looks at commercial arbitration. Subsequent chapters will specifically address labor and employment arbitration, international commercial arbitration, and private judging.

6

INTRODUCTION TO
COMMERCIAL ARBITRATION

CHAPTER HIGHLIGHTS

In this chapter, you will read and learn about the following:

1. The historical development of U.S. statutory and case law on arbitration.
2. Descriptions of voluntary and court-annexed arbitration.
3. The authority and ethical responsibilities of arbitrators.
4. The role of businesspeople and lawyers in arbitration.
5. The main steps in the typical arbitration process.
6. The advantages and disadvantages of voluntary arbitration to resolve a dispute.
7. The major distinctions between court-annexed and voluntary arbitration proceedings.
8. The limitations on a trial de novo or new trial in court-annexed arbitration.

DEFINING ARBITRATION

Arbitration is an adjudicatory ADR mechanism. Parties submit a disagreement to one or more neutral decision makers called arbitrators. Unlike negotiation or mediation, the arbitrator, not the parties, determines the outcome of the dispute along with any applicable remedies. The arbitration process is more formal than other ADR mechanisms and uses abbreviated, trial-like procedures that are adversarial, rather than collaborative, in nature. Although arbitration has just recently become a widely accepted method of dispute resolution in the United States, it has a lengthy history of successful use in other societies.

The Historical Development of Arbitration

http://
Read about the Chartered Institute of Arbitrators at:
http://www. arbitrators.org

Arbitration is one of the oldest forms of ADR, dating back to ancient Persian, Sumerian, Egyptian, Greek, and Roman civilizations. For example, Athenians used arbitration as an alternative to the expense and complexity of the Athenian justice system; reasons echoed today by many disputants who use arbitration. Arbitration also played a role in the resolution of mercantile disputes in Europe. Private tribunals of merchants connected to guilds and trading companies or court-supervised panels of merchant referees oversaw the process. Some of this European experience carried over to the American colonies. In the colonial United States, arbitration can be traced primarily to Dutch settlers in New York and Quakers in Pennsylvania. At this time, arbitrators dealt primarily with disputes between merchants. These arbitrators were often untrained in the law but well versed in business customs and practices. Arbitration was also relied on to handle personal matters, as exemplified by an arbitration clause contained in George Washington's will to resolve any challenges to distribution of his assets.

The evolution of the English courts led to a decline in the use of arbitration at the end of the eighteenth century and into the nineteenth century. English judges began to view arbitration with suspicion, concerned that arbitrators were usurping their powers and lacking the requisite legal training to interpret party rights and responsibilities. English courts began to routinely overturn arbitral awards, supplanting their own views for those of the arbitrators. Eventually, disputants moved away from the use of arbitration. Likewise, the U.S. courts disfavored arbitration as treading on their traditional authority to adjudicate disputes.

http://
Find the U.S. Code at:
http://law.house. gov/usc.html

However, at the start of the twentieth century, arbitration began to be resurrected as a method for resolving disputes between businesspeople. In 1920, New York passed the first state arbitration statute, which allowed courts to enforce contracts between parties seeking to arbitrate future disputes. The New York statute soon became the model for the first federal arbitration statute, the United States Arbitration Act (now commonly referred to as the Federal Arbitration Act), passed in 1925. The **Federal Arbitration Act (FAA)** was pivotal in the growing acceptance of arbitration to resolve business disputes. The statute promoted the use of arbitration to resolve conflicts involving commercial transactions among businesses in different states or transactions between the United States and foreign countries. The FAA provides parties with the opportunity to resolve their dispute through arbitration rather than the courts. The law also allows parties to seek the assistance of the courts in compelling parties to comply with an arbitration agreement and in enforcing both domestic and foreign arbitral awards.

The **Uniform Arbitration Act** is a state model patterned after the 1920 New York arbitration law. Although some states initially passed statutes antagonistic to arbitration, today nearly all of the states have enacted arbitration acts modeled after the Uniform Arbitration Act. The FAA and state arbitration statutes provide a liberal scheme for the enforcement of arbitration agreements, placing arbitration agreements on an equal footing with other commercial contracts. Under these statutes, a written arbitration agreement, similar to any other written contract, is valid, enforceable, and irrevocable. The only exceptions are those legal or equitable grounds for revocation available for any contract under law.

With the passage of the FAA and applicable state laws, the previous judicial hostility toward arbitration began to dissipate. The heavy backlog of court cases and the successful use of arbitration by many disputants have encouraged the courts, and in particular the Supreme Court, to view arbitration more favorably in recent years. Today arbitration is used in a variety of commercial disputes involving business contracts, intellectual and real property rights, government agencies, construction, finances, health care, insurance, international trade, labor, and employment. Although originally viewed as a method to resolve disputes between two or more businesspeople, arbitration is now also used to resolve conflicts between businesses and their customers. Arbitration was even used to help resolve disputes over athlete disqualifications at the 1996 Olympic Games in Atlanta.

The demand for arbitration has skyrocketed. The American Arbitration Association, a leading nonprofit organization, reported that its arbitration filings were up 34% between 1986 and 1991, with 62,000 cases nationwide totaling more than $4.5 billion in dispute claims. The number of securities arbitration filings has also dramatically risen from about 2,800 in 1987 to nearly 6,000 filings in 1997. The following case illustrates how the FAA may preempt state laws that conflict with its broad acceptance and promotion of arbitration to resolve business disputes.

http://

Learn more about the American Arbitration Association by accessing this site: http://www.adr.org

SECURITIES INDUSTRY ASS'N V. CONNOLLY

883 F. 2d 1114 (1st Cir. 1989), cert. denied, 495 U.S. 956 (1990)

FACT SUMMARY

In Massachusetts, the Secretary of State's office has regulatory authority for secured transactions. That office became concerned when investors who opened brokerage accounts were required to give up their right to go to court over investment disputes. In an effort to promote fairness to customers in investment disputes, the Secretary of State's office enacted certain state securities regulations. These regulations indicated, in part, that a mandatory pre-dispute arbitration agreement (PDAA) between investors and brokers was unethical and grounds for revocation of a broker's license. In addition, brokers must provide a complete, written disclosure to investors of the legal impact of agreeing to a PDAA. The Securities Industry Association brought an action against then Secretary of State Michael Connolly, claiming that the regulations were unconstitutional in light of the terms of the FAA. The trial court granted summary judgment for the Securities Industry

Association. The secretary of state's office appealed that decision.

OPINION: *JUDGE SELYA*

Congress passed the Federal Arbitration Act (FAA) . . . to help legitimate arbitration and make it more readily useful to disputants. The hope has long been that the Act could serve as a therapy for the ailment of the crowded docket.

We are asked to decide today if certain regulations . . . are preempted by the FAA. . . .

The Regulations not only regulate, they do so in a manner patently inhospitable to arbitration. . . .

The Supremacy Clause of Article VI of the federal Constitution prevents the states from impinging overmuch on federal law and policy. Preemption—the vehicle by which the Supremacy Clause is generally enforced—always boils down to a matter of congressional intent. And, because Congress has not expressly delineated the preemptive reach of the FAA, our task is to determine the extent of any implied preemption vis-a-vis the state's regulations.

[It] has been said that implied preemption prospers when Congress intends its enactments "to occupy a given field to the exclusion of state law." That is not the case here: Congress did not want the FAA to occupy the entire field of arbitration. State law may also be preempted "when it actually conflicts with federal law."

Whatever labels may be affixed, the pivot upon which our inquiry turns remains constant: Where Congress has failed explicitly to detail the dimensions of displacement, courts must decide if "the state law disturbs too much the congressionally declared scheme. . . ." Put another way, a state law or regulation cannot take root if it looms as an obstacle to

achievement of the full purposes and ends which Congress has itself set out to accomplish.

Congress, we are told, enacted the FAA to relieve parties from what, even two-thirds of a century ago, was characterized as "the costliness and delays of litigation."

In sum, the legislative history of the FAA, like its text, indicates that the courts must receive the Act hospitably and defend its "mechanisms vigilantly and with some fervor."

Appellants conceded before the district court . . . and on appeal that the regulations apply only to arbitration agreements. They suggest, however, that this bespeaks no unfriendliness. The Commonwealth treats arbitration agreements like other contracts between businesses and consumers; that is, it regulates them as extensively as necessary for the public weal. In our view, that self-congratulatory casuistry will not wash. Indeed, we think it evident that it was precisely this sort of categorization error which Congress sought to cure when it enacted the FAA. The FAA prohibits a state from taking more stringent action addressed specifically, and limited, to arbitration contracts.

That is not to say that a state can do nothing about a perceived problem. The Commonwealth's powers remain great, so long as used evenhandedly. The FAA does not prohibit judicial relief from arbitration contracts which are shown to result from fraud or enormous (unfair) economic imbalance of the sort sufficient to avoid contracts of all types.

Appellants also urge us to find that, notwithstanding the general rule, Congress carved out an exception to the Act by permitting states concurrently to regulate securities transactions.

Simply put, nothing in the Securities Act, the Exchange Act, or the grant of concurrent power to the states to regulate securities manifests a congressional intent to limit or prohibit waiver of a judicial forum for a particular claim, or to abridge the sweep of the FAA.

The long and short of it is that we can find no evidence of a clear congressional command to override the unambiguous proarbitration mandate of the FAA in the securities field.

State law need not clash head on with a federal enactment in order to be pre-empted. If state law "stands as an obstacle to the accomplishment of the full purpose and objectives of Congress," it must topple.

http://
Read about the SEC's securities arbitration regulations at this site:
http://www.sec.gov

Discussion Questions

1. According to the appeals court, what was the congressional intent behind the passage of the FAA?
2. What are some bases for judicial relief from arbitration agreements that do not offend the FAA?
3. Do you think that states should have the authority to regulate arbitration agreements to protect investors' access to the courts for securities disputes?

MAIN ASPECTS OF VOLUNTARY ARBITRATION

Most arbitrations are voluntary with parties agreeing to submit their disputes to an arbitrator, who renders a final decision or award. **Voluntary arbitrations** are usually binding, with parties agreeing in advance to comply with the terms of the arbitrator's decision. There is little or no opportunity for a judicial appeal, although in some instances, the parties may decide that the award of the arbitrator will be non-binding or merely advisory. Based on the arbitrator's advisory opinion, the parties may decide whether to negotiate, mediate, or litigate their dispute.

Determining Procedures

As there is no single uniform set of arbitration rules or procedures, numerous community, national, and international entities offer to administer the arbitration process based on their own unique set of procedures. Unlike litigation, the parties can design their own arbitration process, referred to as an **ad hoc proceeding,** or follow the established rules of administering organizations, such as the American Arbitration Association, the International Chamber of Commerce in Paris, or Judicial, Arbitration, and Mediation Services (JAMS)/EnDispute. In some cases, parties may use a number of ADR processes, including arbitration, to handle their conflict. For example, IBM and Fujitsu used a structured ADR process that combined aspects of negotiation, mediation, and arbitration to resolve an intellectual property case concerning operating systems software. A popular hybrid process is called **med-arb.** In med-arb the parties first attempt to mediate the dispute. If unsuccessful, they then have two options: (1) to allow the mediator to take on the

http://
Find out more about JAMS/EnDispute at:
http://www.jams—endispute.com

role of an arbitrator and decide the outcome of the dispute or (2) to dismiss the mediator and select a new third-party neutral advisor to act as arbitrator. In a **rules by reference** proceeding, the disputants elect to follow the established procedures of an administering organization. Although no two arbitrations are identical, most arbitration processes are characterized by an agreement to arbitrate, selection of an arbitrator or arbitral panel, pre-hearing preparation, the arbitration hearing, the arbitration or arbitral award, and post-award actions.

Agreement to Arbitrate

Voluntary arbitration is a creature of contract. A separate arbitration agreement or an arbitration clause within an existing business contract must exist before a disputing party can initiate the arbitration process. In some instances, a court may infer an arbitration agreement based on the business conduct of, or verbal promises made between, the parties. However, to avoid confusion or misunderstanding, it is best to enter into a written agreement to arbitrate. The arbitration agreement will normally outline the types of disputes subject to arbitration, the authority of the arbitrator, the substantive law to be applied to the dispute, and the arbitration rules or procedures to be followed.

There are two types of arbitration agreements: the **pre-dispute arbitration agreement (PDAA)** and the submission agreement. A PDAA is an agreement or clause inserted into a contract *prior to any dispute* that requires the parties to use arbitration if there are any future disagreements. (See Figure 6.1.) For example, the securities industry mandates that customers wishing to open a brokerage account must enter into a PDAA with the brokerage firm. Under the PDAA, the investor and the brokerage house agree that they will use arbitration if they have any future conflicts over trades or other financial dealings.

The second type of written agreement, the **submission agreement,** is a contract to arbitrate that the parties enter into *after a dispute* has already arisen. (See Figure 6.2.) Perhaps two firms have entered into a contract for the purchase of computer hardware and software. The initial sales contract does not contain an arbitration clause. If a dispute arises over the payment terms and warranties for the computers,

---

FIGURE 6.1 Sample Pre-Dispute Arbitration Agreement (PDAA)

Any controversy, dispute, or claim arising out of, in connection with, or in relation to the interpretation, performance, or breach of this agreement shall be resolved, at the request of either party, by a general reference conducted by a retired judge from the panel of Judicial Arbitration & Mediation Services, Inc. (J*A*M*S), appointed pursuant to the provisions of California Code of Civil Procedure Section 638(1) *et seq.* The parties intend this general reference agreement to be specifically enforceable in accordance with said Section 638(1). If the parties cannot agree upon a member of the J*A*M*S panel, one shall be appointed by the Presiding Judge in the County in which the matter is to be heard.

Source: Reprinted with permission of JAMS/EnDispute.

FIGURE 6.2   Sample Submission Agreement

Structuring the Arbitration Hearing

The Submission Agreement is important in that it sets forth the rights of the parties and the rules and procedures to be followed at the arbitration hearing. The parties must decide whether they prefer to plan a potential arbitration proceeding before a dispute arises or if they would rather postpone those determinations until they actually face an arbitration hearing.

EXHIBIT FUTURE DISPUTE SUBMISSION AGREEMENT

Pre-Hearing Conference

The arbitrator(s) shall schedule a pre-hearing conference to reach agreement on procedural matters, arrange for the exchange of information, obtain stipulations, and attempt to narrow the issues.

Discovery

OPTION 1: The parties will submit a proposed discovery schedule to the arbitrator(s) at the pre-hearing conference. The scope and duration of discovery will be within the sole discretion of the arbitrator(s).

OPTION 2: It is our objective to expedite the arbitration proceedings by placing the following limitations on discovery:

a. Each party may propound only one interrogatory requesting the names and addresses of the witnesses to be called at the arbitration hearing.

b. On a date to be determined at the pre-hearing conference, each party may serve one request for the production of documents. The documents are to be exchanged two weeks later.

c. Each party may depose _____ witnesses. Each deposition must be concluded within four hours and all depositions must be taken within thirty (30) days of the pre-hearing conference. Any party deposing an opponent's expert must pay the expert's fee for attending the deposition.

OPTION 3: It is our objective to expedite the arbitration proceedings by eliminating discovery as provided by the Discovery Act pursuant to CCP §1985, et seq. Instead of discovery, the parties agree to the following exchange of information:

a. Either party can make a written demand for lists of the witnesses to be called or the documents to be introduced at the hearing.

The demand must be received prior to the pre-hearing conference.

b. The lists must be served within fifteen (15) days of the demand.

c. No depositions may be taken for discovery.

The Hearing

I. The parties must file briefs with the arbitrator(s) at least three (3) days before the hearing, specifying the facts each intends to prove and analyzing the applicable law.

II. The parties have the right to representation by legal counsel throughout the arbitration proceedings.

III. Judicial rules of evidence and procedure relating to the conduct at the hearing, examination of witnesses, and presentation of evidence do not apply. Any relevant evidence, including hearsay, shall be admitted by the arbitrator if it is the sort of evidence on which responsible persons are accustomed to rely on in the conduct of serious affairs, regardless of the admissibility of such evidence in a court of law.

IV. Within reasonable limitations, both sides at the hearing may call and examine witnesses for relevant testimony, introduce relevant exhibits or other documents, cross-examine or impeach witnesses who shall have testified orally on any matter relevant to the issues, and otherwise rebut evidence, as long as these rights are exercised in an efficient and expeditious manner.

V. Any party desiring a stenographic record may secure a court reporter to attend the proceedings. The requesting party must notify the other parties of the arrangements in advance of the hearing and must pay for the cost incurred.

The Award

I. The decision shall be based on the evidence introduced at the hearing, including all logical and reasonable inferences therefrom. The arbitrator(s) may grant any remedy or relief which is just and equitable.

II. The award must be made in writing and signed by either the arbitrator or a majority of the arbitrators if a panel is used. It shall contain a concise statement of the reasons in support of the decision.

III. The award must by mailed promptly to the parties, but no later than thirty (30) days from the closing of the hearing.

IV. The award can be judicially enforced (confirmed, corrected, or vacated) pursuant to §1285 et seq. of the Code of Civil Procedure. It is final and binding and there is no direct appeal from the award on the grounds of error in the application of the law.

Fees and Expenses
Unless otherwise agreed, each party must pay its own witness fees.

Unless otherwise agreed, each party must pay its pro rata share of the arbitrator's fees.
OPTION 1: The arbitrator has the authority to award attorney fees to the prevailing party.
OPTION 2: The arbitrator must award attorney fees to the prevailing party.
OPTION 3: Each party must pay its own attorney fees.

Source: Reprinted with permission of JAMS/EnDispute.

the parties may decide to arbitrate their conflict and will enter into a submission agreement. Once a PDAA or submission agreement is in place, either party may demand arbitration pursuant to the terms of the agreement. (See Figures 6.3 and 6.4.)

In some instances, critics of arbitration expressed concern that some PDAAs are being unfairly inserted into standardized or form contracts with consumers (adhesion contracts). In selling goods and services to consumers, many businesses use standardized contracts that do not allow for any meaningful negotiation of terms between the parties. Consumers must either accept the contract as written or forfeit the chance to receive the goods or services. In this situation, consumers do not truly have the opportunity to explore and select conflict resolution methods that best meet their needs. For public policy reasons, courts will sometimes not enforce adhesion contracts that are too burdensome on one of the parties.

Even if a valid agreement to arbitrate exists, a court may be called on to decide the issue of arbitrability. Arbitrability deals with a collection of issues regarding whether a particular dispute was truly intended to be, or should be, resolved through arbitration. There are two types of arbitrability: procedural and substantive. In *AT&T Technologies, Inc., v. Communication Workers of America* [475 U.S. 643 (1986)], the Supreme Court defined these concepts and spelled out the split responsibilities between the courts and arbitrators for arbitrability. Unless otherwise specifically agreed to by the parties, arbitrators determine procedural arbitrability, while courts decide issues of substantive arbitrability.

Specifically, **procedural arbitrability** focuses on whether the party seeking arbitration has fully complied with all procedural prerequisites to arbitration. For example, an arbitration clause might require the initiating party (the claimant) to give thirty days' notice of an intention to seek arbitration to the other party (the respondent) in the conflict. If the claimant fails to provide this notice, the arbitrator can determine that the dispute is not procedurally arbitrable until the claimant has done so.

Courts determine **substantive arbitrability** by answering three basic questions: (1) does an agreement to arbitrate exist? (2) is the dispute within the coverage of the arbitration clause? and (3) are there any legal or equitable limits on the use of arbitration to resolve this dispute?

In deciding whether an agreement to arbitrate exists, the court must look at written or verbal agreements as well as any previous dealings between the parties that

FIGURE 6.3 Sample Demand Form for Arbitration

American Arbitration Association

COMMERCIAL ARBITRATION RULES

To institute proceedings, please send three copies of this demand and the arbitration agreement, with the administrative fee as provided in the rules, to the AAA. Send the original demand to the respondent.

DEMAND FOR ARBITRATION

DATE: _____

TO: Name _____
(of the Party on Whom the Demand Is Made)

Address _____

City and State _____ ZIP Code _____

Telephone (   ) _____ Fax _____

Name of Representative _____
(if Known)

Name of Firm (if Applicable) _____

Representative's Address _____

City and State _____ ZIP Code _____

Telephone (   ) _____ Fax _____

The named claimant, a party to an arbitration agreement contained in a written contract, dated _____ _____ and providing for arbitration under the Commercial Arbitration Rules of the American Arbitration Association, hereby demands arbitration thereunder.

THE NATURE OF THE DISPUTE:

THE CLAIM OR RELIEF SOUGHT (the Amount, if Any):

TYPES OF BUSINESS: Claimant _____ Respondent _____

HEARING LOCALE REQUESTED: _____
(City and State)

You are hereby notified that copies of our arbitration agreement and this demand are being filed with the American Arbitration Association at its _____ office, with a request that it commence administration of the arbitration. Under the rules, you may file an answering statement within ten days after notice from the administrator.

Signed _____ Title _____
(May Be Signed by a Representative)

Name of Claimant _____

Address (to Be Used in Connection with This Case) _____

City and State _____ ZIP Code _____

Telephone (   ) _____ Fax _____

Name of Representative _____

Name of Firm (if Applicable) _____

Representative's Address _____

City and State _____ ZIP Code _____

Telephone (   ) _____ Fax _____

☐ **MEDIATION is a nonbinding process. The mediator assists the parties in working out a solution that is acceptable to them. If you wish for the AAA to contact the other parties to ascertain whether they wish to mediate this matter, please check this box (there is no additional administrative fee for this service).**

Form C2–6/93

Source: Reprinted with permission of the American Arbitration Association.

FIGURE 6.4 Sample Submission Form for Dispute Resolution

American Arbitration Association

SUBMISSION TO DISPUTE RESOLUTION

Date: _____

The named parties hereby submit the following dispute for resolution under the _____
_____ Rules* of the American Arbitration Association:

Procedure Selected: ☐ Binding arbitration   ☐ Mediation settlement

                            ☐ Other _____
                                                  (Describe)

FOR INSURANCE CASES ONLY:

_____   _____ to _____   _____
Policy Number   Effective Dates   Applicable Policy Limits

_____   _____
Date of Incident   Location

Insured: _____   Claim Number: _____

Name(s) of Claimant(s)	Check if a Minor	Amount Claimed
_____	☐	_____
_____	☐	_____

Nature of Dispute and/or Injuries Alleged (attach additional sheets if necessary):

Place of Hearing: _____

We agree that, if binding arbitration is selected, we will abide by and perform any award rendered hereunder and that a judgment may be entered on the award.

To Be Completed by the Claimant	*To Be Completed by the Respondent*
Name of Party	Name of Party
Address	Address
City, State, and ZIP Code	City, State, and ZIP Code
( ) _____ Telephone ____ Fax	( ) _____ Telephone ____ Fax
Signature†	Signature†
Name of Party's Attorney or Representative	Name of Party's Attorney or Representative
Address	Address
City, State, and ZIP Code	City, State, and ZIP Code
( ) _____ Telephone ____ Fax	( ) _____ Telephone ____ Fax
Signature†	Signature†

Please file three copies with the A.A.A.

* *If you have a question as to which rules apply, please contact the A.A.A.*
† *Signatures of all parties are required for arbitration.*   Form G1–7/90

Source: Reprinted with permission of the American Arbitration Association.

may show an intention to arbitrate disputes. Often parties may go to court to litigate whether or not an agreement to arbitrate actually exists in their situation. In the following case, the court must decide whether or not the parties have agreed to arbitrate their dispute.

J & C DYEING, INC., V. DRAKON, INC.
93 Civ. 4283, 1994 U.S. Dist. LEXIS 15194 (S.D.N.Y. 1994)

FACT SUMMARY

Between February and June 1992, Drakon, Inc. ("Drakon"), a New Jersey garment manufacturer, submitted purchase orders for yarn to J & C Dyeing, Inc. ("J & C"), a North Carolina yarn dyer and converter. Drakon instructed J & C to ship the yarn directly to Zoltan Toth Knitting Company in Pennsylvania. J & C returned confirmation slips to Drakon, which contained clauses indicating that all disputes between them should be resolved through arbitration in New York City. Drakon never signed the confirmation slips or discussed the use of arbitration with J & C. When problems arose with the yarn, Drakon withheld payment and sued J & C in the Pennsylvania courts in May 1993. J & C then brought a motion to compel arbitration in the New York courts against Drakon, claiming that the parties had an agreement to arbitrate any disputes based on the arbitration clauses contained in the confirmation slips.

OPINION: *JUDGE PIERRE N. LEVAL*

. . . This case presents a classic example of [a] battle of the forms under Section 2–207 of the Uniform Commercial Code. Drakon sent purchase orders to J & C. The shipments of yarn sent by J & C in response to Drakon's orders were accompanied by confirmation slips, all of which contained an arbitration provision. Both parties agree that a contract exists; they disagree as to its terms. The question, then, is whether the arbitration clause contained in the confirmation forms became a term of contract between J & C and Drakon.

U.C.C. § 2-207(2) provides that "additional terms [in an acceptance or confirmation] are to be construed as proposals for addition to the contract." Where, as here, the transaction is between merchants, the additional terms become part of the contract unless (a) the offer expressly limits acceptance to the terms of the offer; (b) they materially alter it; or (c) notification of objection to them has already been given or is given within a reasonable time after notice of them is received. N.Y. U.C.C. § 2-207(2).

Thus, the arbitration clause will be deemed part of the agreement if it falls under one of these three exceptions. Because the parties agree that neither (a) nor (c) apply to their agreement, our analysis is limited to whether the arbitration clause materially alters the contract.

The decision of the New York Court of Appeals in *Marlene Indus. Corp. v. Carnac Textiles, Inc.,* 45 N. Y. 2d 327, 408 N.Y. S. 2d 410, 380 N.E. 2d 239 (N.Y. 1978) is dispositive. (footnote omitted). In *Marlene,* the purchaser placed an oral request for fabrics followed by a written purchase order. An arbitration provision was not mentioned during the oral request and was not included in the purchase order. The seller then sent a confirmation which contained an arbitration clause and instructed the buyer to sign and return a copy of the confirmation. Neither party signed the other's form, and a dispute arose. The seller sought arbitration.

Applying U.C.C. § 2-207(2), the court refused to include the arbitration provision as a term of the parties' agreement. The court explained that "by agreeing to arbitrate a party waives in large part many of his normal rights under substantive and procedural law of the State, and it would be unfair to infer such a significant waiver on the basis of anything less than a clear indication of intent." . . . The court concluded that "it is clear that an arbitration clause is a material addition which can become part of a contract only if it is expressly assented to by both parties." . . .

In certain circumstances, an agreement to arbitrate can be implied from the course of dealing or custom and usage in the trade. However, this must be supported by "evidence which affirmatively establishes that the parties agreed to arbitrate their disputes." . . .

Here, it has not been "affirmatively established" that the parties agreed to arbitrate their disputes. Drakon neither signed any of the confirmation orders, nor otherwise expressly agreed to be bound by the arbitration clause. In addition, the course of dealing between Drakon and J & C does not demonstrate that the parties intended to arbitrate their disputes. Although Drakon did not object to the arbitration clause, the mere retention of confirmation slips without any additional conduct indicative of a desire to arbitrate cannot bind Drakon, for it does not rise to the level of assent required to bind parties to arbitration provisions. . . .

Nor does the fact that arbitration is a common method of dispute resolution in the textile industry require a different outcome. The prevalence of arbitration in the textile industry "is not an acceptable substitute . . . for finding a specific agreement to arbitrate." . . . We likewise find no merit in the fact that Drakon referred to one of J & C's confirmation slips in correspondence. A single reference to a confirmation number, without more, is not a sufficient basis for inferring an agreement to arbitrate. . . .

The second Circuit's decision in *Pervel Indus., Inc. v. T M Wallcovering, Inc.,* 871 F. 2d 7 (2d Cir. 1989) is also distinguishable. There the court held that a fabric purchaser was required to arbitrate where it manifested its assent to arbitration clauses by signing and returning the order confirmations containing the clauses and retained the other forms without objection. See also *Genesco, Inc. v. T. Kakiuchi & Co., Ltd.,* 815 F. 2d 840, 845-46 (2d Cir. 1987)(arbitration clause binding where buyer returned numerous confirmation forms with signatures of high-ranking officers and as to unsigned forms, where buyer and seller enjoyed a "long standing and on-going relationship").

For the foregoing reasons, J & C's petition to compel arbitration is denied.

Discussion Questions

1. Do you think that Drakon should have been required to arbitrate the breach of contract dispute?
2. Do you agree with the court that an arbitration clause materially alters a commercial contract?
3. What should companies like J & C do to ensure compliance with arbitration clauses contained in their confirmation slips?

The second issue of substantive arbitrability considers whether the conflict between the parties is covered under the terms of the arbitration agreement. In some instances, parties may claim that their arbitration agreement did not intend to use arbitration to resolve a particular type of dispute. For example, two businesses enter into a trademark licensing agreement that contains an arbitration clause. The clause states that any disputes that arise under the terms of the contract will be handled through arbitration. At a later point in time, a conflict develops and one of the parties tries to bring a tort claim against the other in court. The claimant may assert that the agreed-upon arbitration clause was only intended to cover contract claims, not tort actions, and therefore does not cover the dispute in question.

Under the earlier-cited *AT&T* case, the courts are expected to broadly interpret arbitration clauses or agreements under the concept of the **presumption of arbitrability.** Today, if a conflict is arguably covered under the terms of the arbitration agreement, courts will normally find that the parties intended that the dispute be processed through arbitration. In determining whether the dispute is within the terms of an arbitration agreement, courts will favor the use of arbitration. When an agreement to arbitrate exists, parties challenging its use face a heavy presumption in favor of the arbitrability of a dispute.

A party may also try to avoid arbitration by claiming that there are legal or equitable limits on the use of arbitration in a particular dispute. Normally, a party will raise standard contract grounds for rendering the arbitration agreement unenforceable. For example, a consumer may have signed an agreement to borrow money from a lending institution. Later, it may be determined that the lender defrauded the consumer in the lending process. Because the consumer had signed the agreement under a fraud, the arbitration clause in that agreement would be invalid.

In certain situations, a party may argue that under law only the judiciary has jurisdiction to resolve particular disputes. For example, earlier courts once determined that only judges could resolve certain statutory disputes such as Title VII or other federal statutory discrimination claims. These claims were viewed as not susceptible to arbitration (not arbitrable). However, recent judicial decisions have begun to expand the nature of disputes that may be arbitrable, which now include the resolution of many statutory and Title VII disputes.

DEGAETANO V. SMITH BARNEY, INC.
1996 U.S. Dist. LEXIS 1140 (S.D. N.Y. 1996), 70 Fair Empl. Prac. Cas. (BNA) 401

FACT SUMMARY

Plaintiff Alicia DeGaetano filed a gender discrimination and tort suit against defendants Smith Barney, Inc., her former employer, and Frederick Hessler, her former manager at Smith Barney. Plaintiff was hired as a financial analyst for Smith Barney in July 1993. When hired, she signed an agreement entitled "Principles of Employment," which included a dispute resolution clause. The clause allowed employment disputes to be handled initially through an internal grievance process and subsequently through binding arbitration administered through the New York Stock Exchange. The clause explicitly stated that the dispute resolution procedures applied to employment discrimination claims under Title VII of the Civil Rights Act of 1964 and any other federal, state, or local antidiscrimination laws. The agreement advised employees that it was their responsibility to review and understand the dispute resolution procedures and to contact Human Resources if they had any questions. In 1993 and 1994, the plaintiff received updated copies of the employee handbook, which restated these dispute resolution procedures and terms.

In March 1994, the plaintiff was assigned to Smith Barney's Public Finance Division's Healthcare Group under the supervision of defendant Hessler. Between August 1994 and January 1995, plaintiff alleged that her supervisor made unwelcome sexual advances and advised her on numerous occasions that her performance evaluations, promotion, and bonuses would depend on whether or not she submitted to his sexual demands. The plaintiff claims she repeatedly told Hessler that she wanted only a professional business relationship. However, he purportedly persisted in his sexual advances and statements. DeGaetano eventually sought intervention from Smith Barney's Human Resources department, but she was told that no action would be taken against Hessler. In February 1995, the plaintiff alleges she was forced to resign from her position because of the continued pressure from Hessler and Smith Barney's refusal to take any action against him.

In January 1995, the plaintiff filed a complaint with the Equal Employment Opportunity Commission which granted her the right to bring her action in federal court. In March 1995, the plaintiff brought this action based on violations of Title VII of the Civil Rights Act of 1964, as well as New York state and city antidiscrimination laws. She also brought a tort action against defendant Hessler for intentional infliction of emotional distress. The defendants demanded arbitration, and the plaintiff refused to submit to arbitration. The defendants made a motion to compel arbitration under the Federal Arbitration Act.

OPINION: *DISTRICT JUDGE DENISE COTE*

The United States Arbitration Act. . . . "reflects a legislative recognition of the 'desirability of arbitration as an alternative to the complications of litigation,'" and "reversed centuries of judicial hostility to arbitration agreements." . . . The Act was designed to allow parties to avoid the costliness and delays of litigation and to place arbitration agreements upon the same footing as other contracts. . . .

The burden of demonstrating. . . . whether Congress intended to preclude the arbitrability of a claim founded on statutory rights—is on the party opposing arbitration. . . . In order to establish that Congress intended to exclude Title VII claims from arbitration under the Act, the Court must look to the statute's text or legislative history, or infer such an intent "from the inherent conflict between arbitration and the statute's underlying purposes." . . . Throughout this inquiry, the Court must keep in mind that "questions of arbitrability must be addressed with a healthy regard for the federal policy favoring arbitration." . . .

As recent Supreme Court decisions have made it clear, the plaintiff is faced with a difficult task in arguing that Congress must have intended to preclude arbitration when it enacted Title VII because of important public policies behind the statute. See *Gilmer*, 500 U.S. at 23 (Age Discrimination in Employment Act ("ADEA") claims may be subject to compulsory arbitration); *Rodriguez de Quijas,* 490 U.S. at 484 (Securities Act of 1933); McMahon, 482 U.S. at 227-38 (Section 10(b) of the Securities Exchange Act of 1934); *Id.* at 234-42 (civil provisions of Racketeers Influenced and Corrupt Organizations Act ("RICO")); *Mitsubishi,* 473 U.S. at 628-40 (Sherman Antitrust Act). The Second Circuit has extended the above-cited line of cases to claims arising under the Employment Retirement Income Security Act ("ERISA"), see *Bird*, 926 F. 2d at 117, and New York's Court of Appeals has followed suit with respect to claims arising under New York's Human Rights Law. . . . Finally, and although not binding authority, other circuits have held that, in the wake of *Gilmer,* Title VII claims are also subject to compulsory arbitration pursuant to the Act. . . .

. . . The plaintiff does not dispute signing the Agreement, which according to its terms, unambiguously obligates plaintiff to comply with the Arbitration Policy. . . .

The crux of plaintiff's argument pertains to . . . whether Congress intended Title VII claims to be nonarbitrable. Plaintiff argues that, as a matter of law, Smith Barney cannot require employees to prospectively waive "substantive rights" under Title VII, including the right to attorney's fees, punitive damages, and injunctive relief. . . .

In making her argument, plaintiff fails to point out where, either in the text of Title VII or its legislative history, Congress has stated its intent "to preclude a waiver of judicial remedies" by means of arbitration. . . . This is not surprising, however, because the text of Title VII, itself evidences a clear Congressional intent to make arbitration an alternative method of dispute resolution. Section 118 of the 1991 amendments to Title VII states, in relevant part:

> Where appropriate and to the extent authorized by law, the use of alternative means of dispute resolution including.
> . . . arbitration, is encouraged to resolve disputes arising under the Acts or provisions of federal law amended by this title.
> (citation omitted) . . . . Further, plaintiff has not shown, and the Court cannot find any evidence in Title VII's legislative history that Congress intended to preclude the arbitrability of claims under Title VII.

Plaintiff's argument, apparently, is to say that even if arbitration is generally permissible under Title VII, this particular arbitration agreement, which, as stated before, precludes certain remedies (attorney's fees, punitive damages, and injunctive relief) is inherently inconsistent with the purposes of Title VII. . . . The mere fact that these statutory remedies may be unavailable in the arbitral forum does not in itself establish that Title VII claims must be resolved in a court of law. As the Supreme Court in Mitsubishi stated:

> Having made the bargain to arbitrate, the party should be held to it unless Congress itself has evinced an intention to preclude a waiver of judicial remedies for the statutory rights at issue.

. . . [T]here is no inherent conflict between arbitration of plaintiff's complaint against Smith Barney and Title VII's underlying purposes. Although arbitration may not afford the full panoply of remedies otherwise available in a court of law,

> "So long as the prospective litigant effectively may vindicate [his or her] statutory cause of action in the arbitral forum, the statute will continue to serve both its remedial and deterrent function."

. . . For the reasons set forth above, defendants' motion to compel arbitration is granted. Defendants' motion for attorneys' fees is denied. The action is hereby stayed pending arbitration.

Discussion Questions

1. Which party has the burden of proving that the discrimination claim is not arbitrable?
2. Why did the court determine that Congress did not intend to preclude the use of arbitration for Title VII claims?
3. Will a limit on the availability of statutory remedies affect the arbitrability of this dispute?

Selection of an Arbitrator or Arbitral Panel

An important aspect of party control over the arbitration process is the selection of the **arbitrator or arbitral panel.** The disputing parties, usually in consultation with their attorneys, are free to choose the third-party decision maker based on the method of selection they have consented to in their arbitration agreement. Depending on the applicable procedures, the parties may decide to choose one arbitrator or a three-arbitrator panel.

The mutually agreed-upon arbitrator is sometimes named in the initial arbitration agreement. Otherwise, the parties may decide to review lists of qualified arbitrators from administering organizations once a dispute arises. For example, the AAA provides parties with identical lists of potential arbitrators. The parties are given ten days to review the list and cross off the names of arbitrators that are unacceptable to them. If a party does not return the list within the allotted time, it is assumed that all the arbitrators on the list are acceptable. The AAA will then compare the lists to find the names of arbitrators acceptable to both parties. If the parties cannot agree on suitable arbitrators, the AAA may select appropriate neutral arbitrators.

In considering an arbitrator, the disputants will usually review a brief biography provided by the administering organization that outlines the arbitrator's professional background, educational credentials, and industry experience. In addition, parties may address other character traits such as the arbitrator's reputation for attentiveness, objectivity, clear judgment, and integrity. Both parties must trust and respect the chosen arbitrator or arbitral panel to feel that their concerns and issues will be properly evaluated.

An arbitrator may be a lawyer, a retired judge, or an experienced businessperson who is familiar with a particular industry or type of dispute. Businesspeople are used to evaluating complex business problems and can bring vital industry knowledge to the decision-making process. For example, in an intellectual property dispute over rights to a new software program, it may be more useful to select a businessperson with extensive experience in the software industry than a lawyer without it.

The arbitrator's substantive and procedural powers derive from the terms of the arbitration agreement. Arbitrators typically possess certain procedural responsibilities, such as helping the parties to determine hearing dates, issuing subpoenas, ordering discovery, presiding over the arbitration hearing, and determining which evidence to accept or reject in a case.

More important, arbitrators have the substantive authority to decide issues of law and fact in the dispute and to render an **arbitral award.** Typically the parties will agree on a choice-of-law provision that specifies which state's or country's substantive law will apply to the dispute. In interpreting the parties' rights, arbitrators may not add to, delete from, or modify the terms of the parties' contractual obligations.

In addition, the arbitrator must fashion appropriate **arbitration remedies** for the award. The arbitrator has broad authority to determine remedies, provided that the remedies do not violate public policy or exceed the arbitrator's contractual authority. Usually arbitrators have the authority to award equitable remedies, including specific performance and injunctive relief. Arbitrators may also award remedies at law, such as compensatory, consequential, and liquidated damages, as well as interest on such damages.

In some arbitration proceedings, the parties may agree in advance to limit the arbitrator's power to award damages to a mutually agreed-upon range of damages, setting a high and a low figure that is not disclosed to the arbitrator. Under **high-low arbitration,** if the arbitrator's award is below the low figure, the losing party will pay the predetermined low figure. If the award exceeds the high figure, the prevailing party will receive only the preset high figure. Parties use this method when the only real issue between them is the amount of damages to be awarded, not the issue of liability.

In the past, courts have implied that arbitrators cannot award punitive damages for a number of public policy reasons. However, in recent years, court decisions have tended to allow arbitrators to award punitive damages as long as they do not expressly violate the arbitrator's contractual authority.

In addition, the use of commercial arbitration to resolve a wide variety of disputes has grown extensively and forms a significant supplement to the judicial system. Commercial arbitrators therefore undertake serious responsibilities to the public as well as to the parties. Arbitrators are bound by certain ethical **canons** or responsibilities aimed at ensuring the fairness, confidentiality, and impartiality of the proceedings. Violating these ethical duties may result in judicial appeal and a reversal of the arbitration award. The complete text of the Code of Ethics for Arbitrators in Commercial Disputes approved by the American Bar Association and the American Arbitration Association is contained in Appendix 11–B of Chapter 11.

http://

Find the ABA Section on Dispute Resolution at: http://www. abanet.org/ dispute

One of the primary ethical duties of arbitrators is to avoid any appearance of bias due to previous or ongoing relationships with the parties, their attorneys, or witnesses. Such relationships would be deemed a conflict of interest. It is essential that arbitrators disclose to the parties any financial, business, professional, social, or familial relationship that may affect their impartiality. If any relationships do exist, arbitrators may withdraw from a case on their own, or upon the request of the parties.

At times, the arbitrator may not become aware of the conflict of interest until after the start of the arbitration hearing. For example, an arbitrator may have carefully reviewed the list of hearing participants and not recognized any conflicts. However, on the day of the hearing, one of the witnesses turns out to be an old college friend who recently married and changed her last name. In this instance, the arbitrator has the ethical duty of **disclosure** as to the prior relationship to the parties, even if the arbitrator believes that he or she can remain objective. The decision concerning whether this earlier relationship affects impartiality should be left up to the disputing parties.

In the following case, an arbitration award was challenged under federal law based on whether an arbitrator had the ethical duty to disclose a prior business relationship.

COMMONWEALTH COATINGS CORP. V. CONTINENTAL CASUALTY CO.
393 U.S. 145 (1968)

FACT SUMMARY

The petitioner, Commonwealth Coatings Corporation (Commonwealth) was a subcontractor that sued the sureties (Continental Casualty Company) on a prime contractor's bond to recover money damages for a painting job. The painting contract included a PDAA to arbitrate controversies under the contract. Under the terms of the PDAA, the subcontractor chose one arbitrator, the prime contractor selected the second arbitrator, and they mutually agreed upon the third arbitrator, Mr. Capacete, who operated an engineering consulting firm in Puerto Rico. The prime contractor was one of the third arbitrator's customers for whom the arbitrator had provided significant and repeated consulting services over the past four to five years. These services included consulting on the same projects as those at issue in this dispute. However, there had been no business dealings between the prime contractor and Mr. Capacete for about a year before the arbitration. Mr. Capacete did not disclose his business relationship with the prime contractor, and the business contacts were unknown to Commonwealth. The outcome of the arbitration hearing was a unanimous decision for the prime contractor. Among other grounds, Commonwealth challenged the award based on bias. The District Court refused to set aside the award, and the Court of Appeals affirmed. The Supreme Court granted certiorari.

OPINION: *MR. JUSTICE BLACK delivered the opinion of the Court*

At issue in this case is the question whether elementary requirements of impartiality taken for granted in every judicial proceeding are suspended when the parties agree to resolve a dispute through arbitration.

. . . .

In 1925, Congress enacted the United States Arbitration Act, 9 U.S.C. sections §§ 1-14, which sets out a comprehensive plan for arbitration of controversies coming under its terms, and both sides here assume that this Federal Act governs this case. Section 10 . . . sets out the conditions upon which awards can be vacated. (footnote omitted) The two counts below held, however, that subsection 10 could not be construed in such a way as to justify vacating the award in this case. We disagree and reverse. Section 10 does authorize vacation of an award where it was "procured by corruption, fraud or undue means" or "[w]here there was evident partiality . . . in the arbitrators." These provisions show a desire of Congress to provide not merely *any* arbitration but an impartial one. It is true that petitioner does not charge before us that the third arbitrator was actually guilty of fraud or bias in deciding this case, and we have no reason, apart from the undisclosed business relationship, to suspect him of any improper motives. But neither this arbitrator nor the prime contractor gave to petitioner any intimation of the close financial relations that had existed between them for a period of years. We have no doubt that if a litigant could show that a foreman of a jury or a judge in a court of justice had,

unknown to litigant, any such relationship, the judgment would be subject to challenge. . . . . It is true that arbitrators cannot sever all their ties with the business world, since they are not expected to get all their income from their work deciding cases, but we should, if anything, be even more scrupulous to safeguard the impartiality of arbitrators than judges, since the former have completely free rein to decide the law as well as the facts and are not subject to appellate review. We can perceive no way in which the effectiveness of the arbitration process will be hampered by the simple requirement that the arbitrators disclose to the parties any dealings that might create an impression of possible bias. . . .

This rule of arbitration and this canon of judicial ethics rests on the premise that any tribunal permitted by law to try cases and controversies not only must be unbiased but also must avoid even the appearance of bias. We cannot believe that it was the purpose of Congress to authorize litigants to submit their cases and controversies to arbitration boards that might reasonably be thought biased against one litigant and favorable to another.

Reversed.

MR. JUSTICE WHITE, with whom Mr. Justice Marshall joins, concurring.

. . . [A]rbitrators are not automatically disqualified by a business relationship with the parties before them if both parties are informed of the relationship in advance, or if they are unaware of the facts but the relationship is trivial. I see no reason automatically to disqualify the best informed and most capable potential arbitrators.

The arbitration process functions best when an amicable and trusting atmosphere is preserved and there is voluntary compliance with the decree, without need for judicial enforcement. This end is best served by establishing an atmosphere of frankness at the outset, through disclosure by the arbitrator of any financial transactions which he has had or is negotiating with either of the parties. In many cases the arbitrator might believe the business relationship to be so insubstantial that to make a point of revealing it would suggest he is indeed easily swayed, and perhaps a partisan of that party. But if the law requires the disclosure, no such imputation can arise. And it is far better that the relationship be disclosed at the outset, when the parties are free to reject the arbitrator or accept him with knowledge of the relationship and continuing faith in his objectivity, than to have the relationship come to light after the arbitration, when suspicious or disgruntled party can seize on it as a pretext for invalidating the award. The judiciary should minimize its role in arbitration as part of the arbitrator's impartiality. That role is best consigned to the parties, who are architects of their own arbitration process, and are far better informed of the prevailing ethical standards and reputations within their business. . . .

MR. JUSTICE FORTAS, with whom Mr. Justice Harlan and Mr. Justice Stewart join, dissenting.

. . . The Court sets aside the arbitration award despite the fact that the award is unanimous and no claim is made of actual partiality, unfairness, bias or fraud.

. . . .

. . . Both courts below held, and peti-

tioner concedes, that the third arbitrator was innocent of any actual partiality, or bias, or improper motive. There is no suggestion of concealment as distinguished from the innocent failure to volunteer information.

The third arbitrator is a leading and respected consulting engineer who has performed services for "most of the contractors in Puerto Rico." He was well-known to petitioner's counsel and they were personal friends. Petitioner's counsel candidly admitted that if he had been told about the arbitrator's prior relationship, "I don't think I would have objected because I know Mr. Capacete [the arbitrator]."

. . . .

I agree that failure of an arbitrator to volunteer information about business dealings with one party will, prima facie, support a claim of partiality or bias. But where there is no suggestion that the nondisclosure was calculated, and where the complaining party disclaims any imputation of partiality, bias, or misconduct, the presumption is clearly overcome. (footnote omitted.)

. . . .

. . . The Court applies to this process rules applicable to judges and not to a system characterized by dealing on faith and reputation for reliability. Such formalism is not contemplated by the Act nor is it warranted in a case where no claim is made of partiality, of unfairness, or of misconduct in any degree.

Discussion Questions

1. Why is the mere appearance of bias sufficient to overturn the award?
2. What should Mr. Capacete have done to avoid the appearance of bias?
3. Who has the primary responsibility for determining whether a business relationship affects arbitrator impartiality?

Pre-Hearing Preparation

Once the arbitrator has been selected, business representatives normally team with their legal representatives to prepare the case for the hearing. However, due to the informality of the proceedings, businesspeople may choose to represent themselves throughout the arbitration process **(pro se).** They should carefully evaluate whether an attorney can more thoroughly prepare and present their case, particularly in instances involving complex legal or factual issues.

As in litigation, each party needs to collect and exchange relevant records and documents in the discovery process. However, in arbitration, the arbitrator sets a much more abbreviated schedule of discovery, yielding a savings in both time and costs for the participants. If documents in the other party's possession are needed, the arbitrator may issue subpoenas for the records, if permissible under the arbitration agreement. In addition, relevant witnesses must be interviewed and prepared for cross-examination. Appropriate arrangements should also be made if the arbitrator will need to visit any company or other relevant site in reviewing the case.

The parties may also decide to participate in a **preliminary hearing** to narrow the issues, exchange relevant documents and witness lists, and determine the dates for the upcoming hearing. The preliminary hearing is an important opportunity to clarify and simplify the factual and legal aspects of a dispute. At its best, the preliminary hearing can help the arbitrator and the parties to run more focused hearing sessions.

The Arbitration Hearing

Generally, the **arbitration hearing** is a less formal, abbreviated, trial-like process. To maintain the integrity of the proceedings, the arbitrators should not have any discussions or contact with the parties beforehand. Similar to judges at trial, arbitrators oversee the hearing process. The arbitration hearing should be conducted in a manner that adheres to basic procedural due process requirements. The parties should have an opportunity to be heard and to have their case decided on the basis of the evidence on the record, as well as the right of legal representation for each party. Arbitrators should strive to keep the process moving forward and to stop any harassing or delaying tactics.

To allow each party to fully present his or her case, arbitrators will allow much latitude in the admission of relevant evidence. Parties may offer testimonial evidence through party or other lay witnesses as well as expert witnesses. Participants may also provide documentary evidence, such as company records, or demonstrative evidence, such as charts and graphs, to support their cases. Courtroom rules of evidence do not apply to arbitration procedures. Formal objections, intended to protect juries from making determinations based on unreliable or irrelevant evidence, are discouraged in arbitration as arbitrators are considered to have the experience and judgment necessary to weigh the credibility and relevance of proffered evidence. Note, however, that an arbitrator's refusal to consider relevant evidence may provide the grounds for a judicial appeal.

Unless a party is appearing pro se, lawyers usually present the case to the arbitrators. Following a brief opening statement that summarizes his or her view of the case and requested remedies, the moving party presents its case through direct testimony of witnesses and documentary evidence and other exhibits. The responding party is then allowed to present its defense. Each party is allowed to cross-examine the other's witnesses. Arbitrators may also ask questions to clarify issues under consideration. During the hearing, the arbitral panel should not comment on the merits of the evidence or give any indication of how it will rule on the dispute. At the end of the hearing, each party may sum up its case in a closing statement.

Depending on the agreed-upon procedures, arbitrators may request that the parties submit post-hearing legal briefs or memoranda to further support their claims and demands for relief. Although they are not required to apply substantive law, arbitrators should carefully evaluate any legal briefs provided during the arbitration process. If allowed under the selected procedures, arbitrators may reopen the hearing process to consider additional evidence. Once all the evidence has been heard, the hearing process is formally closed.

The Arbitration or Arbitral Award

Arbitrators possess broad authority to decide issues of law and fact. Typically, there is no required standard of proof in determining the arbitral outcome, unless otherwise agreed to by the parties. Some arbitrators will look at the general persuasiveness of the evidence, while others may borrow standards from the judicial process, such as the preponderance of the evidence or clear and convincing evidence approaches. For example, in instances in which employees have been discharged for sexual harassment (a violation of Title VII), different arbitral awards have used different standards of proof. Some arbitrators use the higher clear and convincing evidence standard because sexual harassment is a serious allegation and they want to be certain of a decision in which a person may lose his or her livelihood. Others use the preponderance of evidence standard because it is the standard a civil court would use in handling the litigation of employment disputes as well as Title VII matters. Many arbitrators will use the general persuasiveness standard in all arbitral matters, regardless of the nature of the conflict. The arbitral award indicates which party has won the case and any applicable remedies. The arbitral panel may split the award on different issues between the parties. The agreed-upon procedures will outline the number of days that the arbitrator has to make the award. Often, arbitrators take 30 to 45 days after the close of the process to draft their award.

No written opinions explaining the reasons for the outcome or detailing findings of law and fact are required. In fact, such opinions are sometimes avoided to prevent subsequent legal challenges to the award. If written opinions are provided, arbitrators need not defend their decision solely on the basis of substantive law.

Post-Award Actions

Generally, parties comply with the terms of the award. Yet the arbitrators cannot enforce the award. If one party refuses to adhere to the terms of the award, the prevailing party must go to court to seek its enforcement. Arbitrators may not disclose information in post-arbitration proceedings unless specifically required to do so by law.

In a few instances, a losing party may seek to vacate (overturn) or **modify an arbitration award** through a court appeal. However, the FAA and state arbitration laws limit severely the grounds for judicial review of arbitral awards. The main statutory grounds for **vacating the arbitration award** are: (1) arbitrator fraud, corruption, or bias; (2) arbitrator failure to comply with procedural due process requirements, including failing to consider relevant evidence; and (3) arbitrator conduct that exceeds arbitrator authority under the terms of the arbitration agreement. These statutes may also allow modifications of arbitration awards for technical errors committed by the arbitrator, including miscalculating amounts, deciding matters not specifically submitted for review, and drafting awards in an improper form that does not affect the substantive issues.

Grounds for Appeal Under the FAA

The Federal Arbitration Act (FAA) provides limited grounds for court review of arbitral awards. The stated bases for appeal seek to balance the need for fairness in the proceedings with the importance of finality in resolving disputes. An excerpt from the applicable provisions of the FAA dealing with appeals to vacate or modify arbitration decisions follows:

Section 10. Same; vacation; grounds; rehearing

(a) In any of the following cases the United States court in and for the district wherein the award was made may make an order vacating the award upon the application of any party to the arbitration:

(1) Where the award was procured by corruption, fraud, or undue means.

(2) Where there was evident partiality or corruption in the arbitrators, or either of them.

(3) Where the arbitrators were guilty of misconduct in refusing to postpone the hearing, upon sufficient cause shown; or in refusing to hear evidence pertinent and material to the controversy; or of any misbehavior by which the rights of any party have been prejudiced.

(4) Where the arbitrators exceeded their powers, or so imperfectly executed them that a mutual, final, and definite award upon the subject matter submitted was not made.

Grounds for Appeal Under the FAA Continued

(5) Where an award is vacated and the time within which the agreement required the award to be made has not expired the court may, in its discretion, direct a rehearing by the arbitrators. . . .

Section 11. Same; modification or correction; grounds; order
In either of the following cases the United States court in and for the district wherein the award was made may make an order modifying or correcting the award upon the application of any party to the arbitration:

(a) Where there was an evident material miscalculation of figures or an evident material mistake in the description of any person, thing, or property referred to in the award.

(b) Where the arbitrators have awarded upon a matter not submitted to them, unless it is a matter not affecting the merits of the decision upon the matter submitted.

(c) Where the award is imperfect in matter of form not affecting the merits of the controversy.

The order may modify and correct the award, so as to effect the intent thereof and promote justice between the parties.

In *United Steelworkers of America v. Enterprise Wheel & Car Corp.* [363 U.S. 593 (1960)], the Supreme Court determined that courts may not vacate the arbitrator's award simply because they would have interpreted the law or facts of the case differently. In that case, the Court recognized the importance of allowing a decision maker selected by the parties to render a decision, based on his knowledge and experience, without the courts second-guessing his determinations of law and fact.

However, courts will refuse to enforce arbitral awards that explicitly violate law or public policy. Public policy challenges are narrowly defined and cannot be based on generalized assertions about the public interest. Such challenges must be based on a well-recognized public policy concern, and the arbitrator's award must be a clear violation of that policy. The following excerpt from a case involves an employer's challenge to the reinstatement of an employee who had threatened to kill her supervisor based on the arbitrator's factual and legal findings as well as public policy grounds.

COLLINS V. BLUE CROSS BLUE SHIELD OF MICHIGAN

916 F. Supp. 638 (E.D. Mich. 1995)

FACT SUMMARY

The plaintiff, Irma Collins, was a nine-year employee of the defendant, Blue Cross Blue Shield of Michigan (BCBSM), with no prior disciplinary record. In 1993, the plaintiff took a medical leave of absence for the psychiatric treatment of stress. Her treating psychiatrist, Dr. Rosalind Griffin, reported to BCBSM that Ms. Collins was mentally disabled from work due to a psychiatric disorder, and she began to receive short-term disability benefits.

To determine whether the plaintiff continued to be disabled from work, a second psychiatrist, Dr. Joyln Welsh Wagner, undertook an evaluation of the plaintiff. In this evaluation process, Ms. Collins made numerous threats against her female supervisor. The plaintiff made statements about her supervisor such as, "She is living on borrowed time and she doesn't know it" and "I have killed her a thousand times in my mind." Neither Dr. Griffin nor Dr. Wagner believed that the plaintiff would act on these threats.

After reviewing Dr. Wagner's report, BCBSM decided to terminate the plaintiff as her threats violated company policy. When Dr. Griffin determined that the plaintiff was no longer mentally disabled, she authorized Ms. Collins's return to work. Upon her return to work, BCBSM terminated Ms. Collins.

Under an arbitration agreement between the plaintiff and BCBSM, Ms. Collins challenged her termination using arbitration. The arbitrator determined that Ms. Collins had been wrongfully discharged in violation of the Americans with Disabilities Act and the Michigan Handicappers' Civil Rights Act. The arbitrator ordered reinstatement of the plaintiff and awarded her back pay and attorneys' fees.

The plaintiff filed a motion in federal court to confirm the arbitrator's award under the Federal Arbitration Act and the Michigan Arbitration Act. The defendant filed a counterclaim seeking to overturn the arbitrator's award on public policy grounds.

OPINION: *JUDGE LAWRENCE P. ZATKOFF*

. . . .

The manner in which a court is to review an arbitration award under the FAA was set forth by the Sixth Circuit in *Federated Department Stores v. J.V.B. Industries, Inc.,* 894 F. 2d 862, 866 (6th Cir. 1990). The court first noted that the party seeking review must prove that "the arbitrators exceeded their powers, or so imperfectly executed them that a mutual, final, and definite award upon the subject matter submitted was not made." . . . The court then reviewed how other courts have interpreted this language, observing that "the standard of review in arbitration decisions is very narrow." *Id.* at 866.

"As long as the arbitrator is even arguably construing or applying the contract and acting within the scope of his authority, that a court is convinced he committed serious error does not suffice to overturn his decision." *Id.* at 866 (quoting *United Paperworkers International Union v. Misco, Inc.,* 484 U.S. 29, 98 L. Ed. 2d 286, 108 S. Ct. 364 (1987)). The *Federated* court concluded that "arbitrators do not exceed their authority unless they show a manifest disregard of the law." *Id.* at 866.

. . . .

Dr. Griffin determined that plaintiff had recovered from her disability and authorized her return to work on February 1, 1994. The arbitrator found that plaintiff was capable of performing her work despite deficiencies in her writing and editing skills, noting that plaintiff had received a well-qualified rating and had not been disciplined for performance deficiencies.

The Court has no authority to disturb the arbitrator's factual findings that the statements were a product of plaintiff's psychiatric disability. Thus, the statements made by the plaintiff did not disqualify her from employment at BCBSM, and terminating her on the basis of the statements was equivalent to terminating her because of her disability.

BCBSM's second argument is that the Arbitration Award is against public policy because it orders the company to reinstate an employee who has threatened to kill her supervisor.

In *Shelby County Health Care Corporation v. American Federation of State, County and Municipal Employees, Local 1733,* 967 F. 2d 1091 (6th Cir. 1992), the Sixth Circuit laid out the manner in which a court may refuse to enforce an arbitration award that violates public policy:

The public policy exception to the general deference afforded arbitration awards is very limited, and may be exercised only where several strict standards are met. First the decision must violate some explicit public policy that is well defined and dominant. *United Paperworkers International Union v. Misco, Inc.,* 484 U.S. 29, 98 L. Ed. 2d 286, 108 S. Ct. 364 (1987). . . . Second, the conflict between the public policy and the arbitration award must be explicit and clearly shown. Misco, 484 U.S. at 43. Further, it is not sufficient that the "grievant's conduct for which he was disciplined violated some public policy or law" rather, the relevant issue is whether the arbitrator's award "requiring reinstatement of the grievant . . . violated some explicit public policy." *Interstate Brands v. Teamsters Local 135,* 909 F. 2d 885, 893 (6th Cir. 1990).

The defendant's counterclaim states "further, the arbitrator, by ordering reinstatement of an employee who threatens to kill her supervisor, violated public policy." Aside from this conclusory statement, the defendant has failed to show that the arbitrator's decision violated "some explicit public policy that is well defined and dominant." Defendant's assertion that "to threaten to kill another employee is a violation of BCBSM policy . . ." simply will not suffice. Thus, the defendant has failed to show that reinstating the plaintiff will violate some explicit public policy.

IV. CONCLUSION

For the above reasons, the Court finds that the arbitrator did not make an error of law and therefore the Arbitration Award shall be confirmed. . . .

Discussion Questions

1. Do you think it is fair to allow Ms. Collins to return to the workplace?
2. What is the district court stating about the responsibility for fact-finding in an arbitration?
3. What must a party do to support an assertion that an award should be overturned based on public policy grounds?

ADVANTAGES OF VOLUNTARY ARBITRATION

Businesspeople do not like to become entangled in disputes, preferring to focus on the daily operation of their companies. Unfortunately, conflict in business is inevitable, making arbitration an attractive and necessary option for resolving it. Although it uses trial-like procedures, arbitration has many advantages over traditional litigation.

Greater Control.   In standard litigation, the parties have no control over the procedures used to resolve their dispute as the courts already have well-established and complex rules of civil procedure and evidence. In addition, parties do not have the opportunity to decide which judge will review their case or when their case will be heard.

Disputants using arbitration exercise greater control over both the type of procedures and the identity of the decision maker. Businesses electing to use arbitration can either create their own set of procedures or select the rules of a preferred administering agency. They can determine the steps the arbitrator must follow and the standards the arbitrator may use in making an arbitral decision. Normally the courtroom rules of evidence are relaxed during arbitration proceedings, allowing for a freer flow of information. The disputants can choose the person who will decide their disagreement. Parties can identify their chosen arbitrator or arbitral panel in their written agreement or select one from a list of qualified decision makers provided by the administering organization. In addition, the parties, with the assistance of the arbitrator, can work out a mutually agreed-upon schedule of pre-hearing activities and set the date for their arbitration hearing. Because the parties maintain greater control over the arbitration process, they are usually more satisfied and more willing to voluntarily comply with the outcome of the dispute.

Confidentiality.   Under the U.S. legal system, court documents and hearings are generally accessible to the public. Although an important freedom, this can be a drawback to disputing parties. Bad publicity from a lawsuit can seriously damage a company's reputation and its relationships with other businesses and customers, even if the lawsuit proves baseless. At times, a party may even seek to use the pressure of bad publicity to secure an unfair settlement. However, arbitration documents and sessions are private and thus, are not open to public scrutiny and resulting bad publicity. The confidentiality of the arbitration process allows the dispute to be decided solely on its merits and not on outside pressures.

Savings of Time and Money.   Due to court backlogs, lawsuits take an average of nineteen months to be tried. A lengthy discovery process can take months and years, further hampering the quick processing of a dispute. Many businesses cannot afford to wait that long. For example, a small equipment business may be teetering on the edge of bankruptcy because its largest customer has not paid for goods the company shipped. The equipment company could sue its customer in court for nonpayment. However, if it takes years to resolve the dispute in court, the small firm may already be out of business.

As with other ADR mechanisms, arbitration can save parties both time and money. The parties can set their own brisk schedule for the handling of their dispute. In addition, discovery, which accounts for about 80% of all legal fees in a dispute, is limited, helping parties reap added savings in both time and money.

Unfortunately, arbitration does not erase the economic disparities between the parties. A wealthier litigant may be able to afford more and better lawyers, investigators, and expert witnesses. However, arbitration proceedings are normally less expensive than standard litigation, so financial differences may at least be reduced or eased.

Arbitrator Expertise.   A major aspect of the arbitration process is the selection of the arbitrator. Unlike litigation, parties may select a decision maker with the professional experience and industry knowledge vital to understanding the conflict and rendering an appropriate decision. For example, a construction contractor and its subcontractor may have a dispute over whether the subcontractor installed electrical wiring in a commercial building in compliance with government safety codes and architectural drawings. Many judges will not be familiar with the technical aspects of electrical wiring, applicable industry practices, or governmental requirements. The parties may need to spend additional time and money educating the judge about electrical codes, construction practices, and architectural drawings.

http://

Access the Society for Professionals in Dispute Resolution at: http://www.spidr.org

Arbitration allows the parties to choose a decision maker who has the necessary construction background. The arbitrator's expertise can speed the arbitration proceedings along, since the decision maker need not be schooled in the business or technical aspects of the case. Consequently, the parties may feel more confident that the arbitrator better understands the nature of the conflict and the peculiarities of the industry and will be better able to render a fair decision.

Finality of the Award.   Matters handled through litigation may become the subject of seemingly endless court appeals on a number of substantive and procedural technicalities. These appeals can waste time and money. In arbitration, the decisions of the arbitrator are normally viewed as final, with no or few opportunities for appeal. The finality of an award means that the parties can anticipate party compliance soon after the award and can return to their normal business activities without fearing appeals.

Socially Valuable.   Arbitration benefits the general public. The heavy backlog of court cases burdens disputing parties and taxpayers, who must support the court system. Businesses that elect arbitration can ease the court docket by privately resolving their disputes. In addition, arbitration resolves conflicts without a financial cost to the public.

As with other alternatives to litigation, arbitration helps to prompt legal reforms in the court system. Some courts have already begun to adopt arbitration programs that have helped to more quickly and cheaply deal with civil complaints.

ADR IN ACTION

Arbitration Keeps Toyota Sales Rolling

In the 1980s, Toyota car sales were brisk, but trouble was brewing. Toyota had established a policy for determining dealer car allotments based on a dealer's level of sales to ultimate retail customers. Car sales between dealers or between car brokers and dealers were not credited toward dealer car allotments.

Some dealers trying to increase their future shares of cars often bought cars from original dealers or car brokers for resale to retail end users. These second dealers, known as reversal requesting dealers, began to demand that Toyota reassign the first dealer's future car allocation credits to them. The first dealers, known as protesting dealers, were angered by attempts to reduce their future car allotments due to their sales to the second dealers.

Bickering soon broke out between dealers, and many dealers directed their hostility toward Toyota. A number of lawsuits followed. Toyota lost hundreds of thousands of dollars in discovery and other pretrial expenses

alone. Toyota knew it had to do something to save time and money on these dealer disputes and to quell unproductive antagonism between Toyota and its dealers.

In 1985, two Toyota attorneys, William A. Ploude, Jr., and David D. Laufer, developed the Reversal Arbitration Board (RAB). The RAB process established a national network of arbitrators to rapidly and simply process these dealer disputes. Parties are still encouraged to negotiate a resolution to their dispute initially, with RAB as a last resort before litigation. The arbitration process is handled by a third-party nonprofit group, with Toyota paying for the administrative expenses. In the first year of the RAB, the administrative expense for all cases was only $80,000—far less than the pretrial costs for just one lawsuit.

The RAB procedure stresses speed, simplicity, and informality. Each dealer is limited to a two-week discovery period after notice of the hearing. The hearing is before a single arbitrator, and each dealer presents his or her own case with neither lawyers nor Toyota representatives present. There are seldom any outside witnesses. The dealer may appear in person or conduct a telephone conference call, which allows for the rapid handling of interstate disputes. Each session tends to take less than a half hour.

The arbitrator provides a written decision to the dealers and Toyota within a week of the hearing. Each decision becomes a form of internal precedent for dealers, who may review and rely on these awards in future disputes. To highlight the fairness of the process and to encourage the participation of dealers, the RAB decision is binding on Toyota but not on the dealers. Dealers may still appeal the outcome.

Despite its nonbinding nature, the RAB process has been a remarkable success. A survey of dealers indicated that eighty percent of the respondents found the procedure to be fair, while ninety-eight percent stated that the arbitrator was objective. Toyota also found that these types of dealer disputes sharply decreased from 178 in 1985 to a mere three cases in 1992.

No longer was Toyota throwing away hundreds of thousands of dollars in legal fees and related costs in court cases over car allotments. More important, the RAB process helped to preserve essential business relationships and to reduce hostility among dealers and between dealers and Toyota.

DISADVANTAGES OF VOLUNTARY ARBITRATION

Although arbitration provides a number of benefits, business disputants should also be aware of some of the limitations. These disadvantages should be weighed by businesspeople in concert with their attorneys to decide whether arbitration is the appropriate option.

Lack of Precedent.   It is important to recognize that arbitral awards, unlike court decisions, do not establish legal precedent. At times, businesses may wish to set a legal precedent to clearly establish their rights or to defend against future claimants on the same matter. For example, a business may want to prove its proprietary rights to a certain product. If a court determines the company's ownership of the product, the business can use the decision to support its position in, or discourage other parties from bringing, future actions on the same issue. An arbitral award on the company's rights is not binding on other future claimants, therefore, the company cannot use it to prevent or to predict the outcome of future lawsuits.

Adversarial Process.   In negotiation and mediation, the parties must collaborate to determine their own outcome. In these processes, the disputants must open up lines of communication to achieve a "win-win" result. The use of these procedures may not only resolve the current conflict, but they can reduce party hostility and promote a more positive working relationship in the future. Conversely, the "win-lose" result and adversarial nature of arbitration may heighten party hostility and seriously harm the business relationship. In addition, the arbitral process fails to teach the parties how to more effectively deal with each other in future conflicts.

Limits on Discovery.   Limiting discovery can clearly save both time and money for the parties. Yet in certain types of disputes, in-depth discovery may be necessary to effectively prosecute or defend against party claims. A dispute requiring lengthy discovery, such as a technically complex dispute or a discrimination claim, may not be well suited for arbitration. With limits on discovery, these cases may become more difficult to prove, even if the claims have merit.

Consent of Parties.   Unlike litigation, all parties to the dispute must agree to arbitration. Many businesspeople unfamiliar with arbitration will be reluctant to go along with their opponent's desire to use it. Without a PDAA or submission agreement, an arbitrator cannot order parties or witnesses to participate in the proceedings. It may be difficult to persuade the other party to consent to arbitration after the conflict has arisen and animosity has built up between the parties.

Constitutional and Policy Concerns.   A number of people have criticized the use of arbitration on both constitutional and social policy grounds. These critics assert that arbitration sets up a dual system of justice—one for the poor and one for the rich—in violation of equal protection guarantees. Some suggest that arbitration allows wealthier litigants to have their conflicts quickly and cheaply resolved, while poorer litigants must rely on the slower, more expensive court system. Without the involvement of richer litigants in the court system, critics of ADR claim that more powerful voices striving for improvements in the current legal system will be lost.

In addition, others argue that the confidentiality of arbitration proceedings violates standards of due process and the First Amendment right of access to proceedings. Public interest groups and media organizations express concern that certain business disputes involving important policy matters that affect the public interest are being resolved behind closed doors. For example, a nuclear power plant may have a dispute regarding the quality of equipment that a company has provided to the plant. The equipment may have an effect on both the efficiency and safety of the plant. If the parties have agreed to use arbitration, the matter may be resolved privately without the public being made aware of safety risks at the plant or allowed any input into the remedy for the problem.

OVERVIEW OF COURT-ANNEXED ARBITRATION

As more disputants clamor for alternatives to standard civil proceedings, some 1,200 state and federal courts have begun offering ADR options including court-supervised or **court-annexed arbitration.** In certain instances, parties may be required to use arbitration under statutory law, local court rules, or court order. State statutes often mandate court-supervised arbitration programs or provide state courts with the authority to develop detailed rules regarding such programs. Federal statutory law directs each U.S. district court to establish a plan to expedite the processing of disputes and to reduce the time and costs of litigation.

Under these plans, federal courts can develop local court rules or criteria for the use of arbitration. State and federal courts using court-annexed arbitration have set standards for the selection of certain types of cases for arbitration. Many of the cases involve simple factual and legal issues with lower monetary levels of damages being sought. Court-annexed arbitration can be distinguished from voluntary arbitration discussed earlier.

Court-annexed arbitration is not voluntary. As a method for diverting cases from overcrowded court dockets, court-annexed arbitration is often required as a non-binding precondition to a trial. Because the process is involuntary, arbitral awards are not necessarily binding.

Critics of court-annexed arbitration have argued that mandatory arbitration as a precondition to trial violates the Seventh Amendment right to a jury trial. In addition, these critics assert that assigning cases to compulsory arbitration, based primarily on dollar amounts in controversy, deprives only these parties of a right to a jury trial and, therefore, to equal protection of the laws. However, Supreme Court decisions have supported court attempts to increase procedural flexibility under the rules of civil procedure. Court innovation is normally permissible if the change is not **outcome-determinative,** meaning that it does not seriously interfere with or prevent the ultimate determination of the case by a jury. Because court-mandated arbitration is not binding, it is not outcome-determinative. Parties may still request a **trial de novo** or new trial within a specified time period after the arbitration award.

To deter frivolous requests for new trials, some jurisdictions may assess monetary penalties, such as court costs or the other party's arbitration expenses, if the appealing party does not attain a more successful outcome in the new trial. Some critics of court-annexed arbitration contend that these penalties unfairly punish parties for exercising their constitutional right to a jury trial and to equal protection of the laws. Following is a case that challenges a state court-supervised arbitration program as violating both of these rights.

RICHARDSON V. SPORT SHINKO (WAIKIKI CORPORATION)
76 Haw. 494, 880 P. 2d 169 (1994)

FACT SUMMARY

Mrs. Richardson, a disc jockey, was setting up stereo equipment in preparation for a wedding reception at the Queen Kapiolani Hotel in Hawaii. While positioning the equipment and electrical cords, she knelt on the carpet, and a loose carpet staple pierced her left knee through the cartilage and down to the bone. Hotel officials called an ambulance to the scene, and paramedics removed the staple from her knee. She was later treated at a local emergency ward.

Plaintiffs Renee and Thaddeus Richardson brought a negligence action against Sport Shinko, which owned and operated the hotel. Under a Hawaiian law, the case was referred to the state's Court-Annexed Arbitration Program (CAAP). The arbitrator found Sport Shinko liable and awarded the Richardsons $60,441.80 in general and special damages. The Richardsons sought a trial de novo, which was granted. Before the trial, Sport Shinko offered to settle the dispute with the Richardsons for $75,000. The Richardsons rejected the offer, demanding $150,000 in damages.

At trial, the jury determined that Sport Shinko was not negligent and awarded no damages to the Richardsons. Their request for a new trial was rejected. Under a Hawaiian statute (HAR 26), a judge has the discretion to penalize a party that fails to improve its outcome from an arbitration proceeding at the subsequent trial by at least fifteen percent. Sport Shinko then brought an action for sanctions against the

Richardsons and was awarded $5,234.41 in lawyers' fees and court costs. The Richardsons appealed the judgment, which favored Sport Shinko, and the accompanying grant of sanctions. Among a variety of arguments, the Richardsons contended that the referral of their case to the CAAP and the imposition of sanctions violated their right to a jury trial and to equal protection of the laws.

OPINION: *CHIEF JUDGE MOON*

. . . .

A. Right to Trial by Jury in Civil Cases

We deal first with the Richardsons' claim that HAR 26 "impermissibly infringes upon their constitutional right to a jury trial." The resolution of this issue necessarily rests upon the interpretation of state law. . . .

Article I, § 13 of the Hawaii Constitution, as amended in 1978, provides in relevant part: "In suits at common law where the value in controversy shall exceed five thousand dollars, the right of trial by jury shall be preserved." HRCP 38(a)(1990) reaffirms this right providing: "The right of trial by jury as given by the Constitution or a statute of the state or the United States shall be preserved to the parties inviolate." This court acknowledged that article I, § 13 and HRCP 38(a) were patterned after the Seventh Amendment and HRCP 38(a), respectively, and we have therefore deemed the interpretation of those provisions by the federal courts highly persuasive in construing the right to a civil jury trial in Hawaii. . . .

Although trial by jury in civil cases is a "fundamental" right in the State of Hawaii. . . . the right has never been construed so broadly as to prohibit reasonable conditions upon its exercise. Instead, it has been held that "the limitation imposed by the [seventh] amendment is merely that enjoyment of the right of trial by jury be not obstructed, and that the ultimate issues of fact by the jury be not interfered with." . . .

Moreover, in holding that a procedure for non-judicial determinations prior to a jury trial does not violate the seventh amendment, the United States Supreme Court has stated that the seventh amendment "does not prescribe at what stage of an action a trial by jury must, if demanded, be had; or what conditions may be imposed upon the demand of such a trial, consistently with preserving the right to it." . . . This, with regard to mandatory arbitration programs that afford a right to trial de novo, it has been held that the only purpose of the [seventh amendment] is to secure the right of trial by jury before rights of person or property are finally determined. All that it required is that the right of appeal for the purpose of presenting the issue to a jury must not be burdened by the imposition of onerous conditions, restrictions or regulations which would make the right practically unavailable. . . .

Thus, laws, practices, and procedures affecting the right to trial by jury under article I, § 13 are valid as long as they do not significantly burden or impair the right to ultimately have a jury determine issues of fact. In the present case, however, the Richardsons contend that,

although they received a jury trial, the "specter of sanctions" created by HAR 26 impermissibly burdened their exercise of that right. We disagree.

. . . .

. . . HAR 26 serves a necessary and legitimate purpose. Moreover, as we shall discuss, HAR 26 achieves its objectives by reasonable means inasmuch as the authorized sanctions are limited in both amount and application.

First, HAR 26 sanctions are available only if the appealing party does not improve its position, at the present time, by 15% or more, and even then, sanctions are discretionary. Accordingly, every party has the ability to avoid HAR 26 sanctions by undertaking a frank post-arbitration evaluation of the merits of their case.

Second, the potential magnitude of the sanction is not per se unreasonable. Sanctions are presently limited to $5,000.00 in attorneys' fees plus actual "costs" as that term is defined. Many courts have upheld similar or greater potential sanctions as reasonable. . . .

However, although the amount of sanctions authorized by HAR 26 is not per se unconstitutional, "the problem is one of degree rather than kind. . . . The necessity of paying [$75 in arbitrators' fees] as the condition to for the right to appeal [from a mandatory arbitration award] would seemingly operate as a strong deterrent, amounting practically to a denial of that right, if the case should involve only . . . as little as $250.

. . . .

In the present case, the amount in controversy was arguably between $60,441.80 (the arbitration award) and $150,000.00 (the amount the Richardsons demanded in their settlement conference statement filed in the circuit court).

Although no fixed lines can be drawn, we do not believe the $5,234.41 sanction was unreasonable. . . .

When considering the important interests that HAR 26 serves and the limits placed on its use, we cannot say that HAR 26 imposed an unreasonable burden on the Richardsons' right to a civil jury trial. Therefore, we conclude that the sanctions awarded in this case do not violate due process or article I, § 13.

B. Equal Protection of the Laws

Finally, the Richardsons claim that their right to equal protection of the laws under the fourteenth amendment to the United States Constitution was violated "to the extent that [HAR 26] is applied only to a limited class of tort victims exercising their right to a jury trial(.)" Despite their focus on HAR 26, the Richardsons essentially challenge the constitutional validity of the following classifications made by HRS § 601-20(b)(1992), which provides: "All civil actions in tort, having a probable jury award value not reduced by the issue of liability, exclusive of interests and costs, of $150,000 or less, shall be submitted to the [CAAP]." Thus, litigants compelled to participate in the CAAP by HRS § 601-20(b) are subject to HAR 26 sanctions if they exercise their right to a jury trial while other litigants are not. . . .

. . . .

. . . Because mandatory participation in the CAAP by itself does not significantly interfere with a party's constitutional right to a jury trial. . . . we will apply the rational basis test instead.

. . . .

As stated previously, the purpose of the CAAP is "to provide for a procedure to obtain prompt and equitable resolution of certain civil actions in tort through arbitration.". . . We hold that the purpose is a legitimate one. We turn our inquiry then to whether it was reasonable for the legislature to believe that assigning to the CAAP only tort actions having a probable jury award value of $150,000.00 or less would promote its objectives. . . .

First, the legislature could reasonably believe that actions involving more than $150,000.00 would generally require arbitration proceedings of greater length than those intended by the CAAP, and that "the cost of a subsequent trial . . . [would] be very small, relative to the claim itself." . . .

Second, it is fair to presume as a general matter that tort cases will involve only claims for money damages. "In such cases, often the only dispute is over the amount of money owed by one party to the other. In contrast, pleas for equitable relief would probably mean increased complexity and could require continuing supervision of the court. Such cases would be inappropriate for arbitration." . . .

. . . .

Accordingly, we hold that HRS § 601-20(b) does not violate the equal protection clause of the fourteenth amendment.

III. CONCLUSION

Based on the foregoing, we affirm both the judgment and the award of sanctions against the Richardsons.

Discussion Questions

1. Why did the court decide that court-annexed arbitration as a precondition to trial is not overly burdensome? Do you agree with this decision?

2. Would the result of this case be different if court-mandated arbitration was final and binding on parties?

3. Do you think that the sanctions unfairly penalize litigants involved in smaller dollar amount lawsuits?

Unlike voluntary arbitration, court-annexed arbitration rarely gives parties free rein to select the arbitrator or members of the arbitral panel. Arbitrators in court programs are typically individuals certified by the courts, with most being former judges or experienced lawyers. When allowed to choose, the parties are usually limited to court-certified arbitrators; in other instances, the court directly appoints an arbitrator to review the case. Parties are allowed to challenge court-appointed arbitrators on the grounds of bias or lack of impartiality.

Court-annexed arbitration is similar to voluntary arbitration in that there is a limited discovery process. Also, the arbitration hearing tends to be somewhat informal with relaxed procedural rules. However, unlike voluntary arbitrators, court-supervised arbitrators must follow the substantive law of the jurisdiction. In addition, they must apply the standard burden of proof of the preponderance of the evidence rather than one of general persuasiveness.

If the parties do not object to the outcome, the arbitrator's award is entered as a decision of the court. Dissatisfied parties requesting a trial de novo must show that they participated in the court-supervised hearing in good faith. At times, a court may refuse initially to grant an appealing party a new trial if he or she defaulted at the arbitration hearing or sought to otherwise undermine or circumvent the arbitration process. The court may require parties to make good faith use of arbitration before seriously considering a request for a new trial. The following are two cases in which courts considered requests for new trials. Compare the differing outcomes of each case based on the party seeking a trial de novo. The first case involves a plaintiff's lack of participation in a court-mandated arbitration hearing.

HONEYWELL PROTECTION SERVICES V. TANDEM TELECOMMUNICATIONS, INC.
130 Misc. 2d 130, 495 N.Y.S. 2d 130 (Civ. Ct. 1985)

FACT SUMMARY

A dispute between plaintiff Honeywell Protection Services and defendant Tandem Telecommunications, Inc., was referred to a court-annexed arbitration process. At the arbitration hearing, no representative of the plaintiff appeared. The plaintiff's attorney appeared but offered no witnesses or evidence either to support plaintiff's cause of action or to oppose the defendant's counterclaim. As a direct result of the plaintiff's failure to present evidence, the arbitral award was made dismissing the plaintiff's complaint and finding in the defendant's favor on the counterclaim. The plaintiff made a demand for a trial de novo, and the defendant then moved to vacate the call for a new trial.

OPINION: *JUDGE SILBERMANN*

. . . The res governing compulsory arbitration provide that a trial *de novo* may be demanded by any party not in default. (22 NYCRR 28.12[a]). The appearance by an attorney at the hearing does not excuse a default by a party in presenting evidence and proceeding with the hearing. An attorney cannot sit by, listen to his adversaries' proof and demand a trial *de novo* as a result of the failure to affirmatively participate.

The plaintiff herein, in effect, defaulted in proceeding to trial even though it appeared at the hearing by an attorney. The arbitrator noted an appearance by plaintiff's counsel but no appearance by the client.

Plaintiff's counsel contends that "there is no requirement that he must produce a witness at arbitration and a party may prove a claim or a defense by utilizing documents in its possessions [sic] and using the other party's witnesses." Indeed this would be true if the court were to believe that plaintiff had no witnesses or evidence to produce and had in fact presented its entire case before the arbitration panel. In such a case a plaintiff would not be in default and could demand a trial *de novo* (22 NYCRR 28.12[a]).

However, this court having been presented with two motions in separate cases on the same day wherein this same law firm proceeded in almost an identical manner before the arbitration panel has come to the conclusion that this is a ploy to circumvent mandatory arbitration. (citation omitted)

Mandatory arbitration for cases in which the *ad damnum* clause is under $6,000 has been successful in alleviating calendar congestion of the Civil Court. If permitted to succeed such a ruse would create a loophole which would completely undermine compulsory arbitration and incidentally waste the time of the arbitrators and the adverse parties. To permit an attorney to appear at a hearing, not present any evidence and then be free to demand a trial *de novo,* would circumvent the statute providing for compulsory arbitration and render such law a nullity thereby defeating the intent of the arbitration procedure.

. . . . This loophole allows a party to use compulsory arbitration as a forum for free discovery and not for the purpose it was established to resolve disputes and relieve court congestion.

Accordingly, defendant's motion is denied on condition that plaintiff serve and file an affidavit with the court within five days after service of a copy of this order with notice of entry stating that it will present no evidence or witnesses at trial not already produced at the [arbitration] hearing. In the event plaintiff fails to file such an affidavit the motion is granted.

Plaintiff may, if it so elects, move to vacate its default and have this case restored to the arbitration calendar.

Discussion Questions

1. Why did the court determine that the plaintiff was in default and, therefore, unable to request a new trial?
2. What were the intended benefits of the compulsory arbitration program?
3. How might a defaulting party abuse the arbitration hearing process to advance its own claim in a subsequent trial?

This second case considers a defendant's request for a trial de novo, when only the defendant's counsel appeared and did not introduce any evidence at the arbitration hearing.

SAN-DAR ASSOCIATES V. ADAMS
167 Misc. 2d 727, 643 N.Y. S. 2d 880 (1996)

FACT SUMMARY

The plaintiff brought a contract action for monetary damages amounting to $2,650. The action was referred to the court's compulsory arbitration program. At the arbitration hearing, only the defendant's counsel appeared and cross-examined the plaintiff's witness. An award of $1,629 was made to the plaintiff. The defendant made a demand for a trial de novo, and the plaintiff moved to strike the demand. The trial court granted the plaintiff's motion to strike, finding that the defendant's failure to appear at the arbitration was a default precluding him from a new trial. The defendant appealed.

OPINION: *JUDGE P. PARNESS, Judges McCooe and Freedman, concur.*

. . . .

While the failure of a plaintiff to appear or present evidence through his attorney constitutes a default for purposes of compulsory arbitration. . . . the same cannot be said when a defendant, by his attorney, appears and disputes the plaintiff's evidence at the hearing. As a general rule, the plaintiff bears the burden of proof in a civil case. . . . and the defendant is under no obligation to present evidence or witnesses.

Here, the arbitrator's own case report indicates that the matter was contested, since the amount awarded ($1629) was substantially less than the amount demanded ($2650), and the box denominated "failed to appear" was not checked. We therefore conclude that the defendant's appearance by attorney was not a default which would forfeit the remedy of a trial de novo (*Valot v. Allcity Ins. Co.,* 131 Misc. 2d 814, 501 N.Y. S. 2d 597). "The arbitration rules, in particular the procedure governing trial de novo, should not be interpreted too narrowly since the compulsory arbitration program initially deprives the parties of their right to a jury trial." [*Valot,* at 815].

Discussion Questions

1. How does the burden of proof standard influence the court's view as to whether a party may seek a new trial?
2. Will the benefits of mandatory arbitration be lost if defendants need not appear or introduce evidence at the arbitration hearing?
3. Are you concerned that the defendant in this case may be using the arbitration hearing as a chance for free discovery as forewarned in *Honeywell*?

CHAPTER CONCLUSION

After decades of judicial disfavor, arbitration has developed into an important and accepted method for adjudicating business disputes. Statute and case law now look favorably upon both voluntary and court-annexed arbitration. Voluntary arbitration maximizes the opportunity for businesspeople to fashion and participate in an arbitration process that best meets their needs. Court-annexed arbitration helps to expedite and reduce the time and costs of disputes processed through the judicial system. Regardless of the method used, arbitrators bring their special legal and business expertise to the review of business claims and the determination of appropriate awards.

In determining how to best use arbitration, businesspeople should work with their attorneys to evaluate its overall advantages and disadvantages. If arbitration is the selected ADR method, the collaboration between businesspeople and lawyers should continue throughout the process to reap fully the benefits of arbitration.

BEST BUSINESS PRACTICES

Here are some practical tips on how businesspeople can effectively use arbitration to resolve business disputes.

- Work with your attorney or legal staff to create binding arbitration clauses in company contracts with suppliers, vendors, and employees that clearly identify the disputes covered and the processes to be used if conflicts arise.

- Consult your state attorney general's office, local courthouse, Better Business Bureau, or other reputable administering organizations to learn about their arbitration training programs and professional services and to request copies of their standard arbitration clauses and forms.

- Discuss the use of arbitration with other people in your industry to learn about their experiences with the process and to become aware of qualified and respected arbitrators in your field.

- Be prepared to actively participate in the arbitration process, including selecting the arbitrator, collecting relevant company documents, scheduling arbitration proceedings, preparing oral testimony, and coordinating on-site visits, if needed.

- Educate your employees, vendors, and suppliers about the mutual benefits of arbitration to resolve business disputes.

- Evaluate the time and cost savings of your arbitration program and consider updating or revising your procedures to improve its speed and cost-effectiveness.

http://

For example, you can find the University of Massachusetts Dispute Resolution Program at: http://www.umb.edu/disres

KEY TERMS

ad hoc proceeding, p. 161

ADR adjudicatory mechanisms, p. 155

arbitral award, p. 173

arbitration hearing, p. 177

arbitration remedies, p. 173

arbitrator or arbitral panel, p. 172

canons, p. 173

court-annexed arbitration, p. 188

disclosure, p. 174

Federal Arbitration Act (FAA), p. 158

high-low arbitration, p. 173

med-arb, p. 161

modify an arbitration award, p. 179

outcome-determinative, p. 188

pre-dispute arbitration agreement (PDAA), p. 162

pre-hearing preparation, p. 177

preliminary hearing, p. 177

presumption of arbitrability, p. 169

procedural arbitrability, p. 164

pro se, p. 177

rules by reference, p. 162

submission agreement, p. 162

substantive arbitrability, p. 164

trial de novo, p. 188

Uniform Arbitration Act, p. 158

vacating the arbitration award, p. 179

voluntary arbitration, p. 161

ETHICAL AND LEGAL REVIEW

1. Stuart is an arbitrator in an intellectual property dispute between two companies involving ownership of a revolutionary product. During the hearing process, the parties decide to settle the dispute, advising the panel that they intend to merge their companies to pursue this new market together. Later that day, Stuart contacts his broker and buys stock in the merging companies. He does not discuss the arbitration proceeding with his broker. Has Stuart violated any of his ethical obligations? [See Code of Ethics for Arbitrators in Commercial Disputes]

2. During a hearing, an arbitrator named Nancy suggests to the parties that she thinks they should consider settlement. Nancy tells the parties that they could settle the matter easily within a couple of hours and save themselves time and money. Nancy volunteers to help mediate the discussions between the disputing parties. She then directs the parties to dismiss their witnesses, so she can begin the mediation in a confidential setting. Should Nancy have recommended settlement to the parties? Should she have acted to mediate the settlement discussions? [See Code of Ethics for Arbitrators in Commercial Disputes]

3. Two parties, Tracer and NESCO, had entered into a licensing agreement for the use of Tracer's tank and pipeline leak detection process. The licensing agreement contained an arbitration clause covering claims "arising out of this Agreement." After termination of the licensing agreement, Tracer contended that NESCO continued to use its confidential information and trade secrets to market an alternative product. An arbitral panel dismissed Tracer's tort claims for misappropriation of trade secrets as not arbitrable. In turn, Tracer sought to

compel arbitration of these claims. Was a tort claim for the misappropriation of trade secrets arbitrable under the arbitration provision? [*Tracer Research Corp. v. Nat'l Environmental Services Co.* (NESCO), 42 F. 3d 1292 (9th Cir. 1994), *cert. denied,* 116 S. Ct. 37 (1995)]

4. Melinda Broemmer was a pregnant, unmarried, twenty-one-year old high school graduate earning only about $100 a week with no medical benefits. She was under a great deal of physical and emotional stress, since the father-to-be was pressuring her to obtain an abortion and her parents were advising against the procedure. Ultimately, she sought the abortion and, in doing so, was first required to complete three forms, one of which was a separate PDAA. Neither the PDAA nor the arbitration clause was explained to her, and the clinic never provided her with any copies of the documents. Broemmer alleged that she did not recall signing the arbitration agreement and still remains unsure about what arbitration means. Broemmer suffered a punctured uterus during the abortion, which required follow-up medical treatment. She filed a medical malpractice suit against the clinic doctor, and the clinic sought to compel arbitration. Will the court require her to comply with the terms of the PDAA? [*Broemmer v. Abortion Services of Phoenix, Ltd.,* 173 Ariz. 148, 840 P. 2d 1013 (1992)]

5. Antonio and Diana Mastrobuono were an assistant professor of medieval literature and an artist, respectively, who had entered into an investment contract that contained an arbitration clause. The arbitrator in the investment dispute found in favor of the Mastrobuonos and awarded them $400,000 in punitive damages. The dealer's standard investor agreement indicated that the arbitration would be in accordance with the National Association of Securities Dealers (NASD) rules, which allow arbitrators to award punitive damages. However, the agreement also included a choice-of-law provision, which selected the laws of the state of New York to govern any dispute. Under New York case law, arbitrators do not have the authority to award punitive damages. Will the arbitrator's award of punitive damages be upheld? [*Mastrobuono v. Shearson Lehman Hutton,* 115 S. Ct. 1212 (1995)]

SUGGESTED ADDITIONAL READINGS

Blackford, Jason C. "Arbitration Provisions for Business Contracts." *Arbitration Journal.* September 1993, pp. 47–52.

Coulson, Robert. "An Introduction to Commercial Arbitration." *Business Arbitration—What You Need to Know.* American Arbitration Association, 1991, pp. 7–33.

Hoellering, Michael F. "Arbitrability." *Commercial Arbitration for the 1990s.* American Bar Association, 1991, pp.1–13.

7

LABOR AND EMPLOYMENT ARBITRATION

CHAPTER HIGHLIGHTS

In this chapter, you will read and learn about the following:

1. The differences between labor and employment arbitration.
2. The use of voluntary and compulsory arbitration to resolve workplace conflicts.
3. Consideration of statutory and case law regarding labor and employment arbitration.
4. The application of interest arbitration, particularly with regard to public sector employment.
5. An overview of grievance arbitration for public and private sector disputes.
6. Typical exclusions from labor and employment arbitration.
7. The role of businesspeople in the arbitration of workplace disputes.
8. The current debate over the rise in employment arbitration of statutory rights.

In this chapter, we will focus on the use of arbitration to resolve disputes arising in the workplace. Arbitration has long been used to successfully settle disagreements relating to workplace rights and responsibilities. It allows businesses and their employees to remain productive while resolving conflicts. In addition, arbitral awards provide guidance on future conduct between the parties, much like case precedent. Many arbitral decisions are published and offer a detailed analysis of a workplace controversy. This chapter will examine labor and employment arbitration through a combination of pertinent statutory law, seminal court decisions, and recent written arbitral awards.

OVERVIEW OF LABOR AND EMPLOYMENT ARBITRATION

Labor Arbitration

Traditionally, the relationship between management and workers has been adversarial with each party seeking to promote its own interests. In the past, employers and employees have resorted to **self-help remedies** such as pickets, boycotts, strikes, lockouts, and other costly work stoppages to force each other to accept contract concessions or to address workplace complaints. At times, these actions have led to violent clashes resulting in personal injury, property damage, and sometimes even death. The continued normal operation of a private company or government agency is vital to both management and labor. An alternative mechanism was needed to process smoothly and successfully workplace disputes while maintaining industrial productivity or government services. Over time, arbitration has become an important tool for peaceful and constructive resolution of workplace conflicts.

Using its authority to regulate interstate commerce, Congress took the first major step toward the constructive resolution of workplace disputes by enacting the **Arbitration Act of 1888.** The Act was aimed at dealing with costly strikes and work stoppages in the economically vital railway industry. The Act was the first to promote voluntary arbitration of railway conflicts and to provide presidential authority for the appointment of investigatory boards to review the validity of work stoppages.

Although the arbitration provisions were seldom used, the Act provided a foundation for the creation of arbitral panels or tribunals under the later **Railway Labor Act of 1920 (RLA).** The RLA provided an opportunity for clashing parties to consider the use of mediation and arbitration in resolving disputes. The RLA established the **National Mediation Board (NMB)** to handle disputes over the adoption of appropriate terms of labor contracts, and the **National Railroad Adjustment Board (NRAB)** to deal with complaints about the application of such agreements. The NMB sought to apply mediation techniques to break deadlocks in collective bargaining negotiation. If mediation was unsuccessful, the NMB would encourage the parties to engage in voluntary arbitration to resolve their contract differences. The NRAB issued awards, which were to be final and binding on the parties and enforceable in the federal courts. The courts had the power to review NRAB awards on very limited grounds. The RLA was later extended to include the airline industry.

Not long after passage of the RLA, Congress enacted the United States Arbitration Act (now known as the Federal Arbitration Act [FAA]) in 1925, with its broad scheme for the liberal enforcement of arbitration agreements. Soon after, other federal and state laws were passed that promoted the arbitration of disputes between employees and employers in private sector industries and public agencies, particularly those industries or agencies viewed as providing essential services. The drafters of these laws hoped parties would use arbitration to avoid costly work stoppages that might imperil interstate commerce or public health and safety.

In 1935, the **National Labor Relations Act (NLRA)** established the **National Labor Relations Board (NLRB).** The NLRB has the statutory authority over the resolution of claims involving unfair labor practices by labor or management. The primary focus of the NLRB is the protection and interpretation of public rights guaranteed by the NLRA rather than private contractual obligations. Typically, the NLRB will defer to private arbitration, provided that the arbitration meets certain standards, such as obtaining mutual assent to the arbitration process, maintaining the regularity and fairness of the proceedings, and granting awards consistent with the NLRA.

Most of these early laws focused on resolving disputes between employers and workers represented by unions. The arbitration of controversies involving unionized employees is referred to as **labor arbitration.** In most instances, labor arbitration is voluntary, based on the terms of a collective bargaining agreement between employers and the representative union. (See Figure 7.1 for an illustration of the form for Voluntary Labor Arbitration Rules provided by the American Arbitration Association.) A collective bargaining agreement determines the rights and responsibilities of the employer and the union employees. In other cases, arbitration may be compulsory based on statutory or case law directives. In some cases, courts have determined that employees have an obligation not to strike due to the existing binding arbitration clause in a valid collective bargaining agreement.

Employment Arbitration

In certain cases, employers may enter into pre-dispute arbitration agreements (PDAAs) with nonunion employees to resolve their employment disputes. This type of arbitration is referred to as **employment arbitration.** Employment arbitration is not based on a negotiated collective bargaining agreement but may be required as a condition of employment for nonunion employees. The use of employment arbitration has increased significantly, with some employers inserting pre-dispute arbitration clauses into employee manuals, offer letters, promotion awards, and other employment documents in hopes of avoiding litigation costs and procedural and substantive statutory rights and remedies.

Traditionally, few employers resorted to this approach for handling disputes with nonunion workers because the FAA contains an **individual employment contract**

FIGURE 7.1 Voluntary Labor Arbitration Rules

American Arbitration Association

MEDIATION   Please consult the AAA regarding mediation procedures. If you want the AAA to contact the other party and attempt to arrange a mediation, please check this box. ☐

VOLUNTARY LABOR ARBITRATION RULES
DEMAND FOR ARBITRATION

DATE: _____

TO: Name _____
(of the party upon whom the demand is made)

Address _____

City and State _____ ZIP Code _____

Telephone (   ) _____ Fax _____

Name of Representative _____
(if known)

Representative's Address _____

City and State _____ ZIP Code _____

Telephone (   ) _____ Fax _____

The named claimant, a party to an arbitration agreement contained in a written contract, dated _____ _____, providing for arbitration under the Voluntary Labor Arbitration Rules, hereby demands arbitration thereunder.

(Attach the arbitration clause or quote it hereunder.)

NATURE OF DISPUTE:

CLAIM OR RELIEF SOUGHT: (amount, if any)

HEARING LOCALE REQUESTED: _____
(City and State)

You are hereby notified that copies of our arbitration agreement and of this demand are being filed with the American Arbitration Association at its _____ office, with the request that it commence the administration of the arbitration. Under the rules, you may file an answering statement after notice from the administrator.

Signed _____ Title _____
(may be signed by a representative)

Name of Claimant _____

Address (to be used in connection with this case) _____

City and State _____ ZIP Code _____

Telephone (   ) _____ Fax _____

Name of Representative _____

Representative's Address _____

City and State _____ ZIP Code _____

Telephone (   ) _____ Fax _____

To institute proceedings, please send three copies of this demand with the administrative fee, as provided for in the rules, to the AAA. Send the original demand to the respondent.

Form L2–2/90

Source: Reprinted with permission of the American Arbitration Association.

exclusion. This exclusion states explicitly that its policy promoting arbitration does not apply to "contracts of employment of seaman, railroad employees, or any other class of workers engaged in foreign or interstate commerce." Uncertainty about the application of this exclusion discouraged the development of employment arbitration. However, a number of recent federal decisions, including the following excerpted case, have dealt with the breadth of the FAA's individual employment contract exclusion in considering the validity of PDAA clauses.

O'NEIL V. HILTON HEAD HOSPITAL
1997 U.S. App. LEXIS 13904 (4th Cir. 1997)

FACT SUMMARY

Plaintiff Diane O'Neil brought a state court action against her prior employer, defendant Hilton Head Hospital, claiming she was fired in violation of the Family and Medical Leave Act (FMLA). Plaintiff was a respiratory therapist for the hospital who took a leave of absence in 1994 under the FMLA. During her leave of absence, American Medical International (AMI) acquired the hospital and required hospital employees to sign an acknowledgment of the new AMI employee handbook, which included an arbitration provision. In August 1994, the plaintiff signed this acknowledgment. The grievant was then discharged in October 1994, and she brought the state court lawsuit alleging that her dismissal violated the provisions of the FMLA. Her state court action was removed to the federal district court. Citing the provisions of the AMI arbitration agreement, the defendant motioned to stay the district court proceedings under the FAA. The district court denied the motion, and the defendant appealed.

OPINION: *WILKINSON, Chief Judge*

. . . .

In the FAA, Congress endorsed arbitration as a less formal and more efficient means than litigation of resolving disputes. In line with this congressional intent, the Supreme Court has repeatedly emphasized that the FAA represents "a liberal policy favoring arbitration agreements." *Moses H. Cone Memorial Hospital v. Mercury Construction Corp.,* 460 U.S. 1, 24, 74 L. Ed. 2d 765, 103 S. Ct. 927 (1983); *accord Mastrobuono v. Shearson Lehman Hutton, Inc.,* 514 U.S. 52, 115 S. Ct. 1212, 1216, 131 L. Ed. 2d 76 (1995); *Gilmer v. Interstate Johnson/Lane Corp.,* 500 U.S. 20, 26, 144 L. Ed. 2d 26, 111 S. Ct. 1647 (1991). Pursuant to that liberal policy, "any doubts concerning the scope of arbitrable issues should be resolved in favor of arbitration, whether the problem at hand is the construction of the contract language itself or an allegation of waiver, delay, or a like defense to arbitrability." *Moses H. Cone,* 460 U.S. at 24-25.

The federal policy favoring the effective and efficient resolution of disputes through arbitration applies with equal strength to claims created by contract or by statute. . . . Nothing in the Family and

Medical Leave Act suggests that Congress wished to exempt disputes arising under it from the coverage of the FAA (citations omitted).

It is clear that the provisions of the FAA apply here. The FAA exempts from its coverage "contracts of employment of seamen, railroad employees, or any other class of workers engaged in foreign or interstate commerce." 9 U.S.C. §1. The circuit courts have uniformly reasoned that the strong federal policy in favor of arbitration requires a narrow reading of this section 1 exemption. Thus, those courts have limited the section 1 exemption to seamen, railroad workers, and other workers actually involved in the interstate transportation of goods. *See Rojas v. TK Communications, Inc.,* 87 F. 3d 745, 748 (5th Cir. 1996); *Asplundh Tree Expert Co. v. Bates,* 71 F. 3d 592, 600-601 (6th Cir. 1995); *Miller Brewing Co. v. Brewery Workers Local No. 9,* 739 F. 2d 1159, 1162 (7th Cir. 1984); *Erving v. Virginia Squires Basketball Club,* 468 F. 2d 1064, 1069 (2d Cir. 1972); *Dickstein v. Du Pont,* 443 F. 2d 783, 785 (1st Cir. 1971). (footnote omitted) We agree with this uniform body of precedent. If

Congress had wished to exempt all employees from the coverage of the FAA it could have said so. Instead it enumerated an exempt class of employees, which is limited to workers engaged in the shipment and transportation of goods. *See Rojas,* 87 F. 3d at 748. Therefore, since O'Neil was not engaged in the interstate transportation of goods, she does not fall within the section 1 exclusion, and the FAA applies.

. . . .

The Supreme Court has repeatedly emphasized that "questions of arbitrability must be addressed with a healthy regard for the federal policy favoring arbitration." *Gilmer,* 500 U.S. at 26 (quoting *Moses H. Cone,* 460 U.S. at 24). The district court's analysis turned this clear injunction on its head, pursuing every possible avenue to avoid the binding arbitration agreement between O'Neil and her employer. We cannot endorse such an approach. Accordingly, we reverse the judgment of the district court and remand with instructions that O'Neil's action be stayed in accordance with section 3 of the FAA.

Discussion Questions

1. To whom does the FAA's exclusion for individual employment contracts apply under this decision?
2. Does the FMLA limit the right of employers and employees to agree to arbitrate these statutory disputes?
3. Do you think it is fair for an employer to require employees to sign away their access to the courts to keep their jobs?

Aside from narrow judicial interpretation of the individual employment contract exclusion, the recent growth in employment arbitration can be traced to the Supreme Court's decision in *Gilmer v. Interstate/Johnson Lane,* 500 U.S. 20 (1991). In that instance, a securities broker challenged a PDAA contained in a securities industry registration form (U-4 form) and sought to have his age discrimination case under the Age Discrimination in Employment Act (ADEA) reviewed in the federal courts. In *Gilmer,* the Court approved the use of arbitration to resolve statutory employment disputes, even ADEA claims, between employers and nonunion employees. After *Gilmer,* a number of federal court decisions expanded *Gilmer* to embrace the arbitration of a full range of statutory claims, including Title VII actions. The *Gilmer* court did not directly address the issue of the FAA exclusion, but it demonstrated strong support for the use of arbitration to settle employment disputes in a nonunion environment.

Despite the expanded use of PDAAs in employment, the increase in employment arbitration has sparked controversy. In some instances, employees have felt pressured to sign PDAAs to keep their jobs or advance their careers. Some suggest that such PDAAs should not be upheld because of the unequal bargaining power between employers and nonunion employees, who do not have the force of collective bargaining units to help negotiate fair employment terms and conditions. Others claim that mandating employees to sign PDAAs is coercive and therefore violative of standard contract law principles. A number of legislative proposals that would prevent employers from requiring employees to agree to use arbitration before a statutory dispute arises between them have surfaced but have yet to be enacted in Congress.

Administrative agencies, such as the Equal Employment Opportunity Commission (EEOC) and the NLRB, have also expressed serious concerns about the private adjudication of important statutory rights. In particular, the EEOC issued a policy statement in July 1997 asserting that requiring employees to sign PDAAs for employment disputes as a condition of employment was contrary to fundamental principles of civil rights law. The EEOC stated that such agreements were not truly voluntary and would be disregarded in EEOC investigations of discrimination claims. The agency also encouraged parties to bring their employment discrimination claims to court and to challenge the enforceability of such agreements.

There are limits on the use of PDAAs to resolve employment disputes. Like any other contract, arbitration agreements may be challenged on both legal and equitable grounds under the FAA and state arbitration acts. Recent litigation and administrative agency actions have moved from arbitration of statutory rights to questioning of the validity of employment arbitration agreements based on common law contractual and public policy grounds. Considering issues of fundamental fairness, courts have primarily addressed whether parties knowingly and voluntarily waived their right to go to court and whether the arbitration process fairly protects procedural and substantive rights and remedies. Next is a case in which a federal court must decide whether to enforce the PDAA clause in a U-4 form, which the Supreme Court upheld in the *Gilmer* case.

PRUDENTIAL V. LAI

42 F. 3d 1299 (9th Cir. 1994), cert. denied, 116 S. Ct. 61 (1995)

FACT SUMMARY

Justine Lai and Elvira Viernes applied and were hired for entry-level positions as sales representatives with Prudential in 1989. The women were recent immigrants to the United States with limited language skills and no prior securities industry experience. In 1990, the women sued Prudential and their immediate supervisor for rape, sexual harassment, and sexual abuse in a state court action. Prudential filed a separate lawsuit in federal court to compel arbitration, because the women had signed a securities industry registration form (U-4 form) that contained a PDAA.

Based on their claimed inexperience in the securities industry, the women asserted that they were informed by the defendant's representatives that the form was only an application to take a securities license test. They were told to sign the documents and were not given an opportunity to read the form. No mention was ever made about arbitration, nor were the women given a copy of the National Association of Securities Dealers (NASD) manual, which discussed the arbitration process for securities industry employment disputes. The federal district court issued an order to compel arbitration, and the former employees appealed that order.

OPINION: *SHROEDER, Circuit Judge*

. . . .

The only agreement to arbitrate that appellants actually executed was contained in the U-4 form. . . . [which] states:

I agree to arbitrate any dispute, claim or controversy that may arise between me or my firm, or a customer, or any other person, that is required to be arbitrated under the rules, constitutions, or bylaws of the organizations with which I register. . . .

This provision does not in and of itself bind appellants to arbitrate any particular dispute. To see what appellants possibly could have agreed to arbitrate, we must turn to the arbitration requirements of the NASD, which appellants eventually joined. The NASD manual states:

Any dispute, claim or controversy eligible for submission under part I of this Code between or among members and/or associated persons . . . arising in connection with the business of such member(s) or in connection with the activities of such associated person(s), shall be arbitrated under this Code. . . .

Appellants contend that these provisions do not bind them to arbitrate their employment discrimination claims because they were unaware that they signed any document that contained an arbitration clause, they were never given copies of the NASD manual, and they were not otherwise on notice that they might be agreeing to arbitrate employment disputes. They further contend that even if they had known that they were agreeing to the NASD arbitration provision, its language does not cover employment disputes.

Appellants rely on *Alexander v. Gardner Denver,* 415 U.S. 36, 39 L. Ed.

2d 147, 94 S. Ct. 1011 (1974), to support their argument that they are not bound to arbitrate their statutory claims. *Alexander* held that an arbitration clause contained in a collective bargaining agreement could not supplant Title VII's statutory remedies, (footnote omitted), and the decision was widely interpreted as prohibiting any form of compulsory arbitration of Title VII claims. . . . The Supreme Court, however, without overruling *Alexander,* subsequently held that individuals may contractually agree to arbitrate employment disputes and thereby waive the statutory rights to which they would otherwise be entitled. *Gilmer v. Interstate/ Johnson Lane Corp.,* 500 U.S. 20 (1991).

Gilmer, upon which Prudential heavily relies, made it clear that the ADEA does not bar agreements to arbitrate federal age discrimination in employment claims. (footnote omitted). Our circuit has extended *Gilmer* to employment discrimination claims brought under Title VII. . . . The issue before us, however, is not whether employees may ever agree to arbitrate employment claims; they can. The issue here is whether these particular employees entered into such a binding agreement, thereby waiving statutory court remedies otherwise available. . . .

. . . .

Appellants contend in effect that even after the Supreme Court's decision in *Gilmer,* employees cannot be bound by an agreement to arbitrate employment discrimination claims unless they knowingly agreed to arbitrate such claims. We agree with the appellants that Congress intended there to be at least a knowing agreement to arbitrate employment disputes before any employee may be deemed to have waived the comprehensive statutory

rights, remedies and procedural protections prescribed in Title VII and related state statutes. Such congressional intent, which has been noted in other judicial decisions, is apparent from the text and legislative history of Title VII.

. . . .

This congressional concern that Title VII disputes be arbitrated only "where appropriate," and only when such a procedure was knowingly accepted, reflects our public policy of protecting victims of sexual discrimination and harassment through the provisions of Title VII and analogous state statutes. *See Alexander,* 415 U.S. at 47. This is a policy that is at least as strong as our public policy in favor of arbitration. Although the Supreme Court has pointed out that plaintiffs who arbitrate their statutory claims do not "forego the substantive rights afforded by the statute," *Mitsubishi Motors,* 473 U.S. at 628, the remedies and procedural protections available in the arbitral forum can differ significantly from those contemplated by the legislature. In the sexual harassment context, these procedural protections, [such as limits on the discovery and admissibility of a plaintiffs' sexual history], may be particularly significant. (footnote omitted). Thus, we conclude that a Title VII plaintiff may only be forced to forego her statutory remedies and arbitrate her claims if she has knowingly agreed to submit such disputes to arbitration. . . .

. . . .

In this case, even assuming that appellants were aware of the nature of the U-4 form, they could not have understood that in signing it, they were agreeing to arbitrate sexual discrimination suits. The U-4 form did not purport to describe the type of disputes that were subject to arbitration. Moreover, even if appellants had signed a contract containing the NASD arbitration clause, it would not put them on notice that they were bound to arbitrate Title VII claims. That provision did not even refer to employment disputes. . . .

We therefore hold that appellants were not bound by any valid agreement to arbi-trate these employment disputes, because they did not knowingly contract to forego their statutory remedies in favor of arbi-tration.

The order of the district court is VACATED AND THE MATTER RE-MANDED for the district court to dismiss Prudential's complaint.

Discussion Questions

1. Why did the Ninth Circuit refuse to uphold the terms of the PDAA in this employment dispute?
2. Do you think that parties to a con-tract should have to comply with the terms of contracts they sign regard-less of their business experience?
3. Based on this case, what might employers do to ensure that their employees are knowingly and volun-tarily waiving their right to court access?

In *Prudential,* the Ninth Circuit refused to enforce the PDAA clause based on a combination of ambiguity in the arbitration clause and the employees' lack of business acumen. However, a number of other courts have rejected the Ninth Circuit's analysis, asserting that it contradicts the reasoning in *Gilmer* and that parties signing an agree-ment to arbitrate are viewed as having assented to its terms unless fraud or other wrongful conduct can be shown. The field of employment arbitration is currently unsettled, with varying judicial interpretations and potential state and federal legisla-tion on the horizon.

http://

More information about NASD regulations can be found at: http://www. nasd.com

In light of these continuing legal challenges, the NASD issued a proposal in August 1997 to allow employees to bring their statutory employment disputes to the courts. Under the proposed policy revision, the NASD would amend the U-4 form within the next year, so that the arbitration provision would no longer apply to statutory employ-ment disputes. However, other contract and customer disputes would still be covered under the U-4 form's arbitration provision. The proposed change is subject to approval by the Securities and Exchange Commission.

ADR IN ACTION

Recommendations for Greater Fundamental Fairness in Arbitrating Statutory Employment Disputes

The *Gilmer* decision and subsequent federal cases expanding employment arbitration to a broad range of statutory disputes, including Title VII discrimination claims, did not end the debate over the fairness of arbitrating statutory employment disputes. In 1993, President Clinton convened a ten-member Commission on the Future of Worker-Management Relations, headed by former Secretary of Labor John T. Dunlop. The Dunlop Commission considered hours of testimony on the use of alternative dispute resolution (ADR) in the workplace. In January 1995, the Commission released a report strongly favoring ADR use but rejecting mandatory arbitration programs as a condition of employment. The Dunlop Commission also suggested that any fair employment arbitration program should include objective arbitrators well versed in party issues and statutory rights; a reasonable discovery process to aid case presentation; independent legal representation of employees; written arbitral decisions; the authority of the arbitral panel to issue the full range of statutory remedies available in litigation; and adequate opportunities for judicial review of arbitral decisions.

After the Dunlop Commission's report, several congressional proposals to prevent or limit the use of arbitration for statutory employment disputes surfaced. In addition, the EEOC and the NLRB raised objections to arbitration programs that make agreement to binding arbitration of employment discrimination claims a precondition for getting or keeping a job. Both agencies viewed such compulsory programs as improper employer attempts to preclude an individual's right of access to objective administrative processes. In line with these administrative agencies' views, the National Employment Lawyers Association threatened to boycott arbitral organizations that administer employment cases based on mandatory arbitration clauses.

The American Bar Association also tried to wrestle with the issue of arbitrating statutory employment disputes. The ABA created the Task Force on Alternative Dispute Resolution in Employment, made up of representatives from a diverse range of organizations that deal with labor and employment law issues. The Task Force was charged with considering the appropriateness of statutory employment arbitration and creating methods for improving fairness and due process in such proceedings. In May 1995, the Task Force issued its "Due Process Protocol for Mediation and Arbitration of Statutory Disputes Arising out of the Employment Relationship." The

http://

Find the ABA Section on Dispute Resolution at: http://www. abanet.org/ dispute

ADR IN ACTION Continued

Task Force's report encouraged the use of mediation and arbitration to resolve statutory employment disputes but could not reach consensus on whether employers should have the authority to enter into pre-dispute mediation and arbitration agreements as a condition of employment.

The Task Force did issue various guidelines for establishing greater balance and due process in employment mediation and arbitration similar to some of the recommendations of the Dunlop Commission. The following excerpt provides some suggestions to employers for creating and implementing more fundamentally fair arbitration and mediation programs.

B. RIGHT OF REPRESENTATION

1. *Choice of Representative* Employees considering the use of or, in fact, utilizing mediation and/or arbitration procedures should have the right to be represented by a spokesperson of their own choosing. The mediation and arbitration procedure should specify and should include reference to institutions which might offer assistance, such as bar associations, legal services associations, civil rights organizations, trade unions, etc.

2. *Fees for Representation* The amount and method of payment for representation should be determined between the claimant and the representative. We recom-

mend, however, a number of existing systems which provide employer reimbursement of at least a portion of the employee's attorney fees, especially for lower paid employees. The arbitrator should have the authority to provide for fee reimbursement, in whole or in part, as part of the remedy in accordance with applicable law or in the interests of justice.

3. *Access to Information* One of the advantages of arbitration is that there is usually less time and money spent in pre-trial discovery. Adequate but limited pre-trial discovery is to be encouraged and employees should have access to all information reasonably relevant to mediation and/or arbitration of their claims. . . . Necessary pre-hearing depositions consistent with the expedited nature of arbitration should be available. . . .

C. MEDIATOR AND ARBITRATOR QUALIFICATION

1. *Roster and Membership* Mediators and arbitrators selected for such cases should have skill in the conduct of hearings, knowledge of the statutory issues at stake in the dispute, and familiarity with the workplace and employment environment. The roster of available mediators and arbitrators should be established on a non-discriminatory basis, diverse by gender, ethnicity, background, experience, etc. to satisfy the parties. . . .

. . . .

There is a manifest need for mediators and arbitrators with expertise in statutory requirements in the employment field who may, without special training, lack experience in the employment area and in the conduct of arbitration hearings and mediation sessions. . . . The roster of arbitrators and mediators should contain representatives with all such skills in order to meet the diverse needs of this caseload.

Regardless of their prior experience, mediators and arbitrators on the roster must be independent of bias toward either party. They should reject cases if they believe the procedure lacks requisite due process.

2. *Training* The creation of a roster containing the foregoing qualifications dictates the development of a training program to educate existing and potential labor and employment mediators and arbitrators as to the statutes, including substantive, procedural and remedial issues to be confronted and to train experts in the statutes as to employer procedures governing the employment relationship as well as due process and fairness in the conduct and control of arbitration hearings and mediation sessions.

Training in statutory issues should be provided by the government agencies, bar associations, academic institutions, etc., . . . at various locations throughout the country. Such training should be updated periodically and be required of all mediators and arbitrators. . . .

. . . .

3. *Panel Selection* Upon request of the parties, the designating agency should utilize a list procedure such as that of the AAA or select a panel composed of an odd number of mediators and arbitrators from its roster or pool. . . .

4. *Conflicts of Interest* The mediator or arbitrator for a case has a duty to disclose any relationship which might reasonably constitute or be perceived as a conflict of interest. . . .

5. *Authority of the Arbitrator* The arbitrator should be bound by applicable agreements, statutes, regulations and rules or procedure of the designating agency. . . . The arbitrator should be empowered to award whatever relief would be available in court under the law. The arbitrator should issue an opinion and award setting forth a summary of the issues, including the types(s) of dispute(s), the damages and/or other relief requested and awarded, a disposition of any statutory claim(s).

6. *Compensation of the Mediator or Arbitrator* Impartiality is best assured by the parties sharing the fees and expenses of the mediator and arbitrator. In cases in which the economic condition of a party does not permit equal sharing, the parties should make mutually acceptable arrangements to achieve that goal if at all possible. In the absence of such agreement,

INTEREST AND GRIEVANCE ARBITRATION

Two basic types of arbitration address workplace disputes. **Interest arbitration** applies primarily to unionized workplaces, while **grievance or rights arbitration** is used in both labor and employment disputes. It is the nature of the dispute, not the process, that determines the appropriate category of arbitration. Interest arbitration deals with the creation or revision of future rights under a collective bargaining agreement. Grievance arbitration deals with conflicts over perceived violations of existing rights and obligations governing the employer-employee relationship.

Find the Department of Labor at: http://www.dol. gov

For example, under the terms of a collective bargaining agreement or a company policy, a company might have agreed to offer special job training to employees based on seniority. An interest arbitration case might involve a conflict over either labor's or management's proposed changes to the seniority provisions during contract negotiations to revise a collective bargaining agreement due to expire. Grievance arbitration would focus on a situation in which a senior employee is challenging the employer decision to allow junior workers to receive training first, despite the existence of seniority requirements under the agreement or policy. Like a judge at a bench trial, the sole arbitrator or three-person panel will consider relevant demonstrative and testimonial evidence. Unless the law states or the parties have agreed otherwise, the arbitrator is not bound by any specific standard of proof, often employing a standard of general persuasiveness or reasonableness to the determinations made. Normally the awards in interest and grievance arbitration are viewed as final and binding on the parties. Unlike employment arbitration, many labor arbitration awards set forth written findings of fact and conclusions of law. In recognition of the ongoing relationship between the parties, these written and reasoned awards provide guidance on appropriate future conduct between employers and employees in the workplace.

Under both forms of arbitration, the union has a legal duty to act in good faith and to fairly represent all of its members. Failure to perform this duty properly may result in a lawsuit by an employee or group of employees against the union. For example, a union representative may not refuse to bring forward a grievance for an employee because that representative has a personality conflict or is acting in a discriminatory or arbitrary manner toward that person. However, a union representative may refuse to bring forward a claim that is not meritorious as a proper exercise of discretion if that determination has been made in a nonarbitrary and nondiscriminatory manner.

Regardless of whether the dispute requires interest or grievance arbitration, two topics are generally excluded from both forms of arbitration: management prerogative or rights and internal union administration. **Management prerogative or rights** applies to conflicts that focus on the employer's inherent authority to manage the day-to-day operations of the business. Typically, management prerogative or rights focuses on the employer's control over the company's methods of operation, techniques of production, marketing and financial decisions, product development, and employee discipline and discharge for just cause. Such management rights cannot be arbitrated. Similarly, unions stake out their own protected area of authority involving disputes over **internal union administration,** including the investigation and handling of improper activities by union officials.

OVERVIEW OF INTEREST ARBITRATION

Interest arbitration focuses on disputes concerning the formation of or changes to the terms and conditions of new or renegotiated collective bargaining agreements. Such agreements deal with the detailed interrelationship between management and unionized employees including, but not limited to, wages, vacation and holiday accrual, seniority and promotion rights, health care insurance, and retirement or pension benefits. Labor and management successfully negotiate most issues contained in a collective bargaining agreement. However, the parties may resort to interest arbitration on hotly contested terms and conditions on which the parties have deadlocked. Although interest arbitration may concern any proposed or revised terms to a collective bargaining agreement, disputes over wage rates or health care benefits are the most common grounds for interest arbitration.

Interest arbitration is more often found in disputes involving public sector employees. Unlike most private unionized employees, public sector employees are not entitled to use self-help remedies such as strikes or work slowdowns to obtain contract concessions. For example, under the **Federal Service Labor-Management Relations Statute,** federal union employees and their unions may not encourage, participate, or condone any strikes, work stoppages, or slowdowns. In 1981, President Reagan fired more than 11,000 air traffic controllers and decertified their union, PATCO, for striking in violation of the statute. Through court decisions or statutory law, most states have similar no-strike policies. Typically, on a state level, firefighters, police officers, sanitation workers, and schoolteachers are not allowed to walk off the job because of the damaging impact on public health, safety, or welfare. These federal and state no-strike policies are often incorporated into the terms of collective bargaining agreements with public employee unions. Therefore, interest arbitration provides an alternative method for resolving contract differences between labor and management in the public sector.

In interest arbitration, the arbitrator or three-person panel plays a vital role in the continuation of the collective bargaining process. The interest arbitrator's focus is determining the unresolved terms of a new or revised labor-management agreement, with the goal of arriving at a reasonable and fair solution. The provisions of either an existing collective bargaining agreement or an applicable statute will define the breadth of the interest arbitrator's authority. If given broad authority, the interest arbitrator must address broad questions of policy, often without definite or concrete standards on which to rely.

Interest arbitrators may analyze a number of factors, including the employment requirements for the positions in dispute, the ability of the employer to pay new or revised wage rates, a comparison of wages and benefits with similarly situated employers and employees **(comparability groups),** and any relevant concerns about the impact of the agreement on the public interest and welfare. These factors may be spelled out in a valid collective bargaining agreement or applicable statute. The interest arbitrator's determination is usually viewed as final and binding on the parties.

In some instances, the arbitrator may be required by law or agreement to use final offer selection, a method commonly referred to as **baseball arbitration.** Under **final offer selection,** the arbitrator may be limited to selecting one of the final offers of the parties or one of the particular points within a last offer in reaching a final decision. When faced with final offer selection, the parties will usually put together reasonable final proposals in the hope of persuading the arbitrator to choose their contract language as more reasonable or equitable under the circumstances. Once again, the terms of the collective bargaining agreement or the provisions of a statute will normally spell out the standards to be used in selecting the most reasonable offer. Next is a final offer selection decision in which an interest arbitrator must consider the wage and health care provisions of a public sector collective bargaining agreement through an analysis of factors spelled out under state law.

IN RE WATERLOO COMMUNITY SCHOOL DISTRICT AND AMERICAN FEDERATION OF STATE, COUNTY, & MUNICIPAL EMPLOYEES (AFSCME) COUNCIL 61, LOCAL 2749

99 Lab. Arb. (BNA) 385 (1992)

FACT SUMMARY

AFSCME Council 61, Local 2749 (the Union) represents about 222 employees of the Waterloo Community School District in Iowa (the District or Employer), including custodians, maintenance employees, truck drivers, dock workers, bus mechanics, and food service staff. The collective bargaining agreement between the

District and the Union expires on June 30, 1992. The parties have agreed upon all issues except for wages and health care insurance. To resolve these issues, the parties agreed to final and binding interest arbitration.

In essence, the Union sought a $.28 per hour or a three percent increase across the board, which the Union states will avoid a serious cut in employee purchasing power under current cost-of-living data. The Union argues that its wage request is modest in comparison with other districts. In addition, the Union wanted to increase the Employer's share of health care premiums to fifty percent of the family plan. Once again, the Union argued that its health care proposal was comparable to health care benefits provided to employees in other large school districts in Iowa.

The District serves nearly 12,000 students in one of the largest school districts in Iowa. However, due to steadily declining student enrollments, the District has been required to close some 18 school buildings, including a state-of-the-art high school. Also, the state has decreased support for district schools, placing serious fiscal constraints on the District. The District argued that these declining enrollments and financial limitations have resulted in its request for a wage freeze. Recognizing how disappointing its offer appears, the District offered to make a lump sum payment of $104 to employees or a 0.6 percent increase. The District further contended that it would continue to pay a flat $45 per month toward employee premiums under the family health insurance plan.

Under Iowa statute, the interest arbitrator must consider the following factors in making the choice between the final offers of the parties: (1) the past collective bargaining contracts between the parties including the negotiations that led up to the final offers; (2) a comparison of wages, hours, and conditions of employment of the involved public employees with those of other comparable public employees; (3) the interests and welfare of the public, including the ability of the public to pay for any adjustments or the impact on the public to changes in normal services; and (4) the power of the public employer to assess taxes and appropriate funds to conduct its standard operations.

OPINION: *DAVID A. DILTS, Arbitrator*

The parties have two unresolved issues before the Arbitrator. These issues are wages and insurance. There has been no fact finding report and the Arbitrator is limited to select one of the final offers of the parties on each issue. Each of these issues will be examined, in turn, in the following sections of this opinion.

Wages: There is a substantial difference between the parties' final positions concerning wages. The District has offered a one-time payment of $104. . . . The Union's final offer was for $.28 hourly increase. Using the District's estimates there appears to be an approximately $73,096 difference between the parties' final proposals.

The parties contentions focus on standard issues of wage determination. The cost of living, comparability, and the financial abilities of the District are the central issues. Each of these standards will be examined in turn.

Cost of Living: . . . The Union contends that the cost of living has increased by 3.63 percent. . . . If either final position is awarded, according to the Union, the bargaining unit's wages will lose purchasing power. The District argues that comparisons which do not account for the insurance package provided the employees are not valid and cannot be relied upon by the Arbitrator. Further, the District contends that national averages for the cost of living are not known to be valid for this local area.

The cost of living data does not conclusively demonstrate that the bargaining unit would lose purchasing power if the Union's final offer is awarded. The Arbitrator is convinced that the District's final offer will result in a loss of purchasing power for the bargaining unit. The exact amount of the loss of purchasing power cannot be accurately determined from the record of evidence before this Arbitrator.

Comparability: The parties have offered significantly different comparability groups as the appropriate basis for the determination of a reasonable wage. The Arbitrator notes that the Union's comparisons show that the bargaining unit's current relative position will worsen under the District's final offer and that the Union's final offer would more closely maintain the bargaining unit's current positions. The Arbitrator also notes that the District's comparisons show very little negative relative changes would occur under its final offer.

The Arbitrator has closely examined both comparability groups. The District's group contain less than half of the members of the Union's group. The Union's group contains members that are far smaller in enrollment than the District's group. Both comparability groups are widely dispersed geographically. Neither party offered substantial, financial, industrial, or other data concerning the members of the comparability groups that would aid the Arbitrator in determining which comparability group is the most

representative of the truly similarly situated employers and bargaining units.

. . . .

What is clear to this Arbitrator is that the issue of comparability has little clear and convincing evidence that demands the resolution of the issue in favor of either parties' final offer.

District's Financial Situation: The District's financial situation leaves much to be desired. The District has regularly been required to borrow to finance its operations. Further, the District anticipates further cash flow problems because of the school financing law that was recently passed by the legislature. The District has engaged in a strategy to reduce its financial deficits and there is significant evidence that its declining enrollments will continue to adversely affect its financial resources. The historical evidence concerning the District's closing of buildings and loss of enrollments are given significant weight in support of the District's financial history. This Arbitrator, however, cannot give significant weight to the speculations concerning what the new Iowa school financing law will mean for the District's financial resources.

. . . .

The record of evidence contains a substantial amount of financial information. Probably the most convincing evidence in this record is the District's solvency ratio. . . . Close examination of exhibits 13, 14, 15 and 16 convinces this Arbitrator that a financial solvency ratio of -3.0 presents the District with cause for concern. The Union was unable to refute the validity and reliability of this financial evidence.

This Arbitrator is convinced that the financial solvency position of the District places it [in] a position where fiscal measures are both reasonable and prudent to significantly improve the current situation. While this is not clear evidence of an inability to fund the Union's final offer, [t]he financial evidence is clear and convincing that the Union's final offer is less reasonable than the Employer's final offer in the light of the District's current financial position and the potential for further adverse effects on the District's programs.

Overview: This Arbitrator is sympathetic to the Union's position that something more than what the District has offered must be put into the bargaining unit's wages. In fact, this Arbitrator is convinced that the District's position also lacks reason. This Arbitrator is uncomfortable with both parties' final offers. The District's pressing financial needs are clearly reflected in its final offer, but the need for a living wage is also reflected in the Union's proposal. What neither proposal reflects are the needs of the other party. . . .

In the final analysis, even though the Union's position is supported by the cost of living evidence, it is the current financial situation faced by the District that must be given the greatest weight by this Arbitrator. Further, this Arbitrator after lengthy consideration finds that neither parties' position finds support in the comparability evidence. The arbitrator must therefore award the District's final offer.

Insurance: The District's financial position is also a limiting constraint on the funding of the Union's insurance proposal. The comparisons entered into this record also again fail to convince this Arbitrator of the merit of either parties' final offer. The lack of weight placed on the comparability evidence arises, as it did for wages, from two specific sources. The respective comparability groups are not supported by sufficient evidence to demonstrate their validity and reliability for the purposes offered.

Again, as in the case of the wage issue, the difference in comparability groups and the limited information available concerning their respective memberships' characteristics leaves very little upon which the Arbitrator can rely. . . .

. . . .

The Arbitrator is left with a very difficult choice. One that has been the source of anxiety. However, the bottom line is that the same financial considerations that must form the basis of the wage award must also prevail with respect to the insurance issue. The Union's proposal has merit, but it also has limited applicability to the bargaining unit. The bargaining unit will not generally and uniformly benefit from an award of the Union's final offer on insurance. This fact alone is not sufficient for a finding against the Union, but in the District's current financial climate the Arbitrator simply cannot find evidence in the record to justify an additional $50,000 expenditure from the District's budget to fund the Union's final offer. Further, exacerbating the weight of evidence against the Union's final offer is the fact that there has been a decline in the cost of the family coverage premium. This decrease in premiums for the family coverage will be enjoyed by the bargaining unit, even though the single individual coverage benefit will accrue to the District. Even though the District will realize $3,400 in savings from the reduction in the costs of the insurance premium, the bargaining [unit] will also enjoy a significant reduction in the costs employees must pay for family coverage.

There is little compelling evidence in this record that supports either parties' position with respect to any other standard save the financial situation in which the District finds itself. The Arbitrator is left with no alternative save to award the District's position on insurance.

AWARD

1. On the issue of wages, the District's final offer is awarded.
2. On the issue of insurance, the District's final offer is awarded.

Discussion Questions

1. What standard of proof does the arbitrator seem to apply in reviewing the validity of each party's final offer?
2. What factor plays a crucial role in the selection of the final offers on wages and insurance?
3. How might each party have strengthened its position according to the arbitrator?

Businesspeople can limit the number of issues presented in interest arbitration by preparing a reasonable and focused strategy of negotiation prior to the start of collective bargaining negotiations. If issues remain unresolved, managers play an important role in preparing for an upcoming interest arbitration. They may help to better define the offers and arguments placed before the arbitrators based on their business expertise and understanding of the history of the negotiations process. Businesspeople can also gather important technical data on cost-of-living figures, comparisons of wages and benefits provided to other similarly situated employees (comparability groups), and vital budgetary information to aid the arbitrator's decision-making process. In addition, managers may be called on to testify at the arbitration hearing.

OVERVIEW OF GRIEVANCE OR RIGHTS ARBITRATION

While interest arbitration focuses on the creation or revision of a collective bargaining agreement, grievance or rights arbitration considers whether either party has failed to adhere to the agreed-upon terms the employment relationship. Initially, grievance arbitration was viewed as applying to disputes over the violation of the terms of the union employment relationship specified in a collective bargaining agreement. Such an agreement often incorporates existing industry practices as well as state and federal laws. In this type of grievance arbitration, the union represents the individual worker or the entire workforce in a dispute with management.

For example, a collective bargaining agreement may specify that all employees are subject to discipline or discharge for violating the corporate policy on sexual harassment. An arbitration clause may be included in the agreement to help resolve such an issue. Because the obligation to comply with the existing policy is already in place, this violation would be subject to grievance or rights arbitration.

As a result of the *Gilmer* decision, a new form of grievance arbitration may now be found in nonunion employment relationships. In nonunion environments, certain rights and obligations may be created between the parties through an employee handbook or stated company policy or may be derived from relevant statutory laws. For example, the decision in *Gilmer* required the employee to arbitrate his age discrimination claims, which essentially mandated that Gilmer participate in a form of grievance arbitration in compliance with the procedures of the NASD and applicable laws. If the parties have agreed to use arbitration, the nonunion employee and the employer are in essence participating in a form of grievance arbitration. Because no labor union is involved, these nonunion employees may represent themselves or be represented by their own private attorneys in these arbitrations. In addition, most employment arbitration awards do not provide findings of fact or conclusions of law as found in labor arbitration. Without such written decisions, it is difficult for the parties to determine the bases for the arbitral award or to understand fully their obligations toward each other in the future. The applicability of labor grievance awards to employment disputes is yet to be determined.

Any provision of a collective bargaining agreement, agreed-upon company policy, or established statutory employment right may become the subject of grievance arbitration. Examples include disputes over vacation accrual, seniority rights, layoffs, promotions, discharges, and disciplinary actions. In grievance arbitration, the arbitrator or arbitral panel focuses on the interpretation or application of party agreements, relevant laws, or customary practices in an industry. In many instances, they may also rely on judicial decisions and other arbitral awards to make their determinations. Parties select arbitrators based on their industry expertise and their record for either a liberal or strict construction of employment policies and statutory law. The main limit that most parties place on grievance arbitrators is that they may not add to, subtract from, or modify any provision of agreement in making their award. Therefore, unlike interest arbitrators, grievance arbitrators are limited to interpreting and applying existing terms, industry customs, or statutory rights to a situation rather than creating new or revised rights or obligations between employers and employees.

Grievance arbitration in both the public and private sectors is normally viewed as final and binding between the parties. Generally, the courts have been willing to defer to the judgment of the arbitrators, assuming they have the practical industry experience to more effectively handle disputes between labor and management. The issue of judicial deferral is considered in the following Supreme Court case concerning the discharge of an employee for marijuana possession.

UNITED PAPERWORKERS INTERNATIONAL UNION, AFL-CIO V. MISCO, INC.
484 U.S. 29 (1987)

FACT SUMMARY

Misco, Inc. (Misco), operated a paper plant and had a collective bargaining agreement with the United Paperworkers International Union (Union), which represented production and maintenance employees at the plant. The agreement contained a clause specifying that grievances be submitted to final binding arbitration. Under the contract, Misco reserved the right to establish, amend, or enforce rules for the discipline and discharge of employees and the imposition of appropriate discipline. One of the causes listed for discharge is bringing or consuming intoxicants, narcotics, or controlled substances on plant property or reporting for work under the influence of these substances.

Isiah Cooper, a worker represented by the Union, operated a slitter-rewinder machine, which uses sharp blades to cut rolls of paper. Cooper had been reprimanded for deficient performance twice in the past few months.

On January 21, 1983, law enforcement officials searched Cooper's home pursuant to a search warrant and found considerable amounts of marijuana. Police officers then undertook surveillance of Cooper's car at the plant. The officers watched Cooper and two other men enter a white Cutlass not owned by Cooper. The other two men eventually returned to the plant. The police officers arrested Cooper in the backseat of the car and observed marijuana smoke in the air and a lighted marijuana cigarette in the front-seat ashtray. A search of Cooper's car turned up a plastic scales case and marijuana gleanings. Cooper was charged with marijuana possession.

On January 24, Cooper advised Misco that he had been arrested for marijuana possession at his home. On January 27, Misco became aware of the circumstances of Cooper's arrest in the white Cutlass. On February 7, Misco discharged Cooper for violating company rules concerning controlled substances. Cooper filed a grievance protesting his discharge.

Misco only became aware of the marijuana found in Cooper's car a few days before the arbitration hearing. The Union was not informed of this fact until the hearing started.

The arbitrator found that Misco had failed to provide sufficient evidence that Cooper had possessed or used marijuana on company property. The arbitrator also refused to accept evidence about the marijuana seized from Cooper's car, as he had been discharged before Misco had become aware of these facts. The arbitrator upheld Cooper's grievance and ordered Misco to reinstate him with back pay and seniority.

Misco filed suit in District Court seeking to vacate the award on several grounds, including the issue that Cooper's reinstatement would violate public policy. The District Court ruled that reinstatement would violate public policy based on both general safety concerns about the operation of dangerous machinery under the influence of drugs and state criminal laws against marijuana possession. The Court of Appeals affirmed the lower court based solely on the ground that Cooper's reinstatement would violate a public policy about the operation of dangerous machinery under the influence of alcohol or drugs, and not the state's criminal laws. The Supreme Court granted certiorari.

OPINION: *JUSTICE WHITE delivered the opinion of the Court*

The issue for decision involves several aspects of when a federal court may refuse to enforce an arbitration award rendered under a collective-bargaining agreement. . . .

A court's refusal to enforce an arbitrator's award under a collective bargaining agreement because it is contrary to public policy is a specific application of the more general doctrine, rooted in the common law, that a court may refuse to enforce contracts that violate law or public policy. That doctrine derives from the basic notion that no court will lend its aid to one who founds a cause of action upon an immoral or illegal act, and is further justified by the observation that the public's interests in confining the scope of private agreements to which it is not a party will go unrepresented unless the judiciary takes account of those interests when it considers whether to enforce such agreements. . . .

As we see it, the formulation of public policy set out by the Court of Appeals did not comply with the statement that such a policy must be "ascertained" by reference to the laws and legal precedents in order to demonstrate that they establish a "well defined and dominant" policy against the operation of dangerous machinery while under the influence of drugs. Although certainly such a judgment is firmly rooted in common sense, we explicitly held in *W.R. Grace & Co. V. Rubber Workers,* 461 U.S. 757, 766, 103 S. Ct. 2177, 2183, 76 L. Ed. 2d 298 (1983), that a formulation of public policy based only on "general considerations of supposed public interests" is not the sort that permits a court to set aside an arbitration award that was entered in accordance with a valid collective-bargaining agreement.

. . . . In pursuing its public policy inquiry, the Court of Appeals quite properly considered the established fact that traces of marijuana had been found in Cooper's car. Yet the assumed connection between the marijuana gleanings found in Cooper's car and Cooper's actual use of drugs in the workplace is tenuous at best and provides an insufficient basis for holding that his reinstatement would actually violate the public policy identified by the Court of Appeals "against the operation of dangerous machinery by persons under the influence of drugs or alcohol." A refusal to enforce an award must rest on more than speculation or assumption.

In any event, it was inappropriate for the Court of Appeals itself to draw the necessary inference. To conclude from the fact that marijuana had been found in Cooper's car that Cooper had ever been or would be under the influence of marijuana while he was on the job and operating dangerous machinery is an exercise in fact-finding about Cooper's use of drugs and his amenability to discipline, a task that exceeds the authority of a court asked to overturn an arbitration award. The parties did not bargain for the facts to be found by a court, but by an arbitrator chosen by them who had more opportunity to observe Cooper and to be familiar with the plant and its problems. Nor does the fact that it is inquiring into a possible violation of public policy excuse a court for doing the arbitrator's task. . . .

The judgment of the Court of Appeals is reversed.

Discussion Questions

1. Do you think it is fair to allow Cooper to return to the workplace with back pay and full seniority?
2. What is the Supreme Court stating about the responsibility for fact-finding in an arbitration?
3. What must courts do to support an assertion that an award should be overturned based on public policy grounds?

In grievance arbitration, the parties normally agree to a set of procedures for processing a grievance in an orderly fashion. These procedures may require that grievances be in writing, filed within certain time limits, or allowed to progress through certain stages before being submitted to arbitration. Failure to comply with procedural requirements may force an arbitrator to dismiss a grievance without considering its actual substantive merits.

In cases not based solely on procedural defects, the arbitrator can focus on the facts of the dispute and consider the conduct of the employer and employee in making a decision. Here, an arbitrator must determine whether the employer or employee acted properly and in compliance with established policies or laws in a given situation. Often, grievance arbitration awards reflect whether or not an employer has properly disciplined or discharged an employee. These disputes are referred to as **just cause cases** because the arbitrator must determine if the employer had good reason for disciplining or dismissing an employee. The arbitrator will normally consider the employee's work record, the employer's previous enforcement of the alleged policy violation, the customs and practices of the industry, and any applicable laws in rendering a decision.

Business managers can assist counsel by collecting copies of the necessary employee records, relevant employer policies, pertinent industry professional standards, and other company documents needed to support the case. Managers may also testify at the arbitration hearing about such things as the facts leading up to the dispute, the process undertaken in any internal investigation, the employee's past job performance, and the employer's prior enforcement of the alleged violated policies. Maintaining good documentation of alleged employee violations and the steps taken by management prior to discipline or discharge is a critical management responsibility.

After reviewing the evidence, the arbitrator has three options: (1) to uphold the grievance, reinstating an employee with back pay, seniority, and full benefits; (2) to strike down the grievance, upholding the validity of the employer's disciplinary action or discharge; and (3) to offer a mixed result with some aspects of a grievance being upheld and others being struck down, perhaps in the form of a less severe disciplinary action. Following are two grievance arbitration awards that illustrate the different roles of arbitrators in deciding grievance disputes. In the first decision, an arbitrator must address the procedural issue of whether a union has timely filed a grievance on behalf of an employee fired for poor attendance. In the second instance, the arbitrator must decide the substantive merits of a grievance and if the employer has a just cause for firing a worker who refused to return to work early from his vacation.

IN RE MONROE MANUFACTURING, INC. AND UNION OF NEEDLETRADES, INDUSTRIAL & TEXTILE EMPLOYEES, LOCAL 2638

107 Lab. Arb. (BNA) 877 (1996)

FACT SUMMARY

The employer and the union entered into a collective bargaining agreement that included a no fault attendance program as part of the company work rules. The program used a point system based on employee absence and tardiness. Employees accumulating certain point levels were subject to discharge. The grievant had been repeatedly warned by her supervisor, Mr. Burke, that she was accumulating points under the program due to numerous absences and tardies. The union had filed several grievances on her behalf, challenging some of the points that had been charged against her. The discharged employee acknowledged that her supervisor had informed her that she was accumulating points under the program and that he had warned her that another point against her would result in dismissal. Despite this warning, she left work early for a doctor's appointment on October 11, 1995.

The grievant assumed that she had been discharged and did not return to or call in to work for the next three days. The union steward, Ms. Hughes, contacted her through her mother to tell her that she may not have been discharged. On October 17, 1995, she returned to work but was escorted off the company premises. Using the company's work rules as a guide, the company had asserted that she had quit, as she had not reported to work for three days.

At that time, the union steward verbally informed the employee's supervisor and the personnel director, Mr. Santone, that a grievance would be filed on behalf of the dismissed employee. A written request using a grievance form was then submitted to the employer. This initial request was followed by another union request for information on October 31, 1995. When the union had not received any reply from the company by December 1, the union filed a written grievance. The employer argued that the December 1 grievance was not timely but decided to allow the grievance to be processed through other steps in the process without waiving the timeliness issue. Unable to resolve the dispute on their own, the parties submitted the grievance to an arbitrator.

OPINION: *ELVIS C. STEPHENS, Arbitrator*

[The issue is:—]

1. Was the grievance timely filed?. . .

. . . .

The relevant parts of the contract include provisions of Article 11.

Any complaint, grievance or dispute arising under or relating directly or indirectly to the provisions of the Agreement, or the interpretation or performance thereof, shall, in the first instance, be taken up for adjustment in accord with the following steps:

STEP ONE:

The grievance without interruption of any work, should first be presented orally to the immediate supervisor or foreman by the employee or employees concerned. The grievance must be presented within three (3) days (including Saturdays but not Sundays and holidays) of the alleged occurrence or upon an employee's knowledge thereof, but never exceeding seven (7) days. The supervisor must reply within a reasonable time, no later than five (5) working days.

STEP TWO:

If the grievance presented in Step One is not settled, the employee may take the matter up with his steward and/or Local President, who upon verification of the fact that it has been timely filed with the supervisor, shall present the grievance in writing to the Personnel Manager within five (5) working days after receiving the supervisor's reply in Step One. The grievance must be signed by the Union and/or employee, and further identify the contract section(s) violated.

STEP THREE:

If the settlement is not obtained in Step One, the grievance shall be referred to the company's designated representative within five (5) working days from the date of the reply or failure to reply in Step Two.* * *
* * *
All time limits shall be strictly construed.

The Union contends that Ms. Hughes orally filed a grievance on October 17, 1995, the day the grievant was escorted out of the plant. In support of this contention is the testimony of Ms. Hughes, which was not contradicted by Mr. Santone, who testified that he could not recall if Ms. Hughes did state that she was filing a grievance on R's behalf. The Union argues that Union Exhibit No. 3, a request for information (filed on a griev-

ance form) concerning the points assessed R on October 11, 1995, supports its assertion that it did file a grievance for R.

However, if that is true, the problem is that this grievance was never processed to Step 2. The Union contends that the Employer never gave a reply within the time period of Step 1. Since the supervisor was no longer with the Company, we did not have any testimony from him as to whether or not a grievance was filed, and whether or not he orally answered such grievance. The contract does not require the supervisor's answer to be in writing.

The Union contends that since the Company did not reply, it is estopped from using the timeliness defense on this grievance. However, it has been a general practice in arbitration for many years that a failure of an employer to reply to a grievance, without a specific provision calling for such failure to be deemed a granting of the grievance, places a burden on the union to advance the grievance to the next step, if it wishes to pursue such grievance. The contract in question does not contain any clause granting the grievance if the employer fails to respond within the time period set forth in the various steps. Although it might be thought to be inequitable for a failure to meet time limits to reply on the employer's part to simply place the burden on the union to appeal to the next step, but the failure of the union to move the grievance to the next step within the time limits to be deemed a dismissal of the grievance, such is the reality of arbitration practice. (See Elkouri, p. 198)

Also, Step 3 of the grievance process in the contract provides that if no settlement is reached in Step 2 the Union has five days to appeal " . . . from the date of the reply or failure to reply in Step Two." This indicates that the parties intended that the failure of the Employer to reply to a grievance placed the burden on the Union to appeal to the next step. (It should be noted that the parties have failed to specify a time limit for the Employer to reply after a Step 2 meeting.)

Arbitrator J. Reese Johnston, in *Electrical Repair Service Co. and IBEW Local 1871* (69 LA 604) held that the grievance was not arbitrable since the union failed to appeal to the next step within the time limits specified in the contract. This was so even though the employer failed to answer within the time limits. In the instant case the Employer did respond to the Union's grievance filed on December 1, 1995. Joint Exhibit No. 2 shows that Steve Santone, Personnel Director, answered the grievance by denying it on the grounds that the grievance was not filed on a timely basis, and there

was no violation of the contract. Again, although the Union argues that the delay in answering this grievance should be interpreted as the Company having waived time limits, such is not the case. The contract does not have any provisions to that effect, nor was there any evidence that the Union ever requested or secured a waiver of time limits from the Company. Given the provision in the contract that the time limits shall be strictly construed, a waiver must be explicit, not implicit. There is no evidence that the Company has been lax in enforcing time limits for grievances to be processed.

Therefore, based on all of the evidence, the arbitrator concludes that the grievance must be dismissed as being untimely.

AWARD

The grievance is not timely.

Discussion Questions

1. How did the collective bargaining agreement address the issue of time limits?
2. To avoid a finding of untimeliness, what should the union have done

when the company failed to respond to its grievance?
3. Do you think that the grievant was fairly represented by the union in this case?

IN RE GOODMAN BEVERAGE COMPANY, INC., AND TEAMSTERS LOCAL 571
108 Lab. Arb. (BNA) 37 (1997)

FACT SUMMARY

The Goodman Beverage Company, Inc., was a beer and wine distributor with a union workforce represented by the International Brotherhood of Teamsters. The grievant was a twenty-three-year

employee and the second most senior truck driver and deliveryman responsible for a regular route. Based on his seniority and the vacation provisions of the collective bargaining agreement, the employee selected two weeks in April 1996 for his vacation. The grievant had prepaid travel and accommodation expenses for a family vacation to Florida.

After the grievant selected his vacation time, the most senior truck driver announced his retirement from the Company at the end of February 1996. Two weeks before the grievant's vacation, a second junior driver submitted his resignation with two weeks' notice. On March 28, the Company advised the grievant that he could now only take eight days of vacation and would have to return on April 16 rather than April 22. The grievant had previously modified his vacation plans in 1991 and 1995 to accommodate the Company. The Company was aware that the grievant had prepaid many of his vacation expenses. The grievant advised the Company that he would have to ascertain whether or not he could receive a refund and would contact the Company from Florida with an update on his return options.

On April 15, the grievant contacted the Company by telephone and said that the only way he could return by April 16 was to pay $389 for an airplane ticket. The grievant advised the Company that he could not afford to pay that extra amount and would return on April 22. On April 19, the Company sent the grievant a letter indicating that his failure to report back to work on April 16 was a voluntary quit under the terms of the collective bargaining agreement. The Employer further argued that under the management rights clause in the collective bargaining agreement it could alter employee vacations based on the needs of the business operations.

The Union countered that the grievant had clearly not voluntarily quit. The Union pointed out that the Company knew of the grievant's travel circumstances and that the grievant had properly notified the Company that he could not return until April 22. In addition, the Union noted that, under the progressive discipline spelled out in the collective bargaining agreement, the grievant's failure to return merited at most a warning, not a discharge.

OPINION: *CHARLES A. MORGAN, JR., Arbitrator*

The matter that must be addressed initially is the issue as to whether or not the Grievant's actions indicated or proved a voluntary quit. Before leaving on his designated vacation, the Grievant advised the company that he was not sure that he could get a refund and that, once he arrived at his location in Florida, that he would have to ascertain that fact and would call the Company to indicate to them the situation. On April 15 the Grievant did, in fact, call the Company and advised them that he had been advised by the motel that, in accordance with the terms of his reservation, he could not get a refund and that the only way that he could be there in time to work on April 16 was by flying home at a cost of nearly $400.00, which he could not afford without the motel refund, and told the Company that he could not report for work on April 16 but would report at his originally scheduled time on April 22.

It is an almost universally accepted arbitration rule that an employee "must clearly intend and desire to sever the employment relationship in order to effect a voluntary resignation," Elkouri and Elkouri, *How Arbitration Works,* 4th Edition,1985-89 Cumulative Supplement. In the arbitration case of *Continental Whitecap,* 90 LA 1119, Arbitrator Staudohar stated that there are three ways an employee can resign voluntarily: (1) by written statement; (2) by oral statement; or (3) by a course of action or inaction that indicates an intention to sever the employment relationship. In the instant case there was no written or oral resignation and, in the opinion of the Arbitrator, the actions of the grievant did not indicate an intention to sever the employment relationship. Therefore, the termination of the grievant can only be considered a discharge.

Issue Two: Was the discharge of the Grievant for just cause? . . .

Article 13 of the Collective Bargaining Agreement covers vacations. Section 4 thereof states that vacations shall be scheduled according to seniority and requires the Employer to post a list of employees in order of seniority with the number of weeks of eligible vacation as soon as possible after the first year. . . . There is no express contractual language granting the Employer the right to change vacation choice properly selected by an employee in accordance with the provisions of Article 13. . . . Since the right of Management to cancel is not given in an express provision of the Collective Bargaining Agreement, the exercise of it pursuant to the Management Rights Clause would certainly be subject to the doctrine of equitable estoppel.

The doctrine of equitable estoppel is a substantive rule of law, the elements basically of which are a holding out or representation and an acting upon and change of position because of that representation or holding out.

In the instant case, the representation by the Employer was that if the employee selected his vacation period in accordance with the terms of the contract, he would be entitled to that vacation at that time. The employee acted upon that and changed his position by making his reservations and paying for them in advance thereby changing his position to his detriment assuming that he would receive his vacation at the time scheduled. At the time grievant changed his position, he had no reason to anticipate that the Company would later attempt to deny him the vacation period to which he was entitled under the contract. This was reinforced by the fact on the two previous occasions in 1991 and 1995 when the Grievant had had his vacation changed, it was changed only with his acquiescence to the request of the Company that he change his vacation schedule.

It is obvious that the Company attempted to change the vacation schedule due to the shortness of drivers caused by the retirement of one driver and the resignation of the other driver in February and March. That situation was not so serious since the Company felt it could get along without the services of the Grievant.

The Arbitrator is not saying that under no circumstances does the Company have the right to change scheduled vacations, but he is saying that in this case it did not have the right under the existing circumstances. In accordance with the foregoing, the grievance must be and hereby is sustained; the Grievant will be ordered to full reinstatement with back pay and all rights, including the removal of the record of termination. . . .

Discussion Questions

1. How did the arbitrator determine that the grievant's refusal to return early from vacation was not a voluntary quit?
2. What reasons did the arbitrator give to support his award that the grievant had not been discharged for just cause?
3. Do you think that the company acted properly in this situation?

CHAPTER CONCLUSION

Arbitration has become an essential tool for the peaceful resolution of labor and employment disputes. Labor and employment arbitration provide alternatives to litigation for resolving workplace disputes and allowing employers and employees to process conflicts without interrupting industrial productivity and government services. Interest arbitration is used to break deadlocks in contract negotiations, particularly in the public sector, while grievance arbitration addresses disputes concerning the possible violation of existing rights and obligations. Arbitration can only continue to be an effective method of dispute resolution in the workplace if standards of objectivity, fairness, and due process are observed.

BEST BUSINESS PRACTICES

- Maintain a frank and focused negotiation of collective bargaining agreements to limit issues that must be resolved through interest arbitration.
- Provide detailed and objective data based on similarly situated companies or governmental agencies to support party positions or final offers submitted during interest arbitration.
- Establish clear methods for measuring and maintaining employer and union-employee compliance with the terms of collective bargaining agreements, stated company policies, and relevant statutory laws.
- Document important aspects of employee job performance and keep organized records of grievance filings to aid in grievance arbitration hearings.
- Identify clearly the types of disputes to be resolved through arbitration in employment arbitration clauses.
- Advise managers to be open and honest about the inclusion of arbitration clauses in employment documents to help avoid later confusion and litigation over the use of arbitration to resolve employment disputes.
- Collaborate with legal counsel familiar with the recommendations of the Dunlop Commission and the ABA Task Force on Alternative Dispute Resolution in Employment in establishing employment arbitration programs.

KEY TERMS

Arbitration Act of 1888, p. 200
Baseball arbitration, p. 214
Comparability groups, p. 214
Employment arbitration, p. 201

Federal Service Labor-Management
  Relations Statute, p. 213
Final offer selection, p. 214
Grievance or rights arbitration, p. 212

Individual employment contract
  exclusion, p. 201
Interest arbitration, p. 212
Internal union administration, p. 213
Just cause cases, p. 222
Labor arbitration, p. 201
Management prerogative or rights,
  p. 213
National Labor Relations Act (NLRA),
  p. 201

National Labor Relations Board
  (NLRB), p. 201
National Mediation Board (NMB),
  p. 200
National Railroad Adjustment Board
  (NRAB), p. 200
Railway Labor Act of 1920 (RLA),
  p. 200
Self-help remedies, p. 200

ETHICAL AND LEGAL REVIEW

1. The Texas courts considered whether a discharged employee was required to use arbitration for claims of wrongful discharge and disability discrimination. In that case, company supervisors had told Gonzalez, a store manager, that he must sign a particular document to start the process for receiving stock options and to retain his employment. An employment arbitration clause was contained in the document, but it had not been emphasized to the employees. The trial court would not compel the arbitration on various grounds. On appeal, the state appellate court determined that the company's delay in requesting arbitration and the manager's fraudulent representations of the document were grounds for upholding the trial court's refusal to compel arbitration. Will the state's supreme court require the employee to use arbitration to resolve his employment claims? [*EZ Pawn Corp. v. Mancias,* 934 S.W. 2d 87 (1996)]

2. A former NCR employee, Ms. Olson, brought an action for the intentional infliction of emotional distress in the Texas state courts against her former employer and certain individual defendants. The defendants brought a motion to compel arbitration under the terms of a written employment agreement with Olson. The trial court granted the motion, and an arbitration hearing date was set. Before the arbitration hearing, Olson filed a complaint in federal court against the American Arbitration Association (AAA) on her own behalf as well as those similarly situated. She challenged the attempt to compel arbitration under the state's deceptive trade practices law. She also charged that the AAA had misrepresented its arbitral panels as impartial, contending that AAA panels were biased in favor of employers, in part, because the AAA received significant fees and contributions from employers. Finally, she argued that the panels lacked diversity and were overwhelmingly white, male lawyers rather than a cross section of the public. Will the federal court uphold the trial court's order to compel employment arbitration? [*Olson v. American Arbitration Association,* 876 F. Supp. 850 (N.D. Tex. 1995)]

3. River Oaks Imaging and Diagnostic (ROID) is one of the largest medical X-ray companies in Houston with about 150 workers. Six females who had filed sexual harassment charges against a company manager were fired or forced to resign. Soon thereafter, more workers filed retaliation claims with the EEOC based on the situation. In response to the mounting complaints, ROID then moved to require employees to sign arbitration agreements to keep their jobs. The EEOC sought to secure an injunction in federal court against ROID, claiming that the ADR policy was misleading, retaliatory, and inconsistent with the principles of Title VII. Will the EEOC prevail in halting ROID's institution of its ADR policy? [*EEOC v. River Oaks Imaging and Diagnostic (ROID)*, 1995 U.S. Dist. LEXIS 6140, 1 (S.D. Tex. 1995)]

4. The Adams County Highway Department had proposed changing the language of an existing collective bargaining agreement to include a co-pay provision for employees. The provision would require employees to pay 20 percent on the first $2,000 of medical expenses, with an annual limit of $400 for individual plans and $600 for family plans. The county argued that the provision was reasonable in light of an analysis of comparable public employee groups, rising health care costs, and concerns about abuse of the prescription drug program. The union wanted the health care provisions to remain the same, countering that the county had inflated health care cost figures and lacked solid data on actual health benefit costs. Also, the union asserted that there was no evidence to support the notion that employees were abusing the prescription drug program. Furthermore, the union argued that the county must be willing to offer something in exchange for the requested change in the health care benefits. Using final offer selection, which proposal will the arbitrator select as most reasonable in this case? [*Adams County Highway Department and Adams County Highway Employees Union*, 91 Lab. Arb. (BNA) 1340 (1988)]

5. Without prior negotiation and agreement with the union, the Cook County Board of Education sought to adopt workplace AIDS policies aimed at maintaining a healthful environment. The school board unilaterally adopted a contagious disease policy, which threatened to remove teachers from the classroom; mandatory physical examinations; and forced sick leave for teachers. Although the policy applied to all contagious diseases, the school board admitted that the AIDS crisis prompted its enactment of the policy. Under Illinois law and the terms of the collective bargaining agreement, the arbitrator had to decide whether the employer could unilaterally institute the AIDS policy. Will the school board be required to negotiate with the union on an AIDS policy? [*In re Bd. of Education, Cook County and Morton Council Teachers Union, Local 571*, 89 Lab. Arb. Rep. (BNA) 521 (1987)]

SUGGESTED ADDITIONAL READINGS

Bales, Rick, and Reagan Burch. *The Future of Employment Arbitration in the Nonunion Sector.* 45 Lab. L. J. 627, 1994.

Eastman, Hope B., and David M. Rothenstein. *The Fate of Mandatory Employment Arbitration Amidst Growing Opposition: A Call for Common Ground.* 20 Employee Rel. L. J. 595, 1995.

Elkouri, Frank, and Edna Jasper Elkouri. *How Arbitration Works.* 4th Ed. 1985-89 Cumulative Supplement, pp. 1-10, 96-117.

Twomey, David P. *Labor & Employment Law, Text & Cases.* 8th Ed. 1989, pp. 297-320.

8

INTERNATIONAL COMMERCIAL ARBITRATION

CHAPTER HIGHLIGHTS

In this chapter, you will read and learn about the following:

1. The difficulties of using traditional litigation to resolve international commercial disputes.
2. The benefits of international arbitration over traditional litigation.
3. Comparisons between domestic and international commercial arbitration procedures.
4. Judicial recognition and enforcement of international arbitration awards under the New York and Panama Conventions.
5. Prominent international administering organizations supervising international arbitral panels.
6. Grounds for appeal of arbitral awards under international conventions.
7. The selection of ad hoc or institutional arbitration to resolve international disputes.
8. Business and legal considerations in developing international arbitration clauses in commercial agreements.

As businesses operate in an increasingly global marketplace, the result is a growing number of international business disputes. With no uniform system of international laws to regulate commercial activities, businesspeople must contend with a collection of treaties, conventions, customs, national laws, and national judicial decisions when such conflicts arise. Moreover, differences in culture, language, business practices, and national laws complicate the successful resolution of business conflicts. With no standard system of justice for interpreting definitively party rights and responsibilities, there is a clear need for effective, objective, and professional international dispute resolution mechanisms and organizations. In this expanding world economy, **international commercial arbitration** has become the alternative dispute resolution (ADR) method of choice for resolving international business conflicts. Businesspeople typically insert arbitration clauses into their international commercial agreements, and some nations include provisions encouraging arbitration in their bilateral and multilateral trade treaties. Numerous international and regional administering entities have been established throughout the world to assist businesses in resolving their commercial disagreements. In this chapter, we will discuss the importance of international commercial arbitration in resolving international disagreements between private parties.

NATIONAL LITIGATION VERSUS ARBITRATION OF INTERNATIONAL COMMERCIAL DISPUTES

http://

Check out the Uniserv International Commercial Law site at: http://uniserv.edu .au/law/public

In the global marketplace, there is no uniform international justice system. Most international organizations with adjudicatory authority, such as the International Court of Justice or the World Trade Organization, address conflicts between sovereign nations, not between private individuals or businesses. Traditionally, businesses entering into global transactions have resorted to standard litigation in the courts of a specific country (national courts) to resolve international commercial disagreements.

Anticipating future litigation, many businesses include choice-of-law and choice-of-forum clauses in their commercial contracts. Under a **choice-of-law clause,** the businesses agree on which nation's laws will govern any future disputes between them. A provision indicating where and in what national court any upcoming disagreements will be litigated is a **choice-of-forum clause.** Although these clauses are of benefit, some businesspeople worry about the procedural, substantive, practical, and psychological disadvantages of becoming entangled in the national courts of another party. A number of difficulties may arise when seeking redress for international commercial disputes in national courts, including (1) ensuring the neutrality of national courts, (2) processing multiple lawsuits concerning the same dispute in different countries, and (3) enforcing judicial awards in other nations. Businesspeople would be better off including an arbitration clause in their international commercial agreements. (See Figure 8.1 for examples of such clauses.) That way they have a vehicle for avoiding most of these obstacles in the process of resolving successfully an international dispute.

Concerns About Neutrality in International Disputes

A significant concern in the resolving of international disputes is the neutrality of national courts. If a lawsuit is filed in the national court of one of the disputants,

FIGURE 8.1   Sample Clauses for International Arbitration

"All disputes arising in connection with the present contract shall be finally settled under the Rules of Conciliation and Arbitration of the International Chamber of Commerce by one or more arbitrators appointed in accordance with the said Rules."

International Chamber of Commerce[1]

"Any controversy or claim arising out of or relating to this contract shall be determined by arbitration in accordance with the International Arbitration Rules of the American Arbitration Association."

[The parties may wish to consider adding]

- "The number of arbitrators shall be (one or three)";
- "The place of arbitration shall be (city and/or country)" or
- "The language(s) of the arbitration shall be _____."

American Arbitration Association[2]

A. Pre-dispute Clause

"Any controversy or claim arising out of, relating to, or in connection with, this contract, or the breach, termination or validity thereof, shall be settled by arbitration in accordance with the CPR Non-Administered International Arbitration Rules & Commentary, by (a sole arbitrator) (three arbitrators, of whom each party shall appoint one) (three arbitrators, none of whom shall be appointed by either party). Judgment upon the award rendered by the Arbitrator(s) may be entered by any court having jurisdiction thereof. The seat of the arbitration shall be (city, country). The arbitration shall be conducted in the (language). The neutral organization designated to perform the functions specified in Rule 6 and Rules 7.7(b), 7.8 and 7.9 shall be (name of CPR or other organization)."

B. Existing Dispute Submission Agreement

"We, the undersigned parties, hereby agree to submit to arbitration in accordance with the CPR Non-Administered International Arbitration Rules & Commentary (the "Rules") the following controversy:

[Describe briefly]

We further agree that the above controversy shall be submitted to (a sole arbitrator) (three arbitrators, of whom each party shall appoint one) (three arbitrators, none of whom shall be appointed by either party). We further agree that we shall faithfully observe this agreement and the Rules and that we shall abide by and perform any award rendered by the arbitrator(s). Judgment upon the award may be entered by any court having jurisdiction thereof. The seat of the arbitration shall be (city, country). The arbitration shall be conducted in the (language). The neutral organization designated to perform the functions specified in Rule 6 and Rules 7.7(b), 7.8 and 7.9 shall be (name of CPR or other organization)."

The CPR Institute for Dispute Resolution[3]

[1] ICC Rules of Arbitration (1998)—ICC Rules of Conciliation (1998); ICC Publication No. 581—ISBN 92.842.1239.1 (E); Published in its official English version by the International Chamber of Commerce; Copyright 1997—International Chamber of Commerce (ICC), Paris; Available from: *The ICC International Court of Arbitration,* 38 Cours Albert 1er, 75008 Paris, France and ICC *India,* Federation House, Tansen Marg, New Delhi 110 001, India.

[2] Reprinted with permission of the American Arbitration Association.

[3] *The CPR Institute for Dispute Resolution* is a nonprofit initiative of 500 general counsel of major corporations, leading law firms and prominent legal academics in support of private alternatives to the high costs of litigation. Organized in 1979, CPR develops new methods to resolve business and public disputes by alternative dispute resolution (ADR).

the responding party may feel at a disadvantage based on the makeup of the tribunal, the location of the proceedings, the language used in the process, and the application of national laws to the case. In addition, there may be concern that a national court will favor its own local firm in a dispute involving local, commercial, or political issues. For example, a German company might bring a legal action against a Peruvian firm in a national court in Munich. Let's say the German plaintiff is a major employer in the country. The Peruvian company may feel itself to be at a disadvantage when it faces the influential German company in an unfamiliar legal process held in a foreign language and in a foreign country.

However, if the parties agree to international arbitration, concerns about bias are eased. As in domestic commercial arbitration, parties in international arbitration have greater control over the decision-making process. Unlike in national courts, the disputants can mutually agree on the procedures to be followed, the situs of the arbitration, and the language(s) to be used during the process. The parties can also select the law that will apply to their conflict. More important, the conflicting businesses can choose the third-party neutral arbitrator who will determine the outcome of their dispute. To reduce concerns about national bias, the parties may select arbitrators from nations other than their own. For example, an Irish and a Greek company seeking to resolve a commercial dispute would decrease the chances of national bias by only selecting arbitrators from countries other than Ireland or Greece. Such would not be an option in standard litigation in national courts.

Selection of the Arbitral Forum.   In selecting the arbitral forum, the parties must recognize that national laws may affect the procedural and substantive aspects of the arbitration proceeding; while some nations may not even have any laws that apply to international arbitration. Parties should select national laws and national forums that maximize party autonomy and limit judicial intervention over the arbitral process. The Federal Arbitration Act (FAA) and many other nations' laws have liberal schemes that encourage international arbitration. Similarly, the United Nations Commission on International Trade Law (UNCITRAL) set forth the **UNCITRAL Model Law** in 1985, which provides guidance to countries on adopting international arbitration statutes. The Model Law encourages uniformity among international arbitration laws by reducing legal obstacles to international arbitration. The UNCITRAL Model Law has been adopted by a number of nations and by some states in the United States.

http://

See the UNCITRAL site: http://www.un. or.at/uncitral

Ad Hoc or Institutional Arbitration.   In fashioning an international arbitration clause, parties may agree generally to use arbitration without stating what procedures they will follow. In some cases, treaties or national laws will indicate what process will be used if the parties have not specified an applicable set of rules. For example, the UNCITRAL Model Law incorporates a detailed set of rules for an international arbitration process (**UNCITRAL Arbitration Rules**) for parties that have not selected or created their own arbitration procedures. As with domestic arbitration, parties must decide whether or not to create and implement their own arbitration procedures (ad hoc) or follow the procedures and employ the services of an administering organization (institutional).

Parties electing **ad hoc arbitration** normally will develop a clause or separate agreement spelling out their procedures for handling international commercial disputes. This clause addresses the standard aspects of arbitration, such as the location of the arbitration; the national law to be applied by the arbitrators; the selection and authority of the arbitrators; the pre-hearing rights and conduct of the parties; the nature of discovery, if any; the arbitral hearing process; and the determination of the arbitral award. In the international environment, parties must also decide the language(s) to be used throughout the proceedings, the role of nationality in arbitrator selection, and the currency to be used in the payment of the arbitral panel and the arbitral award. (See Figure 8.2 for an example of an international arbitration sum-

FIGURE 8.2   International Arbitration Summary Checklist

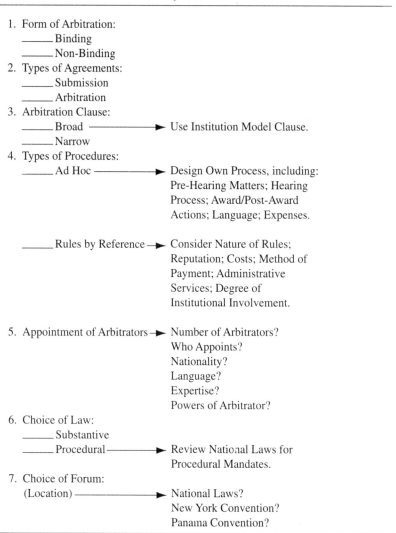

1. Form of Arbitration:
   _____ Binding
   _____ Non-Binding
2. Types of Agreements:
   _____ Submission
   _____ Arbitration
3. Arbitration Clause:
   _____ Broad —————————▶ Use Institution Model Clause.
   _____ Narrow
4. Types of Procedures:
   _____ Ad Hoc —————————▶ Design Own Process, including:
   Pre-Hearing Matters; Hearing
   Process; Award/Post-Award
   Actions; Language; Expenses.

   _____ Rules by Reference —▶ Consider Nature of Rules;
   Reputation; Costs; Method of
   Payment; Administrative
   Services; Degree of
   Institutional Involvement.

5. Appointment of Arbitrators —▶ Number of Arbitrators?
   Who Appoints?
   Nationality?
   Language?
   Expertise?
   Powers of Arbitrator?
6. Choice of Law:
   _____ Substantive
   _____ Procedural —————————▶ Review National Laws for
   Procedural Mandates.
7. Choice of Forum:
   (Location) —————————▶ National Laws?
   New York Convention?
   Panama Convention?

mary checklist.) Due to the complexities of international trade, parties will often rely on an administering organization and its time-tested procedures rather than their own arbitral rules. **Institutional arbitration** is of value with parties living in different countries and speaking different languages. However, parties should carefully evaluate any organization's rules for arbitration before agreeing to use them.

Sometimes businesses seeking to avoid the costs of retaining administering entities may borrow their recognized arbitration procedures, such as the UNCITRAL Arbitration Rules or the Rules of Inter-American Commercial Arbitration Commission. Parties acting without the assistance of an administering agency or using an ad hoc approach should be experienced in international trade matters and international dispute resolution.

ADR IN ACTION

Summary of Major International Administering Organizations

Today, arbitration is a widely accepted method of international dispute resolution. A variety of international arbitration organizations provide facilities, staff, and comprehensive rules and framework for international arbitration. These administering agencies can help disputing parties create or adopt applicable arbitration procedures, select arbitrators, and determine the proper location for the hearing. Below is a brief summary of some of the major organizations that administer international arbitration proceedings between private parties.

The International Chamber of Commerce (ICC) The **International Chamber of Commerce (ICC)** is a well-respected and leading world institution in international arbitration. It created the **International Court of Arbitration (ICC Court)** in 1923. Located in Paris, the ICC Court is assisted by a Secretariat which has more than 30 full-time staff members. In 1995, the ICC Court received more than 400 requests for arbitration proceedings involving parties from 93 different countries and involving amounts exceeding one million U.S. dollars. In addition, the ICC Court appointed and confirmed arbitrators from 62 different nationalities to hear ICC cases. The appointed arbitrators decide the disputes in accordance with the ICC Court's arbitration rules and daily administrative assistance from the ICC's Secretariat. The Secretariat also provides information to parties and their legal representatives in ICC cases. The ICC Court is known for its high level of case monitoring and management, including its review and approval of arbitral awards for proper form and substance. In addition, the ICC requires that parties agree to a document

http://

Learn more about the ICC Court of International Arbitration at: http://www. iccwbo.org

ADR IN ACTION Continued

referred to as **terms of reference,** prior to the start of an ICC arbitration. This document summarizes each party's claims and states the issues to be decided by the arbitrator. The terms of reference aim to help the parties focus on the legal and factual issues under review, to limit the introduction at the hearing of new claims not within the scope of the document, and to outline the specific procedural aspects of the arbitration.

The China International Economic and Trade Commission (CIETAC)/ Hong Kong International Arbitration Centre (HKIAC) Arbitration clauses are commonly found in commercial agreements in China and Hong Kong. Mirroring the enormous economic activity in China and Hong Kong, the combined caseloads of the **China International Economic and Trade Commission (CIETAC)** and the **Hong Kong International Arbitration Centre (HKIAC)** are the largest in the world. In 1995, the CIETAC alone dealt with about 900 cases, and the HKIAC has handled nearly 950 cases since its inception in 1985. The HKIAC benefits from its location in a major world financial center and its proximity to China. In addition, the HKIAC has one of the largest panels of experienced arbitrators, and it operates under a liberal scheme of arbitration laws. The HKIAC will even administer arbitrations under the rules of another administering entity. With the recent return of Hong Kong to Chinese sovereignty, it is unclear if the HKIAC will continue to operate as an independent center. Under Chinese government authority, the CIETAC is the sole international administering organization in China for non-maritime commercial disputes between Chinese businesses and foreign parties. More than half of the CIETAC's cases involve international commercial disputes.

The American Arbitration Association (AAA) Established in 1926, the American Arbitration Association (AAA) is a nonprofit administering agency and a leader in conflict management disputes in the United States. Although most of the AAA's disputes are domestic, the AAA has responded to the growing demand for international arbitration by entering into collaborative agreements with arbitral organizations in more than 50 countries. In 1990, the AAA participated in more than 200 international arbitration proceedings. The AAA has taken a flexible approach to handling international disputes with its network partners. In some instances, the AAA will allow parties to use the rules of a foreign administering entity at its offices in the United States. Similarly, parties may opt to follow the International Arbitration Rules of the AAA at administering organizations in foreign nations.

http://

Check out the Institute of Arbitrators, Australia, at: http://www. instarb.com.au/ index.html

The London Court of International Arbitration (LCIA) The **London Court of International Arbitration (LCIA)** was established as a conflict resolution entity in 1892 under the auspices of the London Chamber of Commerce and Industry, the Corporation of the City of London, and the Chartered Institute of Arbitrators. Major revisions to its procedural rules in 1985 opened the door for the LCIA to become more involved in international commercial disputes. Unlike the ICC, the LCIA promotes greater party autonomy and encourages more rapid dispute resolution through its less stringent administrative presence. The LCIA draws primarily from attorneys who are English Queen's Counsels to serve on its arbitral panels.

The Arbitration Center of the World Intellectual Property Organization (WIPO) Inaugurated in 1994, the **Arbitration Center of the World Intellectual Property Organization (WIPO)** is one of the most recent entrants into the field of international arbitration. This entity was created in response to the growing number of international conflicts focusing on intellectual property rights. The Arbitration Center of the WIPO is a U.N.-sponsored agency that offers arbitration and other conflict resolution services to handle intellectual property disagreements. It has adopted the UNCITRAL Arbitration Rules with some modifications to reflect the processing of intellectual property disputes. Like the LCIA, the Arbitration Center of WIPO stresses party control while offering relatively low-cost administrative assistance to disputing parties.

Fast-Track Arbitration. In international arbitration, the parties may decide to use fast-track arbitration. In a **fast-track arbitration,** the businesspeople agree to resolve certain types of disputes within a fixed time period. A fast-track arbitration provision supplements a general arbitration clause and defines specific categories of disputes to receive expedited treatment. For example, the parties may agree that disputes regarding the terms and conditions of payment will be resolved within a six-month time frame to ensure quick resolution and limited disruption of the business relationship. Disputes not contained in the fast-track arbitration clause are handled in accordance with a general arbitration provision in a commercial contract. Businesspeople should work in concert with their legal counsel to decide whether fast-track arbitration is appropriate for their business relationships and agreements.

Dealing with Multiple Lawsuits in Various Countries

When an international commercial dispute occurs, the moving party may elect to file its action in a court that the claimant believes favors its own position. Even in instances in which the parties have agreed on choices of law and forum specified

http://

Information on the International Trade Law Monitor can be found at:
http:itl.uit.no/ trade_law

in an arbitration clause, a party may decide to challenge the validity of the clause when a dispute arises. In some instances, the selected national court may not be willing to enforce the clause on public policy, jurisdictional, or other contractual or legal grounds. In other instances, parties may have been unable to agree on or specify which country's laws will apply to their disagreements and which nation's court will interpret their obligations.

The responding party may disagree with the choice and file its own lawsuit in another country's court system. Soon the parties are fending off separate court proceedings in which each disputant is challenging the other's selected forum and laws. Each court may resolve the jurisdictional issues differently; one may claim valid jurisdiction over the dispute and apply its own nation's laws, while the other may suggest that a third country is the appropriate forum and possesses the relevant law. Lengthy appeals may follow on jurisdictional issues before any substantive issues are even addressed. Therefore, the use of separate lawsuits in distinct locations can waste the time and resources of all parties involved.

An important benefit of international arbitration is the savings of time and money spent on multiple lawsuits around the globe. By selecting arbitration, the parties are electing to use one process to reconcile their differences. In addition, the disputants can agree in advance on the proper location of the arbitration, preferably in a nation convenient to both participants. In most international arbitration cases, the parties agree to comply with the arbitral award and have little or no opportunity for appeal. Following is a landmark decision in which the Supreme Court states its view on the value of international arbitration and the problem of multiple lawsuits in international commercial disagreements.

SCHERK V. ALBERTO-CULVER CO.
417 U.S. 506 (1973)

FACT SUMMARY

Alberto-Culver Co., a U.S. toiletries and hair care products corporation, sought to expand its international market presence in the 1960s. In 1969, Alberto-Culver entered into an agreement with Fritz Scherk, a German citizen living in Switzerland, who owned three toiletries enterprises organized under the laws of Germany and Liechtenstein. Under the agreement, Scherk would transfer ownership of these businesses, including their trademarks, to Alberto-Culver. The agreement contained an arbitration clause that directed any future controversies to be resolved before the International Chamber of Commerce in Paris using the laws of the state of Illinois in the United States. About a year later, Alberto-Culver discovered that the trademarks were encumbranced and that others may have had superior rights to use them. Alberto-Culver returned the property and offered to rescind the contract. Scherk refused to rescind. Alberto-Culver brought an action against Scherk in an Illinois federal court claiming that fraudulent misrepresentations violated the Securities and Exchange Act of 1934. Scherk countered with a motion to dismiss or alternatively to stay the court action until the matter had been arbitrated at the ICC. In opposing Scherk's motion, Alberto-Culver sought a preliminary injunction restraining the initiation of arbitration proceedings. The district court granted Alberto-Culver's request and stayed the arbitration. The district court had relied on the Supreme Court precedent in *Wilko v. Swan* which indicated that disputes under the Securities and Exchange Act of 1933 were not arbitrable. Scherk appealed, and the Seventh Circuit Court of Appeals affirmed the trial court decision. Scherk petitioned the Supreme Court for review, and the Court granted Scherk's request.

OPINION: *MR. JUSTICE STEWART, delivered the opinion of the Court*

The United States Arbitration Act, (citation omitted), reversing centuries of judicial hostility to arbitration agreements, was designed to allow parties to avoid "the costliness and delays of litigation," and to place arbitration agreements "upon the same footing as other contracts. . . ."

. . . .

The Court [in *Wilko v. Swan*] ruled that an agreement to arbitrate "is a 'stipulation' and [that] the right to select the judicial forum is the kind of 'provision' that cannot be waived under §14 of the Securities Act." 346 U.S. at 434-436, 74 S. Ct. At 186. Thus, Wilko's advance agreement to arbitrate any disputes subsequently arising out of his contract to purchase the securities was unenforceable under the terms of §14 of the Securities Act of 1933.

. . . .

Accepting the premise, however, that the operative portions of the language of the 1933 Act relied upon in *Wilko* are contained in the Securities Act of 1934, the respondent's reliance on *Wilko* in this case ignores the significant and, we find, crucial differences between the agreement involved in *Wilko* and the one signed by the parties here. Alberto-Culver's contract to purchase the business entities belonging to Scherk was truly an international agreement. Alberto-Culver is an American corporation with its principal place of business and vast bulk of its activities in this country, while Scherk is a citizen of Germany whose companies were organized under the laws of Germany and Liechtenstein. The negotiations leading to the signing of the contract in Austria and to the closing in Switzerland took place in the United States, England, and Germany, and involved consultations with legal and trademark experts from each of those countries and from Liechtenstein. Finally, and most significantly, the subject matter of the contract concerned the sale of business enterprises organized under the laws of and primarily situated in European countries, whose activities were largely, if not entirely, directed to European markets.

Such a contract involves considerations and policies significantly different from those found controlling in *Wilko*. In *Wilko*, quite apart from the arbitration provision, there was no question but that the laws of the United States generally, and the federal securities laws in particular, would govern disputes arising out of the stock-purchase agreement. The parties, the negotiations, and the subject matter of the contract were all situated in this country, and no credible claim could have been entertained that any international conflict-of-laws problems would arise. In this case, by contrast, in the absence of the arbitration provision, considerable uncertainty existed at the time of the agreement, and still exists, concerning the law applicable to the resolution of disputes arising out of the contract.

Such uncertainty will almost inevitably exist with respect to any contract touching two or more countries, each with its own substantive laws and conflict-of-laws rules. A contractual provision specifying in advance the forum in which disputes shall be litigated and the law to be applied is, therefore, an almost indispensable precondition to achievement of the orderliness and predictability essential to any international business transaction. Furthermore, such a provision obviates the danger that a dispute under the agreement might be submitted to a forum hostile to the interests of one of the parties or unfamiliar with the problem area involved.

A parochial refusal by the courts of one country to enforce an international arbitration agreement would not only frustrate these purposes, but would invite unseemly and mutually destructive jockeying by the parties to secure tactical litigation advantages. In the present case, for example, it is not inconceivable that if Scherk had anticipated that Alberto-Culver would be able in this country to enjoin resort to arbitration he might have sought an order in France or some other country enjoining Alberto-Culver from proceeding with its litigation in the United States. Whatever recognition the courts of this country might ultimately have granted to the order of the foreign court, the dicey atmosphere of such a legal no-man's land would surely damage the fabric of international commerce and trade, and imperil the willingness and ability of businessmen to enter into international commercial agreements. (footnote omitted).

. . . .

An agreement to arbitrate before a specialized tribunal is, in effect, a specialized kind of forum-selection clause that posits not only the situs of suit but also the procedure to be used in resolving the dispute. (footnote omitted). The invalidation of such an agreement in the case before us would not only allow the respondent to repudiate its solemn promise but would, as well, reflect a "parochial concept that all disputes must be resolved under our laws and in our courts. . . . We cannot have trade and commerce in world markets and international waters exclusively on our terms, governed by our laws, and resolved in our courts." *Id.* at 9, 92 S. Ct. at 1912. (footnote omitted).

For all these reasons we hold that the agreement of the parties in this case to arbitrate any dispute arising out of their international commercial transaction is to be respected and enforced by the federal courts in accord with the explicit provisions of the Arbitration Act. . . .

Discussion Questions

1. According to the Court, what are some of the benefits of using arbitration clauses in international commercial agreements?

2. How did the Court distinguish the *Wilko* case from its decision in this case?

3. How might the Court's refusal to enforce an international arbitration clause affect the actions of the parties in the courts of other foreign nations?

Enforceability of International Arbitration Clauses and Awards

One of the primary problems with using national litigation to resolve international conflicts is the lack of enforceability of national judicial awards. A party suing for breach of contract in another country may be awarded both legal and equitable relief. However, countries will not always accept each other's court orders or legal precedents, unless otherwise required to do so by national law or applicable treaty. No independent world adjudicatory organization can mandate that a court enforce the foreign judgment.

For example, an Iraqi court may have awarded an Iraqi firm $500,000 and injunctive relief against an American firm. The American company can decide not to comply with the award. Let's say the American company has no assets in Iraq. The prevailing party may then seek to enforce the award in the United States. Unless mandated by statute or treaty, however, the U.S. court need not enforce the award. Once again, the claimant might have spent considerable time and money to secure the judgment only to receive nothing in return.

http://

The following site contains the text of New York Convention and current list of signatory nations and text of International Arbitration Rules of AAA: http://www.adr. org

The New York Convention.   Generally, arbitrators have no legal authority to mandate compliance with their award but must rely on domestic courts for enforcement. In most instances, parties who have agreed to use arbitration will also comply with the mandates of an arbitral award. If a party refuses to comply with an award, the prevailing party may seek to enforce it in the relevant national court.

Unlike foreign court judgments and orders, international arbitral awards are much easier to enforce because of the 1958 United Nations Convention on the Recognition and Enforcement of Foreign Arbitral Awards, commonly referred to as the **New York Convention.** Effective since June 7, 1959, signatory nations under this U.N.-sponsored international treaty agree to enforce written arbitration clauses and refuse to allow parties to litigate disputes in their national courts. These ratifying nations also agree to recognize and enforce subsequent international arbitration awards. As of May 1997, some 112 nations have ratified the New York Convention, including the United States, China, Australia, India, Japan, some Middle Eastern countries, and most European and Latin American nations. In 1970, the United States ratified the Convention and provided the federal courts with the subject matter jurisdiction to enforce such arbitral awards by incorporating the Convention's terms into the provisions of the FAA. The U.S. courts have broadly interpreted the terms of the New York Convention to uphold relevant arbitration awards.

In adopting the New York Convention, Congress set forth certain conditions under which the federal courts could have subject matter jurisdiction over arbitral disputes involving the Convention. First, the Convention applies only to nondomestic or international arbitration awards. Under the Convention, the term **nondomestic award** generally means arbitral awards made in the territory of a nation other than the country where the recognition and enforcement of such awards are sought. For example, an arbitration award may be issued in the United States to resolve a business dispute that arose under commercial transactions in the United

States between two U.S. companies. Normally, if one of the parties sought to enforce the award in the United States, it would not be processed under the terms of the Convention.

However, the Convention also allows for national legal differences in defining the term nondomestic. The treaty states further that "[i]t shall also apply to arbitral awards not considered as domestic awards in the State where their recognition and enforcement are sought." Therefore, one must examine the legal interpretations of a particular country to determine whether the Convention applies to the award.

In the United States, statutory law incorporating the New York Convention indicates that arbitration proceedings between solely citizens (individuals or corporations) of the United States do not fall within the coverage of the Convention unless they involve property abroad, the performance or enforcement of the award abroad, or reasonable relation with one or more foreign nations. Under this approach, an arbitral award based on a dispute between two U.S. businesses may be enforceable in the federal courts if the performance of the award were to ocur in a foreign nation. In the following case, a federal court must determine whether an arbitral award is nondomestic or international under the terms of the New York Convention.

DWORKIN-COSELL INTERAIR COURIER SERVICES, INC., ET AL. V. AVRAHAM
728 F. Supp. 156 (S.D. N.Y. 1989)

FACT SUMMARY

A dispute arose between Daniel Avraham, an Israeli citizen; Dworkin-Cosell Interair Courier Services, Inc. (Dworkin-Cosell), a New York corporation; Shigur Express, Ltd. (Shigur), an Israeli corporation; and Moshe Dworkin, a U.S. citizen, who was the president and CEO of Dworkin-Cosell. In 1987, Avraham entered into an employment agreement and a stock purchase and shareholder agreement, both of which contained arbitration clauses. Under the employment agreement, Avraham was to become the vice president and director of Dworkin-Cosell. Avraham also entered into a stock purchase and shareholder agreement in which he and Dworkin would

share in the sale of fifty percent of the outstanding shares of Dworkin-Cosell stock to Shigur. Later that year, Avraham was terminated, and he filed a demand for arbitration claiming breaches of both agreements. After attempts to stay Avraham's demand for arbitration, the court compelled the parties to participate in an arbitration proceeding in New York. The arbitral panel found for Avraham, and Avraham sought to confirm the award in the federal courts in New York. Dworkin-Cosell, Shigur, and Dworkin countered that the court lacked subject matter jurisdiction, in part, because the award was domestic as defined by the New York Convention.

OPINION: *LOUIS L. STANTON, United States District Judge*

Avraham recognizes that unless the Convention on the Recognition and Enforcement of Foreign Arbitral Awards (the "Convention") provides this court with jurisdiction, this court cannot confirm the Award. There is no diversity between the parties, and the Federal Arbitration Act does not provide an independent basis for subject matter jurisdiction.

The Convention is incorporated into United States law at 9 U.S.C. §§201-08. Article I (1) of the Convention states that it shall "apply to arbitral awards not considered domestic awards in the State where their recognition and enforcement are sought." In keeping with Article I(1), at 9 U.S.C. §§202, 203 vests United States' district courts with original jurisdiction, regardless of the amount in controversy, over actions concerning "an arbitration agreement or arbitral award arising out of a legal relationship . . . which is considered as commercial. . . . " However, if the agreement or award arises out of a relationship "which is entirely between citizens of the United States," it does not come under the Convention unless it involves property abroad, "envisages performance or enforcement abroad, or has some reasonable relation with one or more foreign states." 9 U.S.C. §202.

Petitioners contend that the Award does not come under the Convention because it is a "domestic award."

Bergesen v. Joseph Muller Corp., 710 F. 2d 928 (2d Cir. 1983) sets forth this circuit's definition of a nondomestic award:

> The Convention did not define nondomestic awards. The definition appears to have been left out deliberately in order to cover as wide a variety of eligible awards as possible, while permitting the enforcing authority to supply its own definition of 'nondomestic' in conformity with its own national law. . . . We adopt the view that awards 'not considered as domestic' denotes awards which are subject to the Convention not because made abroad, but because made within the legal framework of another country, *e.g., pronounced in accordance with foreign law or involving parties domiciled or having their principal place of business outside the enforcing jurisdiction. Id.* at 932 (emphasis added).

Petitioners contend that "It is conceivable that Congress intended for the mere presence of a foreign shareholder in . . . an employment dispute and a shareholders dispute concerning a New York corporation under New York law, to be sufficient in and of itself to bring such a dispute within the ambit of the convention." . . . Here, the Employment Agreement is between a United States corporation and an Israeli citizen for services to be performed in Israel. The Stock Purchase and Shareholders Agreement, between Israeli citizens (Shigur and Avraham) and American citizens (Dworkin-Cosell and Dworkin), concerns a sale of a New York corporation's stock to an Israeli corporation.

Congress's intent for "the broadest possible implementation of the Convention," (citations omitted) coupled with the factors listed by Avraham in his removal petition, support the conclusion that the Award is not a domestic one:

> The Stock Purchase and Shareholders Agreement . . . relates directly to a sale of the stock of a New York corporation by a United States citizen and an Israeli citizen to an Israeli company (Shigur) and . . . places obligations on the parties concerning engaging in business in air freight and sea freight between the United States and Israel or . . . otherwise engaging in business in New York and

Israel . . . ; [provides] for the Buyer (Shigur) to receive approval of an Israeli company (Clal, Ltd.) with respect to the Shareholders Agreement "and transactions contemplated thereby" . . . ; [and] for the right of first refusal of transfer of shares to be inapplicable to transfers to any entity of which Clal (Israel) Ltd. is a major shareholder. . . . The Employment Agreement . . . is . . . between a New York corporation . . . and . . . a resident and citizen of Israel, providing for [Avraham's] principal place of work being "the Company's principal office in Israel."

Accordingly, petitioners' challenge to this court's jurisdiction is overruled. . . .

Discussion Questions

1. How does the court define the term nondomestic award under the U.S. statutory incorporation of the Convention?
2. What factors does the court evaluate in deciding that this New York arbitral award is a nondomestic one?
3. Does the court illustrate a broad or strict construction of Convention terms in making its decision?

Reciprocity and Commercial Dealings.   In addition to jurisdiction, the recognition and enforcement provisions of the Convention rest on the grounds of reciprocity and commercial dealings. As to **reciprocity,** the Convention requires that nations provide mutual recognition and enforcement of international arbitral awards of other signatories but not those of countries that have not acceded to the Convention. For example, a Venezuelan company and a British company decided to arbitrate a disagreement at an administering organization in a third neutral country, Brazil. The Brazilian arbitrator awarded damages to the Venezuelan company. At that time, however, Brazil was not a signatory to the New York Convention. The British company thus refused to comply with the arbitral award. The Venezuelan company may now seek to enforce the award in the British courts, although the British court would not be required to enforce it due to the lack of reciprocity.

The terms of the Convention apply only to international arbitration awards that are considered commercial in nature. Among these **commercial dealings** are contractual disagreements. Whether or not a conflict arises from a commercial transaction or relationship will depend on the interpretation of the ratifying nation's laws.

Enforcement of the Award.   If the requirements of the Convention are met, a party seeking enforcement need only supply authenticated original or certified copies of the international arbitration award and arbitration agreement to the court. The burden of proving the invalidity of an award falls on the party seeking to challenge it. The grounds for any challenge are limited under the New York Convention and are similar to those outlined in the UNCITRAL Model Law, the FAA, and the national laws of many other countries.

The Convention allows for courts of signatory nations to refuse to recognize and enforce arbitral clauses or awards under these conditions: (1) the arbitration agreement was invalid under the applicable law, such as incapacity of one of the parties; (2) there was a lack of notice of, or a fair opportunity to be heard in, the arbitral proceeding; (3) the composition of the arbitral panel or the arbitral procedures used were not in compliance with the parties' agreement or applicable national law; (4) the arbitral award exceeded the arbitrator's scope of authority under the relevant arbitration agreement; (5) the award is not ripe for review as it has not yet been finalized; (6) the subject matter of the dispute is not arbitrable under laws of the enforcing country; and (7) the award is contrary to the public policy of the enforcing nation. In the following case, a company seeks to challenge the enforcement of an international arbitral award and to have the court undertake a de novo factual and legal review claiming that the award violates public policy.

CELULOSA DEL PACIFICO S.A. V. A. AHLSTROM CORPORATION
1996 U.S. Dist. LEXIS 2747 (S.D. N.Y. 1996)

FACT SUMMARY

The petitioner is a Chilean corporation, Celulosa Del Pacifico S.A. (Pacifico). Pacifico entered into a purchase agreement for pulp mill equipment from a Finnish corporation, A. Ahlstrom Corporation (Ahlstrom), which included an arbitration provision. Under the contract, Pacifico opted to use its own staff to construct Ahlstrom's components and those of other vendors. When the equipment was received from Ahlstrom, Pacifico indicated that it met all contract specifications. However, before the chemical recovery boiler was put into service, it was erected by Pacifico and found to have more than 100 leaks and cracks. Pacifico and Ahlstrom initially agreed that Ahlstrom would provide replacement equipment and additional services pending a determination of the cause of the leaks and cracks. Ultimately, Ahlstrom demanded more than $6 million from Pacifico for the equipment replacement and repair as well as for Pacifico's alleged wrongful call on Ahlstrom's letter of credit. Pacifico rejected Ahlstrom's demand, asserting that the equipment failure was covered under the warranty provisions of the original purchase agreement. In accordance with the purchase agreement, Pacifico demanded arbitration in New York under the rules of the ICC. The arbitral panel found for Ahlstrom. Pacifico filed a motion to vacate the award in the state courts. Ahlstrom ultimately succeeded in removing the dispute to the federal courts for enforcement under the New York Convention.

OPINION: *ROBERT P. PATTERSON, JR., U.S. District Judge*

Pacifico's motion requests this Court to vacate the award as "completely irrational," "contrary to public policy" and "in manifest disregard of the law." In support of its motion, Pacifico attaches a plethora of exhibits from the arbitral proceeding in an effort to persuade the Court to embark on a de novo review of the evidence and make findings of fact and conclusions of law at variance with the arbitral panel's determination.

. . . .

Pacifico's motion is based principally on the majority's determination that certain warranties in the Agreement did not cover the failure of the superheater before it was placed in service. . . .

Pacifico argues that it was "absurd" for the arbitrators to find these warranties applied only to the period after start-up and not to the period before start-up. Comparing the warranty to the type a consumer receives from an electronic retailer, it argued that the warranty also had to apply to the pre-start-up period. It argues that such a warranty has to be implied and must be implied by law. It did not, however, advance an implied warranty theory in its terms of reference or in its post-hearing briefs.

The warranty, here, however, was not a retailer's warranty of a consumer product but a warranty in an agreement between industrial companies which was negotiated at length by those companies. Pacifico undertook to construct the boiler and superheater from Ahlstrom's components and components supplied by other vendors. Under such circumstances, it is entirely reasonable to find, as the majority arbitrators did, that under the agreement reached by the parties, Ahlstrom's warranty of life of its components would not start until the components of the recovery unit had been properly assembled, the recovery unit tested and put into service. It was Ahlstrom's contention that the superheater failed during testing because Pacifico neglected to follow Ahlstrom's guidelines and instructions and not from any action by Ahlstrom. (citation omitted). The majority arbitrators concluded that Pacifico had not carried its burden of establishing that Ahlstrom's actions were the cause of the superheater's failure. (citation omitted). Under the facts of this case, the majority opinion appears to be a well-grounded interpretation of the contract and consistent with the evidence presented. The award is not in the least absurd or irrational. Nor is it contrary to the public policy of this forum.

It is well settled that "the question of interpretation of the . . . agreement is a question for the arbitrator. It is the arbitrator's construction which was bargained for; and so far as the arbitrator's decision concerns construction of the contract, the courts have no business overruling him because their interpretation of the contract is different from his." *United Steel Workers v. Enterprise Wheel & Car Corp.,* 363 U.S. 593, 599, 4 L. Ed. 2d 1424, 80 S. Ct. 1358 (1960).

Pacifico and Ahlstrom are both non-U.S. parties. The award is governed by the New York Convention. (citations omitted). The grounds upon which a party may oppose confirmation are limited to those set out in Article V of the Convention. *Andros Compania Maritima, S.A. v. Marc Rich & Co. A.G.,* 570 F. 2d 691, 699 (2d Cir. 1978); *Fotochrome, Inc., v. Copal, Co., Ltd.,* 517 F. 2d 512, 516 (2d Cir. 1975). The only conceivable ground set out in Article V would be that in Section 2(b), "The recognition of the award would be contrary to public policy of [the forum state]." This provision is to be construed narrowly and to be applied only where enforcement would violate the forum state's most basic notions of morality and justice. *Fotochrome, Inc., v. Copal, Co., Ltd.,* 517 F. 2d 512, 516 (2d Cir. 1975); *Parsons & Whittemore Overseas Co. v.* *Societe Generale* de *L'Industrie du Papier (RAKTA),* 508 F. 2d 969, 974 (2d Cir. 1974); *Andros Compania Maritima, S.A. v. Marc Rich & Co. A.G.,* 570 F. 2d 691, 699 n. 11 (2d Cir. 1978). Review of the award and the record underlying the award reveals no basis whatsoever for finding a violation of basic notions of morality and justice.

The petitioner's motion is denied. . . .

Discussion Questions

1. Will the court broadly interpret the public policy ground for appeal of an international arbitration award?

2. How does the court define what is meant by a violation of public policy under the New York Convention?

3. Does the court defer to the factual and contract determinations of the arbitral panel in this international arbitration proceeding?

Panama Convention.   Aside from the New York Convention, parties planning to use international arbitration should determine whether there are bilateral treaties or regional conventions that may aid in the enforcement of arbitration awards. For example, the Inter-American Convention on International Commercial Arbitration **(Panama or Inter-American Convention)** is a regional version of the New York Convention within the western hemisphere sponsored by the Organization of American States (OAS). The Panama or Inter-American Convention includes similar requirements related to reciprocity and commercial conduct, but applies to the recognition and enforcement of both international and domestic commercial arbitral awards rendered by signatory nations. Between these two conventions, the Panama or Inter-American Convention has primary authority over arbitral awards in the western hemisphere. Canada, the United States, Mexico, Central America, and most South American nations have ratified the Panama or Inter-American Convention. If disputing parties fail to agree on the arbitration rules, this regional convention provides for the application of the current Rules of Inter-American Commercial Arbitration Commission. The U.S. courts have generally used precedent arising from the New York Convention to interpret the Panama or Inter-American Convention. In enforcement proceedings, the Panama or Inter-American Convention uses the same burden of proof and defenses as the New York Convention, although the specific procedures for enforcement are somewhat different. In the following case, the federal court must decide whether it has jurisdiction to enforce an arbitral award under the Panama or Inter-American Convention.

PRODUCTOS MERCANTILES E INDUSTRIALES, S.A. V. FABERGE USA, INC.

23 F. 3d 41 (2nd Cir. 1994)

FACT SUMMARY

In 1971, Productos Mercantiles E Industriales, S.A. (Prome), a Guatemalan corporation, entered into an exclusive licensing agreement with Faberge USA, Inc., a U.S. corporation. Under the agreement, Prome was permitted to use Faberge trademarks on its products in Central America. In 1989, Faberge was acquired by Unilever United States, Inc., which was owned by Unilever, N.V. of the Netherlands and Unilever PLC, a United Kingdom corporation. Unilever assigned its Central American Faberge business to Industrias Unisola, S.A. (Unisola). Faberge informed Prome that it would not renew the licensing agreement when it expired in December 1989. In 1991, Prome filed a claim for arbitration against Faberge and Unisola with the American Arbitration Association in New York. Prome sought to include Unilever in the arbitration, but it refused to participate in the proceeding. The arbitral panel found for $58,949.94 for Prome. Due to a typographical error, the arbitral award was later corrected to $158,949.94 in one paragraph, but not in a second paragraph. Unisola paid the original amount plus interest, but it refused to pay the new amount, which had only been corrected in one paragraph. Prome petitioned the federal court to modify the award to correct the inconsistency and to confirm and enforce the award against Faberge, Unisola, and Unilever. Under the terms of the Panama Convention, Faberge, Unisola, and Unilever moved to dismiss

Prome's action, claiming that the court lacked subject matter jurisdiction over the dispute because the award was domestic, not international. The district court denied their motion, and appeals were taken.

OPINION: *TIMBERS, Circuit Judge*

(A) SUBJECT MATTER JURISDICTION

Appellants contend that the court erred in denying their motion to dismiss for lack of subject matter jurisdiction pursuant to Fed. R. Civ. P. 12(b)(1). Specifically appellants contend that the court erred in finding that the Federal Arbitration Act (FAA), 9 U.S.C. §§ 1-16 (1988 & Supp. IV 1992), in conjunction with the Inter-American Convention on International Commercial Arbitration, done January 30, 1975 O.A.S.T.S. No. 42, reprinted in 9 U.S.C.A. §301(Supp. 1994)(Inter-American Convention), (1) provided the court with subject matter jurisdiction and (2) authorized the court to modify the arbitration award. These contentions are without merit.

(1)Jurisdiction under the Convention

Appellants contend that the court did not have subject matter jurisdiction because the arbitration award was rendered in the United States. Appellants cite the Senate's third reservation to the ratification of the Inter-American Convention, which provides that "the United States of America will apply the Convention, on the basis of reciprocity, to the recognition and enforcement of only those awards made in the territory of another Contracting State." (citation omitted). . . . Appellants contend that these provisions limit the federal courts' jurisdiction over arbitration awards to awards rendered in foreign countries that are signatories to the Inter-American Convention. We disagree.

A plain reading of §304 and the Senate's third reservation indicates that they are intended to bar the enforcement of arbitration decisions rendered in nations not signatories to the Inter-American Convention. The only express prerequisite to the court's jurisdiction is that the dispute between the parties concerns a commercial transaction or agreement. 9 U.S.C.§302 (Supp. IV 1992) (incorporating 9 U.S.C.§§202 and 203(1988)). . . . If Congress had intended to exclude from the court's jurisdiction all awards rendered in the United States, it could have done so by express provision in the enacting legislation. Since it did not do so, we agree with the court that it had the jurisdiction to confirm the arbitration award.

Our decision in *Bergesen v. Joseph Muller Corp.,* 710 F. 2d 928 (2d Cir. 1983), further supports the court's holding that it had subject matter jurisdiction under the Inter-American Convention. In *Bergesen,* we rejected arguments similar to those of appellants in a case involving an analogous treaty. In *Bergesen,* we held that the court had jurisdiction under the Convention on the Recognition and Enforcement of Foreign Arbitral Awards, done June 10, 1958, 21 U.S.T. 2517, 330 U.N.T.S. 38, reprinted in 9 U.S.C.A. §201(Supp. 1994)(New York Convention), to confirm an arbitration award rendered in New York concerning a dispute between two foreign parties. *Id.* at 932-34.

Article I(1) of the New York Convention provides that it applies (1) to the "enforcement of arbitral awards made in the territory of a State other than the State where the recognition and enforcement of such awards are sought" and (2) to "arbitral awards not considered as domestic awards in the State where their recognition and enforcement are sought." *Id.* at 932 n. 2. We held that the court did not have jurisdiction on the first part of this jurisdictional requirement, since the award was rendered in New York. *Id.* We held, however, basis that the arbitration award was a nondomestic award, since it involved a dispute between two foreign parties. *Id.*

In reaching this conclusion, we considered the enacting legislation, which provided that an arbitration award between citizens of the United States was not subject to the New York Convention unless it had some reasonable relation with a foreign state. 9 U.S.C. §202 (1988). We reasoned that Congress also could have excluded from the New York Convention arbitration awards rendered in the United States concerning disputes between foreign parties, but that Congress did not do so. *Bergesen, supra,* 710 F. 2d at 933. We concluded that "it would be anomalous to hold that a district court could direct two aliens to arbitration within the United States under the statute [9 U.S.C. §206] but that it could not enforce the resulting award under the legislation which, in large part, was enacted for just that purpose." *Id.*

A similar situation is presented in the instant action. Prome, a foreign corporation, commenced the arbitration process against Faberge, a domestic corporation, and Unisola, a foreign corporation. The underlying dispute concerned the parties' obligations under the 1971 agreement regarding of Faberge trademarks in

Central America. This award would be considered a nondomestic award under the second part of the New York Convention. Furthermore, the enacting legislation with respect to the Inter-American Convention authorizes the court to "direct that arbitration be held in accordance with the [Inter-American Convention]". 9 U.S.C. §303(Supp. IV 1992).

Appellants contend that *Bergesen* is inapposite, since it involved a different treaty. The legislative history of the Inter-American Convention's implementing statute, however, clearly demonstrates that Congress intended the Inter-American Convention to reach the same results as those reached under the New York Convention:

> "The New York Convention and the Inter-American Convention are intended to achieve the same results, and their key provisions adopt the same standards, phrased in the legal style appropriate for each organization. It is the Committee's expectation, in view of that fact and the parallel legislation under the Federal Arbitration Act that would be applied to the Conventions, that courts in the United States would achieve a general uniformity of results under the two conventions." (citation omitted).

Moreover, the enacting legislation with respect to the Inter-American Convention does not contain language similar to the strict territorial approach provided in the first part of the New York Convention. This is further evidence that Congress did not intend the Inter-American Convention to preclude the enforcement of an arbitration award that is essentially foreign in character simply because the award is rendered in the United States. In the absence of such territorial language, and in light of Congress's intent that the two treaties should produce similar results, we believe that the court had subject matter jurisdiction in the instant action.

We agree with the court's decision that it had subject matter jurisdiction over the arbitration award pursuant to the Inter-American Convention. . . .

Discussion Questions

1. Why did the court apply the Panama or Inter-American Convention rather than the New York Convention in this case?

2. How does the court use the New York Convention to supports its decision involving the Panama or Inter-American Convention?

3. Why does the court decide that Congress did not intend to exclude arbitral awards made in the United States from coverage under the Panama or Inter-American Convention?

DISTINCTIONS BETWEEN DOMESTIC AND INTERNATIONAL COMMERCIAL ARBITRATION

U.S. domestic and international commercial arbitration share many of the same advantages, such as confidentiality, arbitrator expertise, savings in time and money, and greater party control. In most instances, their characteristics are similar, such

For an overview of international arbitration, access this site: http://www.law. vill.edu

as the requirement of an agreement to arbitrate, the party determination of arbitral procedures, the party selection of the arbitrator or arbitral panel, the handling of pre-hearing matters, the actual hearing process, and the arbitral award. However, some important distinctions exist between these two forms of arbitration, which businesspeople need to be aware of when electing to use international commercial arbitration.

Substantive Arbitrability.   As discussed in Chapter 6, courts, not arbitrators, determine the issue of substantive arbitrability for both domestic and international arbitration held in the United States. For example, a party challenging whether an agreement to arbitrate actually exists will go to court before the arbitration hearing to stay the arbitration. If this challenge is deemed frivolous or an attempt to delay arbitration, the parties will lose the benefits of a swift, cost-efficient resolution of the dispute. If the court determines that there is no valid agreement to arbitrate, the parties will not proceed into arbitration and will instead have to resort to litigation of their dispute in national courts.

Generally in international arbitration and under the UNCITRAL Model Law, the arbitrator or arbitral panel initially decides both substantive and procedural arbitrability. The arbitrator's authority can only be challenged in court at the conclusion of the arbitral process. In essence, the arbitrator or panel is viewed as having priority over national courts to determine its own jurisdiction. This approach has been referred to as the **principle of competence-competence** or Kompetenz-Kompetenz. Under competence-competence, the arbitrator or arbitral panel determines initially the existence and validity of an arbitration agreement. To ensure that arbitration will proceed without costly and lengthy court delays based on unfounded or frivolous claims about the existence of an agreement to arbitrate, the courts are required to refer parties back to arbitration if a summary evaluation shows that an arbitration agreement exists. In addition, a party seeking to challenge jurisdiction may ultimately be satisfied with the arbitral award and never dispute the matter in court.

Discovery.   Several important distinctions should be made between the conduct of pre-hearing activities in U.S. domestic and international arbitration. The length and depth of discovery in arbitration differ, depending on the nation's court system and relevant statutes. In the U.S. common law legal system, extensive pretrial discovery is a legal right and a party expectation; one of the benefits of U.S. domestic arbitration is the savings in time and costs through a more limited pre-hearing discovery than one finds in standard litigation. Yet parties in U.S. domestic arbitration usually undertake some discovery prior to the arbitral hearing. Often this process will be on a strict time deadline involving the limited use of interrogatories, depositions, and productions of documents. The FAA allows the arbitrators to order discovery with the federal courts only aiding in the enforcement of valid arbitral discovery orders. However, most international arbitral processes are based in nations with civil law legal systems. In these countries, arbitral proceedings generally do not require pre-hearing discovery or other pre-hearing disclosures. Parties may request discovery, but it is extremely limited and normally allowed only in exceptional circumstances. International arbitral tribunals may order a stringently limited production of documents, but rarely any interrogatories, depositions, or requests for admissions. Businesspeople wishing to preserve the ability to undertake some discovery should specify this in the international arbitration clause.

Provisional Remedies.   Judicial review of party requests for provisional remedies is another area in which U.S. domestic and international arbitration differ. In international arbitration under certain national laws or the UNCITRAL Model Law, parties can request judicial orders for such provisional remedies as temporary restraining orders, injunctions, or attachments based on potential arbitral outcomes. Under these laws, international arbitrators may also independently grant provisional relief.

In accordance with the policies of the FAA, U.S. courts usually defer to the parties' choice of arbitration, preferring not to interfere with or influence the outcome of the process. Also, the FAA does not empower arbitrators to order provisional remedies. At most, U.S. courts will issue provisional remedies that aid rather than inhibit the arbitral process, such as orders to compel arbitration proceedings, to appoint arbitrators, or to confirm arbitration awards. Therefore, while an arbitration is pending, U.S. courts will generally provide no provisional remedies that may impede the arbitrator's decision-making authority or that may be based on assumptions about the potential outcome of a dispute.

For example, a Swedish and an Indian company enter into a contract for the purchase of office furniture. The contract contains an arbitration clause. The Swedish company then alleges that the Indian firm failed to make proper payments for the office furniture shipped to India. The Swedish company may seek to attach the goods shipped or other company assets to protect its interests while the arbitration proceeds. Other national courts may be willing to provide the attachment as a security based on the likely outcome of the arbitration. The U.S. courts, on the other hand, normally will not grant the requested relief, preferring to defer to the authority of the arbitrators and the international arbitral decision before ordering the attachment. In the following case, a Japanese business challenges the jurisdiction of a U.S. federal court to entertain a request for provisional remedies in an international arbitration.

BORDEN, INC. V. MEIJI MILK PRODUCTS CO., LTD.
919 F. 2d 822 (2d Cir.), cert. denied, 500 U.S. 953 (1990)

FACT SUMMARY

Borden, Inc. (Borden), is a New Jersey corporation that manufactures and distributes a variety of dairy, food, and other consumer products throughout the world. Meiji Milk Products Co., Ltd. (Meiji), a Japanese corporation, manufactures milk and milk products in Japan and other countries. Both Borden and Meiji have corporate offices in New York City. In 1983, Borden and Meiji entered into a Trademark License and Technical Assistance Agreement (the agreement) in which Borden licensed to Meiji for seven years the rights to use its name and logo in Meiji's manufacture of margarine products in Japan. The agreement contained an arbitration clause that all disputes be resolved in accordance with the Japanese-American Trade Arbitration Agreement of 1952.

For seven years, Meiji used the Borden name and logo on its packaging. Subsequently, Meiji obtained protection of its package design under the Japanese Design Patent Law. After the agreement expired, Meiji continued to use the same packaging without the Borden logo and trademark. Borden contended that using the same packaging is an improper appropriation of Borden's business goodwill in violation of the agreement. In 1990, Borden brought an action in the federal courts in New York alleging breach of contract and wrongful destruction of goodwill and demanding, in part, that the court issue an injunction ordering Meiji to arbitrate the dispute. The trial court determined that the court possessed subject matter jurisdiction to compel arbitration. An expedited appeal followed.

OPINION: *TIMBERS, Circuit Judge*

As a threshold matter, we address the question of the court's subject matter jurisdiction to entertain the application for preliminary injunctive relief in aid of arbitration.

. . . .

Meiji's argument is that, since the agreement between the parties contains an arbitration clause, the [New York]

Convention is applicable. Article II(3) of the Convention provides that "[t]he court of a Contracting State, when seized of an action in a matter in respect of which the parties have made an agreement within the meaning of this article, shall, at the request of one of the parties, refer the parties to arbitration. . . ." The full text of the Convention is published following 9 U.S.C.A. §201 (West Supp. 1990). Borden concedes that the Convention is applicable, but argues that the Convention does not oust the court of jurisdiction to issue an injunction in aid of arbitration. We agree.

Federal courts are charged with enforcing the Convention. 9 U.S.C. §201(1988). Specifically, a court "may direct that arbitration be held in accordance with the agreement at any place therein provided for. . . . Such court may also appoint arbitrators. . . ." *Id.* at §206. Furthermore, the courts are empowered to confirm an arbitration award once rendered. *Id.* at §207.

Meiji argues that a court's jurisdiction is limited to compelling arbitration or confirming an arbitration award. In the instant case, however, Borden specifically invoked §206, seeking to have the district court compel arbitration and appoint arbitrators. We hold that entertaining an application for a preliminary injunction in aid of arbitration is consistent with the court's powers pursuant to §206. *Cf. McCreary Tire & Rubber Co. v. CEAT S.p.A.,* 501 F. 2d 1032, 1037-38 (3rd Cir. 1974)(district court order refusing to vacate an attachment reversed, because underlying complaint sought to bypass arbitration altogether and "[t]he Convention forbids the courts of a contracting state from entertaining a suit which violates an agreement to arbitrate"); *International Shipping Co. v. Hydra Offshore, Inc.,* 875 F. 2d 388, 391 n. 5 (2d Cir.)(district court properly held that jurisdiction could not be premised on the Convention because "the party invoking its provisions did not seek either to compel arbitration or to enforce an arbitral award"), *cert. denied,* 110 S. Ct. 563 (1989).

In the instant case, far from trying to bypass arbitration, Borden sought to have the court *compel* arbitration. New York law specifically provides for provisional remedies in connection with an arbitrable controversy, N.Y. Civ. Prac. L. & R. (CPLR) §7502(c) (McKinney Supp. 1990), and the equitable powers of federal courts include the authority to grant it. *Murray Oil Products Co. v. Mitsui & Co.,* 146 F. 2d 381 (2d Cir. 1944). Entertaining an application for such a remedy, moreover, is not precluded by the Convention but rather is consistent with its provisions and its spirit. In *Murray,* we held that an arbitration clause, "does not deprive the promisee of the usual provisional remedies. . . ." *Id.* at 384. We held that the desire for speedy decisions in arbitration "is entirely consistent with a desire to make as effective as possible recovery upon awards, *after they have been made,* which is what provisional remedies do." *Id.* (emphasis added).

We hold that the district court properly exercised subject matter jurisdiction. . . .

Discussion Questions

1. Why did the court determine that it possessed subject matter jurisdiction in this dispute?

2. Prior to the issuance of an arbitral award, on what grounds will the federal courts order provisional remedies under the terms of the Convention?

3. How does Borden's request differ from that of the parties in the *McCreary* case?

Hearing Process.   In U.S. domestic arbitration, the hearing is similar to an abbreviated trial with its confrontational style. As with U.S. litigation, parties in domestic arbitration expect the opportunity to provide oral testimony, face cross-examination, and allow their attorneys to advocate their positions in persuasive opening and closing statements. This adversarial approach makes it more difficult for the parties to maintain a positive business relationship after the arbitration. However, international arbitration proceedings tend to be much less confrontational. Parties may request a chance to offer oral testimony. Most party testimony, however, is accepted in written form as is common in most civil law nations. Oral evidence is often limited to questions from the arbitral panel on particular issues for which the panel seeks clarification or further evidence based on the written pleadings or party statements. This approach seldom subjects business executives to uncomfortable cross-examination. The international arbitration process tends to avoid hostile confrontations, and therefore, it is more likely to preserve business relationships after the arbitral process is complete.

Arbitral Award.   As discussed in Chapter 6, lengthy reasoned opinions are not required to support arbitral awards in U.S. domestic arbitration. The arbitral award

http://

The Spanish-language Web page of the International Institute for Training in ADR Methods is at: http://www.inter-mediacion.com

may merely indicate which party has prevailed and the damages to be assessed, if applicable. Often, arbitrators refrain from offering their reasoning to avoid providing a disgruntled party with grounds for appeals to the courts. However, in international arbitral proceedings, arbitrators or arbitral panels generally provide extensive, reasoned opinions to support their awards. The decisions will discuss factual findings and legal interpretations and have been compared to court opinions rendered after bench trials.

ADR IN ACTION

NAFTA Looks to International Arbitration for Cross-Border Disputes

On January 1, 1994, the North American Free Trade Agreement (NAFTA) took effect with the United States, Mexico, and Canada creating the world's largest free trade region with some 360 million consumers in a nearly $7 trillion marketplace. The agreement phases out tariffs, duties, quotas, and other trade barriers in a broad range of industries, including telecommunications, agriculture, financial services, computers, and energy products. NAFTA strives to accelerate investment and other commercial activity among these three nations, and it is anticipated that other Central and South American countries may join the pact in the future. With this rise in commercial activity, it is inevitable that there would be a corresponding increase in the number of commercial disputes. The conflict management provisions of NAFTA provide detailed procedures for resolving disputes, largely between each signatory nation rather than each private business.

Although NAFTA only generally addresses cross-border dispute reso-lution between private parties, it makes a clear statement in favor of international arbitration and ADR to handle these disagreements. Article 2022(1) of NAFTA states that "[e]ach party shall, to the maximum extent possible, encourage and facilitate the use of arbitration and other means of alternative dispute resolution for the settlement of international commercial disputes between private parties in the free trade area."

Also under Article 2022(2), each signatory nation is directed to institute procedures for the recognition and enforcement of such international arbitral awards. Nations that have adopted either the New York or Panama Conventions are viewed as being in compliance with Article 2022(2). In addition, Article 2022(4) calls for the establishment of an Advisory Committee on Private Commercial Disputes made up of individuals with experience or expertise in private international commercial disputes. The Committee is expected to study and report on the availability, use, and effectiveness of

ADR IN ACTION Continued

international arbitration and other conflict resolution methods on commercial disputes in the free trade zone.

The implementation of NAFTA ultimately led to the birth of a new international dispute resolution center to deal with NAFTA-related commercial disagreements. In 1995, the American Arbitration Association, the British Columbia International Commercial Arbitration Centre, the Mexico City National Chamber of Commerce, and the Quebec National and International Commercial Arbitration Centre entered into a cooperative agreement to form the **Commercial Arbitration and Mediation Center for the Americas (CAMCA).** These four prominent organizations came together to provide a forum for the study, administration, and advancement of international arbitration, mediation, and other forms of conflict management for private commercial disputes under NAFTA. CAMCA has assembled a twelve-member Governing Council with four representatives from each of the NAFTA signatory nations, including the chief executive of each of the founding organizations. The Governing Council will establish and monitor applicable rules, procedures, and fees for conflict management procedures for NAFTA disputes. CAMCA is also developing a diverse international roster of arbitrators and mediators, including some 30 neutral panelists from each of the signatory nations supplemented by neutral panelists from other nations. CAMCA also seeks to educate neutral panelists, businesspeople, and legal professionals about international arbitration and other ADR methods as well as the procedures and services of CAMCA. As commercial activity continues to blossom under NAFTA, CAMCA and other administering organizations will continue to promote international arbitration and other ADR mechanisms that will quickly, privately, and cheaply resolve private cross-border commercial disagreements throughout the Americas.

CHAPTER CONCLUSION

Growth in the global marketplace has led to a rise in international commercial disputes between private businesses. With no uniform international legal system, attempts to redress international disagreements in national courts have led to concerns about court neutrality, multiple lawsuits, and judicial enforceability. International arbitration overcomes many of the difficulties associated with the processing of disagreements through national courts. This form of ADR emphasizes party autonomy and control over the decision-making process. Businesspeople may choose to use either ad hoc or institutional arbitration with many reputable administering organizations available to serve their conflict management needs. The existence of national treaties as well as the New York and Panama Conventions make the recognition and enforcement of international arbitral awards much easier than the orders of national courts. With limited grounds for appeal, international arbitration has become an important method for effective and final resolution of business conflicts in world markets.

BEST BUSINESS PRACTICES

- Collaborate with legal counsel to draft international arbitration clauses for inclusion in international commercial agreements.
- Address the benefits and difficulties associated with both ad hoc and institutional arbitration in the global marketplace.
- Consider the reputation, rules, arbitral panels, administrative services, and costs of different administering organizations before directing arbitral proceedings to a specific international entity.
- Make certain that the choice-of-forum statement in an international arbitration clause specifies a nation that is a signatory to either the New York or Panama Convention to aid enforcement.
- Be aware that national laws may affect substantive and procedural aspects of international arbitration and agree to use national laws that strictly limit judicial intervention into arbitral proceedings.
- Decide whether certain disputes may be better handled on an expedited basis using fast-track arbitration.

KEY TERMS

Ad hoc arbitration, p. 237
Arbitration Center of the World
   Intellectual Property Organization
   (WIPO), p. 240
China International Economic and
   Trade Commission (CIETAC),
   p. 239
Choice-of-forum clause, p. 234
Choice-of-law clause, p. 234
Commercial Arbitration and Mediation
   Centre for the Americas (CAMCA),
   p. 259
Commercial dealings, p. 247

Fast-track arbitration, p. 240
Hong Kong International Arbitration
   Centre (HKIAC), p. 239
Institutional arbitration, p. 238
International Chamber of Commerce
   (ICC), p. 238
International commercial arbitration,
   p. 234
International Court of Arbitration (ICC
   Court), p. 238
London Court of International
   Arbitration (LCIA), p. 240
New York Convention, p. 244

Nondomestic award, p. 244
Panama or Inter-American Convention,
  p. 250
Principle of competence-competence,
  p. 254

Reciprocity, p. 247
Terms of reference, p. 239
UNCITRAL Arbitration Rules, p. 236
UNCITRAL Model Law, p. 236

ETHICAL AND LEGAL REVIEW

1. A South African company and a U.S. company have entered into a commercial agreement regarding the licensing and distribution of computer hardware and software. The agreement contained a general arbitration clause to deal with any future disputes between the parties. In 1996, a disagreement over distribution rights arose between the parties, and they agreed to invoke the arbitration provision. In an effort to promote objectivity, the parties decided to hold the arbitration proceeding in a third country, Brazil. Will this choice of location affect the recognition and enforcement of the arbitral award? [See the *1958 United Nations Convention on the Recognition and Enforcement of Foreign Arbitral Awards*]

2. Mitsubishi Motors Corporation, a Japanese company, entered into a joint venture with Chrysler International, S.A., a Swiss company, which is wholly owned by Chrysler Corporation, a U.S. company. Under the joint venture, the companies sought to increase the distribution of Mitsubishi-manufactured vehicles, bearing the Chrysler-Mitsubishi trademarks, through Chrysler dealers outside the United States. Soler Chrysler Plymouth, Inc., a Puerto Rican company, entered into a Sales and Distribution Agreement with Mitsubishi and Chrysler that contained an arbitration clause. A dispute arose when Soler ran into difficulties maintaining its expected sales quota and asked Mitsubishi to delay or cancel the shipment of several vehicle orders. In addition, Soler sought to ship some of its inventory to other dealers in the United States and Latin America. Mitsubishi and Chrysler objected to these requests. Ultimately, Mitsubishi brought an action in the U.S. federal court in Puerto Rico to compel arbitration. Soler countered that the commercial conduct of Mitsubishi and Chrysler was an illegal restraint of trade in violation of the antitrust provisions of the Sherman Act, which must be decided in the federal courts and not through arbitration. Is this international disagreement involving alleged antitrust violations in the global marketplace arbitrable? [See *Mitsubishi Motors Corp. v. Soler Chrysler-Plymouth, Inc.,* 473 U.S. 614 (1985)]

3. Two U.S. firms, Lander Company, Inc., and MMP Investments, Inc., entered into a contract for MMP's distribution of shampoos and other products manufactured by Lander in Poland. The agreement contained an arbitration clause that stated that any future disputes be processed in New York City under the rules of the International Chamber of Commerce (ICC). A disagreement arose,

and the parties undertook arbitration in New York City before an arbitrator who was a New York attorney. The arbitrator found in favor of Lander in the amount of $500,000 plus interest. Lander sought to enforce the award in the United States federal courts. MMP objected to the enforcement of the arbitral award, in part, because it claimed that the court lacked subject matter jurisdiction under the New York Convention because both firms were from the United States and the award was rendered in the United States. Will the federal court have the jurisdiction under the New York Convention to recognize and enforce an award rendered in the United States involving two U.S. companies? [See *Lander Company, Inc., v. MMP Investments, Inc.,* 107 F. 3d 476 (7th Cir. 1997)]

4. Under the Hong Kong Arbitration Ordinance, an arbitrator has the authority to award interest on arbitral awards. In a dispute between the Hong Kong government and a private business, Shimizu Corporation, the arbitrator determined that Shimizu was entitled to compound interest on two arbitral awards against the government. The government appealed the award, claiming that Hong Kong law only empowered arbitrators to award simple and not compound interest. The appellate level Supreme Court determined that the arbitrator had the discretion to award compound interest under the national law. The judge in the appeals decision indicated that "[i]t would not make sense, given the desire to make arbitration attractive and to give Hong Kong an 'edge' in the 'market,' to follow the old formula restricting interest to simple interest, and all commercial practicalities would make it essential to allow compound interest to be awarded in appropriate cases." The government appealed the decision to the higher-level Hong Kong Appeals Court. Will the court's legal interpretation of the national law of Hong Kong affect the arbitrator's compound interest award? [See *Mealey's International Arbitration Reports,* Vol. 12, No. 5 (May 1997)]

5. Creative Tile Marketing, Inc. (CTM), a Florida corporation, entered into an agency agreement with SICIS International, S. r. L. (SICIS), an Italian corporation, that manufactures decorative mosaic tiles. Under the agreement, SICIS appointed CTM as its exclusive agent in various countries, including the United States, Canada, Australia, Singapore, and Taiwan. The agency agreement contained an arbitration clause for future disputes to be resolved through arbitration in Geneva, Switzerland. In 1990, CTM claimed that SICIS had wrongfully terminated the agency relationship and that CTM was entitled to be paid by SICIS for certain sales commissions. CTM sought to block arbitration, alleging that the international arbitration clause was invalid, in part, because it failed to specify the number or procedures for appointing arbitrators. Will the court refuse to enforce the international arbitration provision because it failed to address these issues? [*Creative Tile Marketing, Inc., v. SICIS International, S. r. L.,* 922 F. Supp. 1534 (S.D. Fla. 1996)]

SUGGESTED ADDITIONAL READINGS

Born, Gary. "Arbitration Offers Alternative to Litigation Abroad." *The National Law Journal*. December 4, 1995, p. C8.

Rivkin, David W. "International Arbitration." in *Commercial Arbitration for the 1990s*. American Bar Association, 1991, pp. 123-137.

Wagoner, David E. "Tailoring the ADR Clause in International Contracts." *The Arbitration Journal*. June 1993, pp. 77-82.

9

PRIVATE JUDGING

CHAPTER HIGHLIGHTS

In this chapter, you will read and learn about the following:

1. The use of private judges through court appointment, state reference statutes, and by private contract agreement.
2. Basic procedural aspects of private judging.
3. The role and duties of contract private judges, temporary judges, and referees.
4. Differences between general and special references to private judges.
5. Comparison of private judging versus domestic arbitration.
6. Analysis of constitutional concerns about the private judging process, including equal protection, due process, and First Amendment issues.

Can a retired judge or magistrate continue to play an important role in the adjudication of conflict? Advocates of private judging believe they can. A number of state courts and private parties are using the private judging process. The term *private judging* is derived from the professional background of the decision maker and the nature of the process. Under the **private judging** process, disputing parties or the courts empower a private person, usually a retired judge or magistrate with special expertise, to hear and decide their case after private proceedings. Private judges are not mediators who encourage party settlement, but adjudicators who make findings of fact and law in a dispute. These judges may be employed by the state court system or by private parties, either independently or with the assistance of an alternative dispute resolution (ADR) services provider. Rather than wasting their training and experience, retired judges are putting them to good use to help parties resolve their conflicts in a rapid, cost-effective, and private manner. Advocates of the process claim that private judges have alleviated extensive case backlogs, while critics decry the practice as an abdication of court responsibility that permits only a select group of litigants to secretly dispose of their disputes. In this chapter, we will discuss the benefits and drawbacks of private judging, commonly referred to as **rent-a-judge.**

AN OVERVIEW OF PRIVATE JUDGING

In the United States, the concept of the private judge dates back to the 1800s. Primarily authorized by state statute, state laws called **reference statutes** allowed parties to seek the assistance of a retired judge or magistrate to serve as a temporary judge or referee in their dispute. The practice received little attention until the 1970s when three California lawyers, Hillel Chodos, James F. Craig, and Seth M. Hufstedler, faced with a complex medical billing dispute and an extensive court backlog, looked for another way to resolve their case. They discovered an 1872 statute that gave California courts authority to refer civil disputes to a temporary judge or referee selected and paid for by the parties. With the approval of the court, the three lawyers hired a retired judge who rendered a decision within seven months, saving the parties about $100,000 in attorneys' fees. Chados, Craig, and Hufstedler's research and creativity revived the practice of private judging. Several other states have enacted statutes permitting court referral of disputes to privately compensated judges, but the state court system of California has made the greatest use of the practice. (See Figure 9.1.) Most states also have statutes that permit their courts to refer civil cases to temporary judges who are employed and paid by the state.

The concept of private judging is not restricted to cases referred from the court system. It may also involve parties who have contractually agreed to hire a retired judge or magistrate as a **contract private judge.** These private disputants may supervise the contract private judge on their own or with the aid of a private ADR services provider. The number of disputes handled in this manner is difficult to determine because of the confidential nature of such proceedings.

Private judges usually possess adjudicatory responsibilities similar to those of sitting judges in the state court system. These judges carry out standard procedural duties, such as scheduling the time, date, and location of the proceeding. They supervise discovery and may issue subpoenas or orders for production of relevant documents. Private judges may hold pretrial conferences to narrow legal and factual issues, preside over hearing sessions, and rule on objections. After the hearing, private judges issue decisions spelling out their findings of fact and conclusions of law.

The private judging process can be accessed in three basic ways: (1) by private contract, (2) by court appointment, or (3) by reference statute. Contract private judges are chosen and provide services without any court involvement. On the

FIGURE 9.1   States with Court Referral of Disputes to Private Judges

| California |
| Indiana |
| Kansas |
| Maine |
| Missouri |
| New Hampshire |
| New York |
| North Carolina |
| Ohio |
| Oklahoma |
| South Carolina |
| Texas |
| Washington |

Sources: Anne S. Kim, *Rent-a-Judges and the Costs of Selling Justice,* 44 Duke L. J. 166, 168 n. 10 (1994); Amy L. Litkovitz, *Note & Comment: The Advantages of Using a "Rent-a-Judge" System in Ohio,* 10 Ohio St. J. on Disp. Res. 491, 491 n. 6 (1995).

other hand, the selection of private judges through court appointment or reference statute directly involves the assistance, approval, and supervision of the courts. These state-supervised proceedings only apply to cases that have already been filed in the courts. We will now discuss each of these distinct methods of private judging.

CONTRACT PRIVATE JUDGES

Through private contract, parties can agree in advance or when a dispute arises to refer their conflict to a retired judge or magistrate. The parties select the private judge on their own or with the assistance of an ADR services provider, without the involvement or supervision of the court system. The contract private judge will apply the substantive law of the agreed-upon state or country, not necessarily that of the forum where the proceeding is taking place. The decision of the judge is viewed as binding on the parties, often with no opportunity for appeal. Because the parties retain the flexibility to craft procedures that meet their needs, the parties may allow limited grounds for appeal similar to those permitted for arbitral awards. The contract private judge's findings are not viewed as a decision of the court, and they remain completely confidential.

ADR IN ACTION

A Conversation with a Contract Private Judge

The retired Honorable Kevin R. Doyle never expected to be a contract private judge. In fact, he never set out to be a judge or even a lawyer when he attended Notre Dame University. Both his father and older brother were successful attorneys, but he was not sure if law practice was for him. A two-year stint in the military that exposed him to the military courts fueled his interest in law. After his military service, he attended Boston College Law School, where he graduated first in his class. To put himself through law school, he worked as a claims adjuster and honed his negotiation and conflict resolution skills.

With a classmate, he opened a general practice firm in which he handled a wide range of legal matters, including mergers, acquisitions, and labor negotiations, for some nine years. In 1970, Judge Doyle became a part-time special judge in the Massachusetts district courts, hearing only criminal cases and practicing civil law on the side. Eventually, he became the presiding judge in Waltham District Court, where he served for more than twenty years until his retirement at age 59 in 1993.

That same year, Judge Doyle established KRD ADR Services, Inc., a for-profit ADR firm. His company provides contract private judging and mediation services. Judge Doyle handles about three or four private cases a week (about 150 disputes per year), primarily resolving insurance, construction, and business dissolution disputes. In his new role as a private judge, he remarks that former judges have to "[g]et over the idea that you have the flags, a couple of bailiffs, that you have the power of the state behind you." He notes that as a sitting judge, it is easier to exert pressure over the parties to act reasonably or to settle disputes. But as a private judge, "[y]ou have to be a business person, first and foremost."

Judge Doyle sees an important place for ADR in the resolution of many disputes. He notes that "lawyers often insist on handling every case as a million dollar case, when the average case is a $26,000 case that doesn't justify $25,000 in legal fees." With most cases settling before trial, Judge Doyle observes that private judging offers not only a savings in legal fees, but a savings in time. He adds that lawyers can go to their clients with the private judging alternative and say, "Now look, we can go to court and this may take three-and-a-half years; this is almost as good. We are going to have a real, live judge. He just won't be wearing the robes."

Judge Doyle believes that he can often save the parties up to two years of time and legal expenses. To help the parties realize these savings, he will narrow the legal and factual issues through prehearing stipulations. Although discovery remains limited, he requires the parties to provide each other with any documents they plan to use at the private judging session at least one week in advance. At times, parties may submit a prehearing memorandum for his review.

At the sessions, the parties are seated informally around a conference table. Parties or their representatives make brief opening remarks, call witnesses, offer supportive documents, and make closing presentations. The relaxed and abbreviated procedural environment and Judge Doyle's expertise help to move cases along at a faster pace. "I've seen impossible cases that I was able to work on, and they are very satisfying. . . .You can say to yourself afterwards, 'We got that done in one day.' You know how long that would take to try that case to a jury? At least a week, because you have to proceed more slowly. And you know you are going to put the jury to sleep." To further accelerate resolution, Judge Doyle will provide the parties with his findings of fact and conclusions of law usually within a week of the final private judging session.

Aside from the savings in time and money, Judge Doyle believes that parties are also drawn to private judging services because they can select a decision maker who has expertise in their type of disagreement and is fair. "What people are really looking for in an arbitrator is that detached, disinterested, professional perspective," points out Judge Doyle. He believes that lawyers and clients often feel more comfortable dealing with a former judge whom they know has the depth of experience in rendering decisions. He notes that lawyers may not always agree with his determinations, but they trust his judgment.

In many instances, Judge Doyle's focus as a private judge is not on determining liability for the parties but on deciding the amount of damages that should be awarded. In his view, one of the main obstacles to the settlement of disputes is the inability of lawyers and clients to evaluate objectively the value of their cases. "There are a lot of cases where the plaintiff does not have a realistic idea of the value of the case. They all have a brother-in-law who had a hangnail that got $180,000. And they don't understand why their $180,000 isn't waiting for them." Judge Doyle also remarked that insurance companies may be reluctant to pay claims due to concern about fraud and that claims adjusters may be taking too narrow a view of the merits of the case.

Massachusetts does not have a reference statute in place, and Judge Doyle believes that mandating private judging or arbitration tramples on too many fundamental rights. He prefers that parties come to the process voluntarily. Because there are so many complicated disputes, Judge Doyle asserts that ADR will be an

COURT-SUPERVISED PRIVATE JUDGING

Temporary Judges

If parties have not contractually agreed to use a private judge, the court may select and appoint a temporary judge with the consent of the parties. The consenting disputants are also involved in the selection of the temporary judge. **Temporary judges** are former judges recalled from retirement through a court **order of appointment.** Depending on state statute, these temporary judges are usually employed and compensated by the state to handle civil disputes. They play an important role in helping to alleviate the pressures on overburdened state court dockets. Viewed as part of the state court system, temporary judges retain the full range of judicial authority and are bound by the same canons of judicial ethics as are full-time regular judges. Unlike other quasi-judicial officers, temporary judges may cite and enforce contempt charges against a party. In addition, these judges may impanel juries, sometimes referred to as **rent-a-juries** to distinguish them from jurors participating in trials before full-time state judges.

Temporary judges apply the substantive law of the jurisdiction. However, the litigants may specify the use of relaxed procedural rules in the order of appointment. Unlike that of the contract private judge, the decision of a temporary judge is considered a decision of the court. Although the temporary judge's decision is not subject to trial de novo, the award may be appealed in the same manner as other standard court judgments.

REFERENCE-MANDATED JUDGING

Referees or Special Masters

In some instances, litigants may rely on a state reference statute to implement the private judging process. The parties may file a **voluntary petition** requesting the referral, or the courts may recommend a referral. Under a reference statute, a court must first approve of the reference to the private judge and then issue an order of reference referring a pending civil case to a private judge, called a **referee** or a

special master. In the **order of reference,** the private judge is named, the breadth of the private judge's powers are specified, applicable procedural requirements are identified, and each party's obligation to pay for the private judge's services is stated. At times, state law permits the delegation of the courts' adjudicatory authority to administrative boards. These boards may also refer specific disputes to referees.

Although state reference statutes seek to delegate adjudicatory functions to referees, constitutional mandates limit the role of referees in the federal courts to largely administrative responsibilities. Article III of the U.S. Constitution vests the federal courts with their adjudicatory authority. **Federal Rule of Civil Procedure 53** does allow for federal court references to special masters, including referees, auditors, examiners, and assessors. However, the rule indicates that such appointments should be made only in exceptional cases. Normally, special masters in the federal courts are used to deal with complex discovery matters or to serve as mediators aiding nonbinding settlement discussions in complicated disputes. The primary focus of Federal Rule 53 is to delegate administrative duties to special masters to allow federal judges to focus on their traditional adjudicatory roles under Article III. Therefore, special masters are allowed to aid the parties in reaching a settlement or to rule on discovery issues and other administrative matters, but they may not adjudicate the outcome of the dispute.

Referees often are retired judges or magistrates but are not required to be judges, or even lawyers. The private judge or referee is supervised by the court or the administrative board with adjudicatory authority. As subordinate officers, referees must comply with the ethical standards that apply to full-time judges. For example, referees are expected to recuse themselves from cases in which they may be considered biased due to past personal, financial, or social ties with one of the parties.

The referee's adjudicatory authority is spelled out in the order of reference in compliance with state constitutional and statutory laws. In reviewing the case, the referee is required to apply the substantive law of the jurisdiction. As with temporary judges, the order of reference may allow the parties to relax certain procedural rules. Unlike temporary judges, referees do not retain a full panoply of judicial powers, as they act under the supervision of a judge or an administrative board. For example, referees lack the authority to cite and punish a party for contempt.

General or Special References

General References. Based on state statute, a court may issue an order of reference that is either a general or special reference. Under a **general reference,** the private judge conclusively decides all or part of the issues of law and fact in the dispute. (See Figure 9.2.) The referee's findings of fact and conclusions of law are often referred to as the **referee's report.** The general referee's report is binding on the parties and is entered on the record as if rendered by the court. In these instances, the parties must consent to the general reference and participate in the selection of the general referee.

http://

Information on JAMS/EnDispute can be found at: http://www.jams-endispute.com

FIGURE 9.2 Judicial Arbitration & Mediation Services, Inc. (JAMS) Draft Model
Clause: Party Agreement on Request for Order of General Reference

We hereby agree and covenant with each other to waive and give up the right to a jury trial and
to submit all manner of causes of action, controversies, differences, claims or demands
whatsoever, whether of fact or of law or both, relating to or growing out of this contract, to be
resolved at the request of any party, by a trial on Order of Reference conducted by a retired
judge or justice from the panel of Judicial Arbitration & Mediation Services, Inc. (JAMS),
appointed pursuant to the provisions of California Code of Civil Procedure § 638(1) or any
amendment, addition or successor section thereto to hear the case and report a statement of
decision thereon. The parties intend this general reference agreement to be specifically
enforceable in accordance with said section. If the parties are unable to agree upon a member
of the JAMS panel to act as referee, then one shall be appointed by the Presiding Judge of the
county wherein the hearing is to be held. The parties shall pay in advance, to the referee, the
estimated reasonable fees and costs of the reference, as may be specified in advance by the
referee. The parties shall initially share equally, by paying their proportionate amount of the
estimated fees and costs of the reference. Failure of any party to make such a fee deposit shall
result in a forfeiture by the non-depositing party of the right to prosecute or defend the cause(s)
of action which is (are) the subject of the reference, but shall not otherwise serve to abate, stay,
or suspend the reference proceeding.

Source: Reprinted with permission of JAMS/EnDispute.

Parties objecting to the referee's report may file a motion with the court for a
new trial. The trial court judge will review the referee's report to determine if a new
trial is warranted. When considering the motion, the trial judge has the authority to
vacate the referee's award on several grounds, including bias and errors of law. If
the motion is granted, the trial court judge may revise the referee's findings, reopen
the case for further proceedings, or modify the referee's judgment in whole or in
part. The decision then becomes appealable based on other court awards. In some
instances, the failure to request a new trial may preclude a party from appealing the
judgment.

Special References. Under a **special reference,** the private judge may be called
on to render an advisory decision on all or certain aspects of the dispute. The court
may first refer the matter to the special referee without the parties' prior consent or
involvement in the referee's selection. The special referee then submits a report to
the presiding judge. The trial judge must then independently review the referee's
findings and adopt, modify, or reject them in whole or in part. Because there is a
lack of party consent, the special referee's report is viewed as nonbinding and subject to trial de novo review by the presiding trial judge. Depending on the relevant
state statute, the parties may file objections to the findings and request a rehearing
of the matter. If no party objects and the trial judge agrees with the report, it will
be entered into the court record as a decision of the court. The litigants retain the
same appeal and enforcement rights as with a traditional court award.

In the following case, the court must decide whether litigants have properly consented to a court's order of reference under state law. In this opinion, the court distinguishes between general and special references based on the issue of party
consent.

AETNA LIFE INS. CO. V. THE SUPERIOR COURT OF SAN DIEGO COUNTY

182 Cal. App. 3d 431 (1986)

FACT SUMMARY

Mary Ellen Hammer brought an action on behalf of herself and the estate of her deceased husband, John Hammer, against Aetna Life Insurance Company (Aetna) for tortious breach of a health insurance contract. Mrs. Hammer claimed that Aetna had refused to pay for immuno-augmentative therapy (IAT) that Mr. Hammer had received for his cancer at the Immunology Researching Centre in the Bahamas. Mr. Hammer subsequently died, and the Bahamian facility was closed after traces of the AIDS virus were found in the IAT serum. Aetna argued that its policy only covered necessary medical treatment that is widely accepted in the medical profession. Both parties agree that IAT is not a generally accepted cancer therapy. Mrs. Hammer argued that the language regarding the treatments covered under the policy was vague and ambiguous.

The court issued an order assigning a local attorney, Louis A. Tepper, as a "special referee" to decide all issues of law and fact regarding the policy's coverage. In his written findings, Mr. Tepper determined that the insurance policy was ambiguous and did not conclusively exclude coverage for the IAT treatment. Aetna requested that the trial court judge view the referee's findings as merely advisory and hold a hearing on the referee's report. The court denied Aetna's requests and accepted the referee's report as an order of the court. Aetna appealed that court order.

OPINION: *JUSTICE BUTLER, with Justices Kremer and Work concurring*

Section 638 of the Code of Civil Procedure broadly authorizes consensual references "[t]o try any and all of the issues in an action or proceeding. . . ." However, the statute calls for "the agreement of the parties filed with the clerk, or judge, or entered in the minutes . . ." or alternatively requires there be a written contract or lease with specific authorization for a reference of disputes under the agreement. Here, although the parties did not object to the reference, they did not agree to it in writing and therefore did not meet the statutory conditions.

The superior court has no power to assign matters to a reference for decision without explicit statutory authorization. (citations omitted)

. . . .

Particularly, the court has no power to make an unconsented to general reference, which conclusively decides all or part of a matter, because not only is such a general reference not authorized except by explicit agreement of the parties (§638, *supra*), but also, the California Constitution prevents delegation of judicial powers except for the performance of "subordinate judicial duties." (Cal. Const., art. VI, §22; see *In re Perrone C.* (1979) 26 Cal. 3d 49 [160 Cal. Rptr. 704, 603 P. 2d 1300]; *In re Edgar M.,* (1975) 14 Cal. 3d 727 [122 Cal. Rptr. 574, 537 P. 2d 406].) Deciding a major legal issue in a case, which will probably determine liability, is not a subordinate judicial duty. The Supreme Court said in *In re Edgar M.*

a referee can make a binding determination only in a consensual general reference. In re Edgar M., supra, at p. 734; see §§638, 644; Estate of Hart, 11 Cal. 2d 89, 91 [77 P. 2d 1082].

The statutes carefully preserve the distinctions of special and general reference to comply with the constitutional mandate; a general reference has binding effect, but must be consensual, whereas a special reference may be ordered without consent but is merely advisory, not binding on the superior court. (see §§644, 645; Estate of Bassi (1965) 234 Cal. App. 2d 529, 536-537 [44 Cal. Rptr. 541]; 6 Witkin, Cal. Procedure (3rd ed. 1985) Proceedings Without Trial, §§50, 51.)

Here, the reference order purported to be a special reference, under section 639, subdivision (d); it even referred to the referee as "special." (footnote omitted). Yet, the superior court treated the referee's findings and conclusions of law as binding and determinative of the issue. No rehearing procedure was provided, and there is no evidence the superior court judge who made the final order ever considered the matter himself, independently of the referee's decision. He simply entered judgment on the referee's report as though it were a binding decision of the court itself. Yet, as we have stated, the reference was not a consensual general reference, the record being wholly lacking in any evidence of a written agreement of the parties to such a binding general reference. We view this action as an abdication of judicial responsibility not authorized by law and contravening the constitutional restrictions upon the exercise of judicial power.

Some cases suggest failure to object to an erroneous reference waives error. (citations omitted). Here, however, although Aetna may not have objected to the ref-

eree hearing the law and motion matter in the capacity of the special referee, it did most emphatically object to the court's treating the reference as general and the referee's findings as binding. . . .

III.

Hammer urges us to treat Aetna's voluntary participation in the reference hearing as a waiver of the legal infirmity, saying (1) the reference consumed much time and money and (2) the referee is a panelist in an organization known as Alternatives to Litigation, which has saved much time and money in civil litigation in San Diego County, and our invalidation of the reference here might chill the actions of that organization in helping to alleviate local congestion in the trial courts.

While Alternatives to Litigation enjoys increasing public acceptance, the superior court may not delegate its constitutionally conferred judicial power except strictly in accordance with legal requirements. The admittedly desirable goal of reducing the burden of the backlog of cases in the trial courts does not compel ratification of an illegal reference. Efficiency is not more important than preserving the constitutional integrity of the judicial process.

Moreover, we do not perceive a compelling public policy to validate the reference procedure used by the court. Commentators have expressed some reservations about California's practice of permitting litigants to hire private judges. (citations omitted). One commentator has noted that extensive use of private references may impair the intellectual development of common law precedent: "Referee trials, however, graft the private aspects of arbitration onto the public aspects of judicial proceedings. A referee's decision has all the authority of a judicial determination but is made within the private context normally associated with arbitration. Lacking the judge's ultimate responsibility to the public, the referee is interested only in litigants who hired him. . . . Any significant shift of litigation to reference trials would adversely affect society as cases that would have been part of an important development in the law are decided through a mechanical application of principles that may not reflect current legal developments." (citation omitted.) We mention these considerations not in derogation of Alternatives to Litigation, but to simply show that the practice is not without its problems. Accordingly, no public policy compels us to strain to validate what was in fact an invalid procedure.

Discussion Questions

1. How does the court distinguish between special and general references?

2. What policies cause the appeals court to question the use of judicial references?

3. Do you think the court's decision will have a chilling effect on the use of private judging?

PRIVATE JUDGING VERSUS COMMERCIAL ARBITRATION

The private judging process offers many of the same benefits found in arbitration and other forms of ADR. (See Table 9.1.) All of these ADR procedures aim to save disputants both time and money in resolving their disputes. In each instance, an expert decision maker is chosen to aid in the rapid adjudication of a conflict. The public benefits through the preservation of limited judicial resources and the alleviation of congested court dockets.

Private judging may appear to be merely another form of arbitration. This statement is largely accurate when applied to contract private judges. Like arbitration, the parties in a private judging procedure agree to submit their dispute to a third-party neutral. In both methods, the parties retain control over the procedures to be used and the substantive law to be applied. The decision of the contract private judge, as in arbitration, is private and may be subject to little or no appeal depending on the terms of the party agreement. In contract private judging, the neutral will always be a retired judge or magistrate; in arbitration, the parties may select a decision maker who is an experienced lawyer or respected business executive, rather than a retired judge or magistrate.

Some important differences exist between the roles of arbitrators and contract private judges as compared with temporary judges and referees. Arbitrators and contract private judges are not considered to be judicial officers. Temporary judges retain the full scope of judicial powers, while referees are subordinate officers who

http://

Learn more about the American Arbitration Association at: http://www.adr.org

TABLE 9.1   Summary Comparison of Private Arbitration and Private Judging Forms

	Standard Arbitration	Contract Private Judging	Temporary Judge	General Referee	Special Referee
Party consent required?	Yes	Yes	Yes	Yes	No
Party participation in selecting decision maker?	Yes	Yes	Yes	Yes	No
Bound by canons of judicial ethics?	No	No	Yes	Yes	Yes
Who usually pays decision maker?	Party disputants	Party disputants	State court system	Party disputants	Party disputants
Proceedings confidential?	Yes	Yes	Yes	Yes	Yes
Award binding?	Yes, unless otherwise agreed by parties	Yes, unless otherwise agreed by parties	Yes, viewed as decision of court	Yes, if not objected to by parties becomes decision of court	No, only advisory, must obtain court approval of report
Award appealable?	Only as agreed by parties	Only as agreed by parties	Yes, standard channels available	Yes, standard channels available	Yes, standard channels available
Final award as precedent?	No	No	Yes	Yes	Yes

possess limited judicial powers. Both temporary judges and referees are court-supervised and are expected to comply with judicial ethics. On the other hand, as nonjudicial decision makers, arbitrators and contract private judges are not bound by canons of judicial ethics, although they may independently follow ethical guidelines set forth by their administering agencies or professional organizations. Parties should be aware that no regulatory or licensing authorities directly oversee the conduct of private arbitrators or contract private judges. Business disputants should ensure that their chosen neutral is truly qualified and objective. In selecting a contract private judge, businesspeople should thoroughly review their biographies, evaluate their credentials, and ascertain their reputations as ADR providers in their community.

In addition, the proceedings and awards of arbitrators and contract private judges are completely private. In some instances, this confidentiality allows business disputants to protect their business reputations and proprietary or competitive information. However, these decisions do not carry any precedential weight and will not discourage future claimants. Conversely, the decisions of temporary judges and referees become part of the court record and are viewed as decisions of the court. Although litigants lose confidentiality with regard to their awards, they gain a precedent that may be used to block future claimants. For example, a decision by an arbitrator or contract private judge binding two businesses disputing the ownership of a particular parcel of land cannot be used to deter future litigants. If this same dispute was to be resolved by a temporary judge or referee, the decision could be used to formally establish ownership of the property and to prevent future lawsuits over that same issue.

Lastly, the grounds for appeal differ between these mechanisms. In arbitration or contract private judging, there may be few or no grounds for appeal, depending on the parties' agreement. (See Chapter 6, Introduction to Commercial Arbitration.) Because they are treated as decisions of the court, decisions rendered by temporary judges or referees are subject to the same grounds for appeal as any other court order or decision. Temporary judges or referees provide a businessperson the speed, informality, and decisionmaking expertise of arbitration and contract private judging, coupled with the opportunity to preserve the full range of appellate channels.

In the following case, the court must first determine what type of proceeding the parties have agreed on before addressing what, if any, channels of appellate review are available.

OLD REPUBLIC INS. CO. V. ST. PAUL FIRE & MARINE INS. CO.
45 Cal. App. 4th 631 (1996)

FACT SUMMARY

The dispute was between two insurance carriers over the responsibility to pay the defense and indemnity costs that arose out of two personal injury lawsuits. The two actions involved injuries suffered in the collision between a tractor trailer and another vehicle. After the settlement of the personal injury claims, Old Republic Insurance Company (Old Republic) sued St. Paul Fire & Marine Insurance Company (St. Paul), which countersued for the defense and indemnity costs. The insurance companies agreed to a stipulation appointing the Honorable Robert E. Rickles, a retired appeals court justice, to hear and decide their dispute. The agreement was entitled "Stipulation for Binding Arbitration Before Special Master." The terms of the stipulation suggested that the decision of the private judge would be binding on the parties and would be entered as a decision of the trial court. The stipulation indicated that any objections to the findings of fact or conclusions of law would be reviewed at the appellate court level. The retired justice found in favor of Old Republic, and the award was confirmed by the trial court. St. Paul appealed the confirmation of the award and sought a **plenary review** of the retired justice's report by the appellate court.

**OPINION: *JUSTICE RYLAARSDAM,
with Justices Sills and Crosby concurring***

. . . .

DISCUSSION

1. WHEN IS A DECISION OF A QUASI-JUDICIAL OFFICER SUBJECT TO PLENARY APPELLATE REVIEW?

Several alternative dispute resolution procedures result in decisions by quasi-judicial officers which are subject to varying scopes of judicial and appellate review. Depending upon the nature of the procedure adopted, these range from no judicial review to plenary review.

Common alternative dispute resolution procedures are judicial and contractual arbitration and references to special master. Judicial arbitrations are governed by Code of Civil Procedure (footnote omitted) §1141.10 et seq. and California Rules of Court, rule 1600 et seq.; contractual arbitrations by section 1280 et seq.; and references by §638 et seq. Although not usually categorized as alternative dispute resolution, we need also consider whether Justice Rickles acted as a "temporary judge." Such judicial officers are authorized to perform judicial functions pursuant to California Constitution, article VI, §21 and their powers are governed by California Rules of Court, rule 244. Such a temporary judge has the power to render a judgment which is appealable in the same manner as one rendered by a constitutional judge. (*In re Marriage of Assemi* (1994) 7 Cal. 4th 896, 908 30 Cal. Rptr. 2d 265, 872 P. 2d 1190)

After a judicial arbitration, a dissatisfied litigant is entitled to a trial de novo. (§1141.20, subd. (b).) Following such a trial on the merits, parties have the same rights of appeal as in all other cases tried in the superior court. However, absent a timely request for a trial de novo, the arbitration award constitutes a final, nonappealable judgment. (§1141.20, subd. (a).)

The scope of judicial review of the decisions of contractual arbitrators is delineated in *Moncharsh v. Heily & Blase, supra,* 3 Cal 4th 1: "The merits of the controversy between the parties are not subject to judicial review." (*Id.* at p. 11, quoting *O'Malley v. Petroleum Maintenance Co.* (1957) 48 Cal. 2d 107, 111 [308 P. 2d 9].) Since one of the reasons for the rule is that "it vindicates the intentions of the parties" (*Moncharsh v. Heily & Blase, supra,* 3 Cal 4th at p. 11), the issue arises whether a contrary intention of the parties, as expressed in the stipulation herein, overrides the general rule. We consider this issue below.

Review of the decision of a referee or special master is governed by section 644. The decision of the referee, unless objected to under section 645, is treated as a decision of the court, and "judgment may be entered thereon in the same manner as if the action had been filed by the court." (§644.) Such a judgment is subject to appeal in the same manner as any other judgment.

We therefore need to determine whether the stipulation constituted an agreement for the appointment of a temporary judge, for judicial or contractual arbitration, or for reference by a special master.

. . . .

Did the stipulation provide for the appointment of a temporary judge? The California Constitution requires an oath of office before a temporary judge may act as such. (*In re Marriage of Assemi, supra,* 7 Cal. 4th at p. 908.) Additionally, California Rules of Court, rule 244(a) requires approval by the presiding judge. Nothing in the record demonstrates such an oath was taken or such approval obtained. In addition, a temporary judge renders a judgment, an action not contemplated by the parties to the stipulation. Here, the parties contemplated that Justice Rickles's decision be confirmed as a judgment by the assigned judge. Therefore, Justice Rickles cannot have acted as a constitutionally authorized temporary judge.

Did the stipulation provide for judicial or contractual arbitration? The stipulation provides "the procedure to be followed in connection with the hearing of the arbitration shall be governed by the provisions of California Rules of Court, Rules 1607, 1609, 1610, 1611, 1612, 1613, 1614 and 1615." These rules govern judicial arbitrations. There is, of course, nothing which precludes parties to a contractual arbitration from agreeing that the arbitration is to be governed by the rules for judicial arbitration. We need not determine whether the agreement, assuming it constitutes an agreement to arbitrate, provides for judicial or contractual arbitration. If it is the former, the absence of the request for trial de novo precludes an appeal. (§1141.20, subd. (a).) If it is the latter, the plenary scope of review sought here is not available. (*Moncharsh v. Heily & Blase, supra,* 3 Cal 4th 1.)

Did the stipulation provide for a reference? Section 638 permits the court to order a reference upon the stipulation of the parties. "In a consensual general reference on all issues, the general referee's decision 'stands as the decision of the court.'" (citations omitted.) "The decision of the referee . . . may be excepted to and reviewed in like manner as if made by the court." (§645.) This means that, upon a motion for a new trial, the trial judge, "can . . . modify the statement of decision, reopen the proceedings for further evidence, or modify the judgment in whole or in part." (citations omitted.) When considering such a motion for a new trial, the trial judge would be authorized to vacate the award of the referee on several bases, including error of law (§657), the very basis for the appeal here. The judgment based on a decision of the referee is appealable in the same manner as if it were a judgment of the court. (§645.)

In their stipulation, the parties limited the power of the trial court providing "The Court's review of the findings of fact and conclusions of law submitted by the Special Master shall be governed by Code of Civil Procedure sections 1286, 1286.2, 1286.4, 1286.6, and 1286.8." These statutory provisions delineate the power of the trial court in connection with the enforcement of an arbitration award and, as distinguished from its power under a motion for a new trial, do not permit the trial court to subject the arbitrator's decision to the same scope of review as the parties' stipulation sought to extend to this court. (*Moncharsh v. Heily & Blase, supra,* 3 Cal 4th at p. 26.)

Considering the general tenor of the stipulation and particularly taking into account the limitations the parties placed upon the trial judge, limiting his function to one determining a motion to confirm an arbitration award, we conclude that in spite of their use of the term "special master," the parties entered into an arbitration agreement. For reasons discussed above, on a judgment confirming an arbitration award, we are precluded from considering whether the arbitrator committed legal error.

3. EFFECT OF THE STIPULATION FOR APPEALABILITY

The parties attempted, by their stipulation, to empower this court to review the legal correctness of the award. Such an attempt is inconsistent with some of the primary purposes of arbitration, quicker results and early finality. Furthermore, because of the flexibility in the consideration of both evidence and law afforded to arbitrators (*Moncharsh v. Heily & Blase, supra,* 3 Cal 4th at p. 11), appellate courts are ill suited to extend plenary appeal rights to a party to an agreement to arbitrate. Most importantly, the Court of Appeals reviews judgments. Because the trial court entered judgment in accordance with the stipulation of the parties, there is

nothing for us to review. . . .

. . . .

No appeal can be taken except from an appealable order or judgment, as defined in the statutes and developed by case law. (citation omitted.) There is no constitutional right to an appeal. (citation omitted.) The parties cannot by their stipulation confer jurisdiction upon this court where none exists. . . .

Discussion Questions

1. How does the court determine that the parties did not agree to use a temporary judge?
2. Why does the court decide that the parties did not make a reference to a special master, even though they used the term *special master* in their stipulation?
3. What aspect of the stipulation causes the court to view the process as an arbitration?

As the above-cited case illustrates, parties must consult applicable state laws and court rules to determine the proper process for using temporary judges and referees. Merely including these terms in a conflict resolution agreement or court stipulation without following applicable procedures will fail to ensure the opportunity for appellate review. Businesses should work with an attorney to fashion an agreement that complies with state laws and court rules.

CONSTITUTIONAL CONCERNS ABOUT PRIVATE JUDGING

One of the main benefits of private judging is that the private judge's determination may become the decision of the court. This process saves time and money, while providing parties with enforceable court determinations and opportunities for standard appellate review. However, these benefits have yielded a number of constitutional objections to private judging focusing on due process, equal protection, and the First Amendment. We will discuss each of these constitutional issues in turn.

Due Process

Procedural Protections.   As stated earlier, temporary judges and referees must apply the substantive law of the jurisdiction, but they may relax procedural rules in carrying out their duties. Parties that elect to litigate their disputes, rather than use

ADR options, expect or desire the full panoply of procedural protections. Objections have been raised that parties appearing before temporary judges and referees will not receive the full procedural protections of the court in violation of due process rights.

Private Payment and Bias.   Referees are typically paid by the parties, not by the state. Private payment could lead to bias and a lack of objectivity in the referee, procedural abuses, and the loss of fundamental fairness in the proceedings. For example, let's say that a referee is selected to resolve a dispute between an individual policyholder and a major insurance carrier that regularly appears before the courts. The referee might show favoritism to the insurance carrier to obtain future business from this litigant, rather than to the policyholder, who may never be involved in another legal dispute. If the referee's fees are not split evenly, the referee might be more friendly to the party who is footing more of the bill.

Concerns about pecuniary interest and its impact on objectivity are troubling ones. However, supporters of private judging argue that the process is court-supervised and that the findings are merely advisory in nonconsensual processes before special referees. In addition, parties retain the option for objective court review through motions for a new trial or appeals challenging a private judge's decision. From a practical perspective, private judges who exhibit biases will likely be recognized and weeded out by parties who participate in the evaluation and selection of referees.

Impact on the Quality of the Court System.   Some have raised general due process concerns regarding the quality of judging in the state system and the overall practice of court referrals to private judges. Critics have suggested that lucrative private judging opportunities will lure high-quality judges away from the state system to private ADR firms. Consequently, they are concerned that the quality of the public court system will suffer. In addition, these critics note that presiding judges may use referees to assist their former colleagues who have left the public system for more lucrative private practice.

In the following case, a litigant challenges in the federal courts the referral of her case to a special referee in a state court. The litigant alleges that her bias concerns are derived from the pecuniary interest of California state court judges in the private judging industry.

ROOT V. HONORABLE FLOYD SCHENK
953 F. Supp. 1115 (S.D. Ca. 1997)

FACT SUMMARY

Plaintiff Andrea Root brought an action in federal court against the Honorable Floyd H. Schenk, a state court trial judge. Ms. Root was a defendant in a state court action brought by Health Industries of America. Among other things, she objected to Judge Schenk's referral of the discovery portion of her dispute to referee William Sheffield, a retired state court judge. Ms. Root requested that the special referee refrain from making any discovery rulings until a motion could be brought challenging Judge Schenk's referral. The referee did not await the motion, ruled against Root, and recommended sanctions against Root and her counsel. The referee also recommended that Root be required to pay the referee's fees, amounting to nearly $5,000. Judge Schenk approved and signed the referee's report, except the recommendation regarding the sanctions. Root then brought this action in federal court against Judge Schenk on due process, equal protection, and First Amendment free speech issues. She claimed that the state courts were too biased to objectively review and determine her federal constitutional claims.

OPINION: *JUDGE ALICEMARIE H. STOTLER*

Plaintiff asserts that the judge abdicated his "fast-track" responsibilities by referring discovery issues to a retired judge. . . . Plaintiff says that judges of Orange County Superior Court are bombarded with a massive marketing device by retired judges in the private sector to leave the bench and earn similar lucrative fees and are in a conflict of interest position when they refer cases to their former colleagues; the sitting judges now make use of a form order to refer all pending and future discovery motions to a referee without determining if it is appropriate in a particular case. Plaintiff's objections to the procedure and high fees were met with a retaliatory denial and shortened time to pay and comply with the order. Plaintiff further asserts that the California statute authorizing the use of referees, Cal. Code of Civ. Proc. §639, provides no criteria for determining when it is appropriate to appoint a discovery referee. These mandatory and coerced referrals violate due process and equal protection guarantees. It would be futile to seek further review through the California courts, says plaintiff, because the judges there are also subject to the same barrage of overtures to join the private sector and thus the same conflicts of interest. . . .

. . . .

[The Plaintiff asserts that the] alleged appearance of bias here is Judge Schenk's pecuniary interest in the matter. The public perception of bias is increased by the fact that there are newspaper ads and articles discussing the market for referees and other hired judges. Since Judge Schenk is 73, and approaching retirement, there is a greater appearance of pecuniary interest. Plaintiff queries "might a sitting state trial court judge strain to avoid interfering with the retirement nest of his friends, their brethren, and possibly themselves?"

. . . .

(a) Does Bias Render the State Tribunal Incompetent such that Plaintiff Does not Have the Opportunity to Raise the Federal Claims Before a Competent State Tribunal?

In *Partington v. Gedan,* 880 F. 2d 116, 125 n. 3 (9th Cir. 1989), the Ninth Circuit stated that in order for a litigant to have an adequate opportunity in the state proceedings to raise his or her constitutional challenges. . . . there must not be incompetency of the state tribunal caused by bias. *Id.* The Ninth Circuit has referred to this as "the 'extraordinary circumstance' that the state tribunal is incompetent by reason of bias." *Hirsh v. Justices of the Supreme Court,* 67 F. 3d 708, 713 (9th Cir. 1995).

This case is not one that demonstrates the extraordinary circumstances where the tribunal is incompetent due to bias. While it is true that many state judges retire to become private judges, and that the more success this system has, the more job opportunities there will be, this is not sufficient interest to disqualify all state judges as biased, which the plaintiff suggests.

. . . .

In *Tumey v. Ohio,* 273 U.S. 510, 71 L. Ed. 749, 47 S. Ct. 437 (1927), the statute at issue authorized a court to retain a portion of the fines of any defendant convicted before a judge. The Supreme Court held that while the question of what is sufficient financial interest to disqualify a judge for bias may often be difficult, it definitely deprives a party of due process where the judge has a direct, personal,

substantial pecuniary interest in reaching a conclusion against him. *Id.*

. . . .

However, an adjudicator is presumed to be unbiased, and to overcome this presumption, a litigant must make a showing of conflict of interest or other specific reason for disqualification *Yamaha Motor Corp., U.S.A. v. Rhiney,* 21 F. 3d 793, 798 (8th Cir. 1994).

. . . Here, the allegations of the complaint do not establish that state judges do not want to stunt the growth of private judging because they want a job on retirement. . . . Here, any interest that Judge Schenk or the other judges of the Superior Court of Orange County have is speculative only, and this is not sufficient to overcome the presumption of fairness.

. . . .

. . . [T]he judge did not show bias in ordering that the parties "initially share equally" in the reference fees. While under California law, the district court cannot make an automatic equal provisional allocation without considering the appropriate factors and exercising its discretion, the "trial court will be presumed to have done so, in the absence of a showing to the contrary" and there is no requirement that a trial court "explain the details of its exercise of discretion, [or] . . . announce in conclusory fashion that it has reviewed the law, weighed all appropriate factors, and exercised its discretion." *DeBlase v. Superior Court,* 41 Cal. App. 4th 1279, 1286 (1996). Plaintiff's allegations do not make out a case of court bias.

. . . .

. . . [T]here is no set of facts alleged that show that he is biased and cannot fairly adjudicate these federal claims.

Discussion Questions

1. Who has the burden of showing bias in this case?

2. What standard does the court use in determining whether Judge Schenk is too biased to continue as the trial judge in this case?

3. What might the state courts do to avoid the appearance of bias based on the marketing efforts and career opportunities afforded private judging firms?

Equal Protection

A common criticism of ADR is that it provides swift justice only for wealthy litigants, not for indigent and middle-class individuals and struggling small businesses. This criticism becomes particularly acute when private judging involves general and special referees. In these proceedings, the parties must pay the hourly rates of the referees, who review and handle all or certain aspects of their cases, such as discovery rulings; sitting or temporary judges are paid normally through state taxes. Although this same concern can be raised about the costs of mediation and arbitration, neither of these processes delivers a court decision on the record.

In a general reference, the parties must agree to use a referee and therefore must be in the financial position to pay the private judge's rates. These rates could be as high as $200 to $300 per hour with some private judges commanding fees of $5,000 per day. The general referee's findings allow wealthy litigants to obtain a rapid court decision, while economically disadvantaged disputants may have to wait years for the same chance. In addition, the general reference process permits wealthier litigants to jump ahead of those in the standard court system in the line for appeals, as they retain the option for standard appellate review. While the economically disadvantaged may see little benefit from private judging, wealthier litigants will receive quick justice at the trial phase and a healthy head start that pushes them years ahead on the enforcement of their judgments and any appeals of their cases.

In a special reference situation, the referee's decision is merely advisory, so the presiding judge does not have to secure the consent of all parties. If a judge determines that some aspect of a case can be handled by a special referee, indigent and middle-class individuals or financially weak businesses may have to split the lucrative fees of a private judge rather than rely on the services of state-compensated judges. The costs of the special referee may prevent parties of modest means from initiating or continuing with meritorious cases. Clearly, many judges will consider the economic status of the parties before referring a matter to an expensive private judge. But the potential for economic hardship exists, particularly when congested court dockets make it difficult for judges to assess the economic circumstances of the parties. This argument also brings in a due process concern that the special referee process may prevent meaningful prosecution of lawsuits by economically disadvantaged litigants.

Supporters of private judging contend that there is no intentional discrimination between rich and poor and no constitutional right to equal access to the civil courts. They note that inequities currently exist in the court system, as wealthier litigants can already afford better lawyers and expert witnesses. These supporters suggest that such aspects of our society as better schools, homes, and lifestyles are already more accessible to those with wealth and that the litigation process merely reflects this societal reality. They add that the use of private judges allows court resources to be focused on fewer cases, helping speed the process for all litigants, regardless of economic circumstances.

In the following case, indigent parties challenge the expense of a special referee during the discovery process based on equal protection grounds.

SOLORZANO V. THE SUPERIOR COURT OF LOS ANGELES COUNTY
18 Cal. App. 4th 603 (1993)

FACT SUMMARY

Plaintiffs/petitioners Ada Solorzano, America Rodriguez, and Dolores Morales were elderly people who brought an action against respondent/defendant Family Health Plan (FHP) alleging, in part, unfair business practices and misleading advertising regarding FHP's senior health care plan under California's Medi-Cal and Medicaid programs. The plaintiffs filed the lawsuit both as individuals and on behalf of the general public and sought injunctive relief and compensatory and punitive damages against FHP. At the trial and appeals court stages, the plaintiffs were certified as indigent (*in forma pauperis*) and were represented by a public interest organization and a private law firm serving *pro bono publico*. During the discovery phase, the plaintiffs requested the production of a number of FHP documents including records of its contacts with government agencies, sales

and marketing materials, and information regarding similar complaints against FHP. The defendant refused to supply these materials, contending that it need only provide documents that specifically related to the named plaintiffs. On January 7, 1992, the trial court made a special reference to William F. Powers to handle the contentious discovery issues. The plaintiffs objected to the referral, indicating that they were indigent and unable to pay his fees, which were $200 per hour.

On January 14, 1992, Referee Powers sent the parties a letter outlining his fees and indicating that they would be split equally absent a showing of good cause for some alternative allocation. In letters dated January 23 and 30, 1992, the plaintiffs advised Referee Powers of their indigent status and requested a deferral of any fee assessment. Referee Powers rejected the request, and the public interest organization representing the plaintiffs sent him a retainer check for $500 on January 31, 1992. Referee Powers temporarily stayed discovery and on February 26, 1992, the plaintiffs received in forma pauperis status from the trial court. On March 3, 1992, Referee Powers sent the plaintiffs a bill for $1,490 and a subsequent invoice for $420.

On March 12, 1992, Referee Powers recommended in writing that discovery be stayed once more, except as to records involving the named plaintiffs, to allow FHP to seek a writ of mandate from the appeals court on a federal preemption issue. Referee Powers also indicated that part of the plaintiffs' document requests may infringe on the right of privacy of FHP's patients in violation of patient-physician privilege, and he recommended that plaintiffs narrow their production of documents request. After this stay, Referee Powers exchanged letters with the plaintiffs regarding payment of his invoices.

On November 2, 1992, FHP's request for a writ of mandate was denied, and discovery resumed. The trial court heard the plaintiffs' continuing objections about fees and reiteration of their indigency on November 18, 1992. At that time, the plaintiffs further advised the court of an April 7, 1992 offer from Judicial Arbitration and Mediation Services, Inc. (JAMS), for free referee services under its pro bono program. FHP refused to consider the JAMS offer, asserting that it was an inappropriate ex parte contact and that plaintiffs should be required to pay for referee services to avoid abuse of the discovery process. Because of the dispute between the plaintiffs and Referee Powers over his fees, the court then appointed a second referee, L. Thaxton Hanson.

Referee Hanson charged $300 per hour which fees would be split evenly. Plaintiffs objected, reasserting their indigent status. The trial court responded that "fees are not going to be waived. If you are going to litigate, you are going to pay." The plaintiffs sought a writ of mandate in the appeals court to vacate the trial court order and to issue a new order relieving the plaintiffs of the obligation to pay discovery fees.

OPINION: *JUSTICE P. KLEIN, with Justices Coskey and Kitching concurring*

CONTENTIONS

Plaintiffs contend that the requirement they pay a referee to resolve discovery disputes denies them meaningful access to the courts and violates their rights to equal protection and due process.

FHP responds, inter alia, plaintiffs should be estopped from seeking free discovery based on their conduct before the trial court. FHP also argues plaintiffs are not "involuntary participants" in this litigation and the discovery dispute has been caused by the plaintiffs' inclusion of private attorney general theories of recovery for which FHP should not have to finance.

DISCUSSION

1. THE PLAINTIFFS' CONSTITUTIONAL ASSERTIONS

Plaintiffs argue the imposition of discovery referee fees on indigent litigants in the present context violates public policy and settled principles of constitutional law. They claim the trial court's order inhibits access to the courts and impermissibly infringes the rights to counsel, equal protection, and due process. Plaintiffs further allege the requirement that plaintiffs pay such fees rewards FHP for its abuse of the discovery process. (footnote omitted.)

All amici curiae have sided with the plaintiffs. (footnote omitted.) They stress the importance of discovery in complex litigation and the need for resolution of such disputes without cost to indigent litigants. They argue pro bono counsel and public interest legal organizations will be forced to absorb substantial discovery fees, and may decline representation of the poor in cases where there is a likelihood of contentious discovery disputes.

. . . .

3. THE TRIAL COURT ABUSED ITS DISCRETION BY ITS DISCOVERY ORDER.

A. PRIVATELY COMPENSATED REFEREES UNAVAILABLE TO THE TRIAL COURT HERE

Numerous federal and state cases have established the right of indigent litigants to avoid the payment of various court costs and fees which otherwise would prevent meaningful access to the courts. (footnote omitted.) In line with this authority, the California Rules of Court list various court fees and costs, without limitation, which are waived for indigents proceeding in forma pauperis. (footnote omitted.)

. . . .

We recognize that the fees in issue here are not court fees but fees paid to a privately compensated discovery referee. As such, the trial court cannot waive them.

However, no one can deny the indispensability of discovery in the prosecution of a lawsuit. Further, prior to the addition of subdivision (e) to section 639 and the enactment of section 645.1 in 1981 (Stats. 1981, ch. 299, §1, p. 1429, §2, p. 1430), all discovery was "free." Discovery disputes were presided over and resolved by the trial courts.

When the Legislature amended section 639 and enacted section 645.1 in 1981, it obviously intended to give the overburdened trial courts the opportunity to utilize the paid expertise of retired judges in the resolution of complicated, time-consuming discovery disputes. Here, the trial court readily availed itself of that welcomed option. However, in the circumstances of this case, use of those services was inappropriate.

Fees of $200 and $300 per hour charged by privately compensated discovery referees allow affluent litigants to avoid discovery compliance by pricing enforcement of legitimate discovery demands beyond the means of indigent plaintiffs. This advantage based on wealth flows directly from the trial court's order imposing equal division of fees between indigent plaintiffs and an adverse litigant of far superior financial means.

Section 645.1 makes no provision for indigent litigants proceeding in forma pauperis. However, such parties are by definition unable to pay court-ordered reference fees regardless of how they are allocated. That is, no division or allocation of hourly fees for the services of a privately compensated discovery referee that imposes a monetary burden on impecunious litigants can achieve the fair and reasonable goal of section 645. Therefore, based on the present record, we conclude section 645.1 does not constitute authority for the trial court to appoint a privately compensated discovery referee to resolve the instant dispute.

B. TRIAL COURT VIGILANCE NEEDED IN OTHER DISCOVERY REFERENCE ORDERS

Sections 639 and 645.1 are similarly silent with respect to the dilemma of a party of modest means who does not qualify for the cost protection afforded by proceeding in forma pauperis. Reference to a discovery referee imposes a substantial economic burden on such a party. It is therefore incumbent on trial courts utilizing the relief afforded by these sections to look beyond the benefit realized by the judicial system and consider the economic impact the order of reference will have on the parties. Accordingly, trial courts should review discovery motions carefully to differentiate between those motions that can be retained by the court and those which are appropriate for reference.

The trial court also must avoid the appearance of delegating judicial functions to referees. In *Aetna Life Ins. Co. v. Superior Court* (1986) 182 Cal. App. 3d 431 [227 Cal. Rptr. 460], the trial court made an order assigning all law and motion for summary judgment proceedings to a referee. The referee heard motions for summary judgment and prepared a written report which included findings of fact and conclusions of law. The trial court denied a hearing on the report and adopted the findings of the referee. *Aetna* held the reference order was not authorized by statute and constituted an impermissible delegation of judicial power. In so doing the *Aetna* court observed, "[e]fficiency is not more important than preserving the constitutional integrity of the judicial process." (*Id.*, at p. 437.)

The justice system not only must be fair to all litigants; it must appear to be so. The increasingly common practice of referring discovery matters, without regard to the financial burden imposed upon litigants, threatens to undermine both of these goals.

. . . .

E. APPROPRIATE ALTERNATIVE DISCOVERY ORDERS

In their briefs, the parties and amici curiae have suggested several options by which the discovery dispute might be resolved. These include a pro bono referee, a retired judge of the superior court sitting by assignment, or retention of the matter by the trial court. Any of these alternatives may be appropriate.

We conclude that it is the trial court's responsibility to form a fair means of discovery dispute resolution which takes into consideration the financial status of the parties. . . .

The petition for writ of mandate is granted. The trial court's order is reversed, and the matter remanded to the trial court to make whatever new order it deems appropriate, consistent with the views expressed herein.

Discussion Questions

1. How does the court resolve the referral of issues to privately compensated referees when indigent parties are involved in a legal action?

2. What does the court assert that trial judges must evaluate when considering the use of private judges in cases not specifically involving indigent litigants?

3. What options are available to the trial court in dealing with the discovery disputes in this case?

The First Amendment

A final constitutional criticism focuses on the public's, and particularly, the media's right of access to private judging proceedings and documents. Typically, private judging sessions, either contract or court-supervised, are closed to the public. Contract judging is analogous to arbitration, which allows parties to resolve their disputes in private. Yet the findings of referees or temporary judges are on the record. Thus, some argue that it makes sense to allow the public and media access to these proceedings to preserve the integrity of the court system. No court decision has been rendered regarding First Amendment rights and court-supervised private judging.

However, the courts in the *Cincinnati Gas* case (discussed in Chapter 5) did provide a basis for determining whether court-supervised ADR procedures should be open to the public. The *Cincinnati Gas* court sought to preserve the integrity of the judicial process by striking a balance between the right of access and the need for relaxed and confidential proceedings. In that case, the court applied the *Press Enterprise II* standards to a court-supervised, nonbinding summary jury trial and determined that the process could remain closed to the media and the public. The *Press Enterprise II* standards inquire, (1) Does the process have tradition of accessibility? and (2) Does public access play a significant role in the proper functioning of the process?

Under the first prong of this test, although there is no constitutional right of access to civil trials, both civil and criminal trials have historically been open to the public. Because referee and temporary judge proceedings may result in final court decisions, one may argue that these processes are part of standard litigation and should be open to the public. On the other hand, one can assert that referees and temporary judges are supplements to, and not part of, the normal litigation process and that courts using these mechanisms have traditionally kept them private.

Second, whether public involvement is important to the fair functioning of the process depends to a large extent on the case. If the dispute involves a matter that may impact the public, one could argue that the media and public should be allowed access to the proceedings. For example, a controversy between two landholders over the ownership of forest land may be important to the public if it involves the protection of local forestry jobs or the destruction of an environmentally sensitive area. However, a battle between two local firms over a failure to make timely payment under the terms of a computer maintenance contract may not benefit significantly from public access. At this time, it may be best for judges considering court-supervised private judging to screen out cases that involve matters of public interest and to only recommend temporary judges or referees for private business conflicts.

CHAPTER CONCLUSION

Retired judges or magistrates can play key roles in adjudicating business conflicts. Through court appointment, state reference statutes, and private contract agreements, disputing businesses may empower a private person to hear and decide their case. With contract private judging, the parties maximize their control through the development of their own procedures, their selection of the private judge, and the confidentiality of the proceeding and its outcome. Under reference statutes or court appointments, retired judges help courts to alleviate extensive case backlogs and to provide a more rapid, informal, and often less costly resolution of business conflicts. These procedures provide the added benefits of obtaining a court decision on the record and retaining standard channels of appellate review available to business litigants. However, businesses and individual citizens must be vigilant about court-supervised private judging practices to ensure that they are being used effectively and that they do not represent an unacceptable abdication of court responsibility or abuse of court discretion. Therefore, it is important for businesspeople to work with their legal counsel to understand the distinctions between the various forms of private judging and to use those methods that are best suited to their dispute.

BEST BUSINESS PRACTICES

- Be familiar with the differences in your state between contract private judges, temporary judges, general referees, or special referees when faced with these alternatives in business litigation.

- Contact local courts and well-established ADR service providers for more information on private judging practices and for lists of potential private judges.

- When selecting a private judge, carefully review with the assistance of counsel the reputation, professional experience, and educational credentials of a number of private judges.

- Consider the option of a general reference rather than private arbitration to gain the privacy and speed of an arbitration with the benefits of a court decision on the record and traditional channels of appellate review.

- Collaborate fully with your attorney in special reference proceedings, particularly when discovery issues are at stake, to effectively protect the legal interests of your business.

KEY TERMS

Contract private judge, p. 266
Federal Rule of Civil Procedure 53,
   p. 271
General reference, p. 271
Order of appointment, p. 270
Order of reference, p. 271

Plenary review, p. 277
Private judging, p. 265
Referee, p. 270
Referee's report, p. 271
Reference statutes, p. 266
Rent-a-judge, p. 266

Rent-a-jury, p. 270
Special master, p. 271
Special reference, p. 272

Temporary judges, p. 270
Voluntary petition, p. 270

ETHICAL AND LEGAL REVIEW

1. In a hypothetical situation, Judge Smith has been appointed by a trial court to serve as a general referee in an insurance dispute between Allright Insurance Company and Ginny Moore, an individual policyholder. Ms. Moore claims that Allright is required to compensate her for damage to her home from a winter snowstorm under the terms of her homeowner's insurance policy. Allright claims the damage does not come within the terms of her policy protections. Judge Smith has handled five private contract judging cases involving Allright Insurance and has found in its favor four of those times. Should Judge Smith disclose these contacts to the court and to Ms. Moore? [See *ABA Model Code for Judicial Conduct* (1990)]

2. In a hypothetical case, a major television station, WRDS, has fired one of its news anchors, Crystal Summers. Ms. Summers has sued the station, claiming both age and gender discrimination as the reasons for her dismissal. She alleges that the station thought that she was too old to attract younger viewers, even though her co-anchor, Ken Brightman, is five years older than her. There has been a great deal of public and media interest in the dispute. The trial court has appointed a temporary judge to handle the thorny conflict. Applying the standards of *Cincinnati Gas,* consider whether the proceedings should be open to the public. Do you think the public has an important role to play in this employment dispute? [*Cincinnati Gas and Electric Co. v. General Electric Co.,* 854 F. 2d 900 (6th Cir. 1988), *cert. denied,* 489 U.S. 1033 (1989)]

3. Plaintiff Edgar Rushing brought an action against Lancaster Radiology Medical Group and several others for wrongful discharge based on race discrimination. The trial court appointed a discovery referee even though the plaintiff objected to the order, claiming that he could not afford to pay a special referee. The referee ultimately submitted a bill for more than $18,000 and recommended that each party pay half. The plaintiff objected and ultimately did not pay his allocated portion. Will the plaintiff's attorney be required to pay the plaintiff's outstanding share of the fees? [*McMillan v. Super. Ct. of Los Angeles County,* 50 Cal. App. 4th 246 (1996)]

4. Russell J. Clark owns a 4.42-acre lot in the private Rancho Santa Fe community development. Property in this exclusive community is subject to numerous land use and aesthetic regulations. As his family's trustee, Clark applied to subdivide the Rancho Santa Fe Association property, a request that the association denied.

He challenged the decision in court, and the parties ultimately agreed to a general reference before the Honorable Charles W. Froehlich, Jr. Referee Froehlich determined that the Association had not abused its discretion in rejecting Clark's application, and the superior court entered the judgment on the record. Clark brought a motion for a new trial, which the trial court referred to Referee Froehlich, who denied the request as untimely. Clark appealed. Can a trial court delegate a motion for a new trial to a general referee? [*Clark v. Rancho Santa Fe Ass'n.,* 216 Cal. App. 3d 606 (1989)]

5. A trial court appointed a superior court commissioner to serve as a temporary judge in a divorce and child support action brought by Dorothy Sarracino against Ernest Sarracino. Mr. Sarracino was personally served with summonses, initial pleadings, and a notice of the upcoming hearing. He filed responsive pleadings in both matters but did not appear at the hearing. In his absence, the temporary judge issued dissolution and support orders. Mr. Sarracino sought to vacate the orders, partly alleging that the court did not have the authority to appoint the commissioner as a temporary judge without his agreement. May the court appoint a temporary judge in a dissolution and child support matter without the agreement of both parties? [*Sarracino v. Super. Ct. of Los Angeles County,* 13 Cal. 3d 1 (1974)]

SUGGESTED ADDITIONAL READINGS

Alternative Methods of Dispute Resolution, 37 Vand. L. Rev. 845, 1015-1030, 1984.

Kim, Anne S. *Rent-a-Judges and the Costs of Selling Justice.* 44 Duke L. J. 166, October 1994.

Litkovitz, Amy L. *Note & Comment: The Advantages of Using a "Rent-A-Judge" System in Ohio.* 10 Ohio St. J. on Disp. Resol. 491, 1995.

Part IV

CREATING THE ADR ENVIRONMENT

Chapter 10: Business Dispute Resolution Systems

Chapter 11: The Future of Business ADR

Chapters 10 and 11 conclude our review of alternative dispute resolution for business with practical considerations for businesspersons using processes discussed in the previous chapters. In Chapter 10, business dispute resolution systems are covered. Specifically, the chapter describes approaches to managing and resolving both internal and external business disputes through comprehensive preemptive planning. Chapter 11 considers the ethical obligations of practitioners of alternative dispute resolution as well as consumers of ADR and predicts likely legislative and judicial trends in the field that have the potential of impacting business.

10

BUSINESS DISPUTE RESOLUTION SYSTEMS

CHAPTER HIGHLIGHTS

In this chapter, you will read and learn about the following:

1. Establishing procedures to resolve internal disputes involving employees, managers, and shareholders, including employee training, employee contracts and handbook language, and company ombudsmen.
2. Establishing procedures to resolve external disputes involving customers, business partners, and competitors, including use and supervision of outside counsel, relations with insurance carriers, and customer contracts and agreements.

The preceding chapters have described in detail the various alternative dispute resolution processes used to resolve business disputes. ADR processes range from informal, settlement-oriented negotiation to formal, adjudicative arbitration. Each process has advantages and disadvantages as well as proper and improper applications. This chapter will provide guidance on incorporating ADR processes into an effective business dispute resolution program. We will address the creation of structures for resolving both internal and external business disputes. The chapter concludes with exercises designed to assist you in evaluating the needs of various types of businesses with respect to dispute resolution system design.

AN OVERVIEW OF BUSINESS DISPUTE RESOLUTION SYSTEMS

Ten years ago, Chief Justice Warren Burger wrote in an article entitled "Our Vicious Legal Circle," "The notion that ordinary people want black-robed judges, well-dressed lawyers and fine courtrooms as settings to resolve their disputes is incorrect. People with problems, like people with pains, want relief, and they want it as quickly and inexpensively as possible." The same can be said of businesses. Both businesses and individuals want a system that provides them some measure of humanity, a system that allows them to participate in resolving their own dispute. They seek to be heard directly, not eliminated from the process through expensive and arcane legal procedures. They desire, in short, access to the processes that are used to solve their problems. The premise of the preceding chapters has been that ADR processes provide such access. Consequently, wise businesspeople develop companywide, programmatic approaches to implementing dispute resolution.

Successful companies manage both internal and external conflict. Internal dispute resolution mechanisms resolve conflict between members of the organization, such as employees, while external dispute resolution mechanisms target disputes involving those with whom the company does business, such as vendors and suppliers. The best company dispute resolution policy is a comprehensive and preemptive one that addresses both types of disputes as early as possible.

http://

For information on the Foundation for Prevention and Early Conflict Resolution, see http://wwwz. conflictresolution .org/perg/index. html

In deciding to implement policies favoring ADR, companies must answer three initial questions relating to internal and external disputes. How should the company balance facilitative, evaluative, and adjudicative processes? Should the company favor binding or nonbinding processes? And, what benefits is the company most interested in achieving with an ADR program? These benefits, at minimum, often include economic savings, relationship preservation, and quick dispute resolution.

The most effective method of balancing facilitative, evaluative, and adjudicative processes, both binding and nonbinding, is to employ them in that sequence. Negotiation and mediation are the least expensive and most expeditious facilitative processes, and they pose no threat to future adjudication. When they prove unsuccessful, the minitrial or summary jury trial, evaluative processes that allow party-driven settlement but introduce an advisory third party charged with considering the merits of the case in an advisory capacity may be used. If the evaluative process fails, an adjudicative process, whether private arbitration or public trial, remains available. This progression of relatively simple processes saves time, money, and important commercial relationships by resolving many cases early. It also saves costly adjudication for cases in which early settlement proves impossible. This progression allows businesses to rely on nonbinding, negotiated processes that initially preserve party control over outcomes and to relinquish control in adjudicative processes only when necessary. Finally, this progression recognizes the fact that business dispute resolution is primarily concerned with economics. As such, length of time to resolution, reduction of resolution costs, and preservation of important commercial relationships contribute to both narrow process and broad policy decisions.

ADR IN ACTION

United Parcel Service Delivers an Employment ADR Program

Two years of research and planning by a core group drawn from the legal, human resources, employee relations, communications, training, and labor departments ended recently for UPS with the creation of its pilot Employment Dispute Resolution Program. This program covers approximately 5,000 nonunion management, administrative, technical, and specialist employees in two company regions. Ultimately, the program will cover all 70,000 workers in these categories around the world. The planning group visited six companies with similar programs, studied twenty-five additional corporate ADR initiatives, and consulted extensively with the American Arbitration Association before finalizing plans for the program.

The program, which complements other ADR efforts by the company, including incorporation of ADR into many company contracts and documents, covers claims such as discipline, discrimination, harassment, termination, and interference with other legal rights. The program moves a dispute through three internal and two external processes. A dispute may be sent through three in-house processes including "open door," facilitation, and peer review. Outside processes used to resolve disputes are private mediation and arbitration. The first four steps of the program, open door through media-

tion, are processes that allow voluntary negotiation of disputes and only end with mutually agreed-upon conclusions. It is only at the fifth and final stage that a third party may impose an outcome on the company or employee. "We want to do everything we can to maintain a positive relationship while the dispute is in process, so that ideally, when the dispute is satisfactorily resolved, we all go back to work and move forward," said Joseph Shaginaw, UPS corporate employee relations manager.

Extensive in-house training and promotion will accompany the rollout of the full program. UPS hopes the economic benefits of the program will be considerable. Indeed, they hope to shave as much as eighty percent from the $10 million spent annually on legal expenses. Still, Jeff Paquin, who handles ADR and litigation for the company, says, "A lot of companies start the process because they want to save money. But if you do it for that reason only, you're not going to get too far. We began with the principle that we wanted to do this to resolve disputes in a way that is fair to employees and the company. And if you save money, reduce the amount of time to resolve a dispute, maintain confidentiality, and do all these things, that's great. But always remember the real objective: preserving working relationships."

INTERNAL DISPUTE RESOLUTION POLICIES

http://

For information on training and simulations, see the Harvard Negotiation Project site: http://www.law.harvard.edu/Programs/PON/

In-house employee training is a significant effort companies can make to reduce **internal disputes** or conflict in the workplace. Training is preemptive inasmuch as it endeavors to empower employees to solve problems informally and early. Indeed, interactive training in interest-based and nonadversarial conflict resolution can improve the workplace by avoiding formal conflict resolution processes altogether.

Employee contracts and handbooks calling for ADR processes present two noteworthy opportunities to promote the ADR philosophy in the company. For many years, courts have enforced contract provisions and grievance processes that use ADR principles. In 1991, the U.S. Supreme Court decided in *Gilmer v. Interstate/Johnson Lane Corp.* that an arbitration clause requiring an employee to submit an age discrimination claim to arbitration and waiving a right to trial was enforceable. The Court held that an employee who signs such an agreement is simply choosing an alternative forum in which to resolve a claim. Courts have reached largely consistent results since then, although courts will decline to enforce agreements that they believe to be unconscionable or otherwise insufficient in contract terms. Indeed, some recent decisions have scaled back support for mandatory arbitration agreements. These provisions enable businesses to use rapid and cost-effective means offered by alternative dispute resolution to resolve claims and avoid litigation with and between employees altogether.

http://

The complete text of Gilmer v. Interstate/Johnson may be found at: http://caselaw.findlaw.com/cgi-bin/getcase.pl?court=US&vol=500&invol=20

Employers wishing to use handbook provisions and contracts for the purposes of ADR should be mindful of several potential pitfalls. They should not, for example, treat contracts and handbooks as equivalent. In *Heurtebise v. Reliable Business Computers,* 550 NW 2d 243 (1996), where a handbook allowed the employer to modify the contents at its sole discretion, a court declined to enforce an arbitration provision, finding that no intent to be bound was present. Although courts normally affirm such provisions, judges are willing to void them when they pose an injustice to the employee. To be effective and enforceable, ADR provisions in either a contract or handbook must be:

1. *Fair.* Provisions should, at a minimum, include an impartial third-party advisor, an opportunity for parties to state their case following a reasonable period of preparation, and a range of remedies generally equivalent to those available in a public forum. In *Stirlen v. Supercuts,* 60 Cal. Rptr. 2d 138 (1997), the court struck down a provision that provided that only actual damages could be recovered, and that those damages were subject to further limitations for mitigation.

2. *Inexpensive.* Courts have voided arbitration clauses that shifted a disproportionate amount of proceeding expenses to the employee. Companies are well advised to divide ADR expenses to avoid the appearance of placing an undue economic burden on the employee.

3. *Consistent.* The commitment to ADR should apply to all populations. If the provision appears to deprive a single class of employees from using the courts,

while ensuring the right of the business to do so, courts will be cautious about enforcing it. In *Stirlen v. Supercuts,* the court declined to enforce a provision that also allowed the company to avoid arbitration while requiring it of the employee.

4. *Voluntary.* Courts have expressed reservations about **adhesion contracts** that condition employment, new or continued, upon employee acceptance of an ADR provision that waives the right to court access.

5. *Clear.* The principles of contract are followed closely in analyzing pre-dispute clauses and handbook provisions, and these principles disfavor clauses that are not explicit and prominently displayed. They should, at a minimum, identify the employees covered by the provision, the case types covered, the nature of the procedure used to address each particular case, the allocation of process-related expenses, and the right to counsel.

The following case illustrates many of these principles as it considers the enforceability of an employment handbook and contract package requiring employees to use arbitration to resolve claims against the company.

GIBSON V. NEIGHBORHOOD HEALTH CLINICS

(7th U.S. Circuit, 1997)

FACT SUMMARY

Gibson, who had previously been employed by Neighborhood Health Clinics under circumstances not relevant to this case, was rehired by NHC on December 22, 1994. On December 30, 1994, at which time Gibson, although rehired, had not yet returned to work, NHC held a meeting at which all employees were presented with a new Associates Policy Manual and required to sign a new Associates Understanding. Gibson was not required to attend the meeting, and in fact, she did not. The Understanding included the following language:

> I agree to the grievance and arbitration provisions set forth in the Associates Policy Manual. I understand that I am waiving my right to a trial, including a jury trial, in state or federal court of the class of disputes specifically set forth in the grievance

and arbitration provisions on pages 8–10 of the Manual.

The Manual states that when an employee alleges a violation of his or her rights under the ADA or Title VII:

> Then it is clearly intended and agreed that the sole and exclusive means for the resolution of all disputes, issues, controversies, claims, causes of action, or grievances by an employee against neighborhood health clinics shall be through the process of arbitration.

The opening two paragraphs of the Manual include the following language:

> Neighborhood Health Clinics reserves the right at any time to modify, revoke, suspend, terminate, or change any or all terms of this Manual, plans, policies, or procedures, in whole or in part, without having to consult or

reach agreement with anyone, at any time, with or without notice. . . .

[W]hile Neighborhood Health Clinics intends to abide by the policies and procedures described in this Manual, it does not constitute a contract nor promise of any kind. Therefore, employees can be terminated at any time, with or without notice, and with or without cause.

The arbitration provisions were not part of the terms of employment during Gibson's previous tenure with NHC.

When Gibson was rehired in December 1994, she was told to report to work on January 9, 1995. On that date, she met with NHC's personnel director, Chris Baxter, who handed her a stack of papers to sign, including insurance and tax forms. Among the papers was the Associates Understanding. Gibson testified at her deposition that when she asked Baxter about the Associates Understanding, Baxter told her that it was a form that everybody signed so that complaints about time off could be settled through a grievance procedure. The Manual referenced in the Associates Understanding was not given to Gibson at that time; Baxter was only able to locate a copy of the Manual later that day, at which time she provided it to Gibson. Although she signed the Associates Understanding, Gibson never signed the Manual.

NHC fired Gibson on April 6, 1995. On May 15, 1995, Gibson filed a discrimination claim with the Equal Employment Opportunity Commission, alleging sex and disability discrimination. NHC was informed of this charge shortly thereafter. Gibson then filed her complaint in the district court. NHC moved to dismiss Gibson's complaint on the ground that she had waived her right to a judicial determination of her claims against NHC by agreeing to submit such disputes to arbi-

The complete text of Alexander v. Gardner-Denver may be found at:
http://caselaw.findlaw.com/scripts/getcase.pl?navby=case&court=US&vol=415&page=36

For the complete text of Pierce v. Atchison, Topeka, see this site:
http://caselaw.findlaw.com/cgi-bin/getcase.pl?court=7th&navby=case&no=943057

tration. The district court agreed, concluding that the Manual in connection with the Associates Understanding created an enforceable arbitration agreement, and granted the motion for dismissal. In addition, because Gibson failed to abide by the deadline for submitting her claim to arbitration, the dismissal effectively foreclosed her ability to obtain redress. The district court therefore entered final judgment, from which Gibson now appeals.

OPINION: *FLAUM, Circuit Judge*

On appeal, the parties debate an important issue: whether the prerogative of litigating one's ADA and **Title VII claims** in federal court is the type of important right the relinquishment of which requires a **knowing and voluntary waiver.** The Supreme Court indicated in *Alexander v. Gardner-Denver Co.,* 415 U.S. 36 (1974), that an employee could not forfeit substantive rights under Title VII absent a voluntary and knowing waiver. In *Pierce v. Atchison, Topeka & Santa Fe Ry. Co.,* 65 F.3d 562 (7th Cir. 1995), we applied the knowing and voluntary standard set out in *Alexander* to an employee's release of age and race discrimination claims against his employer. Thus, before an employee cedes a substantive right grounded in federal statutory law, she must understand and freely make the decision to do so.

Less clear is whether the right to have one's federal claims determined judicially rather than in an arbitration proceeding qualifies for this added protection. The Supreme Court has not reached this issue, but in dicta has stated that in agreeing to arbitrate a federal claim, a party "does not forgo the substantive rights afforded by the statute; it only submits to their resolution in an arbitral, rather than a judicial, forum." *Gilmer v. Interstate/Johnson Lane Corp.,* 500 U.S. 20 (1991). Conversely, we have noted that by being forced into binding arbitration [employees] would be surrendering their right to trial by jury—a right that civil rights plaintiffs fought hard for and finally obtained in the 1991 amendments to Title VII. This issue is further complicated by the strong federal policy in favor of arbitration as embodied in the substantive provisions involved in this case. Thus, an employee's contractual agreement to submit her federal claims to arbitration implicates competing policy concerns.

Obviously, the strongest case for a court's finding that an employer and employee agreed to submit claims to arbitration will arise when the record indicates the employee has knowingly agreed to do so. If parties operate under these conditions, we believe that the twin goals of protecting federal rights and resolving claims where possible through arbitration will be effected. Moreover, the formation of arbitration agreements upon terms that both parties understand need not be unduly burdensome. The course that NHC undertook to alert those already employed to the change in policy (the convening of a meeting and the presentation of the appropriate documentation) demonstrates the feasibility of achieving this objective. While we therefore stress the advantage of arbitration agreements that are the product of an employee's knowing and voluntary consent, we decline today to decide whether such consent is a prerequisite to the validity of an agreement to arbitrate federal civil rights claims. To resolve this appeal, we need look no further than the state law of contract that generally governs arbitration agreements.

The parties agree that an employee and employer may contractually agree to submit federal claims, including Title VII and ADA claims, to arbitration. An agreement to arbitrate is treated like any other contract. If there is no contract, there is to be no forced arbitration. In determining whether a valid arbitration agreement arose between the parties, a federal court should look to the state law that ordinarily governs the formation of contracts.

It is a basic tenet of contract law that in order for a promise to be enforceable against the promisor, the promisee must have given some consideration for the promise. Consideration is defined as bargained for exchange whereby the promisor (here Gibson) receives some benefit or the promisee (here NHC) suffers a detriment. Thus, in order for Gibson's agreement to be enforceable, there must be detriment to NHC or benefit to Gibson that was bargained for in exchange for Gibson's promise to arbitrate all disputes.

Often, consideration for one party's promise to arbitrate is the other party's promise to do the same. In the present case, however, NHC cannot point to its own promise to arbitrate in order to make enforceable Gibson's promise to do likewise. The Understanding contains no promise on NHC's part to submit claims to arbitration. It is worded entirely in terms of Gibson's obligation to submit her claims to arbitration (using phrases such as "I agree" "I understand" "I am waiving"); it contains no promise on NHC's part. In order for a contract to be enforceable, both parties must be bound by its terms. Although Indiana courts will not find that there was a lack of obligation on the part of one party when "a reasonable and logical interpretation will render the contract valid and enforceable," *Id.* at 645, there is no gloss we can apply to the language of the Understanding that would suggest that NHC was also required to forgo a judicial forum in favor of arbitration. To find that NHC was required to arbitrate any claim brought by Gibson would not give recognition to an obligation that was clearly present yet imperfectly expressed, but rather would lend arcane meaning to the clear language chosen by NHC; to find an obligation here would be to weave a contract out of loose threads. Therefore, we conclude that the Understanding itself did not contain consideration for Gibson's promise in the form of a promise by NHC to submit disputes to arbitration.

In contrast to the one-sided obligation contained in the wording of the Understanding, the Manual contains language that arguably could be read to bind NHC. We conclude, however, that any promise NHC made in the Manual cannot serve as consideration for Gibson's promise to arbitrate. The absence of a meaningful link between Gibson's promise, contained in the Understanding, and NHC's obligation, set forth in the Manual, precludes reading these provisions as complementary components of a bargained for exchange. To be sure, contract terms may be incorporated by reference to a separate document, including an employee handbook, and consideration for the promise in one instrument may be contained in another. Nevertheless, whatever the physical form by which a contract is memorialized (if any), proper consideration must consist of benefit or detriment given in exchange for the promise in question. The principal purposes of this consideration requirement are the "cautionary function of bringing home to the promisor the fact that his promise is legally enforceable and an evidentiary function . . . of making it more likely that an enforceable promise was intended." *Scholes v. Lehmann*, 56 F.3d 750 (1995). Neither of these functions is served when a promisor does not know of the promise that purportedly serves as consideration. Here, Gibson was unaware

of the terms of the Manual (even if the Understanding's reference to the Manual alerted her to its existence) at the time she signed the Understanding. The promise that she made in the Understanding, therefore, was not given in exchange for any promise that NHC made in the Manual. In addition, although the Manual contains language that could be read to bind Gibson as well as NHC, Gibson did not (even in the objective or constructive sense) assent to the terms of the Manual, either when she signed the Understanding (at which point the Manual was not made available), or when she received the Manual. Consequently, there is no promise on the part of NHC that can serve as consideration for Gibson's promise to arbitrate.

Nor was Gibson's promise to submit claims to arbitration supported by consideration in the form of NHC's promise to hire her or to continue to employ her, or by its reasonable reliance on her promise. An initial offer of employment may constitute consideration for an employee's promise, such as a covenant not to compete. However, NHC's offer of employment to Gibson was not made in exchange for her promise to arbitrate, for she had already been hired at the time she made the promise. Once again, the element of bargained for exchange is lacking. An employer's specific promise to continue to employ an at-will employee may provide valid consideration for an employee's promise to forgo certain rights. In the present case, however, NHC never made a promise to continue Gibson's employment in exchange for her promise to submit claims to arbitration. That is, it never communicated to her that if she signed the Understanding she could continue to work there, and that if she did not her status would be uncertain. It is true that NHC continued to employ her. Yet when an employer has made no specific promise, the mere fact of continued employment does not constitute consideration for the employee's promise.

Finally, while in the employment context it has been held that one party's partial performance in reliance upon the other party's promise may be sufficient consideration to make the promise enforceable, there is no indication in the present case that NHC was induced to rely on Gibson's promise. It had made its decision to hire her prior to her agreeing to the terms of the Understanding, and there is no evidence that its decision to continue to employ her following her signing of the Understanding (on the day she returned to work) was based upon her agreeing to the terms contained therein. We therefore conclude that Gibson's promise to submit her claims against NHC to arbitration did not give rise to an enforceable contract.

Reversed and Remanded.

Discussion Questions

1. Do cases involving civil rights present particularly compelling claims deserving of formal court adjudication, regardless of any ADR clause contained in an employment contract or handbook?

2. Does the interest in judicial economy and in support of ADR outweigh the employee's interest in public adjudication of statutory and constitutional claims?

3. Is employment, whether continued or new, an acceptable incentive to enter into an ADR agreement with an employer? How would consideration of public policy affect your answer?

4. Why should employees be compelled to arbitrate and thus forfeit their right of access to a court trial by a jury of their peers?

ADR IN ACTION

National Franchise Mediation Program

The CPR Institute for Dispute Resolution operates a National Franchise Mediation Program. A diverse group of fifty companies, including Burger King, UNOCAL, McDonald's, Dollar-Rent-A-Car, Holiday Inn, Jiffy Lube International, and Meineke Discount Muffler Shops, participate. The participating companies commit to resolving franchisor/franchisee disputes through direct negotiation and, in the event of failure, through a formal ADR process. Franchisee participation is voluntary, but franchisors must participate if a franchisee initiates a dispute resolution procedure. The program has addressed successfully a wide variety of disputes, including encroachment, lease claims, customer service matters, and contract violation allegations.

http://

For a complete description of the CPR National Franchise Mediation program, including statistics and members, see this site: http://www. cpradr.org/fran _397.htm

Use of company ombuds is a long-standing method of internal dispute management and resolution. The **ombudsman** is a company-employed internal problem solver. Ombudsmen offer employees a confidential, relatively powerful office through which to resolve claims that they would otherwise have to address through formal grievance procedures or litigation. Likewise, they offer the employer an opportunity to diffuse potentially serious workplace disputes prior to the initiation of either in-house grievance procedures or external lawsuits. The ombudsman position is a difficult one to maintain in terms of loyalty and privilege, because it is normally one through which promises of neutrality and confidentiality are made to the employee and employer alike. The following two cases give opposing answers to the question of whether the files maintained by an ombudsman can later be discovered in litigation. Ironically, both cases involve the same company and ombudsman, but were decided by different courts.

KIENTZY V. MCDONNELL DOUGLAS CORPORATION
33 F.R.D. 570 (U.S.D.C. Eastern Dist. Miss, 1991)

FACT SUMMARY

Plaintiff Mary Kientzy alleges that McDonnell Douglas Aircraft Corporation (MDC) terminated her from her position as a security officer in violation of Title VII. The plaintiff has noticed Therese Clement for deposition and would depose other company personnel about their statements to ombudsman Clemente. Clemente is employed as a senior staff assistant in the ombudsman program of the defendant's subsidiary McDonnell Douglas Aircraft Company (McAir). Clemente has been employed in the McAir Ombudsman Office since the ombudsman program began in 1985. The purpose of the ombudsman program and office is to mediate, in a strictly confidential environment, disputes among MDC employees and between employees and management.

Plaintiff Kientzy was terminated from employment in August 1988, following the decision of a company disciplinary committee. After the committee made its decision, the plaintiff went to Ms. Clemente in her position as ombudsman; MDC nevertheless terminated her. The plaintiff argues that Ms. Clemente received information about her situation from company employees, including a member of the disciplinary committee who has since died.

This action is before the court upon the motion of Therese Clemente for an order under Federal Rule of Civil Procedure 26(c)(1), protecting from pretrial discovery by both plaintiff and defendant the communications she received in her position as a company ombudsman of defendant MDC. MDC argues in support of Clemente's position. The plaintiff argues that any such ombudsman **privilege** should not include the information sought.

OPINION: *DAVID D. NOCE, U.S. Magistrate Judge*

Plaintiff argues that the information received by Clemente is relevant to the trial of the action and is discoverable on two grounds. First, she argues that the statements made to Clemente by defendant's personnel may evidence discriminatory animus in the decision to terminate her. Second, she argues that the ombudsman program is a company procedure for appealing her dismissal and that the ombudsman thus participated in the final decision to terminate her. For the reasons set forth below, the court agrees with movant that the confidential communications made to her are protected from disclosure by Federal Rule of Evidence 501.

Rule 501 requires that this Court assay the ombudsman's claim of privilege by interpreting the principles of the common law "in light of reason and experience." Four cardinal factors have been discerned for this purpose.

> (1) The communication must be one made in the belief that it will not be disclosed; (2) confidentiality must be essential to the maintenance of the relationship between the parties; (3) the relationship should be one that society considers worthy of being fostered; and (4) the injury to the relationship incurred by disclosure must be greater than the benefit gained in the correct disposal of litigation.

First, ombudsman Clemente received the subject communications in the belief that they would be kept confidential. The McAir ombudsman office is constituted as an independent and neutral entity. It has no authority to make company policy. Its head has the position of company vice-president, independent of the company's human resources and personnel offices. The office has direct access to the company president. Ombudsman Clemente is bound by the Code of Ethics of the Corporate Ombudsman Association, which provides for the confidentiality of communications. The office has adopted procedures to assure such confidentiality. The McAir Ombudsman Office has given its strict pledge of confidentiality to all employees and to the company. All new employees are so advised and defendant has repeatedly restated to its employees that they may rely on the confidentiality of the ombudsman's office. Since it opened in 1985, the McAir ombudsman's office has received approximately 4800 communications. Defendant has sought, but has been refused, access to the ombudsman's files and records regarding plaintiff. The company has indicated it will not request them in the future.

Second, confidentiality of communications is essential to relationships between the ombudsman's office and defendant's employees and defendant's management. The function of the McAir ombudsman's office is communications and to remedy workplace problems, in a strictly confidential atmosphere. Without this confidentiality, the office would be just one more nonconfidential opportunity for employees to air disputes. The ombudsman's office provides an opportunity for complete disclosure, without the specter of retaliation, that does not exist in the other available nonconfidential grievance and complaint procedures.

Third, the relationship between the ombudsman office and defendant's employees and management is worthy of societal support. The Court takes judicial notice of the fact that MDC and McAir are very large federal government contractors in the aircraft, space, and other industries. It is important that their employees have an opportunity to make

http://

For a complete version of the Federal Rules of Evidence, including Rule 501, see the Cornell Law School site: http://www.law.cornell.edu/rules/fre/overview.html

confidential statements and to receive confidential guidance, information, and aid to remedy workplace problems, to benefit themselves and possibly the nation. This is true in spite of the possibility that such actions may be perceived by an employee to be against company or fellow employees' interests.

Fourth, the harm caused by a disruption of the confidential relationship between the ombudsman's office and others in plaintiff's case would be greater than the benefit to plaintiff by disclosure. A successful ombudsman program resolves many problems informally and more quickly than other formal procedures, including court actions. A court order that Clemente disclose the information communicated to her in confidence, or that her informants disclose what they told her in confidence about plaintiff, would destroy the reputation and principle of confidentiality that the McAir ombudsman program and office now enjoys and needs to perform its function. The utility of that program and office, in resolving disputes in this workplace and thus diminishing the need for more formal resolution procedures, is founded on the confiden-

tiality of its communications to and from company officials and employees. Federal Rule of Evidence 408 has recognized the utility of confidential settlement discussions. The societal benefit from this confidentiality is paramount to plaintiff's need for disclosure.

The Court is persuaded in the case at bar that the plaintiff's need for relevant information can be satisfied, in spite of the privilege, by deposing all relevant fact witnesses, including the remaining members of the disciplinary committee, about the events leading to plaintiff's termination. Indeed, the depositions of these persons is expected to occur soon. Plaintiff may not ask these witnesses to disclose their statement to the company ombudsman. Plaintiff may ask these witnesses about facts known by them, even though those facts were contained in their statements to the ombudsman. Because there has been no showing that ombudsman Clemente has nonconfidential, relevant information, plaintiff may not depose her at all.

For the reasons set forth above, IT IS HEREBY ORDERED that the motion of Therese Clemente for a protective order is sustained.

CARMAN V. MCDONNELL DOUGLAS CORPORATION
114 F.3d 790 (8th Cir. 1997)

FACT SUMMARY

In October 1992, McDonnell Douglas Aircraft Corporation laid off Frank Carman as part of a reduction in its management staff. Carman then sued McDonnell Douglas, claiming that his termination violated the Age Discrimination

in Employment Act, the Missouri Human Rights Act, and the Employee Retirement Income Security Act of 1974. In the course of discovery, the District Court denied Carman's request for the production of certain documents, holding that they were protected by the "Ombudsman Privilege." The District Court later granted summary judgment to McDonnell Douglas, a decision which Carman now appeals. We hold that the District Court lacked sufficient justification for creating an ombudsman privilege and denying Carman's discovery request.

In June 1994, Carman requested 54 sets of documents from McDonnell Douglas. Item No. 53 was a request for "[a]ll notes and documents reflecting data known to . . . Clemente [a company ombudsman] . . . concerning "the plaintiff, a number of other individuals, and various topics, including "[m]eeting notes regarding lay-offs in Plaintiff's Division" and "[m]eeting notes regarding Plaintiff Frank Carman." McDonnell Douglas objected to this and many other requests as vague, overbroad, and irrelevant. McDonnell Douglas further objected with regard to documents known to Therese Clemente, because her activities as an ombudsman were considered confidential, and any information and documents relating to her activities are immune from discovery. In response, the plaintiff filed a motion to compel production of certain documents. The Court granted the motion in part and ordered the defendants to produce a number of documents, including those requested in Item No. 53. Two months later, however, in clarifying its order with respect to Item No. 53, the Court ruled that the "defendant is not required to produce documents protected by the Ombudsman Privilege."

OPINION: *ARNOLD, Chief Judge*

In the context of this case, the term "ombudsman" refers to an employee outside of the corporate chain of command whose job is to investigate and mediate workplace disputes. The corporate ombudsman is paid by the corporation

and lacks the structural independence that characterizes government ombudsmen in some countries and states, where the office of ombudsman is a separate branch of government that handles disputes between citizens and government agencies. Nonetheless, the corporate ombudsman purports to be an independent and neutral party who promises strict confidentiality to all employees and is bound by the Code of Ethics of the Corporate Ombudsman Association, which requires the ombudsman to keep communications confidential. McDonnell Douglas argues for recognition of an evidentiary privilege that would protect corporate ombudsmen from having to disclose relevant employee communications to civil litigants.

Federal Rule of Evidence 501 states that federal courts should recognize evidentiary privileges according to "the principles of the common law" interpreted "in the light of reason and experience." The beginning of any analysis under Rule 501 is the principle that "the public has a right to every man's evidence." Hardwicke, L.C.J., quoted in 12 Cobbett's Parliamentary History 675, 693 (1742). Accordingly, evidentiary privileges "are not lightly created." *United States v. Nixon,* 418 U.S. 683, 710 (1974). A party that seeks the creation of a new evidentiary privilege must overcome the significant burden of establishing that permitting a refusal to testify or excluding relevant evidence has a public good transcending the normally predominant principle of utilizing all rational means for ascertaining truth.

The first important factor for assessing a proposed new evidentiary privilege is the importance of the relationship that the privilege will foster. The defendant argues that ombudsmen help resolve workplace disputes prior to the commencement of

http://

For a sample Code of Ethics, see this site: http://www-leland.stanford.edu/dept/ocr/ombudsperson/standards.html

expensive and time-consuming litigation. We agree that fair and efficient alternative dispute resolution techniques benefit society and are worthy of encouragement. To the extent that corporate ombudsmen successfully resolve disputes in a fair and efficient manner, they are a welcome and helpful addition to a society that is weary of lawsuits.

Nonetheless, far more is required to justify the creation of a new evidentiary privilege. First, McDonnell Douglas has failed to present any evidence, and indeed has not even argued, that the ombudsman method is more successful at resolving workplace disputes than other forms of alternative dispute resolution, nor has it even pointed to any evidence establishing that its own ombudsman is especially successful at resolving workplace disputes prior to the commencement of litigation. In recognizing a privilege for the McDonnell Douglas ombudsman's office in 1991, the court in *Kientzy v. McDonnell Douglas Corp.,* 133 F.R.D. 570, 572 (E.D. Mo. 1991), found that the office had received approximately 4,800 communications since 1985, but neither the court nor McDonnell Douglas in the present case provides us with any context to evaluate the significance of this statistic.

Second, McDonnell Douglas has failed to make a compelling argument that most of the advantages afforded by the ombudsman method would be lost without the privilege. Even without a privilege, corporate ombudsmen still have much to offer employees in the way of confidentiality, for they are still able to promise to keep employee communications confidential from management. Indeed, when an aggrieved employee or an employee-witness is deciding whether or not to confide in a company ombudsman, his greatest concern is not likely to be that the statement will someday be revealed in civil discovery. More likely, the employee will fear that the ombudsman is biased in favor of the company, and that the ombudsman will tell management everything that the employee says. The denial of an ombudsman privilege will not affect the ombudsman's ability to convince an employee that the ombudsman is neutral, and creation of an ombudsman privilege will not help alleviate the fear that she is not.

We are especially unconvinced that "no present or future [McDonnell Douglas] employee could feel comfortable in airing his or her disputes with the Ombudsman because of the specter of discovery." See Appellee's Br. 45. An employee either will or will not have a meritorious complaint. If he does not and is aware that he does not, he is no more likely to share the frivolousness of his complaint with a company ombudsman than he is with a court. If he has a meritorious complaint that he would prefer not to litigate, then he will generally feel that he has nothing to hide and will be undeterred by the prospect of civil discovery from sharing the nature of his complaint with the ombudsman. The dim prospect that the employee's complaint might someday surface in an unrelated case strikes us as an unlikely deterrent. Again, it is the perception that the ombudsman is the company's investigator, a fear that does not depend upon the prospect of civil discovery, that is most likely to keep such an employee from speaking openly.

McDonnell Douglas also argues that failure to recognize an ombudsman privilege will disrupt the relationship between management and the ombudsman's office. In cases where management has nothing to hide, this is unlikely. It is probably true that management will be less likely to share damaging information with an ombudsman if there is no privilege.

Nonetheless, McDonnell Douglas has provided no reason to believe that management is especially eager to confess wrongdoing to ombudsmen when a privilege exists, or that ombudsmen are helpful at resolving disputes that involve violations of the law by management or supervisors. If the chilling of management-ombudsman communications occurs only in cases that would not have been resolved at the ombudsman stage anyway, then there is no reason to recognize an ombudsman privilege.

McDonnell Douglas relies on the analysis of the court in *Kientzy,* supra, apparently one of only two federal courts to have recognized a corporate-ombudsman privilege. We do not find the reasoning of that opinion convincing. For example, the *Kientzy* opinion argues that confidentiality is essential to ombudsman-employee relationships because the function of that relationship is to receive communications and to remedy workplace problems in a strictly confidential atmosphere. Without this confidentiality, the office would just be one more nonconfidential opportunity for employees to air disputes. The ombudsman's office provides an opportunity for complete disclosure, without the specter of retaliation, that does not exist in the other available, nonconfidential grievance and complaint procedures. As we have said, the corporate ombudsman will still be able to promise confidentiality in most circumstances even with no privilege. To justify the creation of a privilege, McDonnell Douglas must first establish that society benefits in some significant way from the particular brand of confidentiality that the privilege affords. Only then can a court decide whether the advantages of the proposed privilege overcome the strong presumption in favor of disclosure of all relevant information. The creation of a wholly new evidentiary privilege is a big step. This record does not convince us that we should take it.

We disagree with the District Court's holding that employee communications to Therese Clemente were protected from discovery by an ombudsman privilege. The judgment is reversed, and the cause remanded for further proceedings consistent with this opinion. On remand, the District Court should order the production of the evidence it had believed the privilege protected, unless there are other reasons why discovery of this evidence would not be appropriate.

It is so ordered.

Discussion Questions

1. If ombudsman confidentiality is not preserved, is there any reason to believe that the use of ombuds has any long-term future? Under what circumstances do you expect that an employee would use an ombudsman if absolute confidentiality is not guaranteed?

2. Are the circumstances in these cases sufficiently dissimilar to justify the differing rulings? Is the absence of judicial certainty on this matter troubling?

3. Is private, outside dispute resolution an acceptable substitute for in-house, ombud dispute resolution in jurisdictions in which there is no clear judicial finding in favor of ombud proceeding confidentiality?

4. Would a statutory privilege be preferable to a judicial privilege? Why or why not?

ADR IN ACTION

Peers Judging Peers: A Corporate Cost-Cutting Strategy

Peer review programs, ones in which employees judge other employees in-house and without lawyers, have become a popular form of alternative dispute resolution for companies. Darden Restaurants, Inc., the owner of Red Lobster, the nation's largest seafood chain, and Olive Garden, the top casual Italian restaurant chain, is one of several companies, including TRW, Inc., Marriott International, Inc., and Rockwell International Corp., who have recently created peer review programs. Darden permits employees who have been disciplined or fired to appeal such decisions to a panel of several coworkers who may hear testimony from the appealing party and other employees. The panel receives evidence and, on the basis of that testimony and evidence, has the authority to affirm or overturn the management decision. The panel can even award money damages to any employee who brings a claim deemed to have merit by the panel. Each panel comprises volunteers from other restaurants as well as company management employees.

Darden, the largest casual restaurant dining group in the world, characterizes its program as highly successful. The company believes the program helps protect valuable employees from unfair dismissal and asserts that it has reduced racial tensions between employees and with customers. In addition, company General Counsel Clifford Whitehall claims the program cuts $1 million from annual legal expenses, which now total $3.5 million. The program saves on legal expenses by providing Darden's 114,500 employees with an alternative to employee litigation against the company. Indeed, although roughly 100 cases go through peer review each year, only about 10 or so ultimately result in litigation.

EXTERNAL DISPUTE RESOLUTION POLICIES

The Role of Outside Counsel

External disputes present a different set of options. Companies wishing to make broad use of ADR will likely need to closely supervise outside legal counsel. As this text has demonstrated, counsel—particularly outside firms—are sometimes reluctant to use ADR processes. Many are reluctant for substantive reasons, such as the absence of regulatory authority over most private ADR providers. Others, principally practitioners not schooled in law during the past decade, are unfamiliar with the processes and prefer to litigate in the familiar courtroom setting rather than learn new advocacy skills and process rules. Still others anticipate the potential loss of revenue through the use of ADR processes designed to eliminate the time and acrimony of the trial and its associated costs.

Companies have several options with respect to the use and supervision of outside counsel. First, they may require that in all cases a **choice of process memorandum** be created by counsel and reviewed in-house before any decision is made. In such a document, counsel must explain the reasons for choosing a particular dispute resolution process, whether trial or ADR. Second, companies may require that some percentage of all business referred to outside counsel be sent to an ADR process. Counsel could select from among the cases referred, but they would be required to show a good-faith effort to resolve a stated percentage of all cases through an ADR process. Third, companies could create a more significant role for in-house counsel, one that expressly includes managing cases through ADR processes. Cases on which a decision to litigate has been made in-house could be sent to outside counsel; many of the remaining cases could be managed to conclusion by in-house counsel. Finally, ADR agreements between companies that deal regularly with one another can eliminate the question of process choice altogether. When companies with ongoing commercial relationships agree to refer some or all cases to a form of ADR, perhaps using the following American Arbitration Association predispute contract clauses, counsel is only left with process execution, not with the process decision.

Enforcement of ADR provisions in commercial contracts is governed by essentially the same rules that were previously described for use in employee agreements. When such provisions are between business partners, courts virtually always enforce them because they are rarely adhesion contracts that raise the concerns of unilateral bargaining power found in some employment contracts. The appendix to this chapter includes a number of **predispute contract clauses** provided by the American Arbitration Association for use in commercial agreements. Most of the clauses are consistent with one another, so that they can be layered for different processes in a contract as described at the beginning of this chapter.

The Role of the Insurer

A solid working relationship with one's insurer is also helpful. Most carriers are intensely interested in reducing the cost of defending suits. Thus, where a business communicates its willingness to engage in ADR processes, the insurer is in a position to bring additional pressure to bear on the attorneys representing the company. Most business insurance policies cover both fees and settlements or judgments. Consequently, the insurer has, to a very significant extent, veto power over counsel's choice of a dispute resolution process.

The Role of Customers

Contracts with customers may specify the use of ADR processes. Many customers find it attractive to participate in less formal processes to resolve claims against a company. However, customers may wish to resolve a dispute in court. The following case examines the enforceability of a clause contained in a mail-order computer purchase contract requiring arbitration, rather than litigation, of all claims against the company. The case is presented for two reasons: (1) to further elucidate the nature of knowing and voluntary assent to an arbitration clause and (2) to provide a context in which to consider the impact on customer relations resulting from enforcement of such a clause.

HILL V. GATEWAY 2000, INC.
105 F.3d 1147 (7th Cir. 1997)

FACT SUMMARY

A customer picks up the phone, orders a computer, and gives a credit card number. Presently a box arrives, which contains the computer and a list of terms that apply unless the customer returns the computer within 30 days. Are these terms effective as the parties' contract, or is the contract term-free because the order-taker did not read any terms over the phone or elicit the customer's assent?

One of the terms in the box containing a Gateway 2000 system was an arbitration clause. Rich and Enza Hill, the customers, kept the computer more than 30 days before complaining about its components and performance. They filed suit in federal court arguing, among other things, that the product's shortcomings make Gateway a racketeer (mail and wire fraud are said to be the predicate offenses), leading to treble damages under RICO for the Hills and all other purchasers. Gateway asked the district court to enforce the arbitration clause; the judge refused, writing that "[t]he present record is insufficient to support a finding of a valid arbitration agreement between the parties or that the plaintiffs were given adequate notice of the arbitration clause." Gateway took an immediate appeal.

OPINION: *EASTERBROOK, Circuit Judge*

The Hills say that the arbitration clause did not stand out: they concede noticing the statement of terms but deny reading it closely enough to discover the agreement to arbitrate, and they ask us to conclude that they therefore may go to court. Yet an agreement to arbitrate must be enforced "save upon such grounds as exist at law or in equity for the revocation of any contract." 9 U.S.C. sec. 2. *Doctor's Associates, Inc. v. Casarotto*, 116 S. Ct. 1652 (1996), holds that this provision of the Federal Arbitration Act is inconsistent with any requirement that an arbitration clause be prominent. A contract need not be read to be effective; people who accept take the risk that the unread terms may in retrospect prove unwelcome. Terms inside Gateway's box stand or fall together. If they constitute the parties' contract because the Hills had an opportunity to return the computer after reading them, then all must be enforced.

ProCD, Inc. v. *Zeidenberg*, 86 F.3d 1447 (7th Cir. 1996), holds that terms inside a box of software bind consumers who use the software after an opportunity to read the terms and to reject them by returning the product. Likewise, *Carnival Cruise Lines, Inc.* v. *Shute,* 499 U.S. 585

(1991), enforces a forum-selection clause that was included among three pages of terms attached to a cruise ship ticket. *ProCD* and *Carnival Cruise Lines* exemplify the many commercial transactions in which people pay for products with terms to follow; *ProCD* discusses others. The district court concluded in *ProCD* that the contract is formed when the consumer pays for the software; as a result, the court held, only terms known to the consumer at that moment are part of the contract, and provisos inside the box do not count. Although this is one way a contract could be formed, it is not the only way: A vendor, as master of the offer, may invite acceptance by conduct, and may propose limitations on the kind of conduct that constitutes acceptance. A buyer may accept by performing the acts the vendor proposes to treat as acceptance. Gateway shipped computers with the same sort of accept-or-return offer ProCD made to users of its software. ProCD relied on the Uniform Commercial Code rather than any peculiarities of Wisconsin law; both Illinois and South Dakota, the two states whose law might govern relations between Gateway and the Hills, have adopted the UCC; neither side has pointed us to any atypical doctrines in those states that might be pertinent; *ProCD* therefore applies to this dispute.

Plaintiffs ask us to limit *ProCD* to software, but where's the sense in that? *ProCD* is about the law of contract, not the law of software. Payment preceding the revelation of full terms is common for air transportation, insurance, and many other endeavors. Practical considerations support allowing vendors to enclose the full legal terms with their products. Cashiers cannot be expected to read legal documents to customers before ringing up sales. If the staff at the other end of the phone for direct-sales operations such as Gateway's had to read the four-page statement of terms before taking the buyer's credit card number, the droning voice would anesthetize rather than enlighten many potential buyers. Others would hang up in a rage over the waste of their time. And oral recitation would not avoid customers' assertions (whether true or feigned) that the clerk did not read term X to them, or that they did not remember or understand it. Writing provides benefits for both sides of commercial transactions. Customers as a group are better off when vendors skip costly and ineffectual steps such as telephonic recitation, and use instead a simple approve-or-return device. Competent adults are bound by such documents, read or unread. For what little it is worth, we add that the box from Gateway was crammed with software. The computer came with an operating system, without which it was useful only as a boat anchor. Gateway also included many application programs. So the Hills' effort to limit *ProCD* to software would not avail them factually, even if it were sound legally which it is not.

For their second sally, the Hills contend that *ProCD* should be limited to executory contracts (to licenses in particular), and therefore does not apply because both parties' performance of this contract was complete when the box arrived at their home. This is legally and factually wrong: legally because the question at hand concerns the formation of the contract rather than its performance, and factually because both contracts were incompletely performed. *ProCD* did not depend on the fact that the seller characterized the transaction as a license rather than as a contract; we treated it as a contract for the sale of goods and reserved the question whether for other purposes a

http://

The complete text of ProCD v. Zeidenberg may be found at this site: http://caselaw.findlaw.com/cgi-bin/getcase.pl?court=7th&navby=case&no=961139

http://

The complete text of Carnival Cruise Lines v. Shute may be found at this site: http://caselaw.findlaw.com/scripts/getcase.pl?navby=case&court=US&vol=499&page=585

"license" characterization might be preferable. All debates about characterization to one side, the transaction in *ProCD* was no more executory than the one here: Zeidenberg paid for the software and walked out of the store with a box under his arm, so if arrival of the box with the product ends the time for revelation of contractual terms, then the time ended in *ProCD* before Zeidenberg opened the box. But of course ProCD had not completed performance with delivery of the box, and neither had Gateway. One element of the transaction was the warranty, which obliges sellers to fix defects in their products. The Hills have invoked Gateway's warranty and are not satisfied with its response, so they are not well positioned to say that Gateway's obligations were fulfilled when the motor carrier unloaded the box. What is more, both ProCD and Gateway promised to help customers to use their products. Long-term service and information obligations are common in the computer business, on both hardware and software sides. Gateway offers "lifetime service" and has a round-the-clock telephone hotline to fulfill this promise. Some vendors spend more money helping customers use their products than on developing and manufacturing them. The document in Gateway's box includes promises of future performance that some consumers value highly; these promises bind Gateway just as the arbitration clause binds the Hills.

Next the Hills insist that *ProCD* is irrelevant, because Zeidenberg was a "merchant" and they are not. Section 2-207(2) of the UCC, the infamous battle-of-the-forms section, states that "additional terms [following acceptance of an offer] are to be construed as proposals for addition to a contract." Between merchants such terms

become part of the contract. Plaintiffs tell us that *ProCD* came out as it did only because Zeidenberg was a "merchant" and the terms inside ProCD's box were not excluded by the "unless" clause. This argument pays scant attention to the opinion in *ProCD,* which concluded that, when there is only one form, "sec. 2-207 is irrelevant." The question in *ProCD* was not whether terms were added to a contract after its formation, but how and when the contract was formed—in particular, whether a vendor may propose that a contract of sale be formed, not in the store (or over the phone) with the payment of money or a general "send me the product," but after the customer has had a chance to inspect both the item and the terms. *ProCD* answers "yes," for merchants and consumers alike. Yet again, for what little it is worth we observe that the Hills misunderstand the setting of *ProCD.* A "merchant" under the UCC "means a person who deals in goods of the kind or otherwise by his occupation holds himself out as having knowledge or skill peculiar to the practices or goods involved in the transaction," sec. 2-104(1). Zeidenberg bought the product at a retail store, an uncommon place for merchants to acquire inventory. His corporation put ProCD's database on the Internet for anyone to browse, which led to the litigation but did not make Zeidenberg a software merchant.

At oral argument the Hills propounded still another distinction: the box containing ProCD's software displayed a notice that additional terms were within, while the box containing Gateway's computer did not. The difference is functional, not legal. Consumers browsing the aisles of a store can look at the box, and if they are unwilling to deal with the prospect of additional terms can leave the box alone, avoiding the transactions costs of returning the package after reviewing its contents. Gateway's box, by contrast, is just a shipping carton; it is not on display anywhere. Its function is to protect the product during transit, and the information on its sides is for the use of handlers ("Fragile!" "This Side Up!") rather than would-be purchasers.

Perhaps the Hills would have had a better argument if they were first alerted to the bundling of hardware and legalware after opening the box and wanted to return the computer in order to avoid disagreeable terms, but were dissuaded by the expense of shipping. What the remedy would be in such a case—could it exceed the shipping charges?—is an interesting question, but one that need not detain us because the Hills knew before they ordered the computer that the carton would include some important terms, and they did not seek to discover these in advance. Gateway's ads state that their products come with limited warranties and lifetime support. How limited was the warranty—30 days, with service contingent on shipping the computer back, or five years, with free onsite service? What sort of support was offered? Shoppers have three principal ways to discover these things. First, they can ask the vendor to send a copy before deciding whether to buy. The Magnuson-Moss Warranty Act requires firms to distribute their warranty terms on request; the Hills do not contend that Gateway would have refused to enclose the remaining terms too. Concealment would be bad for business, scaring some customers away and leading to excess returns from others. Second, shoppers can consult public sources (computer magazines, the Web sites of vendors) that may contain this information. Third, they may inspect the documents after the product's delivery. Like Zeidenberg, the Hills took the third option. By keeping the computer beyond 30 days, the Hills accepted Gateway's offer, including the arbitration clause.

The Hills' remaining arguments, including a contention that the arbitration clause is unenforceable as part of a scheme to defraud, do not require more than a citation to *Prima Paint Corp. v. Flood & Conklin Mfg. Co.,* 388 U.S. 395 (1967). Whatever may be said pro and con about the cost and efficacy of arbitration (which the Hills disparage) is for Congress and the contracting parties to consider. Claims based on RICO are no less arbitrable than those founded on the contract or the law of torts. *Shearson/ American Express, Inc. v. McMahon,* 482 U.S. 220, 238-42 (1987). The decision of the district court is vacated, and this case is remanded with instructions to compel the Hills to submit their dispute to arbitration.

Discussion Questions

1. Is a company's interest in ADR sufficient grounds to enforce it over the objection of a customer under circumstances similar to the ones described in the case?

2. How prominently should ADR provisions that substantially affect the rights of a consumer be displayed? Do the facts in this case suggest a good-faith effort on the part of Gateway to communicate these essential terms? Does this case represent an example of an adhesion contract?

3. What is the long-term effect on ADR if provisions like the ones in this case are enforced? Is it possible that such an enforcement will work to the disadvantage of ADR? Why or why not?

CHAPTER CONCLUSION

Businesses that choose to use the full range of dispute resolution processes in a systematic fashion can expect to reap considerable gains. ADR offers the possibility of quick and inexpensive resolution of both internal and external disputes. Companies wishing to preserve important relationships in either setting may do so most effectively by designing dispute resolution systems that address problems preemptively and by choosing processes and legal counsel carefully.

BEST BUSINESS PRACTICES

Here are some practical tips for managers on the design of systems for the resolution of business disputes.

- In designing company dispute resolution processes, differentiate between internal and external disputes and understand the benefits of particular processes in each context.

- Do not be tempted to neglect internal and informal conflicts that may sap productivity and employee morale. The cost in confidentiality of an ombudsman's office is likely offset by the gains realized through employee productivity.

- Centralize decision making related to dispute resolution to ensure consistent application of procedural rules and maximum internal and external cost savings. In doing so, note the likelihood that corporate outside counsel will often neglect to use mediation, preferring arbitration and litigation instead.

- Mediation should precede adversarial processes in both internal and external systems, as it provides an opportunity for a negotiated settlement that may preserve important, ongoing business relationships.

- Understand that advocacy is important in the context of any dispute resolution process and that it must be tailored to the specific process being used to address a particular case.

- Anticipate the expectations and needs of international clients as you consider processes and methods for dispute resolution.

KEY TERMS

Adhesion contracts, p. 299
Arbitration within monetary limits,
   p. 321
Choice of process memorandum,
   p. 311
Discovery, p. 319
Dispute Review Board, p. 321
Employee contracts and handbooks,
   p. 298

External disputes, p. 310
Internal disputes, p. 298
Knowing and voluntary waiver, p. 300
Ombudsman, p. 304
Predispute contract clauses, p. 311
Privilege, p. 304
Title VII claims, p. 300

ETHICAL AND LEGAL REVIEW

Consider the needs of the following companies with respect to alternative dispute resolution policy. Design a system for each that describes responses to internal and external disputes. Create systems consistent with the needs and resources of each company.

1. Nichecom, LLP is a small, closely held family business that sells retail office machines. The company has a base of both corporate and individual clients who purchase machines, service contracts, and supplies. The company occasionally struggles to collect from clients, both corporate and individual, and is unsure how to address such occurrences short of collection lawsuits. In addition, Nichecom builds into its service agreements factory warranties for the machines it sells to clients, and it does repair work only when the warranty does not provide independent coverage. Nichecom's clients often struggle with manufacturers to obtain service, and Nichecom feels caught in the middle. With whom should Nichecom have ADR agreements? What sorts of agreements should the parties create and why should they create them?

2. Agile, Ltd. is a mid-sized, publicly traded manufacturing concern with a unionized production workforce of 100 and a managerial contingent of 20. The relationship between the company and the union is acrimonious, although there has never been a work stoppage. Although a grievance procedure is in place, it is rarely used and is subject to revision during the imminent collective bargaining round. In addition, Agile, a maker of rollerblades and other Generation X sports gear, is faced with mounting legal expenses related to use of its gear. What provisions should the Agile ADR program include?

3. Megalith Incorporated is an international conglomerate. It holds contracts around the world, has a large staff of in-house lawyers, and uses outside counsel extensively. Megalith designs and produces a variety of products and services and is an industry leader in research and development. Megalith operates in many highly competitive areas in which trade secrets are vital, and litigation

is to be avoided. What sorts of ADR clauses might Megalith include in contracts with its employees and vendors? What other uses of ADR might benefit Megalith? Why would ADR utilization benefit Megalith?

4. Expert Services, Chartered is a mid-sized consulting and service firm built on relationships with long-standing clients who rely upon experienced firm employees to service their accounts. Loss of a client has a significant impact on Expert, and maintaining high employee morale is therefore essential. What ADR approaches could Expert undertake to preserve both employee and customer loyalty?

SUGGESTED ADDITIONAL READINGS

Blake, Robert R., and Jane S. Mouton. *Solving Costly Organizational Conflicts: Achieving Intergroup Trust, Cooperation, and Teamwork.* Jossey-Bass, 1984.

Cooley, John W. *Mediation Advocacy.* National Institute for Trial Advocacy, 1996.

Cooley, John W., and Steven Lubet. *Arbitration Advocacy.* National Institute for Trial Advocacy, 1997.

Costantino, C., and C. Merchant. *Designing Conflict Management Systems: A Guide to Creating Productive and Healthy Organizations.* Jossey-Bass, 1996.

Gleason, S., ed. *Workplace Dispute Resolution: Directions for the Twenty-First Century.* Michigan State University Press, 1997.

Weise, R. H. "The ADR Program at Motorola." *5 Negotiation Journ. 381.* 1989.

CHAPTER APPENDIX 10A:

PREDISPUTE CONTRACT CLAUSES FROM THE AMERICAN ARBITRATION ASSOCIATION

Predispute Contract Clause Calling for Negotiation

In the event of any dispute, claim, question, or disagreement arising from or relating to this agreement or the breach thereof, the parties hereto shall use their best efforts to settle the dispute, claim, question, or disagreement. To this effect, they shall consult and negotiate with each other in good faith and, recognizing their mutual interests, attempt to reach a just and equitable solution satisfactory to both parties. If they do not reach such solution within a period of 60 days, then, upon notice by either party to the other, all disputes, claims, questions, or differences shall be finally settled by arbitration administered by the American Arbitration Association in accordance with the provisions of its Commercial Arbitration Rules.

Predispute Contract Clause Calling for Mediation

If a dispute arises out of or relates to this contract, or the breach thereof, and if the dispute cannot be settled through negotiation, the parties agree first to try in good faith to settle the dispute by mediation administered by the American Arbitration Association under its Commercial Mediation Rules before resorting to arbitration, litigation, or some other dispute resolution procedure.

Predispute Contract Clause Calling for Arbitration

Any controversy or claim arising out of or relating to this contract, or the breach thereof, shall be settled by arbitration administered by the American Arbitration Association in accordance with its Commercial [or other] Arbitration Rules [including the Emergency Interim Relief Procedures], and judgment on the award rendered by the arbitrator(s) may be entered in any court having jurisdiction thereof.

Clauses Providing Details Related to Arbitration

Arbitrator Selection.   Within 15 days after the commencement of arbitration, each party shall select one person to act as arbitrator and the two selected shall select a third arbitrator within 10 days of their appointment. If the arbitrators selected by the parties are unable or fail to agree upon the third arbitrator, the third arbitrator shall be selected by the American Arbitration Association.

or

In the event that arbitration is necessary, [name of specific arbitrator] shall act as the arbitrator.

Arbitrator Qualifications.   The arbitrator shall be a certified public accountant.

or

The arbitrator shall be a practicing attorney [or a retired judge of the [specify] Court].

or

The arbitration proceedings shall be conducted before a panel of three neutral arbitrators, all of whom shall be members of the bar of the state of [specify], actively engaged in the practice of law for at least 10 years.

Discovery.   Consistent with the expedited nature of arbitration, each party will, upon the written request of the other party, promptly provide the other with copies of documents [relevant to the issues raised by any claim or counterclaim on which the producing party may rely in support of or in opposition to any claim or defense]. Any dispute regarding discovery, or the relevance or scope thereof, shall be determined by the [arbitrator(s) or chair of the arbitration panel], which determination shall be conclusive. All discovery shall be completed within [45 or 60] days following the appointment of the arbitrator(s).

or

At the request of a party, the arbitrator(s) shall have the discretion to order examination by deposition of witnesses to the extent the arbitrator deems such additional discovery relevant and appropriate. Depositions shall be limited to a maximum of [three] [insert number] per party and shall be held within 30 days of the making of a request. Additional depositions may be scheduled only with the permission of the [arbitrator(s) or chair of the arbitration panel], and for good cause shown. Each deposition shall be limited to a maximum of [three hours, six hours, or one day's] duration. All objections are reserved for the arbitration hearing except for objections based on privilege and proprietary or confidential information.

The Award.   The award shall be made within nine months of the filing of the notice of intention to arbitrate (demand), and the arbitrator(s) shall agree to comply with this schedule before accepting appointment. However, this time limit may be extended by agreement of the parties or by the arbitrators, if necessary.

or

The arbitrators will have no authority to award punitive or other damages not measured by the prevailing party's actual damages, except as may be required by statute.

or

In no event shall an award in an arbitration initiated under this clause exceed [insert amount].

or

Any award in an arbitration initiated under this clause shall be limited to monetary damages and shall include no injunction or direction to any party other than the direction to pay a monetary amount.

or

If the arbitrator(s) find liability in any arbitration initiated under this clause, they shall award liquidated damages in the amount of [insert amount].

or

Any monetary award in an arbitration initiated under this clause shall include pre-award interest at the rate of [insert percentage] from the time of the act(s) giving rise to the award.

Confidentiality.   Except as may be required by law, neither a party nor an arbitrator may disclose the existence, content, or results of any arbitration hereunder without the prior written consent of both parties.

Predispute Contract Clause Calling for Final Offer Arbitration

Each party shall submit to the arbitrator and exchange with each other in advance of the hearing their last, best offers. The arbitrator shall be limited to awarding only one or the other of the two figures submitted.

Predispute Contract Clause Calling for Arbitration Within Monetary Limits

Any award of the arbitrator in favor of [specify a party] and against [specify a party] shall be at least [specify a dollar amount] but shall not exceed [specify a dollar amount]. [Specify a party] expressly waives any claim in excess of [specify a dollar amount] and agrees that its recovery shall not exceed that amount. Any such award shall be in satisfaction of all claims by [specify a party] against [specify a party].

or

In the event that the arbitrator denies the claim or awards an amount less than the minimum amount of [specify], then this minimum amount shall be paid to the claimant. Should the arbitrator's award exceed the maximum amount of [specify], then only this maximum amount shall be paid to the claimant. It is further understood between the parties that, if the arbitrator awards an amount between the minimum and maximum stipulated range, then the exact awarded amount will be paid to the claimant. The parties agree that this agreement is private between them and will not be disclosed to the arbitrator.

Predispute Contract Clause Calling for a Dispute Review Board

The parties shall impanel a **Dispute Review Board** of three members in accordance with the Dispute Review Board Procedures of the American Arbitration Association. The DRB, in close consultation with all interested parties, will assist and recommend the resolution of any disputes, claims, and other controversies that might arise among the parties.

Predispute Contract Clause Calling for a Minitrial

Any controversy or claim arising from or relating to this contract shall be submitted to the American Arbitration Association under its Minitrial Procedures.

Predispute Contract Clause Calling for Mediation-Arbitration

If a dispute arises from or relates to this contract or the breach thereof, and if the dispute cannot be settled through direct discussions, the parties agree to endeavor first to settle the dispute by mediation administered by the American Arbitration

Association under its Commercial Mediation Rules before resorting to arbitration. Any unresolved controversy or claim arising from or relating to this contract or breach thereof shall be settled by arbitration administered by the American Arbitration Association in accordance with its Commercial Arbitration Rules, and judgment on the award rendered by the arbitrator may be entered in any court having jurisdiction thereof. If the parties agree, a mediator involved in the parties' mediation may be asked to serve as the arbitrator.

Clauses for Use in International Disputes

Any controversy or claim arising out of or relating to this contract shall be determined by arbitration administered by the American Arbitration Association under its International Arbitration Rules.

Any dispute, controversy, or claim arising out of or relating to this contract, or the breach thereof, shall be finally settled by arbitration administered by the Commercial Arbitration and Mediation Center for the Americas in accordance with its rules, and judgment on the award rendered by the arbitrator(s) may be entered in any court having jurisdiction thereof.

Any dispute, controversy, or claim arising from or relating to this contract, or the breach, termination, or invalidity thereof, shall be settled by arbitration in accordance with the Rules of Procedure of the Inter-American Commercial Arbitration Commission in effect on the date of this agreement.

Any dispute, controversy, or claim arising out of or relating to this contract, or the breach, termination, or invalidity thereof, shall be settled by arbitration under the UNCITRAL Arbitration Rules in effect on the date of this contract. The appointing authority shall be the American Arbitration Association. The case shall be administered by the American Arbitration Association under its Procedures for Cases under the UNCITRAL Arbitration Rules.

Source: Reprinted with permission of the American Arbitration Association.

11

THE FUTURE OF BUSINESS ADR

CHAPTER HIGHLIGHTS

In this chapter, you will read and learn about the following:

1. Ethical issues involved in integrating ADR into the business setting.
2. Institutionalizing ADR for the business community through court-annexed and private processes.
3. Likely trends related to ADR use and regulation in the business community.
4. Codes of ADR professional conduct.

Alternative dispute resolution has, it appears, become a permanent feature of the American legal landscape. Both companies and individual consumers are becoming increasingly sophisticated in their use of ADR processes to resolve both simple and complex business disputes. In addition, demand for many of these processes continues to grow. However, because ADR is relatively new, it is still a largely unregulated field. Although arbitration is supported by considerable legal authority, very little case law or statutory authority exists on mediation, private judging, summary jury trials, and the minitrial. Furthermore, ADR practitioners are not normally licensed, certified, or subject to professional conduct oversight. In short, ADR remains an emerging area of professional practice.

This final chapter considers the future of business ADR in greater detail. Some of the ethical dimensions of ADR and the pitfalls they raise for businesses seeking to use private ADR regularly will be discussed. We will address the expected direction of ADR use, its regulation, and the role of business in developing ADR as a more formal institution. The chapter concludes with several difficult ethical scenarios for your consideration.

ETHICAL CONCERNS ARISING FROM THE USE OF ADR

ADR practitioners face a variety of difficult ethical issues, some of which can reasonably be expected to affect business consumers of ADR services. Some of the issues can be resolved by reference to an ADR code of professional conduct, and many ADR practitioners now voluntarily comply with rules promulgated by various professional organizations. However, until a uniform statute or system of state regulations is created, ethical questions will continue to be raised regarding such issues as the boundaries of confidentiality and conflicts of interest.

http://

Find the American Bar Association at:
http://www.
abanet.org

The American Bar Association, the American Arbitration Association, and the Society of Professionals in Dispute Resolution have created Model Standards of Conduct for Mediators; these standards are included as an appendix to this chapter. The American Arbitration Association Code of Ethics for Commercial Arbitrators is also provided as an appendix to this chapter. These codes are representative of those offered by other professional ADR organizations. It is important to note that none of the organizations may discipline a practitioner. However, a careful review of these codes will provide the business consumer of ADR services with a fairly extensive understanding of the ethical responsibilities accepted by most practitioners. Before submitting a case to an ADR professional, consumers are well advised to ask the practitioner whether he or she follows a code and, if so, which one.

http://

Read about the American Arbitration Association at:
http://www.adr.
org/

Businesses using ADR also face ethical questions, among them the use of **coerced participation.** For example, the *Gateway 2000* case covered earlier raises the question of whether it is proper to enforce against an unsophisticated consumer a fine-print agreement to submit a case to arbitration. Although the court saw nothing illegal in doing so, the parties apparently felt deceived. That deception may later cost the company business, if the provision and its enforcement against a consumer become widely publicized. In addition, the question of whether to attempt to persuade a reluctant employee to waive his or her right to trial in favor of an arbitration clause in a contract of employment raises thorny ethical issues for business.

http://

Information on the Society of Professionals in Dispute Resolution can be found at:
http://www.igc.
apc.org/spidr

A second ethical issue for industry concerns the nature of the agreements reached in private ADR processes. Does a company have an obligation to agree only to those things that serve the public interest? Courts are able to factor such considerations into the judgments reached through litigation; mediators may not be able to do so in a private settlement conference. **Nonfiling and nonassistance covenants** provide an interesting example of this dilemma. Such an agreement might contain a covenant binding an employee who settles with the company to refrain from filing or assisting anyone else who files any claim against the company. An agreement might even bind a nonemployee settling with the company from voluntarily providing any assistance to persons or entities also asserting claims against the company. The court in the following case considers the service of public interests in settlement agreements; it specifically addresses the use of private ADR to reach such agreements. The case is helpful not only because it explores the value of settlement agreements, but because it recognizes some limitations on the terms of settlement.

E.E.O.C V. ASTRA USA, INC.
94 F.3d 738 (1st Cir. 1996)

FACT SUMMARY

In this case of first impression, Astra USA, Inc., challenges a preliminary injunction restraining it from entering into or enforcing settlement agreements containing provisions that prohibit settling employees both from filing charges of sexual harassment with the Equal Employment Opportunity Commission and from assisting the Commission in its investigation of any such charges.

The EEOC investigated three sexual harassment charges filed against Astra. At least two of these charges alleged class-wide improprieties. The controversy arose when the Commission found its investigation hampered by certain settlement agreements entered into between Astra and various employees who had pursued sexual harassment claims but were unable to disclose information on the claims due to prior confidential settlement agreements. One employee, who expressed reluctance about speaking with an EEOC investigator, refused to say whether she had entered into a settlement agreement at all. When the EEOC contacted ninety employees and requested information, only twenty-six replied. The Commission

found this widespread unresponsiveness to be sinister, although its cause was unproven. The Commission did not use its subpoena power to compel any recalcitrant employee to furnish relevant information.

The record revealed that Astra entered into at least eleven private settlement agreements with employees who claimed to have been subjected to, or to have witnessed, sexual harassment. The details of the agreements varied, but they all contained versions of four provisions that are relevant to this appeal. The settling employee (1) agreed not to file a charge with the EEOC, (2) agreed not to assist others who file charges with the EEOC, (3) released all employment-related claims against Astra, and (4) assented to a confidentiality scheme under which she would be barred from discussing the incident(s) that gave rise to her claim and from disclosing the terms of her settlement agreement.

The EEOC asked Astra to rescind those portions of the settlement agreements that prohibited individuals from filing charges with the Commission and from aiding its investigations. Astra defended both the nonfiling and the nonassistance provisions and maintained that employees who have signed settlement agreements may not volunteer any information to the Commission that is beyond the scope of an ongoing investigation.

OPINION: *SELYA, Circuit Judge*

We turn to those provisions of the settlement agreements that prohibit employees from aiding the EEOC in its investigation of charges. Astra objects to the portion of the injunction that bans it from either introducing or enforcing these provisions on two grounds. First, it claims that the injunction was issued without a satisfactory showing of irreparable harm. Second, it claims that the injunction is unnecessary because it now interprets the settlement agreements to permit various types of communication with the EEOC. Both claims lack force.

We start this phase of our inquiry by addressing whether a broad nonassistance agreement is void as against public policy. If it is overwhelmingly clear that the provisions prohibiting settlors from assisting in EEOC investigations offend public policy, a lesser showing that those provisions are causing irreparable harm will suffice to support a preliminary injunction barring their enforcement.

We build on bedrock. "[A] promise is unenforceable if the interest in its enforcement is outweighed in the circumstances by a public policy harmed by enforcement of the agreement." *Town of Newton v. Rumery,* 480 U.S. 386, 392 (1987). In performing that balancing here, we must weigh the impact of settlement provisions that effectively bar cooperation with the EEOC on the enforcement of Title VII against the impact that outlawing such

provisions would have on private dispute resolution.

Congress entrusted the Commission with significant enforcement responsibilities in respect to Title VII. See 42 U.S.C. Section(s) 2000e-5(a). To fulfill the core purposes of the statutory scheme, "it is crucial that the Commission's ability to investigate charges of systemic discrimination not be impaired." *EEOC v. Shell Oil Co.,* 466 U.S. 54, 69 (1984). Clearly, if victims of or witnesses to sexual harassment are unable to approach the EEOC or even to answer its questions, the investigatory powers that Congress conferred would be sharply curtailed and the efficacy of investigations would be severely hampered.

What is more, the EEOC acts not only on behalf of private parties but also "to vindicate the public interest in preventing employment discrimination." *General Tel. Co. v. EEOC,* 446 U.S. 318, 326 (1979). In many cases of widespread discrimination, victims suffer in silence. In such instances, a sprinkling of settlement agreements that contain stipulations prohibiting cooperation with the EEOC could effectively thwart an agency investigation. Thus, any agreement that materially interferes with communication between an employee and the Commission sows the seeds of harm to the public interest.

To complete the balance we must next address what impact the injunction against nonassistance covenants might have on private dispute resolution. We do not doubt that public policy strongly favors encouraging voluntary settlement of employment discrimination claims. Yet we fail to see that this portion of the injunction creates a substantial disincentive to settlement, and Astra makes no plausible argument to the contrary. Simply put, this admonition does nothing at all to promote further litigation between Astra and the settling employee or to disturb the finality of the negotiated settlement. Thus, weighing the significant public interest in encouraging communication with the EEOC against the minimal adverse impact that opening the channels of communication would have on settlement, we agree wholeheartedly with the lower court that nonassistance covenants which prohibit communication with the EEOC are void as against public policy.

We now return to Astra's principal assertion: that, because the EEOC could obtain the information it seeks through the use of its subpoena power, there is no evidence of irreparable harm and, hence, no basis for fashioning the disputed segment of the injunction. This boils down to a contention that employees who have signed settlement agreements should speak only when spoken to. We reject such a repressive construct. It would be most peculiar to insist that the EEOC resort to its subpoena power when public policy so clearly favors the free flow of information between victims of harassment and the agency entrusted with righting the wrongs inflicted upon them. Such a protocol would not only stultify investigations but also significantly increase the time and expense of a probe.

We need not add hues to the rainbow. The district court neither misperceived the law nor misused its discretion in enjoining the utilization of settlement provisions that prohibit employees from assisting the EEOC in investigating charges of discrimination. Consequently, employees who have signed such settlement agreements may respond to questions from EEOC investigators and also may volunteer information concerning sexual harassment at Astra to the EEOC.

In addition to enjoining Astra from entering into or enforcing the nonassistance provisions of the settlement agreements, the district court also enjoined Astra from entering into or enforcing those provisions that ban employees from filing charges with the EEOC. Astra argues that public policy favors the enforcement of such covenants; that the EEOC will not suffer irreparable harm in the absence of an injunction; and that the restraint exceeds the bounds authorized under 42 U.S.C. Section(s) 2000e-5(f)(2). Because we agree that the EEOC has made no showing that it will suffer irreparable harm in the absence of this portion of the injunction, we decline to reach Astra's other claims.

Our analysis of this issue does not evolve from an exploration of the relation between irreparable harm and likelihood of success on the merits. That inquiry is most utilitarian in instances in which the issue is whether the degree of harm is sufficient to warrant injunctive relief. Here, however, there is no significant risk of irreparable harm—and that fact alone is dispositive.

This conclusion rests on the role that the filing of a charge plays in the statutory scheme. The EEOC has no authority to conduct an investigation based on hunch or suspicion, no matter how plausible that hunch or suspicion may be. The reverse is true: the Commission's power to investigate is dependent upon the filing of a charge of discrimination. Unlike other federal agencies that possess plenary authority to demand to see records relevant to matters within their jurisdiction, the EEOC is entitled to access only to evidence relevant to the charge under investigation.

Once a charge is filed with the EEOC, the situation changes dramatically. The allegations contained in the charge do not narrowly circumscribe the Commission's investigation. Rather, the charge serves as a jurisdictional springboard enabling the Commission to investigate whether the employer is engaged in any discriminatory practices. So viewed, the charge is capable of supporting an EEOC investigation into both the discrimination described in the charge itself and into the surrounding circumstances (including a full probing of any evidence of discriminatory practices unearthed during the course of the initial investigation).

Given this set of rules, the EEOC's claim of irreparable harm cannot withstand scrutiny. The EEOC is already investigating three charges against Astra, two of which allege classwide sexual harassment in the workplace. These charges provide the EEOC with jurisdiction to conduct a thorough investigation into incidents of sexual harassment, invidious practices, and other prohibited conduct that may have occurred at Astra over time. Additionally, the portion of the injunction that prevents the enforcement of the settlement agreements' nonassistance provisions—a portion of the injunction that we uphold—ensures that employees will be able to cooperate freely with the EEOC's investigators.

The short of it is that, once an injunction issues prohibiting Astra from enforcing the nonassistance covenants, this case offers no prospect of irreparable harm to the EEOC. Thus, the judicial restraint that the district court imposed against enforcement of the nonfiling covenants violates the tenet that "injunctive relief should be no more burdensome to the defendant than necessary to provide complete relief to the plaintiffs." *Califano v. Yamasaki,* 442 U.S. 682, 702 (1978).

This case is an especially attractive candidate for application of the Yamasaki

doctrine. The difficult, highly ramified questions that surround the validity of nonfiling covenants counsel persuasively against reaching out past what is required during the preliminary injunction phase. Consequently, we believe it was inadvisable—and legally incorrect—for the district court, on the sparse evidence contained in this record, to attempt to confront the thorny question of whether agreements not to file charges with the EEOC are void as against public policy. Courts should take care not to yearn for the blossom, when only the bud is ready.

In an effort to coax a different result, the EEOC bemoans the increased burden that it would face if it had to compel potential witnesses' cooperation by subpoena. As applied to this portion of the preliminary injunction, the Commission's asseveration is a non sequitur. As long as enforcement of the nonassistance covenants is enjoined, the EEOC's current investigations will not be impeded even if settling parties cannot file additional charges. And as we have already noted, those investigations are sufficiently broad in scope to permit the Commission to get to the bottom of the unsavory (but, as yet, unproven) allegations that are swirling around the company.

To be sure, we are cognizant of the possibility that additional charges filed with the EEOC perhaps could serve as a basis to expand the temporal scope of the ongoing investigations. Thus, the nonfiling covenants, if left undisturbed, theoretically could limit the claims of some class members against Astra, and this limitation might in turn provide a basis for a finding of irreparable harm. But that is sheer speculation on this exiguous record. Absent any hard evidence that anyone who signed a settlement agreement with Astra now seeks to press charges with the EEOC

http://

Find the complete text of the case Califano v. Yamasaki, 442 U.S. 682 at: http://caselaw. findlaw.com/ scripts/getcase. pl?navby=case& court=US&vol= 442&page=682

which, if filed, would expand the investigations' scope, the disputed portion of the injunction is unwarranted. If the EEOC's investigations subsequently reveal that such a situation actually exists, that is the time to renew the quest for an injunction against enforcement of the nonfiling provisions contained in Astra's settlement agreements.

We therefore affirm that portion of the injunction and vacate the portion enjoining Astra from entering into or enforcing nonfiling covenants in connection with those agreements.

Discussion Questions

1. What public policy interest suggests that a private, voluntary agreement between an aggrieved party and the perpetrator should be overturned? Can a clear standard for enforcing that public interest be articulated?

2. Does the neutral advisor have any responsibility to safeguard the public during the course of an ADR proceeding to ensure that an agreement created as a result is not violative of some public interest? If so, how can the unbiased neutral advisor, who assures the parties that he or she will not give legal advice, do so?

3. Assuming that the public has an interest in the economical use of judicial resources, should not settlement agreements reached outside the courtroom be enforced in virtually all circumstances?

INSTITUTIONALIZING DISPUTE RESOLUTION: FUTURE TRENDS IN ADR

As previously noted, alternative dispute resolution remains an emerging institution. It has, in the last decade, begun to be taught widely at both business and law schools. As a practice area, therefore, it is roughly only ten years old. Its principal competitor is the established system of court adjudication. The legal system in this country is centuries old, and it is based on an English system commenced centuries before that. As a result, it is not surprising that, after just ten years, ADR methods continue to be refined and standardized, and that practitioners are only now beginning to be regulated. Nor is it surprising that some of those who practice in the long-established legal system seek to restrain the development of ADR. In his keynote address at the 1996 Illinois Supreme Court dinner, Justice Moses Harrison offered an assessment of the impact of ADR on the Illinois judiciary and judicial system. His remarks were largely disapproving, but they represent the protectiveness some legal practitioners feel for the traditional system.

> Generally speaking, I'm opposed to dispute resolution and mediation. I know that we need some means to dispose of small cases, but I don't believe that sitting around trying to talk things over is an adequate substitute for formal proceedings governed by

rules of evidence and presided over by an experienced judge. Our current system is the culmination of centuries of experience, experience which has shown that without rules of evidence, real justice is difficult to achieve. Alternative dispute resolution may make the courts' statistics look good, but good statistics don't necessarily reflect an improvement. After all, Mussolini made the trains run on time in Italy, but so what? He had to turn his country into a fascist state to do it. Mediation and alternative dispute resolution proposals are seductive because they promise to reduce costs, but they are dangerous because they are also a means for reducing the power of the courts. These proposals are in direct competition with our court system. Indeed, they threaten to destroy the very system that is the very basis of our profession. They undermine the judiciary by diverting scarce resources away from the courts and by placing the process under the control of people who do not know and have no reason to know any law or rules of evidence. The result, I believe, will be a cut-rate brand of rough justice that is neither fair nor consistent, but merely cheap.

http://

See further details about the Cornell/Price Waterhouse study at:
http://www.news
.cornell.edu/busi
ness/May97/AD
Rstudy.html

It seems clear, despite such criticism, that ADR is becoming a crucial component of business dispute resolution. Perhaps this is because courts face mounting dockets, preventing ready access to adjudicated outcomes. Perhaps it is the result of client dissatisfaction with adjudicative outcomes. Or, perhaps it is due to client misgivings about the costs, both economic and intangible, associated with adjudication. Whatever the reasons, businesses are turning to ADR with greater frequency than ever. Indeed, a Cornell University study for Price Waterhouse found that nearly one fourth of U.S. corporations surveyed use some form of ADR to resolve in-house grievances. Mediation is the most popular form, used by eighty-eight percent of the companies. Some form of arbitration was used by seventy-nine percent.

http://

Additional CPR Institute survey data can be found at this address:
http://www.
cpradr.org/poll
_597.htm

Another study, undertaken by the CPR Institute for Dispute Resolution in 1996, yielded similar statistics. The survey found that business respondents use ADR in nearly seventeen percent of their cases, both internal and external, up from eight percent in 1993. In addition, the study shows that sixty-two percent of responding companies conduct in-house ADR training and that fifty-one percent employ an ADR specialist or have an ADR committee. Respondents reported cost savings of seventy-one percent when comparing mediation with litigation and forty-four percent when comparing arbitration with litigation. Finally, thirty-one percent indicated that they use ADR expertise and utilization as express criteria in evaluating an attorney's performance. A final set of data is provided by the American Arbitration Association, which also reports steadily increasing use of ADR. In 1986, 46,700 cases were resolved by AAA neutral advisors; in 1996, that number had jumped to 70,500 cases.

http://

The Survey of Federal Court ADR Programs is found at this address:
http://www.c
pradr.org/
setfedct.htm

In addition to greater business demand for ADR, it appears that, Justice Harrison's comments notwithstanding, many courts and legislators continue to advance ADR as a means of reducing the demands on the courts. The following case excerpt describes the commitment to ADR processes expected of judges and parties by the Colorado Supreme Court. It provides a clear mandate to lawyers and clients to use ADR and signals a judicial willingness to support contractual clauses designating ADR as the process of first choice to resolve business disputes. In short, it offers a response to the position taken by Justice Harrison.

CITY AND COUNTY OF DENVER V. THE DISTRICT COURT IN AND FOR THE CITY AND COUNTY OF DENVER

939 P.2d 1353 (Supreme Court of Colorado, 1997)

FACT SUMMARY

This case involves a dispute between the city and county of Denver, Colorado and a general contractor. The city and county of Denver entered into a series of contracts with PCL-Harbert. The contracts required PCL to perform all the work necessary to complete construction of the terminal building at Denver International Airport. As part of its mission, PCL subcontracted with Corradini Corporation for the installation of terrazzo flooring in the terminal building. Disputes arose over work performed under the contracts, and the parties engaged in unsuccessful informal settlement discussions. PCL brought suit against the city and county of Denver in Denver District Court, claiming breach of contract and promissory estoppel and requesting declaratory judgment. In addition, Corradini filed one claim against the city and county of Denver, alleging breach of contract. The city and county of Denver moved to dismiss PCL's claims for lack of jurisdiction and failure to state a claim, arguing that PCL was required to submit its claims through the nonarbitration ADR procedures set forth in the contracts. The city and county of Denver also sought to stay Corradini's claim, pending outcome of the ADR procedures regarding the disputes between the city and county of Denver and PCL.

OPINION: *BENDER, Justice*

Alternative dispute resolution mechanisms are favored in Colorado as a convenient, efficient alternative to litigation. We issued a rule to the district court to show cause because enforcement of nonarbitration ADR procedures in appropriate cases provides guidance and fosters stability for those seeking the benefits of similar dispute resolution procedures in their business dealings. We now make the rule absolute.

The right of parties to contract encompasses the correlative power to agree to a specific procedure for the resolution of disputes. Failure to follow the mandates of a valid ADR clause contravenes Colorado's public policy of supporting ADR as well as frustrates the intent of the parties who originally agreed to an alternate remedy to resolve their disputes. PCL may not avoid a portion of the Contract, the ADR procedure, while retaining the benefits of the Contract. The ADR clause of the Contract is broad in scope, and we apply a presumption in favor of alternative dispute resolution to PCL's claims.

The district court's denial of Denver's motion to dismiss PCL's claims and Denver's request to stay proceedings raises issues of substantial public importance. The General Assembly has provided for a permissive immediate appeal of the denial of a motion to compel arbitration. This case involves enforcement of ADR provisions not involving arbitration, and the party seeking to compel ADR has no immediate appellate remedy for an abuse of discretion by the district court. Colorado possesses a tradition of supporting alternative dispute resolution mechanisms when agreed to by the parties. ADR procedures promote settlement of controversies in a manner which avoids the cost of litigation and contributes to the efficient functioning of our judicial system. Enforcement of ADR procedures in appropriate cases provides guidance and fosters stability for those who seek to use similar mechanisms in their business dealings. Appellate review after litigation of PCL's claims against Denver would be an inadequate remedy for Denver because litigation would not only frustrate the intent of the parties in this case, but would also violate Colorado's strong public policy of encouraging alternative dispute resolution.

We turn to precedent in arbitration jurisprudence, which we also find helpful in our assessment of the applicability and scope of the ADR clauses in the Contract. Arbitration has long been recognized in Colorado as a convenient, speedy and efficient alternative to settling disputes by litigation. An ADR provision requiring the parties to resolve disputes through an administrative process serves the same public policy interests as does an ADR provision which requires the parties to submit to arbitration. Both ADR provisions allow the parties to agree upon an alternate nonjudicial forum to resolve disputes which is simpler and more expedient than normally encountered in our judicial system.

Under the Federal Arbitration Act, courts resolve any doubts regarding the scope of arbitrable issues in favor of arbitration and apply a presumption of arbitration because of the strong public policy of encouraging alternative dispute resolution. Similarly, Colorado has followed federal precedent to determine the scope of an arbitration clause by requiring the district court to apply the presumption favoring arbitrability and to prohibit litigation unless the court can say with positive assurance that the arbitration provision is not susceptible of any interpretation that encompasses the subject matter of the dispute.

As part of the process of determining whether a specific dispute falls within the scope of the ADR clause, the district court must ascertain the reasonable expectations of the parties by applying the language chosen by the parties for the ADR clause to the factual nature of the dispute. An ADR clause may be very expansive or limited to a few subject matters. A broad or unrestricted arbitration clause makes the strong presumption favoring arbitration apply with even greater force.

Thus we hold that the district court must compel ADR unless the court can say with positive assurance that the ADR clause is not susceptible of any interpretation that encompasses the subject matter of the dispute. We also hold that the district court must accord the parties a presumption in favor of ADR and must resolve doubts about the scope of the ADR clause in favor of the ADR mechanism. Failure to follow the mandates of a valid ADR clause contravenes Colorado's public policy of supporting ADR as well as frustrates the intent of the parties who initially agreed to an alternate remedy to resolve their disputes.

We therefore remand with instructions allowing all of PCL's claims to be heard under the ADR procedures and direct the district court to stay proceedings on Corradini's claim pending determination of all of PCL's claims in the ADR proceedings.

Discussion Questions

1. Has the court overstated the importance of ADR? Is public policy this clear?
2. Does forcing a party to participate in an ADR process diminish ADR by making it just another kind of adversarial process?

FUTURE TRENDS IN BUSINESS ADR

Several trends have emerged in the ADR field. ADR practitioners and consumers have begun to position ADR as a complementary, rather than competitive, component within the legal system. Instead of regarding the courthouse as a competitor for business, many in the ADR field have begun to see it as an ally in resolving certain claims that are unsuitable for private resolution, while seeking to establish other claims as within the province of ADR. No attorney, judge, or businessperson has failed to note the trend away from fully litigated cases in favor of settlement. Furthermore, only a small percentage of all business disputes actually result in formal litigation being commenced, and the overwhelming majority of cases filed result in a pretrial settlement. Consequently, the use of professional settlement practitioners can be expected to continue to increase in the future.

Mandatory court-annexed ADR programs have proliferated and will continue to flourish in many jurisdictions, representing another significant development in the short-term future of ADR. For ADR practitioners, the proliferation of court-annexed ADR programs is a mixed blessing. Although many think that increased use of ADR processes in any setting will likely result in growth for the field as a whole, others regard the court-annexed processes, largely arbitration, as likely to diminish the standing of private ADR practitioners. Those who object to court-annexed programs point to their often diminished status and poor funding as proof of this assertion. In any event, it seems probable that cases in court-annexed settings involving increasingly significant dollar amounts will force more cases out of the courtroom and into arbitration and related ADR processes. Indeed, many parties may voluntarily move cases to private ADR practitioners to avoid court-annexed programs.

Common law has developed and will continue to develop in the area of ADR. This text has covered many of the interesting new rules resulting from judicial decisions that affect the practice and consumption of ADR in the United States. Courts may soon address more directly the questions of confidentiality limits and the creation of a mediator's privilege at both the state and federal levels. They are also likely to address more specifically the enforceability of settlement contracts reached in private ADR settings. Rulings on ADR practitioner malpractice are another inevitable, though unfortunate, result of increased ADR use and common-law development.

The still largely unregulated ADR practice will continue to see state and federal laws aimed at standardizing the **licensing and regulation of ADR professionals,** the processes in which they engage, and the legal effect of ADR agreements. The 1990 Civil Justice Reform Act requires all federal courts to implement "expense and delay reduction" programs that include the use of ADR. The next broad movements in ADR legislation will probably include licensing and concomitant disciplinary oversight. Some suggest that a uniform statute, akin to the Uniform Commercial Code, may be of assistance in establishing ADR more effectively. In the Price Waterhouse survey cited previously, uncertainty about the qualifications of arbitrators and mediators was a major reason to avoid private ADR. The following ADR in Action makes it clear that many attorneys are troubled by the absence of oversight and licensing or registration.

ADR IN ACTION

Do Attorneys Actually Use Mediation?

A 1996 North Central College study of Illinois attorneys seeking frequency of mediation usage data revealed the following information. The average annual number of cases handled by the responding attorneys was 64.4, the highest case load reported was 400, and the lowest was 5. Twenty-seven practice areas were identified as the most frequently handled case types. They included personal injury, workers' compensation, contract disputes, securities fraud, employer discrimination, torts, commercial litigation, medical malpractice, legal malpractice, divorce, probate, real estate, labor disputes, personnel disputes, grievances, insur-ance, bankruptcy, utility/regulatory litigation, business litigation, municipal liability, professional liability, product liability, intellectual property, patent, trademark, copyright, and franchise. The average percentage of those cases in which mediation was used was only 4.3 percent. The number of respondents indicating that they had taken courses or continuing legal education in alternative dispute resolution (ADR) was 46.3 percent.

The results of the survey can be summarized as follows. The overwhelming percentage of attorneys manage significant case loads, but they use mediation very infrequently despite their significant knowledge of and training in it and its availability in their geographic area. Attorneys who use the process indicated a variety of reasons for doing so. "Reduced time to settle," "method of negotiation used in mediation," and "attorney/client control over outcome" were, in that order, the highest ranked reasons. Those who avoided using mediation gave several reasons for doing so, with "effectiveness of mediation," "type of cases handled are inappropriate for mediation," and "qualifications and/or licensing of mediators," in that order, being the top reasons.

The most striking finding of the study is the rather low level of mediation usage by responding attorneys. This finding is even more significant when the relatively high level of knowledge and training in ADR the lawyers professed to have is considered. One would expect broad educational exposure to correlate with higher use; it does not appear to do so in any significant way.

The leading reasons for avoidance are also interesting. Not surprising is ineffectiveness of the process as the most highly ranked response. One suspects, though data were not solicited on the subject, that many attorneys considered a mediation ineffective in which they settled for less than what they perceived a trier of fact would have awarded their client. However, this is likely not an accurate or meaningful measure of success or failure, in and of itself. Mediation success may involve other less readily calculated factors, such as the value of a continuing relationship between litigants.

The fact that case type ranked second is significant, given the practice areas of the responding attorneys. Legally, very few case types, as a class, are inappropriate for mediation. Consequently, for attorneys engaged in practices that are largely nontransactional, as the respondents are, one would expect a higher percentage of cases to be deemed suitable for mediation and actually mediated. The data suggest that attorneys rule out cases as a class, rather than individually.

It is not surprising that attorneys regard qualifications and/or licensing as a reason to avoid mediation, but it does indicate the need for the introduction of some form of standardized mediation practice qualifications. One suspects that attorneys, all of whom *are* licensed and *have* taken a prescribed course of study, are hesitant to use mediators in states like Illinois, where there are no threshold qualifications, no binding codes of **professional conduct,** and no process for terminating the practice privileges of those who do not perform competently or ethically.

CHAPTER CONCLUSION

Alternative dispute resolution processes are increasingly becoming the first choice of managers for resolving both internal and external business disputes. As an institution, ADR is a response to the vastly overcrowded and often unresponsive court system. Many important questions remain unanswered relating to the ethical concerns faced by practitioners and consumers alike. Business has an important role to play in the development of these processes, not simply as a consumer, but as an agent for the adoption of appropriate regulation.

BEST BUSINESS PRACTICES

Here are some practical tips for managers on the use of ADR for the settlement of business disputes.

- Be aware of the uncertainty present in ADR ethics. Because it is unlikely that any mediator or arbitrator is answerable to a licensing or certification disciplinary committee, a thorough understanding of the processes and potential ethical lapses to which practitioners may succumb is essential.

- Insofar as the agreements reached in ADR may later be reviewed for compliance with the public interest, craft settlement agreements and/or releases to meet the test of public judicial scrutiny.

- Expect in-house and outside counsel to be familiar with the emerging common law in ADR, as it will very likely address issues of significance to clients, such as confidentiality and conflicts of interest.

- Be mindful not only of the economic benefits that may accrue by using ADR, but of the benefits to the larger society in the form of reduced court dockets and more rapid and meaningful access to justice, created by your prudent use of ADR.

KEY TERMS

Coerced participation, p. 324
Common law, p. 333
Licensing and regulation of ADR
  professionals, p. 334
Mandatory court-annexed ADR
  programs, p. 333

Nonfiling and nonassistance covenants,
  p. 324
Professional conduct, p. 335

ETHICAL AND LEGAL REVIEW

Consider the ethical obligations of each party, including the ADR professional, counsel, and disputants, in the following scenarios.

1. Documents produced in the private settlement of litigation involving a tobacco company are maintained by the company as confidential, despite public requests to review them. Does the public have a right to review private settlement material? Is the likelihood of settlement diminished if the public obtains the documents? [*Brown & Williamson v. FTC,* 710 F. 2d 1165 (6th Circuit, 1983)]

2. At a performance review, the employee is presented with an employment contract containing an arbitration clause providing that any dispute arising from her employment will be resolved in arbitration. The employee initialed each page of the contract and signed the last page in full. The employee is terminated following a lengthy medical leave and seeks to charge the company with disability discrimination. The company seeks to dismiss the suit and move to arbitration. Should the company seek to enforce the agreement? Would the analysis be different if the person was still employed by the company? Should the judge allow a case involving federal discrimination law to be voided and sent to private arbitration? [*Miller v. Public Storage Management,* 96-10670 (5th Circuit, 1997)]

3. A mediation conference regarding a products liability claim against a large company commences. The plaintiff seeks $625,000 for alleged serious injuries resulting from use of the company's product. The mediation takes place before all of the potential witnesses have been deposed and before all of the evidence has been completely gathered and reviewed. It becomes clear during the conference that the defendant and defense counsel have a mistaken understanding of the permanence and extent of the plaintiff's injuries, thinking them to be more substantial than in truth they are; the plaintiff has not created this misunderstanding but would likely benefit from it. Should the mediator clarify this misunderstanding? Should the plaintiff or plaintiff's counsel clarify the misunderstanding, even if it might reduce the amount of the settlement?

4. During an ADR process a company discovers information not likely to be learned or discovered elsewhere. The information is valuable to its case but is inaccessible as a matter of proof unless the neutral advisor can be made to testify. The company agreed to keep all communications in the process confidential but believes now that it can force the neutral advisor to testify, notwithstanding its earlier agreement to refrain from doing so, under a court order because the case is being heard in a jurisdiction that has not established a mediator privilege. Should the company endeavor to do so?

5. An insurer that regularly uses ADR offers a contract to a neutral guaranteeing referral of a minimum number of cases per year and offering to pay all fees associated with their resolution. Should the neutral enter into such an agreement? Is

the agreement ethically defensible if parties in the cases are advised by the neutral of the relationship with the insurer?

SUGGESTED ADDITIONAL READINGS

Buehring-Uhle, C. "The IBM-Fujitsu Arbitration: A Landmark in Innovative Dispute Resolution." *2 AM. Rev. Intl. Arb. 113, 1991.*

Cavenagh, T. "A Quantitative Analysis of the Use and Avoidance of Mediation by the Cook County, Illinois, Legal Community." *14 Med. Quart. 4, 1997.*

Crowley, T. *Settle It out of Court.* John Wiley & Sons, 1994.

Edelman, P. "Institutionalizing Dispute Resolution Alternatives." *9 Just. System Jour. 134, 1984.*

Galanter, M. "Reading the Landscape of Disputes: What We Know and Don't Know (And Think We Know) About Our Alleged Contentious Society." *31 UCLA L. Rev. 4, 1983.*

Kritek, P. *Negotiating at an Uneven Table.* Jossey-Bass, 1994.

Menkel-Meadow, C. "Public Access to Private Settlements: Conflicting Legal Policies." *6 Alternatives 85, 1993.*

Morgan, T., and R. Rotunda. *Model Code of Professional Responsibility, Model Rules of Professional Conduct & Other Selected Standards on Professional Responsibility.* Foundation Press, 1995.

Articles on the use of ADR in the federal courts can be found at the following World Wide Web addresses:

ADR & Settlement in the Federal Courts http://www.fjc.gov/ALTDISRES/ adrsource/adrblurb.html

Alternatives to Litigation: Do They Have a Place in the Federal Courts? http://www.fjc.gov/ALTDISRES/altlitig/altlitig.html

Mediation and Conference Programs in the Federal Courts http://www.fjc. gov/ALTDISRES/mediconf/mediconf.html

CHAPTER APPENDIX 11A:

MODEL STANDARDS OF CONDUCT FOR MEDIATORS

The Model Standards of Conduct for Mediators were prepared from 1992 through 1994 by a joint committee composed of two delegates from the American Arbitration Association, John D. Feerick, Chair, and David Botwinik, two from the American Bar Association, James Alfini and Nancy Rogers, and two from the Society of Professionals in Dispute Resolution, Susan Dearborn and Lemoine Pierce.

The Model Standards have been approved by the American Arbitration Association, the Litigation Section and the Dispute Resolution Sections of the American Bar Association, and the Society of Professionals in Dispute Resolution. The views set out in this publication have not been considered by the American Bar Association House of Delegates and do not constitute the policy of the American Bar Association.

Introductory Note

The initiative for these standards came from three professional groups: The American Arbitration Association, the American Bar Association, and the Society of Professionals in Dispute Resolution.

The purpose of this initiative was to develop a set of standards to serve as a general framework for the practice of mediation. The effort is a step in the development of the field and a tool to assist practitioners in it—a beginning, not an end. The model standards are intended to apply to all types of mediation. It is recognized, however, that in some cases the application of these standards may be affected by laws or contractual agreements.

Preface

The Model Standards of Conduct for Mediators are intended to perform three major functions: to serve as a guide for the conduct of mediators; to inform the mediating parties; and to promote public confidence in mediation as a process for resolving disputes. The standards draw on existing codes of conduct for mediators and take into account issues and problems that have surfaced in mediation practice. They are offered in the hope that they will serve an educational function and provide assistance to individuals, organizations, and institutions involved in mediation.

I. Self-Determination: A Mediator shall Recognize that Mediation is Based on the Principle of Self-Determination by the Parties.

> Self-determination is the fundamental principle of mediation. It requires that the mediation process rely upon the ability of the parties to reach a voluntary, un-coerced agreement. Any party may withdraw from mediation at any time.

COMMENTS:

- The mediator may provide information about the process, raise issues, and help parties explore options. The primary role of the mediator is to facilitate a voluntary resolution of a dispute. Parties shall be given the opportunity to consider all proposed options.

- A mediator cannot personally ensure that each party has made a fully informed choice to reach a particular agreement, but it is a good practice for the mediator to make the parties aware of the importance of consulting other professionals, where appropriate, to help them make informed decisions.

II. Impartiality: A Mediator shall Conduct the Mediation in an Impartial Manner.

The concept of mediator impartiality is central to the mediation process. A mediator shall mediate only those matters in which she or he can remain impartial and even-handed. If at any time the mediator is unable to conduct the process in an impartial manner, the mediator is obligated to withdraw.

COMMENTS:

• A mediator shall avoid conduct that gives the appearance of partiality toward one of the parties. The quality of the mediation process is enhanced when the parties have confidence in the impartiality of the mediator.

• When mediators are appointed by a court or institution, the appointing agency shall make reasonable efforts to ensure that mediators serve impartially.

• A mediator should guard against partiality or prejudice based on the parties' personal characteristics, background or performance at the mediation.

III. Conflicts of Interest: A Mediator shall Disclose all Actual and Potential Conflicts of Interest Reasonably Known to the Mediator. After Disclosure, the Mediator shall Decline to Mediate unless all Parties Choose to Retain the Mediator. The Need to Protect Against Conflicts of Interest also Governs Conduct that Occurs During and After the Mediation.

A conflict of interest is a dealing or relationship that might create an impression of possible bias. The basic approach to questions of conflict of interest is consistent with the concept of self-determination. The mediator has a responsibility to disclose all actual and potential conflicts that are reasonably known to the mediator and could reasonably be seen as raising a question about impartiality. If all parties agree to mediate after being informed of conflicts, the mediator may proceed with the mediation. If, however, the conflict of interest casts serious doubt on the integrity of the process, the mediator shall decline to proceed.

A mediator must avoid the appearance of conflict of interest both during and after the mediation. Without the consent of all parties, a mediator shall not subsequently establish a professional relationship with one of the parties in a related matter, or in an unrelated matter under circumstances which would raise legitimate questions about the integrity of the mediation process.

COMMENTS:

• A mediator shall avoid conflicts of interest in recommending the services of other professionals. A mediator may make reference to professional referral services or associations which maintain rosters of qualified professionals.

- Potential conflicts of interest may arise between administrators of mediation programs and mediators and there may be strong pressures on the mediator to settle a particular case or cases. The mediator's commitment must be to the parties and the process. Pressure from outside of the mediation process should never influence the mediator to coerce parties to settle.

IV. Competence: A Mediator shall Mediate Only When the Mediator has the Necessary Qualifications to Satisfy the Reasonable Expectations of the Parties.

Any person may be selected as a mediator, provided that the parties are satisfied with the mediator's qualifications. Training and experience in mediation, however, are often necessary for effective mediation. A person who offers herself or himself as available to serve as a mediator gives parties and the public the expectation that she or he has the competency to mediate effectively. In court-connected or other forms of mandated mediation, it is essential that mediators assigned to the parties have the requisite training and experience.

COMMENTS:

- Mediators should have information available for the parties regarding their relevant training, education and experience.
- The requirements for appearing on the list of mediators must be made public and available to interested persons.
- When mediators are appointed by a court or institution, the appointing agency shall make reasonable efforts to ensure that each mediator is qualified for the particular mediation.

V. Confidentiality: A Mediator shall Maintain the Reasonable Expectations of the Parties with Regard to Confidentiality.

The reasonable expectations of the parties with regard to confidentiality shall be met by the mediator. The parties' expectations of confidentiality depend on the circumstances of the mediation and any agreements they may make. The mediator shall not disclose any matter that a party expects to be confidential unless given permission by all parties or unless required by law or other public policy.

COMMENTS:

- The parties may make their own rules with respect to confidentiality, or other accepted practice of an individual mediator or institution may dictate a particular set of expectations. Since the parties' expectations regarding confidentiality are important, the mediator should discuss these expectations with the parties.
- If the mediator holds private sessions with a party, the nature of these sessions with regard to confidentiality should be discussed prior to undertaking such sessions.

- In order to protect the integrity of the mediation, a mediator should avoid communicating information about how the parties acted in the mediation process, the merits of the case, or settlement offers. The mediator may report, if required, whether parties appeared at a scheduled mediation.

- Where the parties have agreed that all or a portion of the information disclosed during a mediation is confidential, the parties' agreement should be respected by the mediator.

- Confidentiality should not be construed to limit or prohibit the effective monitoring, research, or evaluation of mediation programs by responsible persons. Under appropriate circumstances, researchers may be permitted to obtain access to the statistical data and, with the permission of the parties, to individual case files, observations of live mediations, and interviews with participants.

VI. Quality of the Process: A Mediator shall Conduct the Mediation Fairly, Diligently, and in a Manner Consistent with the Principle of Self-Determination by the Parties.

- A mediator shall work to ensure a quality process and to encourage mutual respect among the parties. A quality process requires a commitment by the mediator to diligence and procedural fairness. There should be adequate opportunity for each party in the mediation to participate in the discussions. The parties decide when and under what conditions they will reach an agreement or terminate a mediation.

COMMENTS:

- A mediator may agree to mediate only when he or she is prepared to commit the attention essential to an effective mediation.

- Mediators should only accept cases when they can satisfy the reasonable expectations of the parties concerning the timing of the process. A mediator should not allow a mediation to be unduly delayed by the parties or their representatives.

- The presence or absence of persons at a mediation depends on the agreement of the parties and the mediator. The parties and mediator may agree that others may be excluded from particular sessions or from the entire mediation process.

- The primary purpose of a mediator is to facilitate the parties' voluntary agreement. This role differs substantially from other professional-client relationships. Mixing the role of a mediator and the role of a professional advising a client is problematic, and mediators must strive to distinguish between the roles. A mediator should therefore refrain from providing professional advice. Where appropriate, a mediator should recommend that parties seek outside professional advice, or consider resolving their dispute through arbitration, counseling, neutral evaluation, or other processes. A mediator who undertakes, at the request of the parties, an additional dispute resolution role in the same matter assumes increased responsibilities and obligations that may be governed by the standards of other processes.

- A mediator shall withdraw from a mediation when incapable of serving or when unable to remain impartial.
- A mediator shall withdraw from a mediation or postpone a session if the mediation is being used to further illegal conduct, or if a party is unable to participate due to drug, alcohol, or other physical or mental incapacity.
- Mediators should not permit their behavior in the mediation process to be guided by a desire for a high settlement rate.

VII. Advertising and Solicitation: A Mediator shall be Truthful in Advertising and Solicitation for Mediation

Advertising or any other communication with the public concerning services offered or regarding the education, training, and expertise of the mediator shall be truthful. Mediators shall refrain from promises and guarantees of results.

COMMENTS:

- It is imperative that communication with the public educate and instill confidence in the process.
- In an advertisement or other communication to the public, a mediator may make reference to meeting state, national, or private organization qualifications only if the entity referred to has a procedure for qualifying mediators and the mediator has been duly granted the requisite status.

VIII. Fees: A Mediator shall fully Disclose and Explain the Basis of Compensation, Fees, and Charges to the Parties.

The parties should be provided sufficient information about fees at the outset of a mediation to determine if they wish to retain the services of a mediator. If a mediator charges fees, the fees shall be reasonable, considering among other things, the mediation service, the type and complexity of the matter, the expertise of the mediator, the time required, and the rates customary in the community. The better practice in reaching an understanding about fees is to set down the arrangements in a written agreement.

COMMENTS:

- A mediator who withdraws from a mediation should return any unearned fee to the parties.
- A mediator should not enter into a fee agreement which is contingent upon the result of the mediation or amount of the settlement.

- Co-mediators who share a fee should hold to standards of reasonableness in determining the allocation of fees.
- A mediator should not accept a fee for referral of a matter to another mediator or to any other person.

IX. Obligations to the Mediation Process: Mediators have a Duty to Improve the Practice of Mediation.

COMMENT:

- Mediators are regarded as knowledgeable in the process of mediation. They have an obligation to use their knowledge to help educate the public about mediation; to make mediation accessible to those who would like to use it; to correct abuses; and to improve their professional skills and abilities.

Source: Reprinted with permission of the American Arbitration Association.

CHAPTER APPENDIX 11B:

THE CODE OF ETHICS FOR ARBITRATORS IN COMMERCIAL DISPUTES

The Code of Ethics for Arbitrators in Commercial Disputes was prepared in 1977 by a joint committee consisting of a special committee of the American Arbitration Association and a special committee of the American Bar Association. It has been approved and recommended by both organizations.

Preamble

The use of commercial arbitration to resolve a wide variety of disputes has grown extensively and forms a significant part of the system of justice on which our society relies for fair determination of legal rights. Persons who act as commercial arbitrators therefore undertake serious responsibilities to the public as well as to the parties. Those responsibilities include important ethical obligations.

Few cases of unethical behavior by commercial arbitrators have arisen. Nevertheless, the American Bar Association and the American Arbitration Association believe that it is in the public interest to set forth generally accepted standards of ethical conduct for guidance of arbitrators and parties in commercial disputes. By establishing this code, the sponsors hope to contribute to the maintenance of high standards and continued confidence in the process of arbitration.

There are many different types of commercial arbitration. Some cases are conducted under arbitration rules established by various organizations and trade associations, while others are conducted without such rules. Although most cases are arbitrated pursuant to voluntary agreement of the parties, certain types of dispute are submitted to arbitration by reason of particular laws. This code is intended to apply to all such proceedings in which disputes or claims are submitted for decision to one or more arbitrators appointed in a manner provided by an agreement of the parties, by applicable arbitration rules, or by law. In all such cases, the persons who have the power to decide should observe fundamental standards of ethical conduct. In this code all such persons are called "arbitrators" although, in some types of case, they might be called "umpires" or have some other title.

Various aspects of the conduct of arbitrators, including some matters covered by this code, may be governed by agreements of the parties, by arbitration rules to which the parties have agreed, or by applicable law. This code does not take the place of or supersede such agreements, rules, or laws and does not establish new or additional grounds for judicial review of arbitration awards.

While this code is intended to provide ethical guidelines in many types of arbitration, it does not form a part of the arbitration rules of the American Arbitration Association or of any other organization, nor is it intended to apply to mediation or conciliation. Labor arbitration is governed by the Code of Professional Responsibility for Arbitrators of Labor-Management Disputes, not by this code.

Arbitrators, like judges, have the power to decide cases. However, unlike full-time judges, arbitrators are usually engaged in other occupations before, during, and after the time that they serve as arbitrators. Often, arbitrators are purposely chosen from the same trade or industry as the parties in order to bring special knowledge to the task of deciding. This code recognizes these fundamental differences between arbitrators and judges. In some types of arbitration, there are three or more arbitrators. In such cases, it is sometimes the practice for each party, acting alone, to appoint one arbitrator and for the other arbitrators to be designated by those two, by the parties, or by an independent institution or individual. The sponsors of this code believe that it is preferable for parties to agree that all arbitrators should comply with the same ethical standards. However, it is recognized that there is a long-established practice in some types of arbitration for the arbitrators who are appointed by one party, acting alone, to be governed by special ethical considerations. Those special considerations are set forth in the last section of the code, headed "Ethical Considerations Relating to Arbitrators Appointed by One Party." Although this code is sponsored by the American Arbitration Association and the American Bar Association, its use is not limited to arbitrations administered by the AAA or to cases in which the arbitrators are lawyers. Rather, it is presented as a public service to provide guidance in all types of commercial arbitration.

Canon I.

An Arbitrator Should Uphold the Integrity and Fairness of the Arbitration Process.

A. Fair and just processes for resolving disputes are indispensable in our society.
   Commercial arbitration is an important method for deciding many types of dis-

putes. In order for commercial arbitration to be effective, there must be broad public confidence in the integrity and fairness of the process. Therefore, an arbitrator has a responsibility not only to the parties but also to the process of arbitration itself, and must observe high standards of conduct so that the integrity and fairness of the process will be preserved. Accordingly, an arbitrator should recognize a responsibility to the public, to the parties whose rights will be decided, and to all other participants in the proceeding. The provisions of this code should be construed and applied to further these objectives.

B. It is inconsistent with the integrity of the arbitration process for persons to solicit appointment for themselves. However, a person may indicate a general willingness to serve as an arbitrator.

C. Persons should accept appointment as arbitrators only if they believe that they can be available to conduct the arbitration promptly.

D. After accepting appointment and while serving as an arbitrator, a person should avoid entering into any financial, business, professional, family or social relationship, or acquiring any financial or personal interest, which is likely to affect impartiality or which might reasonably create the appearance of partiality or bias. For a reasonable period of time after the decision of a case, persons who have served as arbitrators should avoid entering into any such relationship, or acquiring any such interest, in circumstances which might reasonably create the appearance that they had been influenced in the arbitration by the anticipation or expectation of the relationship or interest.

E. Arbitrators should conduct themselves in a way that is fair to all parties and should not be swayed by outside pressure, by public clamor, by fear of criticism or by self-interest.

F. When an arbitrator's authority is derived from an agreement of the parties, the arbitrator should neither exceed that authority nor do less than is required to exercise that authority completely. Where the agreement of the parties sets forth procedures to be followed in conducting the arbitration or refers to rules to be followed, it is the obligation of the arbitrator to comply with such procedures or rules.

G. An arbitrator should make all reasonable efforts to prevent delaying tactics, harassment of parties or other participants, or other abuse or disruption of the arbitration process.

H. The ethical obligations of an arbitrator begin upon acceptance of the appointment and continue throughout all stages of the proceeding. In addition, wherever specifically set forth in this code, certain ethical obligations begin as soon as a person is requested to serve as an arbitrator, and certain ethical obligations continue even after the decision in the case has been given to the parties.

Canon II.

An Arbitrator Should Disclose Any Interest or Relationship Likely to Affect Impartialiy or Which Might Create an Appearance of Partiality or Bias.

INTRODUCTORY NOTE

This code reflects the prevailing principle that arbitrators should disclose the existence of interests or relationships that are likely to affect their impartiality or that might reasonably create an appearance that they are biased against one party or favorable to another. These provisions of the code are intended to be applied realistically so that the burden of detailed disclosure does not become so great that it is impractical for persons in the business world to be arbitrators, thereby depriving parties of the services of those who might be best informed and qualified to decide particular types of case. This code does not limit the freedom of parties to agree on whomever they choose as an arbitrator. When parties, with knowledge of a person's interests and relationships, nevertheless desire that individual to serve as an arbitrator, that person may properly serve.

DISCLOSURE

A. Persons who are requested to serve as arbitrators should, before accepting, disclose
   1. any direct or indirect financial or personal interest in the outcome of the arbitration;
   2. any existing or past financial, business, professional, family or social relationships which are likely to affect impartiality or which might reasonably create an appearance of partiality or bias. Persons requested to serve as arbitrators should disclose any such relationships which they personally have with any party or its lawyer, or with any individual whom they have been told will be a witness. They should also disclose any such relationships involving members of their families or their current employers, partners or business associates.
B. Persons who are requested to accept appointment as arbitrators should make a reasonable effort to inform themselves of any interests or relationships described in the preceding paragraph A.
C. The obligation to disclose interests or relationships described in the preceding paragraph A is a continuing duty which requires a person who accepts appointment as an arbitrator to disclose, at any stage of the arbitration, any such interests or relationships which may arise, or which are recalled or discovered.
D. Disclosure should be made to all parties unless other procedures for disclosure are provided in the rules or practices of an institution which is administering the arbitration. Where more than one arbitrator has been appointed, each should inform the others of the interests and relationships which have been disclosed.
E. In the event that an arbitrator is requested by all parties to withdraw, the arbitrator should do so. In the event that an arbitrator is requested to withdraw by less than all of the parties because of alleged partiality or bias, the arbitrator should withdraw unless either of the following circumstances exists.

1. If an agreement of the parties, or arbitration rules agreed to by the parties, establishes procedures for determining challenges to arbitrators, then those procedures should be followed; or,

2. if the arbitrator, after carefully considering the matter, determines that the reason for the challenge is not substantial, and that he or she can nevertheless act and decide the case impartially and fairly, and that withdrawal would cause unfair delay or expense to another party or would be contrary to the ends of justice.

Canon III.

An Arbitrator in Communicating with the Parties Should Avoid Impropriety or the Appearance of Impropriety.

A. If an agreement of the parties or applicable arbitration rules referred to in that agreement establishes the manner or content of communications between the arbitrator and the parties, the arbitrator should follow those procedures notwithstanding any contrary provision of the following paragraphs B and C.

B. Unless otherwise provided in applicable arbitration rules or in an agreement of the parties, arbitrators should not discuss a case with any party in the absence of each other party, except in any of the following circumstances.

1. Discussions may be had with a party concerning such matters as setting the time and place of hearings or making other arrangements for the conduct of the proceedings. However, the arbitrator should promptly inform each other party of the discussion and should not make any final determination concerning the matter discussed before giving each absent party an opportunity to express its views.

2. If a party fails to be present at a hearing after having been given due notice, the arbitrator may discuss the case with any party who is present.

3. If all parties request or consent to it, such discussion may take place.

C. Unless otherwise provided in applicable arbitration rules or in an agreement of the parties, whenever an arbitrator communicates in writing with one party, the arbitrator should at the same time send a copy of the communication to each other party. Whenever the arbitrator receives any written communication concerning the case from one party which has not already been sent to each other party, the arbitrator should do so.

Canon IV.

An Arbitrator Should Conduct the Proceedings Fairly and Diligently.

A. An arbitrator should conduct the proceedings in an evenhanded manner and treat all parties with equality and fairness at all stages of the proceedings.

B. An arbitrator should perform duties diligently and conclude the case as promptly as the circumstances reasonably permit.

C. An arbitrator should be patient and courteous to the parties, to their lawyers and to the witnesses and should encourage similar conduct by all participants in the proceedings.

D. Unless otherwise agreed by the parties or provided in arbitration rules agreed to by the parties, an arbitrator should accord to all parties the right to appear in person and to be heard after due notice of the time and place of hearing.

E. An arbitrator should not deny any party the opportunity to be represented by counsel.

F. If a party fails to appear after due notice, an arbitrator should proceed with the arbitration when authorized to do so by the agreement of the parties, the rules agreed to by the parties or by law. However, an arbitrator should do so only after receiving assurance that notice has been given to the absent party.

G. When an arbitrator determines that more information than has been presented by the parties is required to decide the case, it is not improper for the arbitrator to ask questions, call witnesses, and request documents or other evidence.

H. It is not improper for an arbitrator to suggest to the parties that they discuss the possibility of settlement of the case. However, an arbitrator should not be present or otherwise participate in the settlement discussions unless requested to do so by all parties. An arbitrator should not exert pressure on any party to settle.

I. Nothing in this code is intended to prevent a person from acting as a mediator or conciliator of a dispute in which he or she has been appointed as arbitrator, if requested to do so by all parties or where authorized or required to do so by applicable laws or rules.

J. When there is more than one arbitrator, the arbitrators should afford each other the full opportunity to participate in all aspects of the proceedings.

Canon V.

An Arbitrator Should Make Decisions in a Just, Independent and Deliberate Manner.

A. An arbitrator should, after careful deliberation, decide all issues submitted for determination. An arbitrator should decide no other issues.

B. An arbitrator should decide all matters justly, exercising independent judgment, and should not permit outside pressure to affect the decision.

C. An arbitrator should not delegate the duty to decide to any other person.

D. In the event that all parties agree upon a settlement of issues in dispute and request an arbitrator to embody that agreement in an award, an arbitrator may do so, but is not required to do so unless satisfied with the propriety of the terms of settlement. Whenever an arbitrator embodies a settlement by the parties in an award, the arbitrator should state in the award that it is based on an agreement of the parties.

Canon VI.

An Arbitrator Should Be Faithful to the Relationship of Trust and Confidentiality Inherent in that Office.

A. An arbitrator is in a relationship of trust to the parties and should not, at any time, use confidential information acquired during the arbitration proceeding to gain personal advantage or advantage for others, or to affect adversely the interest of another.

B. Unless otherwise agreed by the parties, or required by applicable rules or law, an arbitrator should keep confidential all matters relating to the arbitration proceedings and decision.

C. It is not proper at any time for an arbitrator to inform anyone of the decision in advance of the time it is given to all parties. In a case in which there is more than one arbitrator, it is not proper at any time for an arbitrator to inform anyone concerning the deliberations of the arbitrators. After an arbitration award has been made, it is not proper for an arbitrator to assist in post-arbitral proceedings, except as is required by law.

D. In many types of arbitration it is customary practice for the arbitrators to serve without pay. However, in some types of cases it is customary for arbitrators to receive compensation for their services and reimbursement for their expenses. In cases in which any such payments are to be made, all persons who are requested to serve, or who are serving as arbitrators, should be governed by the same high standards of integrity and fairness as apply to their other activities in the case. Accordingly, such persons should scrupulously avoid bargaining with parties over the amount of payments or engaging in any communications concerning payments which would create an appearance of coercion or other impropriety. In the absence of governing provisions in the agreement of the parties or in rules agreed to by the parties or in applicable law, certain practices relating to payments are generally recognized as being preferable in order to preserve the integrity and fairness of the arbitration process. These practices include the following.

1. It is preferable that before the arbitrator finally accepts appointment the basis of payment be established and that all parties be informed thereof in writing.

2. In cases conducted under the rules or administration of an institution that is available to assist in making arrangements for payments, the payments should be arranged by the institution to avoid the necessity for communication by the arbitrators directly with the parties concerning the subject.

3. In cases where no institution is available to assist in making arrangement for payments, it is preferable that any discussions with arbitrators concerning payments should take place in the presence of all parties.

Canon VII.

Ethical Considerations Relating to Arbitrators Appointed by One Party.

INTRODUCTORY NOTE

In some types of arbitration in which there are three arbitrators, it is customary for each party, acting alone, to appoint one arbitrator. The third arbitrator is then appointed by agreement either of the parties or of the two arbitrators, or, failing such agreement, by an independent institution or individual. In some of these types of arbitration, all three arbitrators are customarily considered to be neutral and are expected to observe the same standards of ethical conduct. However, there are also many types of tripartite arbitration in which it has been the practice that the two arbitrators appointed by the parties are not considered to be neutral and are expected to observe many but not all of the same ethical standards as the neutral third arbitrator. For the purposes of this code, an arbitrator appointed by one party who is not expected to observe all of the same standards as the third arbitrator is called a "nonneutral arbitrator." This Canon VII describes the ethical obligations that nonneutral party-appointed arbitrators should observe and those that are not applicable to them.

In all arbitrations in which there are two or more party-appointed arbitrators, it is important for everyone concerned to know from the start whether the party-appointed arbitrators are expected to be neutrals or nonneutrals. In such arbitrations, the two party-appointed arbitrators should be considered nonneutrals unless both parties inform the arbitrators that all three arbitrators are to be neutral or unless the contract, the applicable arbitration rules, or any governing law requires that all three arbitrators be neutral. It should be noted that, in cases conducted outside the United States, the applicable law might require that all arbitrators be neutral. Accordingly, in such cases, the governing law should be considered before applying any of the following provisions relating to nonneutral party-appointed arbitrators.

A. *Obligations under Canon I.* Nonneutral party-appointed arbitrators should observe all of the obligations of Canon I to uphold the integrity and fairness of the arbitration process, subject only to the following provisions.

   1. Nonneutral arbitrators may be predisposed toward the party who appointed them but in all other respects are obligated to act in good faith and with integrity and fairness. For example, nonneutral arbitrators should not engage in delaying tactics or harassment of any party or witness and should not knowingly make untrue or misleading statements to the other arbitrators.

   2. The provisions of Canon I.D relating to relationships and interests are not applicable to nonneutral arbitrators.

B. *Obligations under Canon II.* Nonneutral party-appointed arbitrators should disclose to all parties, and to the other arbitrators, all interests and relationships which Canon II requires be disclosed. Disclosure as required by Canon II is for the benefit not only of the party who appointed the nonneutral arbitrator, but also for the benefit of the other parties and arbitrators so that they may know of any bias which may exist or appear to exist. However, this obligation is subject to the following provisions.

1. Disclosure by nonneutral arbitrators should be sufficient to describe the general nature and scope of any interest or relationship, but need not include as detailed information as is expected from persons appointed as neutral arbitrators.

2. Nonneutral arbitrators are not obliged to withdraw if requested to do so by the party who did not appoint them, notwithstanding the provisions of Canon II.E.

C. *Obligations under Canon III.* Nonneutral party-appointed arbitrators should observe all of the obligations of Canon III concerning communications with the parties, subject only to the following provisions.

1. In an arbitration in which the two party-appointed arbitrators are expected to appoint the third arbitrator, nonneutral arbitrators may consult with the party who appointed them concerning the acceptability of persons under consideration for appointment as the third arbitrator.

2. Nonneutral arbitrators may communicate with the party who appointed them concerning any other aspect of the case, provided they first inform the other arbitrators and the parties that they intend to do so. If such communication occurred prior to the time the person was appointed as arbitrator, or prior to the first hearing or other meeting of the parties with the arbitrators, the nonneutral arbitrator should, at the first hearing or meeting, disclose the fact that such communication has taken place. In complying with the provisions of this paragraph, it is sufficient that there be disclosure of the fact that such communication has occurred without disclosing the content of the communication. It is also sufficient to disclose at any time the intention to follow the procedure of having such communications in the future and there is no requirement thereafter that there be disclosure before each separate occasion on which such a communication occurs.

3. When nonneutral arbitrators communicate in writing with the party who appointed them concerning any matter as to which communication is permitted under this code, they are not required to send copies of any such written communication to any other party or arbitrator.

D. Nonneutral party-appointed arbitrators should observe all of the obligations of Canon IV to conduct the proceedings fairly and diligently.

E. Nonneutral party-appointed arbitrators should observe all of the obligations of Canon V concerning making decisions, subject only to the following provision.

1. Nonneutral arbitrators are permitted to be predisposed toward deciding in favor of the party who appointed them.

F. Nonneutral party-appointed arbitrators should observe all of the obligations of Canon VI to be faithful to the relationship of trust inherent in the office of arbitrator, subject only to the following provision.

1. Nonneutral arbitrators are not subject to the provisions of Canon VI.D with respect to any payments by the party who appointed them.

Source: Reprinted with permission of the American Arbitration Association.

Appendix A

UNIFORM ARBITRATION ACT

1. Validity of Arbitration Agreement

A written agreement to submit any existing controversy to arbitration or a provision in a written contract to submit to arbitration any controversy thereafter arising between the parties is valid, enforceable, and irrevocable, save upon such grounds as exist at law or in equity for the revocation of any contract. This act also applies to arbitration agreements between employers and employees or between their respective representatives [unless otherwise provided in the agreement].

2. Proceedings to Compel or Stay Arbitration

(a) On application of a party showing an agreement described in Section 1 and the opposing party's refusal to arbitrate, the Court shall order the parties to proceed with arbitration, but if the opposing party denies the existence of the agreement to arbitrate, the Court shall proceed summarily to the determination of the issue so raised and shall order arbitration if found for the moving party. Otherwise, the application shall be denied.

(b) On application, the Court may stay an arbitration proceeding commenced or threatened on a showing that there is no agreement to arbitrate. Such an issue, when in substantial and bona fide dispute, shall be forthwith and summarily tried and the stay ordered if found for the moving party. If found for the opposing party, the Court shall order the parties to proceed to arbitration.

(c) If an issue referable to arbitration under the alleged agreement is involved in an action or proceeding pending in a court having jurisdiction to hear applications under subdivision (a) of this Section, the application shall be made therein. Otherwise and subject to Section 18, the application may be made in any court of competent jurisdiction.

(d) Any action or proceeding involving an issue subject to arbitration shall be stayed if an order for arbitration or an application therefor has been made under this Section or, if the issue is severable, the stay may be with respect thereto only. When the application is made in such action or proceeding, the order for arbitration shall include such stay.

(e) An order for arbitration shall not be refused on the ground that the claim in issue lacks merit or bona fides or because any fault or grounds for the claim sought to be arbitrated have not been shown.

3. Appointment of Arbitrators by Court

If the arbitration agreement provides a method of appointment of arbitrators, this method shall be followed. In the absence thereof, or if the agreed method fails or for any reason cannot be followed, or when an arbitrator appointed fails or is unable to act and his successor has not been duly appointed, the Court on application of a party shall appoint one or more arbitrators. An arbitrator so appointed has all the powers of one specifically named in the agreement.

4. Majority Action by Arbitrators

The powers of the arbitrators may be exercised by a majority unless otherwise provided by the agreement or by this act.

5. Hearing

Unless otherwise provided by the agreement:
(a) The arbitrators shall appoint a time and place for the hearing and cause notification to the parties to be served personally or by registered mail not less than five days before the hearing. Appearance at the hearing waives such notice. The arbitrators may adjourn the hearing from time to time as necessary and, on request of a party and for good cause or upon their own motion, may postpone the hearing to a time not later than the date fixed by the agreement for making the award, unless the parties consent to a later date. The arbitrators may hear and determine the controversy upon the evidence produced notwithstanding the failure of a party duly notified to appear. The Court on application may direct the arbitrators to proceed promptly with the hearing and determination of the controversy.

(b) The parties are entitled to be heard, to present evidence material to the controversy, and to cross-examine witnesses appearing at the hearing.

(c) The hearing shall be conducted by all the arbitrators, but a majority may determine any question and render a final award. If, during the course of the hearing, an arbitrator for any reason ceases to act, the remaining arbitrator or arbitrators appointed to act as neutrals may continue with the hearing and determination of the controversy.

6. Representation by Attorney

A party has the right to be represented by an attorney at any proceeding or hearing under this act. A waiver thereof, prior to the proceeding or hearing, is ineffective.

7. Witnesses, Subpoenas, and Depositions

(a) The arbitrators may issue (cause to be issued) subpoenas for the attendance of witnesses and for the production of books, records, documents, and other evidence, and shall have the power to administer oaths. Subpoenas so issued shall be served and, upon application to the Court by a party or the arbitrators, enforced in the manner provided by law for the service and enforcement of subpoenas in a civil action.

(b) On application of a party and for use as evidence, the arbitrators may permit a deposition to be taken, in the manner and upon the terms designated by the arbitrators, of a witness who cannot be subpoenaed or is unable to attend the hearing.

(c) All provisions of law compelling a person under subpoena to testify are applicable.

(d) Fees for attendance as a witness shall be the same as for a witness in the Court.

8. Award

(a) The award shall be in writing and signed by the arbitrators joining in the award. The arbitrators shall deliver a copy to each party personally, by registered mail, or as provided in the agreement.

(b) An award shall be made within the time fixed therefor by the agreement or, if not so fixed, within such time as the Court orders on application of a party. The parties may extend the time in writing either before or after the expiration thereof. A party waives the objection that an award was not made within the time required, unless he notifies the arbitrators of his objection prior to the delivery of the award to him.

9. Change of Award by Arbitrators

On application of a party or, if an application to the Court is pending under Sections 11, 12, or 13, on submission to the arbitrators by the Court under such conditions as the Court may order, the arbitrators may modify or correct the award upon the grounds stated in paragraphs (1) and (3) of subdivision (a) of Section 13 or for the purpose of clarifying the award. The application shall be made within twenty days after delivery of the award to the applicant. Written notice thereof shall be given forthwith to the opposing party, stating he must serve his objections thereto, if any, within ten days from the notice. The award so modified or corrected is subject to the provisions of Sections 11, 12, and 13.

10. Fees and Expenses of Arbitration

Unless otherwise provided in the agreement to arbitrate, the arbitrators' expenses and fees, together with other expenses, not including counsel fees, incurred in the conduct of the arbitration shall be paid as provided in the award.

11. Confirmation of an Award

Upon application of a party, the Court shall confirm an award, unless within the time limits hereinafter imposed grounds are urged for vacating or modifying or correcting the award, in which case the Court shall proceed as provided in Sections 12 and 13.

12. Vacating an Award

(a) Upon application of a party, the Court shall vacate an award where:

(1) The award was procured by corruption, fraud, or other undue means;

(2) There was evident partiality by an arbitrator appointed as a neutral, corruption in any of the arbitrators, or misconduct prejudicing the rights of any party;

(3) The arbitrators exceeded their powers;

(4) The arbitrators refused to postpone the hearing upon sufficient cause being shown therefor or refused to hear evidence material to the controversy or otherwise so conducted the hearing, contrary to the provisions of Section 5, as to prejudice substantially the rights of a party; or

(5) There was no arbitration agreement, the issue was not adversely determined in proceedings under Section 2, and the party did not participate in the arbitration hearing without raising the objection; but the fact that the relief was such that it could not or would not be granted by a court of law or equity is not ground for vacating or refusing to confirm the award.

(b) An application under this Section shall be made within ninety days after delivery of a copy of the award to the applicant, except that, if predicated upon corruption, fraud, or other undue means, it shall be made within ninety days after such grounds are known or should have been known.

(c) In vacating the award on grounds other than stated in clause (5) of Subsection (a), the Court may order a rehearing before new arbitrators chosen as provided in the agreement, or in the absence thereof, by the Court in accordance with Section 3; or if the award is vacated on grounds set forth in clauses (3) and (4) of Subsection (a), the Court may order a rehearing before the arbitrators who made the award or their successors appointed in accordance with Section 3. The time within which the agreement requires the award to be made is applicable to the rehearing and commences from the date of the order.

(d) If the application to vacate is denied and no motion to modify or correct the award is pending, the Court shall confirm the award. As amended August 1956.

13. Modification or Correction of Award

(a) Upon application made within ninety days after delivery of a copy of the award to the applicant, the Court shall modify or correct the award where:

    (1) There was an evident miscalculation of figures or an evident mistake in the description of any person, thing, or property referred to in the award;

    (2) The arbitrators have awarded upon a matter not submitted to them, and the award may be corrected without affecting the merits of the decision upon the issues submitted; or

    (3) The award is imperfect in a matter of form, not affecting the merits of the controversy.

(b) If the application is granted, the Court shall modify and correct the award so as to effect its intent and shall confirm the award as so modified and corrected. Otherwise, the Court shall confirm the award as made.

(c) An application to modify or correct an award may be joined in the alternative with an application to vacate the award.

14. Judgment or Decree on Award

Upon the granting of an order confirming, modifying, or correcting an award, judgment or decree shall be entered in conformity therewith and be enforced as any other judgment or decree. Costs of the application and of the proceedings subsequent thereto and disbursements may be awarded by the Court.

15. Judgment Roll, Docketing

(a) On entry of judgment or decree, the clerk shall prepare the judgment roll consisting, to the extent filed, of the following:

(1) The agreement and each written extension of the time within which to make the award;

(2) The award;

(3) A copy of the order confirming, modifying, or correcting the award; and

(4) A copy of the judgment or decree.

(b) The judgment or decree may be docketed as if rendered in an action.

16. Applications to Court

Except as otherwise provided, an application to the Court under this act shall be by motion and shall be heard in the manner and upon the notice provided by law or rule of court for the making and hearing of motions. Unless the parties have agreed otherwise, notice of an initial application for an order shall be served in the manner provided by law for the service of a summons in an action.

17. Court, Jurisdiction

The term "Court" means any court of competent jurisdiction of this State. The making of an agreement described in Section 1, providing for arbitration in this State, confers jurisdiction on the Court to enforce the agreement under this Act and to enter judgment on an award thereunder.

18. Venue

An initial application shall be made to the Court of the [county] in which the agreement provides the arbitration hearing shall be held or, if the hearing has been held, in the county in which it was held. Otherwise the application shall be made in the [county] where the adverse party resides or has a place of business or, if he has no residence or place of business in this State, to the Court of any [county]. All subsequent applications shall be made to the Court hearing the initial application, unless the Court otherwise directs.

19. Appeals

(a) An appeal may be taken from:

(1) An order denying an application to compel arbitration made under Section 2;

(2) An order granting an application to stay arbitration under Section 2(b);

(3) An order confirming or denying confirmation of an award;

(4) An order modifying or correcting an award;

(5) An order vacating an award without directing a rehearing; or

(6) A judgment or decree entered pursuant to the provisions of this act.

(b) The appeal shall be taken in the manner and to the same extent as from orders or judgments in a civil action.

20. Act Not Retroactive

This act applies only to agreements made subsequent to the taking effect of this act.

21. Uniformity of Interpretation

This act shall be so construed as to effectuate its general purpose to make uniform the law of those states which enact it.

Appendix B

THE UNITED STATES ARBITRATION ACT 9 U.S.C. 1-16

9 U.S.C. 1 "Maritime transactions" and "commerce" defined; exceptions to operation of title

"Maritime transactions," as herein defined, means charter parties, bills of lading of water carriers, agreements relating to wharfage, supplies furnished vessels or repairs to vessels, collisions, or any other matters in foreign commerce which, if the subject of controversy, would be embraced within admiralty jurisdiction; "commerce," as herein defined, means commerce among the several States or with foreign nations, or in any Territory of the United States or in the District of Columbia, or between any such Territory and another, or between any such Territory and any State or foreign nation, or between the District of Columbia and any State or Territory or foreign nation, but nothing herein contained shall apply to contracts of employment of seamen, railroad employees, or any other class of workers engaged in foreign or interstate commerce.

9 U.S.C. 2 Validity, irrevocability, and enforcement of agreements to arbitrate

A written provision in any maritime transaction or a contract evidencing a transaction involving commerce to settle by arbitration a controversy thereafter arising out of such contract or transaction, or the refusal to perform the whole or any part thereof, or an agreement in writing to submit to arbitration an existing controversy arising out of such a contract, transaction, or refusal, shall be valid, irrevocable, and enforceable, save upon such grounds as exist at law or in equity for the revocation of any contract.

9 U.S.C. 3 Stay of proceedings where issue therein referable to arbitration

If any suit or proceeding be brought in any of the courts of the United States upon any issue referable to arbitration under an agreement in writing for such arbitration, the Court in which such suit is pending, upon being satisfied that the issue involved in such suit or proceeding is referable to arbitration under such an agreement, shall on application of one of the parties stay the trial of the action until such arbitration has been had in accordance with the terms of the agreement, providing the applicant for the stay is not in default in proceeding with such arbitration.

9 U.S.C. 4 Failure to arbitrate under agreement; petition to United States court having jurisdiction for order to compel arbitration; notice and service thereof; hearing and determination

A party aggrieved by the alleged failure, neglect, or refusal of another to arbitrate under a written agreement for arbitration may petition any United States District Court which, save for such agreement, would have jurisdiction under Title 28 in a civil action or in admiralty of the subject matter of a suit arising out of the controversy between the parties for an order directing that such arbitration proceed in the manner provided for in such agreement. Five days' notice in writing of such application shall be served upon the party in default. Service thereof shall be made in the manner provided by the Federal Rules of Civil Procedure. The Court shall hear the parties, and upon being satisfied that the making of the agreement for arbitration or the failure to comply therewith is not in issue, the Court shall make an order directing the parties to proceed to arbitration in accordance with the terms of the agreement. The hearing and proceedings, under such agreement, shall be within the district in which the petition for an order directing such arbitration is filed. If the making of the arbitration agreement or the failure, neglect, or refusal to perform the Same be in issue, the Court shall proceed summarily to the trial thereof. If no jury trial be demanded by the party alleged to be in default or if the matter in dispute is within admiralty jurisdiction, the Court shall hear and determine such issue. Where such an issue is raised, the party alleged to be in default may, except in cases of admiralty, on or before the return day of the notice of application, demand a jury trial of such issue; and upon such demand, the Court shall make an order referring the issue or issues to a jury in the manner provided by the Federal Rules of Civil Procedure, or may specially call a jury for that purpose. If the jury find that no agreement in writing for arbitration was made or that there is no default in proceeding thereunder, the proceeding shall be dismissed. If the jury find that an agreement for arbitration was made in writing and that there is a default in proceeding thereunder, the Court shall make an order summarily directing the parties to proceed with the arbitration in accordance with the terms thereof.

9 U.S.C. 5 Appointment of arbitrators or umpire

If in the agreement provision be made for a method of naming or appointing an arbitrator or arbitrators or an umpire, such method shall be followed; but if no method be provided therein, or if a method be provided and any party thereto shall fail to avail himself of such method, or if for any other reason there shall be a lapse in the naming of an arbitrator or arbitrators or umpire, or in filling a vacancy, then upon the application of either party to the controversy the Court shall designate and appoint an arbitrator or arbitrators or umpire, as the case may require, who shall act under the said agreement with the same force and effect as if he or they had been specifically named therein; and unless otherwise provided in the agreement, the arbitration shall be by a single arbitrator.

9 U.S.C. 6 Application heard as motion

Any application to the Court hereunder shall be made and heard in the manner provided by law for the making and hearing of motions, except as otherwise herein expressly provided.

9 U.S.C. 7 Witnesses before arbitrators; fees; compelling attendance

The arbitrators selected either as prescribed in this title or otherwise, or a majority of them, may summon in writing any person to attend before them or any of them as a witness and in a proper case to bring with him or them any book, record, document, or paper which may be deemed material as evidence in the case. The fees for such attendance shall be the same as the fees of witnesses before masters of the United States courts. Said summons shall issue in the name of the arbitrator or arbitrators, or a majority of them, and shall be signed by the arbitrators, or a majority of them, and shall be directed to the said person and shall be served in the same manner as subpoenas to appear and testify before the Court; if any person or persons so summoned to testify shall refuse or neglect to obey said summons, upon petition the United States District Court for the district in which such arbitrators, or a majority of them, are sitting may compel the attendance of such person or persons before said arbitrator or arbitrators, or punish said person or persons for contempt in the same manner provided by law for securing the attendance of witnesses or their punishment for neglect or refusal to attend in the courts of the United States.

9 U.S.C. 8 Proceedings begun by libel in admiralty and seizure of vessel or property

If the basis of jurisdiction be a cause of action otherwise justiciable in admiralty, then, notwithstanding anything herein to the contrary, the party claiming to be aggrieved may begin his proceeding hereunder by libel and seizure of the vessel or other property of the other party according to the usual course of admiralty proceedings, and the Court shall then have jurisdiction to direct the parties to proceed with the arbitration and shall retain jurisdiction to enter its decree upon the award.

9 U.S.C. 9 Award of arbitrators; confirmation; jurisdiction; procedure

If the parties in their agreement have agreed that a judgment of the Court shall be entered upon the award made pursuant to the arbitration, and shall specify the Court, then at any time within one year after the award is made any party to the arbitration may apply to the Court so specified for an order confirming the award, and thereupon the Court must grant such an order unless the award is vacated, modified, or corrected as prescribed in Sections 10 and 11 of this title. If no court is specified in the agreement of the parties, then such application may be made to the United States court in and for the district within which such award was made. Notice of the application shall be served upon the adverse party, and thereupon the Court shall have jurisdiction of such party as though he had appeared generally in the proceeding. If the adverse party is a resident of the district within which the award was made, such service shall be made upon the adverse party or his attorney as prescribed by law for service of notice of motion in an action in the same court. If the adverse party shall be a nonresident, then the notice of the application shall be served by the marshal of any district within which the adverse party may be found in like manner as other process of the Court.

9 U.S.C. 10 Same; vacation; grounds; rehearing

(a) In any of the following cases the United States court in and for the district wherein the award was made may make an order vacating the award upon the application of any party to the arbitration:

(1) Where the award was procured by corruption, fraud, or undue means.

(2) Where there was evident partiality or corruption in the arbitrators, or either of them.

(3) Where the arbitrators were guilty of misconduct in refusing to postpone the hearing, upon sufficient cause shown, or in refusing to hear evidence pertinent and material to the controversy or of any other misbehavior by which the rights of any party have been prejudiced.

(4) Where the arbitrators exceeded their powers or so imperfectly executed them that a mutual, final, and definite award upon the subject matter submitted was not made.

(5) Where an award is vacated and the time within which the agreement required the award to be made has not expired, the Court may, in its discretion, direct a rehearing by the arbitrators.

(b) The United States District Court for the district where an award was made that was issued pursuant to Section 580 of title 5 may make an order vacating the award upon the application of a person, other than a party to the arbitration, who is adversely affected or aggrieved by the award, if the use of arbitration or the award is clearly inconsistent with the factors set forth in Section 572 of title 5.

9 U.S.C. 11   Same; modification or correction; grounds; order

In either of the following cases, the United States court in and for the district wherein the award was made may make an order modifying or correcting the award upon the application of any party to the arbitration:

(a) Where there was an evident material miscalculation of figures or an evident material mistake in the description of any person, thing, or property referred to in the award.

(b) Where the arbitrators have awarded upon a matter not submitted to them, unless it is a matter not affecting the merits of the decision upon the matter submitted.

(c) Where the award is imperfect in matter of form not affecting the merits of the controversy.

The order may modify and correct the award, so as to effect the intent thereof and promote justice between the parties.

9 U.S.C. 12   Notice of motions to vacate or modify; service; stay of proceedings

Notice of a motion to vacate, modify, or correct an award must be served upon the adverse party or his attorney within three months after the award is filed or delivered. If the adverse party is a resident of the district within which the award was made, such service shall be made upon the adverse party or his attorney as prescribed by law for service of notice of motion in an action in the same court. If the adverse party shall be a nonresident, then the notice of the application shall be served by the marshal of any district within which the adverse party may be found in like manner as other process of the Court. For the purposes of the motion, any judge who might make an order to stay the proceedings in an action brought in the same court may make an order to be served with the notice of motion, staying the proceedings of the adverse party to enforce the award.

9 U.S.C. 13   Papers filed with order on motions; judgment; docketing; force and effect; enforcement

The party moving for an order confirming, modifying, or correcting an award shall, at the time such order is filed with the clerk for the entry of judgment thereon, also file the following papers with the clerk:

(a) The agreement: the selection or appointment, if any, of an additional arbitrator or umpire; and each written extension of the time, if any, within which to make the award.

(b) The award.

(c) Each notice, affidavit, or other paper used upon an application to confirm, modify, or correct the award, and a copy of each order of the Court upon such an application.

The judgment shall be docketed as if it was rendered in an action.

The judgment so entered shall have the same force and effect, in all respects, as, and be subject to all the provisions of law relating to, a judgment in an action; and it may be enforced as if it had been rendered in an action in the Court in which it is entered.

9 U.S.C. 14 Contracts not affected

This title shall not apply to contracts made prior to January 1, 1926.

9 U.S.C. 15 Inapplicability of the Act of State doctrine

Enforcement of arbitral agreements, confirmation of arbitral awards, and execution upon judgments based on orders confirming such awards shall not be refused on the basis of the Act of State doctrine.

9 U.S.C. 16 Appeals

(a) An appeal may be taken from:

(1) an order:

(A) refusing a stay of any action under Section 3 of this title,

(B) denying a petition under Section 4 of this title to order arbitration to proceed,

(C) denying an application under Section 206 of this title to compel arbitration,

(D) confirming or denying confirmation of an award or partial award, or

(E) modifying, correcting, or vacating an award;

(2) an interlocutory order granting, continuing, or modifying an injunction against an arbitration that is subject to this title; or

(3) a final decision with respect to an arbitration that is subject to this title.

(b) Except as otherwise provided in Section 1292(b) of title 28, an appeal may not be taken from an interlocutory order:

(1) granting a stay of any action under Section 3 of this title;

(2) directing arbitration to proceed under Section 4 of this title;

(3) compelling arbitration under Section 206 of this title; or

(4) refusing to enjoin an arbitration that is subject to this title.

Appendix C

THE CONVENTION ON THE RECOGNITION AND ENFORCEMENT OF FOREIGN ARBITRAL AWARDS 9 U.S.C. 201-208

9 U.S.C. 201 Enforcement of convention

The Convention on the Recognition and Enforcement of Foreign Arbitral Awards of June 10, 1958, shall be enforced in United States courts in accordance with this chapter.

9 U.S.C. 202 Agreement or award falling under the convention

An arbitration agreement or arbitral award arising out of a legal relationship, whether contractual or not, which is considered as commercial, including a transaction, contract, or agreement described in Section 2 of this title, falls under the Convention. An agreement or award arising out of such a relationship which is entirely between citizens of the United States shall be deemed not to fall under the Convention unless that relationship involves property located abroad, envisages performance or enforcement abroad, or has some other reasonable relation with one or more foreign states. For the purpose of this Section, a corporation is a citizen of the United States if it is incorporated or has its principal place of business in the United States.

9 U.S.C. 203 Jurisdiction; amount in controversy

An action or proceeding falling under the Convention shall be deemed to arise under the laws and treaties of the United States. The district courts of the United States (including the courts enumerated in Section 460 of title 28) shall have original jurisdiction over such an action or proceeding, regardless of the amount in controversy.

9 U.S.C. 204 Venue

An action or proceeding over which the district courts have jurisdiction pursuant to Section 203 of this title may be brought in any such court in which save for the arbitration agreement an action or proceeding with respect to the controversy between the parties could be brought, or in such court for the district and division which embraces the place designated in the agreement as the place of arbitration if such place is within the United States.

9 U.S.C. 205 Removal of cases from state courts

Where the subject matter of an action or proceeding pending in a State court relates to an arbitration agreement or award falling under the Convention, the defendant or the defendants may, at any time before the trial thereof, remove such action or proceeding to the District Court of the United States for the district and division embracing the place where the action or proceeding is pending. The procedure for removal of causes otherwise provided by law shall apply, except that the ground for removal provided in this Section need not appear on the face of the complaint but may be shown in the petition for removal. For the purposes of Chapter 1 of this title, any action or proceeding removed under this Section shall be deemed to have been brought in the District Court to which it is removed.

9 U.S.C. 206 Order to compel arbitration; appointment of arbitrators

A court having jurisdiction under this chapter may direct that arbitration be held in accordance with the agreement at any place therein provided for, whether that place is within or without the United States. Such court may also appoint arbitrators in accordance with the provisions of the agreement.

9 U.S.C. 207 Award of arbitrators; confirmation; jurisdiction; proceeding

Within three years after an arbitral award falling under the Convention is made, any party to the arbitration may apply to any court having jurisdiction under this chapter for an order confirming the award as against any other party to the arbitration.

The Court shall confirm the award, unless it finds one of the grounds for refusal or deferral of recognition or enforcement of the award specified in the said Convention.

9 U.S.C. 208 Chapter 1; residual application

Chapter 1 applies to actions and proceedings brought under this chapter to the extent that that chapter is not in conflict with this chapter or the Convention as ratified by the United States.

Appendix D

AMERICAN ARBITRATION ASSOCIATION COMMERCIAL ARBITRATION RULES

American Arbitration Association Commercial Arbitration Rules as Amended and Effective on July 1, 1996, all rights are reserved by the American Arbitration Association.

1. Agreement of Parties

The parties shall be deemed to have made these rules a part of their arbitration agreement whenever they have provided for arbitration by the American Arbitration Association (hereinafter AAA) under its Commercial Arbitration Rules. These rules and any amendment of them shall apply in the form obtaining at the time the demand for arbitration or submission agreement is received by the AAA. The parties, by written agreement, may vary the procedures set forth in these rules.

2. Name of Tribunal

Any tribunal constituted by the parties for the settlement of their dispute under these rules shall be called the Commercial Arbitration Tribunal.

3. Administrator and Delegation of Duties

When parties agree to arbitrate under these rules, or when they provide for arbitration by the AAA and arbitration is initiated under these rules, they thereby authorize the AAA to administer the arbitration. The authority and duties of the AAA are prescribed in the agreement of the parties and these rules and may be carried out through such of the AAA's representatives as it may direct.

4. National Panel of Arbitrators

The AAA shall establish and maintain a National Panel of Commercial Arbitrators and shall appoint arbitrators as provided in these rules.

5. Regional Offices

The AAA may, at its discretion, assign the administration of an arbitration to any of its regional offices.

6. Initiation under an Arbitration Provision in a Contract

Arbitration under an arbitration provision in a contract shall be initiated in the following manner:

(a) The initiating party (hereinafter claimant) shall, within the time period, if any, specified in the contract(s), give written notice to the other party (hereinafter respondent) of its intention to arbitrate (demand), which notice shall contain a statement setting forth the nature of the dispute, the amount involved, if any, the remedy sought, and the hearing locale requested, and;

(b) shall file at any regional office of the AAA three copies of the notice and three copies of the arbitration provisions of the contract, together with the appropriate filing fee as provided in the schedule on page 19.

The AAA shall give notice of such filing to the respondent or respondents. A respondent may file an answering statement in duplicate with the AAA within ten days after notice from the AAA, in which event the respondent shall at the same time send a copy of the answering statement to the claimant. If a counterclaim is asserted, it shall contain a statement setting forth the nature of the counterclaim, the amount involved, if any, and the remedy sought. If a counterclaim is made, the appropriate fee provided in the schedule on page 19 shall be forwarded to the AAA with the answering statement. If no answering statement is filed within the stated time, it will be treated as a denial of the claim. Failure to file an answering statement shall not operate to delay the arbitration.

7. Initiation under a Submission

Parties to any existing dispute may commence an arbitration under these rules by filing at any regional office of the AAA three copies of a written submission to arbitrate under these rules, signed by the parties. It shall contain a statement of the matter in dispute, the amount involved, if any, the remedy sought, and the hearing locale requested, together with the appropriate filing fee as provided by the schedule.

8. Changes of Claim

After filing of a claim, if either party desires to make any new or different claim or counterclaim, it shall be made in writing and filed with the AAA, and a copy shall be mailed to the other party who shall have a period of ten days from the date of such mailing within which to file an answer with the AAA. After the arbitrator is appointed, however, no new or different claim may be submitted except with the arbitrator's consent.

9. Applicable Procedures

Unless the AAA in its discretion determines otherwise, the Expedited Procedures shall be applied to any case where no disclosed claim or counterclaim exceeds $50,000, exclusive of interest and arbitration costs. Parties may also agree to using the Expedited Procedures in cases involving claims in excess of $50,000. The Expedited Procedures shall be applied as described in Sections 53 through 57 of these rules, in addition to any other portion of these rules that does not conflict with the Expedited Procedures. All other cases shall be administered in accordance with Sections 1 through 52 of these rules.

10. Administrative Conference, Preliminary Hearing, and Mediation Conference

At the request of any party or at the discretion of the AAA, an administrative conference with the AAA and the parties and/or their representatives will be scheduled in appropriate cases to expedite the arbitration proceedings. There is no administrative fee for this service.

In large or complex cases, at the request of any party or at the discretion of the arbitrator or the AAA, a preliminary hearing with the parties and/or their representatives and the arbitrator may be scheduled by the arbitrator to specify the issues to be resolved, to stipulate to uncontested facts, and to consider any other matters that will expedite the arbitration proceedings. Consistent with the expedited nature of arbitration, the arbitrator may, at the preliminary hearing, establish (1) the extent of and schedule for the production of relevant documents and other information, (2) the identification of any witnesses to be called, and (3) a schedule for further hearings to resolve the dispute. There is no administrative fee for the first preliminary hearing.

With the consent of the parties, the AAA at any stage of the proceeding may arrange a mediation conference under the Commercial Mediation Rules in order to facilitate settlement. The mediator shall not be an arbitrator appointed to the case. Where the parties to a pending arbitration agree to mediate under the AAA's rules, no additional administrative fee is required to initiate the mediation.

11. Fixing a Locale

The parties may mutually agree on the locale where the arbitration is to be held. If any party requests that the hearing be held in a specific locale and the other party files no objection thereto within ten days after notice of the request has been sent to it by the AAA, the locale shall be the one requested. If a party objects to the locale requested by the other party, the AAA shall have the power to determine the locale, and its decision shall be final and binding.

12. Qualifications of an Arbitrator

Any neutral arbitrator appointed pursuant to Sections 13, 14, 15, or 54 or selected by mutual choice of the parties or their appointees, shall be subject to disqualification for the reasons specified in Section 19. If the parties specifically so agree in writing, the arbitrator shall not be subject to disqualification for those reasons.

Unless the parties agree otherwise, an arbitrator selected unilaterally by one party is a party-appointed arbitrator and not subject to disqualification pursuant to Section 19.

The term "arbitrator" in these rules refers to the arbitration panel, whether composed of one or more arbitrators and whether the arbitrators are neutral or party appointed.

13. Appointment from Panel

If the parties have not appointed an arbitrator and have not provided any other method of appointment, the arbitrator shall be appointed in the following manner: immediately after the filing of the demand or submission, the AAA shall send simultaneously to each party to the dispute an identical list of names of persons chosen from the panel.

Each party to the dispute shall have ten days from the transmittal date in which to strike names objected to, number the remaining names in order of preference, and return the list to the AAA. In a single-arbitrator case, each party may strike three names on a peremptory basis. In a multi-arbitrator case, each party may strike five names on a peremptory basis. If a party does not return the list within the time specified, all persons named therein shall be deemed acceptable. From among the persons who have been approved on both lists and in accordance with the designated order of mutual preference, the AAA shall invite the acceptance of an arbitrator to serve. If the parties fail to agree on any of the persons named, or if acceptable arbitrators are unable to act, or if for any other reason the appointment cannot be made from the submitted lists, the AAA shall have the power to make the appointment from among other members of the panel without the submission of additional lists.

14. Direct Appointment by a Party

If the agreement of the parties names an arbitrator or specifies a method of appointing an arbitrator, that designation or method shall be followed. The notice of appointment, with the name and address of the arbitrator, shall be filed with the AAA by the appointing party. Upon the request of any appointing party, the AAA shall submit a list of members of the panel from which the party may, if it so desires, make the appointment.

If the agreement specifies a period of time within which an arbitrator shall be appointed and any party fails to make the appointment within that period, the AAA shall make the appointment.

If no period of time is specified in the agreement, the AAA shall notify the party to make the appointment. If within ten days thereafter an arbitrator has not been appointed by a party, the AAA shall make the appointment.

15. Appointment of Neutral Arbitrator by Party-Appointed Arbitrators or Parties

If the parties have selected party-appointed arbitrators or if such arbitrators have been appointed as provided in Section 14 and the parties have authorized them to appoint a neutral arbitrator within a specified time and no appointment is made within that time or any agreed extension, the AAA may appoint a neutral arbitrator who shall act as chairperson.

If no period of time is specified for appointment of the neutral arbitrator and the party-appointed arbitrators or the parties do not make the appointment within ten days from the date of the appointment of the last party-appointed arbitrator, the AAA may appoint the neutral arbitrator who shall act as chairperson.

If the parties have agreed that their party-appointed arbitrators shall appoint the neutral arbitrator from the panel, the AAA shall furnish to the party-appointed arbitrators, in the manner provided in Section 13, a list selected from the panel, and the appointment of the neutral arbitrator shall be made as provided in that Section.

16. Nationality of Arbitrator in International Arbitration

Where the parties are nationals or residents of different countries, any neutral arbitrator shall, upon the request of either party, be appointed from among the nationals of a country other than that of any of the parties. The request must be made prior to the time set for the appointment of the arbitrator as agreed by the parties or set by these rules.

17. Number of Arbitrators

If the arbitration agreement does not specify the number of arbitrators, the dispute shall be heard and determined by one arbitrator, unless the AAA, in its discretion, directs that a greater number of arbitrators be appointed.

18. Notice to Arbitrator of Appointment

Notice of the appointment of the neutral arbitrator, whether appointed mutually by the parties or by the AAA, shall be sent to the arbitrator by the AAA, together with a copy of these rules, and the signed acceptance of the arbitrator shall be filed with the AAA prior to the opening of the first hearing.

19. Disclosure and Challenge Procedure

Any person appointed as neutral arbitrator shall disclose to the AAA any circumstance likely to affect impartiality, including any bias, any financial or personal interest in the result of the arbitration, or any past or present relationship with the parties or their representatives. Upon receipt of such information from the arbitrator or another source, the AAA shall communicate the information to the parties and, if it deems it appropriate to do so, to the arbitrator and others. Upon objection of a party to the continued service of a neutral arbitrator, the AAA shall determine whether the arbitrator should be disqualified and shall inform the parties of its decision, which shall be conclusive.

20. Vacancies

If for any reason an arbitrator is unable to perform the duties of the office, the AAA may, on proof satisfactory to it, declare the office vacant. Vacancies shall be filled in accordance with the applicable provisions in these rules.

In the event of a vacancy in a panel of neutral arbitrators after the hearings have commenced, the remaining arbitrator or arbitrators may continue with the hearing and determination of the controversy, unless the parties agree otherwise.

21. Date, Time, and Place of Hearing

The arbitrator shall set the date, time, and place for each hearing. The AAA shall send a notice of hearing to the parties at least ten days in advance of the hearing date, unless otherwise agreed by the parties.

22. Representation

Any party may be represented by counsel or other authorized representative. A party intending to be represented shall notify the other party and the AAA of the name and address of the representative at least three days prior to the date set for the hearing in which that person is first to appear. When such a representative initiates arbitration or responds for a party, notice is deemed to have been given.

23. Stenographic Record

Any party desiring a stenographic record shall make arrangements directly with a stenographer and shall notify the other parties of these arrangements in advance of the hearing. The requesting party or parties shall pay the cost of the record. If the transcript is agreed by the parties to be, or determined by the arbitrator to be, the official record of the proceeding, it must be made available to the arbitrator and to the other parties for inspection at a date, time, and place determined by the arbitrator.

24. Interpreters

Any party wishing an interpreter shall make all arrangements directly with the interpreter and shall assume the costs of the service.

25. Attendance at Hearings

The arbitrator shall maintain the privacy of the hearings, unless the law provides to the contrary. Any person having a direct interest in the arbitration is entitled to attend hearings. The arbitrator shall otherwise have the power to require the exclusion of any witness, other than a party or other essential person, during the testimony of any other witness. It shall be discretionary with the arbitrator to determine the propriety of the attendance of any other person.

26. Postponements

The arbitrator for good cause shown may postpone any hearing upon the request of a party or upon the arbitrator's own initiative and shall also grant such postponement when all of the parties agree.

27. Oaths

Before proceeding with the first hearing, each arbitrator may take an oath of office and, if required by law, shall do so. The arbitrator may require witnesses to testify under oath administered by any duly qualified person and, if it is required by law or requested by any party, shall do so.

28. Majority Decision

All decisions of the arbitrators must be by a majority. The award must also be made by a majority, unless the concurrence of all is expressly required in the arbitration agreement or by law.

29. Order of Proceedings and Communication with Arbitrator

A hearing shall be opened by the filing of the oath of the arbitrator, where required; by the recording of the date, time, and place of the hearing and the presence of the arbitrator, the parties, and their representatives, if any; and by the receipt by the arbitrator of the statement of the claim and the answering statement, if any.

The arbitrator may, at the beginning of the hearing, ask for statements clarifying the issues involved. In some cases, part or all of the above will have been accomplished at the preliminary hearing conducted by the arbitrator pursuant to Section 10.

The complaining party shall then present evidence to support its claim. The defending party shall then present evidence supporting its defense. Witnesses for each party shall submit to questions or other examination. The arbitrator has the discretion to vary this procedure but shall afford a full and equal opportunity to all parties for the presentation of any material and relevant evidence.

Exhibits, when offered by either party, may be received as evidence by the arbitrator.

The names and addresses of all witnesses and a description of the exhibits in the order received shall be made a part of the record.

There shall be no direct communication between the parties and neutral arbitrator other than at oral hearing, unless the parties and the arbitrator agree otherwise. Any other oral or written communication from the parties to the neutral arbitrator shall be directed to the AAA for transmittal to the arbitrator.

30. Arbitration in the Absence of a Party or Representative

Unless the law provides to the contrary, the arbitration may proceed in the absence of any party or representative who, after due notice, fails to be present or fails to obtain a postponement. An award shall not be made solely on the default of a party. The arbitrator shall require the party who is present to submit such evidence as the arbitrator may require for the making of an award.

31. Evidence

The parties may offer such evidence as is relevant and material to the dispute and shall produce such evidence as the arbitrator may deem necessary to an understanding and determination of the dispute. An arbitrator or other person authorized by law to subpoena witnesses or documents may do so upon the request of any party or independently.

The arbitrator shall be the judge of the relevance and materiality of the evidence offered, and conformity to legal rules of evidence shall not be necessary. All evidence shall be taken in the presence of all of the arbitrators and all of the parties, except where any of the parties is absent in default or has waived the right to be present.

32. Evidence by Affidavit and Posthearing Filing of Documents or Other Evidence

The arbitrator may receive and consider the evidence of witnesses by affidavit but shall give it only such weight as the arbitrator deems it entitled to after consideration of any objection made to its admission.

If the parties agree or the arbitrator directs that documents or other evidence be submitted to the arbitrator after the hearing, the documents or other evidence shall be filed with the AAA for transmission to the arbitrator. All parties shall be afforded an opportunity to examine such documents or other evidence.

33. Inspection or Investigation

An arbitrator finding it necessary to make an inspection or investigation in connection with the arbitration shall direct the AAA to so advise the parties. The arbitrator shall set the date and time, and the AAA shall notify the parties. Any party who so desires may be present at such an inspection or investigation. In the event that one or all parties are not present at the inspection or investigation, the arbitrator shall make a verbal or written report to the parties and afford them an opportunity to comment.

34. Interim Measures

The arbitrator may issue such orders for interim relief as may be deemed necessary to safeguard the property that is the subject matter of the arbitration, without prejudice to the rights of the parties or to the final determination of the dispute.

35. Closing of Hearing

The arbitrator shall specifically inquire of all parties whether they have any further proofs to offer or witnesses to be heard. Upon receiving negative replies or if satisfied that the record is complete, the arbitrator shall declare the hearing closed.

If briefs are to be filed, the hearing shall be declared closed as of the final date set by the arbitrator for the receipt of briefs. If documents are to be filed as provided in Section 32 and the date set for their receipt is later than that set for the receipt of briefs, the later date shall be the date of closing of the hearing. The time limit within which the arbitrator is required to make the award shall commence to run, in the absence of other agreements by the parties, upon the closing of the hearing.

36. Reopening of Hearing

The hearing may be reopened on the arbitrator's initiative, or upon application of a party, at any time before the award is made. If reopening the hearing would prevent the making of the award within the specific time agreed on by the parties in the contract(s) out of which the controversy has arisen, the matter may not be reopened unless the parties agree on an extension of time. When no specific date is fixed in the contract, the arbitrator may reopen the hearing and shall have thirty days from the closing of the reopened hearing within which to make an award.

37. Waiver of Oral Hearing

The parties may provide, by written agreement, for the waiver of oral hearings in any case. If the parties are unable to agree as to the procedure, the AAA shall specify a fair and equitable procedure.

38. Waiver of Rules

Any party who proceeds with the arbitration after knowledge that any provision or requirement of these rules has not been complied with and who fails to state an objection in writing shall be deemed to have waived the right to object.

39. Extensions of Time

The parties may modify any period of time by mutual agreement. The AAA or the arbitrator may for good cause extend any period of time established by these rules, except the time for making the award. The AAA shall notify the parties of any extension.

40. Serving of Notice

Each party shall be deemed to have consented that any papers, notices, or process necessary or proper for the initiation or continuation of an arbitration under these rules; for any court action in connection therewith; for the entry of judgment on any award made under these rules may be served on a party by mail addressed to the party or its representative at the last known address or by personal service, in or outside the state where the arbitration is to be held, provided that reasonable opportunity to be heard with regard thereto has been granted to the party.

The AAA and the parties may also use facsimile transmission, telex, telegram, or other written forms of electronic communication to give the notices required by these rules.

41. Time of Award

The award shall be made promptly by the arbitrator and, unless otherwise agreed by the parties or specified by law, no later than thirty days from the date of closing the hearing, or, if oral hearings have been waived, from the date of the AAA's transmittal of the final statements and proofs to the arbitrator.

42. Form of Award

The award shall be in writing and shall be signed by a majority of the arbitrators. It shall be executed in the manner required by law.

43. Scope of Award

The arbitrator may grant any remedy or relief that the arbitrator deems just and equitable and within the scope of the agreement of the parties, including, but not limited to, specific performance of a contract. The arbitrator shall, in the award, assess arbitration fees, expenses, and compensation as provided in Sections 48, 49, and 50 in favor of any party and, in the event that any administrative fees or expenses are due the AAA, in favor of the AAA.

44. Award upon Settlement

If the parties settle their dispute during the course of the arbitration, the arbitrator may set forth the terms of the agreed settlement in an award. Such an award is referred to as a consent award.

45. Delivery of Award to Parties

Parties shall accept as legal delivery of the award the placing of the award or a true copy thereof in the mail addressed to a party or its representative at the last known address, personal service of the award, or the filing of the award by any other manner that is permitted by law.

46. Release of Documents for Judicial Proceedings

The AAA shall, upon the written request of a party, furnish the party, at its expense, certified copies of any papers in the AAA's possession that may be required in judicial proceedings relating to the arbitration.

47. Applications to Court and Exclusion of Liability

(a) No judicial proceeding by a party relating to the subject matter of the arbitration shall be deemed a waiver of the party's right to arbitrate.

(b) Neither the AAA nor any arbitrator in a proceeding under these rules is a necessary party in judicial proceedings relating to the arbitration.

(c) Parties to these rules shall be deemed to have consented that judgment upon the arbitration award may be entered in any federal or state court having jurisdiction thereof.

(d) Neither the AAA nor any arbitrator shall be liable to any party for any act or omission in connection with any arbitration conducted under these rules.

48. Administrative Fees

As a not-for-profit organization, the AAA shall prescribe filing and other administrative fees and service charges to compensate it for the cost of providing administrative services. The fees in effect when the fee or charge is incurred shall be applicable.

The filing fee shall be advanced by the initiating party or parties, subject to final apportionment by the arbitrator in the award.

The AAA may, in the event of extreme hardship on the part of any party, defer or reduce the administrative fees.

49. Expenses

The expenses of witnesses for either side shall be paid by the party producing such witnesses. All other expenses of the arbitration, including required travel and other expenses of the arbitrator, AAA representatives, and any witness and the cost of any proof produced at the direct request of the arbitrator, shall be borne equally by the parties, unless they agree otherwise or unless the arbitrator in the award assesses such expenses or any part thereof against any specified party or parties.

50. Neutral Arbitrator's Compensation

Unless the parties agree otherwise, members of the National Panel of Commercial Arbitrators appointed as neutrals on cases administered under the Expedited Procedures with claims not exceeding $10,000 will customarily serve without compensation for the first day of service. Thereafter, arbitrators shall receive compensation as set forth herein.

Arbitrators shall charge a rate consistent with the arbitrator's stated rate of compensation, beginning with the first day of hearing in all cases with claims exceeding $10,000.

If there is disagreement concerning the terms of compensation, an appropriate rate shall be established with the arbitrator by the Association and confirmed to the parties.

Any arrangement for the compensation of a neutral arbitrator shall be made through the AAA and not directly between the parties and the arbitrator.

51. Deposits

The AAA may require the parties to deposit in advance of any hearings such sums of money as it deems necessary to cover the expense of the arbitration, including the arbitrator's fee, if any, and shall render an accounting to the parties and return any unexpended balance at the conclusion of the case.

52. Interpretation and Application of Rules

The arbitrator shall interpret and apply these rules insofar as they relate to the arbitrator's powers and duties. When there is more than one arbitrator and a difference arises among them concerning the meaning or application of these rules, it shall be decided by a majority vote. If that is not possible, either an arbitrator or a party may refer the question to the AAA for a final decision. All other rules shall be interpreted and applied by the AAA.

EXPEDITED PROCEDURES

53. Notice by Telephone

The parties shall accept all notices from the AAA by telephone. Such notices by the AAA shall subsequently be confirmed in writing to the parties. Should there be a failure to confirm in writing any notice hereunder, the proceeding shall nonetheless be valid if notice has, in fact, been given by telephone.

54. Appointment and Qualifications of Arbitrator

(a) Where no disclosed claim or counterclaim exceeds $50,000, exclusive of interest and arbitration costs, the AAA shall appoint a single arbitrator from the National Panel of Commercial Arbitrators, without submission of lists of proposed arbitrators.

(b) Where all parties request that a list of proposed arbitrators be sent, the AAA upon payment of the service charge as provided in the Administrative Fees shall submit simultaneously to each party an identical list of five proposed arbitrators drawn from the National Panel of Commercial Arbitrators, from which one arbitrator shall be appointed. Each party may strike two names from the list on a peremptory basis. The list is returnable to the AAA within seven days from the date of the AAA's mailing to the parties.

   If for any reason the appointment of an arbitrator cannot be made from the list, the AAA may make the appointment from among other members of the panel without the submission of additional lists.

(c) The parties will be given notice by telephone by the AAA of the appointment of the arbitrator, who shall be subject to disqualification for the reasons specified in Section 19. The parties shall notify the AAA, by telephone, within seven days of any objection to the arbitrator appointed. Any objection by a party to the arbitrator shall be confirmed in writing to the AAA with a copy to the other party or parties.

55. Date, Time, and Place of Hearing

The arbitrator shall set the date, time, and place of the hearing. The AAA will notify the parties by telephone, at least seven days in advance of the hearing date. A formal notice of hearing will also be sent by the AAA to the parties.

56. The Hearing

Generally, the hearing shall be completed within one day, unless the dispute is resolved by submission of documents under Section 37. The arbitrator, for good cause shown, may schedule an additional hearing to be held within seven days.

57. Time of Award

Unless otherwise agreed by the parties, the award shall be rendered not later than fourteen days from the date of the closing of the hearing.

Source: Reprinted with permission of the American Arbitration Association.

Appendix E

AMERICAN ARBITRATION ASSOCIATION COMMERCIAL MEDIATION RULES

American Arbitration Association Commercial Mediation Rules as Amended and in Effect January 1, 1992, All Rights Are Reserved by the American Arbitration Association.

1. Agreement of Parties

Whenever, by stipulation or in their contract, the parties have provided for mediation or conciliation of existing or future disputes under the auspices of the American Arbitration Association (AAA) or under these rules, they shall be deemed to have made these rules, as amended and in effect as of the date of the submission of the dispute, a part of their agreement.

2. Initiation of Mediation

Any party or parties to a dispute may initiate mediation by filing with the AAA a submission to mediation or a written request for mediation pursuant to these rules, together with the appropriate Filing Fee. Where there is no submission to mediation or contract providing for mediation, a party may request the AAA to invite another party to join in a submission to mediation. Upon receipt of such a request, the AAA will contact the other parties involved in the dispute and attempt to obtain a submission to mediation.

3. Requests for Mediation

A request for mediation shall contain a brief statement of the nature of the dispute and the names, addresses, and telephone numbers of all parties to the dispute and those who will represent them, if any, in the mediation. The initiating party shall simultaneously file two copies of the request with the AAA and one copy with every other party to the dispute.

4. Appointment of the Mediator

Upon receipt of a request for mediation, the AAA will appoint a qualified mediator to serve. Normally, a single mediator will be appointed, unless the parties agree otherwise or the AAA determines otherwise. If the agreement of the parties names a mediator or specifies a method of appointing a mediator, that designation or method shall be followed.

5. Qualifications of the Mediator

No person shall serve as a mediator in any dispute in which that person has any financial or personal interest in the result of the mediation, except by the written consent of all parties. Prior to accepting an appointment, the prospective mediator shall disclose any circumstance likely to create a presumption of bias or prevent a prompt meeting with the parties. Upon receipt of such information, the AAA shall either replace the mediator or immediately communicate the information to the parties for their comments. In the event that the parties disagree as to whether the mediator shall serve, the AAA will appoint another mediator. The AAA is authorized to appoint another mediator, if the appointed mediator is unable to serve promptly.

6. Vacancies

If any mediator shall become unwilling or unable to serve, the AAA will appoint another mediator, unless the parties agree otherwise.

7. Representation

Any party may be represented by persons of the party's choice. The names and addresses of such persons shall be communicated in writing to all parties and to the AAA.

8. Date, Time, and Place of Mediation

The mediator shall fix the date and the time of each mediation session. The mediation shall be held at the appropriate regional office of the AAA or at any other convenient location agreeable to the mediator and the parties, as the mediator shall determine.

9. Identification of Matters in Dispute

At least ten days prior to the first scheduled mediation session, each party shall provide the mediator with a brief memorandum setting forth its position with regard to the issues that need to be resolved. At the discretion of the mediator, such memoranda may be mutually exchanged by the parties.

At the first session, the parties will be expected to produce all information reasonably required for the mediator to understand the issues presented.

The mediator may require any party to supplement such information.

10. Authority of the Mediator

The mediator does not have the authority to impose a settlement on the parties but will attempt to help them reach a satisfactory resolution of their dispute. The mediator is authorized to conduct joint and separate meetings with the parties and to make oral and written recommendations for settlement. Whenever necessary, the mediator may also obtain expert advice concerning technical aspects of the dispute, provided that the parties agree and assume the expenses of obtaining such advice. Arrangements for obtaining such advice shall be made by the mediator or the parties, as the mediator shall determine.

The mediator is authorized to end the mediation whenever, in the judgment of the mediator, further efforts at mediation would not contribute to a resolution of the dispute between the parties.

11. Privacy

Mediation sessions are private. The parties and their representatives may attend mediation sessions. Other persons may attend only with the permission of the parties and with the consent of the mediator.

12. Confidentiality

Confidential information disclosed to a mediator by the parties or by witnesses in the course of the mediation shall not be divulged by the mediator. All records, reports, or other documents received by a mediator while serving in that capacity shall be confidential. The mediator shall not be compelled to divulge such records or to testify in regard to the mediation in any adversary proceeding or judicial forum.

The parties shall maintain the confidentiality of the mediation and shall not rely on, or introduce as evidence in any arbitral, judicial, or other proceeding:

(a) views expressed or suggestions made by another party with respect to a possible settlement of the dispute;

(b) admissions made by another party in the course of the mediation proceedings;

(c) proposals made or views expressed by the mediator; or

(d) the fact that another party had or had not indicated willingness to accept a proposal for settlement made by the mediator.

13. No Stenographic Record

There shall be no stenographic record of the mediation process.

14. Termination of Mediation

The mediation shall be terminated:

(a) by the execution of a settlement agreement by the parties;

(b) by a written declaration of the mediator to the effect that further efforts at mediation are no longer worthwhile; or

(c) by a written declaration of a party or parties to the effect that the mediation proceedings are terminated.

15. Exclusion of Liability

Neither the AAA nor any mediator is a necessary party in judicial proceedings relating to the mediation.

Neither the AAA nor any mediator shall be liable to any party for any act or omission in connection with any mediation conducted under these rules.

16. Interpretation and Application of Rules

The mediator shall interpret and apply these rules insofar as they relate to the mediator's duties and responsibilities. All other rules shall be interpreted and applied by the AAA.

17. Expenses

The expenses of witnesses for either side shall be paid by the party producing such witnesses. All other expenses of the mediation, including required traveling and other expenses of the mediator and representatives of the AAA and the expenses of any witness and the cost of any proofs or expert advice produced at the direct request of the mediator, shall be borne equally by the parties, unless they agree otherwise.

Source: Reprinted with permission of the American Arbitration Association.

Appendix F

AMERICAN ARBITRATION ASSOCIATION RULES FOR THE RESOLUTION OF EMPLOYMENT DISPUTES

INTRODUCTION

Federal and state laws reflecting societal intolerance for certain workplace conduct, as well as court decisions interpreting and applying those statutes, have redefined responsible corporate practice and employee relations. Increasingly, employers and employees face workplace disputes involving alleged wrongful termination, sexual harassment, or discrimination based on race, color, religion, sex, national origin, age, and disability.

As courts and administrative agencies become less accessible to civil litigants, employers and their employees now see alternative dispute resolution (ADR) as a way to promptly and effectively resolve workplace disputes. ADR procedures are becoming more common in contracts of employment, personnel manuals, and employee handbooks. Increasingly, corporations and their employees look to the American Arbitration Association as a resource in developing prompt and effective employment procedures for employment-related disputes.

These rules have been developed for employers and employees who wish to use a private alternative to resolve their disputes, enabling them to have complaints heard by an impartial person with expertise in the employment field. These procedures benefit both the employer and the individual employee by making it possible to resolve disputes without extensive litigation.

THE FAIRNESS ISSUE: THE DUE PROCESS PROTOCOL

The Due Process Protocol for Mediation and Arbitration of Statutory Disputes Arising Out of the Employment Relationship was developed in 1995 by a special task force composed of individuals representing management, labor, employment, civil rights organizations, private administrative agencies, government, and the American Arbitration Association. The Due Process Protocol, which was endorsed by the Association in 1995, seeks to ensure fairness and equity in resolving workplace disputes. The Due Process Protocol encourages mediation and arbitration of statutory disputes, provided there are due process safeguards. It conveys the hope that ADR will reduce delays caused by the huge backlog of cases pending before administrative agencies and the courts. The Due Process Protocol "recognizes the dilemma inherent in the timing of an agreement to mediate and/or arbitrate statutory disputes" but does not take a position on whether an employer can require a pre-dispute, binding arbitration program as a condition of employment.

The Due Process Protocol has been endorsed by organizations representing a broad range of constituencies. They include the American Arbitration Association, the American Bar Association Labor and Employment Section, the American Civil Liberties Union, the Federal Mediation and Conciliation Service, the National Academy of Arbitrators, and the National Society of Professionals in Dispute Resolution. The National Employment Lawyers Association has endorsed the substantive provisions of the Due Process Protocol. It has been incorporated into the ADR procedures of the Massachusetts Commission Against Discrimination (MCAD) and into the Report of the United States Secretary of Labor's Task Force in Excellence in State and Local Government.

NOTIFICATION

If an employer intends to utilize the dispute resolution services of the Association in an employment ADR plan, it shall, at least thirty (30) days prior to the planned effective date of the program: (1) notify the Association of its intention to do so, and (2) provide the Association with a copy of the employment dispute resolution plan. If an employer does not comply with this requirement, the Association reserves the right to decline its administrative services.

TYPES OF DISPUTES COVERED

The dispute resolution procedures contained in this booklet can be inserted into an employee personnel manual, an employment application of an individual employment agreement, or can be used for a specific dispute. They do not apply to disputes arising out of collective bargaining agreements.

NATIONAL RULES FOR THE RESOLUTION OF EMPLOYMENT DISPUTES

1. Applicable Rules of Arbitration

The parties shall be deemed to have made these rules a part of their arbitration agreement whenever they have provided for arbitration by the American Arbitration Association (hereinafter AAA) or under its National Rules for the Resolution of Employment Disputes. If a party establishes that an adverse material inconsistency exists between the arbitration agreement and these rules, the arbitrator shall apply these rules.

If, within thirty (30) days after the Association's commencement of administration, a party seeks judicial intervention with respect to a pending arbitration, the Association will suspend administration for sixty (60) days to permit the party to obtain a stay of arbitration from the Court. These rules, and any amendment of them, shall apply in the form obtaining at the time the demand for arbitration or submission is received by the AAA.

2. Notification

An employer intending to incorporate these rules or to refer to the dispute resolution services of the AAA in an employment ADR plan, shall, at least thirty (30) days prior to the planned effective date of the program:

(a) notify the Association of its intention to do so; and,

(b) provide the Association with a copy of the employment dispute resolution plan.

Compliance with this requirement shall not preclude an arbitrator from entertaining challenges as provided in Section 1. If an employer does not comply with this requirement, the Association reserves the right to decline its administrative services.

3. AAA as Administrator of the Arbitration

When parties agree to arbitrate under these rules or when they provide for arbitration by the AAA and an arbitration is initiated under these rules, they thereby authorize the AAA to administer the arbitration. The authority and duties of the AAA are prescribed in these rules and may be carried out through such of the AAA's representatives as it may direct.

4. Initiation of Arbitration

Arbitration shall be initiated in the following manner:

(a) The parties may submit a joint request for arbitration.

(b) In the absence of a joint request for arbitration:

  (1) The initiating party (hereinafter Claimant[s]) shall:

    (A) File a written notice (hereinafter Demand) of its intention to arbitrate at any regional office of the AAA, within the time limit established by the applicable statute of limitations if the dispute involves statutory rights. If no statutory rights are involved, the time limit established by the applicable arbitration agreement shall be followed. Any dispute over such issues shall be referred to the arbitrator. The filing shall be made in duplicate, and each copy shall include the applicable arbitration agreement. The Demand shall set forth the names, addresses, and telephone numbers of the parties; a brief statement of the nature of the dispute; the amount in controversy, if any; the remedy sought; and requested hearing location.

    (B) Simultaneously mail a copy of the Demand to the party (hereinafter Respondent[s]).

    (C) Include with its Demand the applicable filing fee, unless the parties agree to some other method of fee advancement.

  (2) The Respondent(s) shall file an Answer with the AAA within ten (10) days after the date of the letter from the AAA acknowledging receipt of the Demand. The Answer shall provide the Respondent's brief response to the claim and the issues presented. The Respondent(s) shall make its filing in duplicate with the AAA and simultaneously shall mail a copy of the Answer to the Claimant.

  (3) The Respondent(s):

    (A) May file a counterclaim with the AAA within ten (10) days after the letter from the AAA acknowledging receipt of the Demand. The filing shall be made in duplicate. The counterclaim shall set forth the nature of the claim, the amount in controversy, if any, and the remedy sought.

    (B) Simultaneously shall mail a copy of any counterclaim to the Claimant.

    (C) Shall include with its filing the applicable filing fee provided for by these rules.

(4) The Claimant shall file an Answer to the counterclaim with the AAA within ten (10) days after the date of the letter from the AAA acknowledging receipt of the counterclaim. The Answer shall provide Claimant's brief response to the counterclaim and the issues presented. The Claimant shall make its filing in duplicate with the AAA and simultaneously shall mail a copy of the Answer to the Respondent(s).

The form of any filing in these rules shall not be subject to technical pleading requirements.

5. Changes of Claim

Before the appointment of the arbitrator, if either party desires to offer a new or different claim or counterclaim, such party must do so in writing by filing a written statement with the AAA and simultaneously mailing a copy to the other party(s), who shall have ten (10) days from the date of such mailing within which to file an Answer with the AAA. After the appointment of the arbitrator, a party may offer a new or different claim or counterclaim only at the discretion of the arbitrator.

6. Administrative and Mediation Conferences

Before the appointment of the arbitrator, any party may request, or the AAA, in its discretion, may schedule an administrative conference with a representative of the AAA and the parties and/or their representatives. The purpose of the administrative conference is to organize and expedite the arbitration, explore its administrative aspects, establish the most efficient means of selecting an arbitrator, and to consider mediation as a dispute resolution option. There is no administrative fee for this service.

At any time after the filing of the Demand, with the consent of the parties, the AAA will arrange a mediation conference under its Mediation Rules to facilitate settlement. The mediator shall not be any arbitrator appointed to the case, except by mutual agreement of the parties. There is no administrative fee for initiating a mediation under AAA Mediation Rules for parties to a pending arbitration.

7. Discovery

The arbitrator shall have the authority to order such discovery, by way of deposition, interrogatory, document production, or otherwise, as the arbitrator considers necessary to a full and fair exploration of the issues in dispute, consistent with the expedited nature of arbitration.

8. Arbitration Management Conference

As soon as possible after the appointment of the arbitrator but not later than sixty (60) days thereafter, the arbitrator shall conduct an Arbitration Management

Conference with the parties and/or their representatives, in person or by telephone, to explore and resolve matters that will expedite the arbitration proceedings. The specific matters to be addressed include:

(a)   The issues to be arbitrated;

(b)   The date, time, place, and estimated duration of the hearing;

(c)   The resolution of outstanding discovery issues and establishment of discovery parameters;

(d)   The law, standards, rules of evidence, and burdens of proof that are to apply to the proceeding;

(e)   The exchange of stipulations and declarations regarding facts, exhibits, witnesses, and other issues;

(f)   The names of witnesses (including expert witnesses), the scope of witness testimony, and witness exclusion;

(g)   The value of bifurcating;

(h)   Arbitration into a liability phase and damages phase;

(i)   The need for a stenographic record;

(j)   Whether the parties will summarize their arguments orally or in writing;

(k)   The form of the award;

(l)   Any other issues relating to the subject or conduct of the arbitration; and

(m) The allocation of attorneys' fees and costs.

The arbitrator shall issue oral or written orders reflecting his or her decisions on the above matters and may conduct additional conferences when the need arises.

There is no AAA administrative fee for an Arbitration Management Conference.

9. Location of the Arbitration

The parties may designate the location of the arbitration by mutual agreement. In the absence of such agreement before the appointment of the arbitrator, any party may request a specific hearing location by notifying the AAA in writing and simultaneously mailing a copy of the request to the other party(s). If the AAA receives no objection within ten (10) days of the date of the request, the hearing shall be held at the requested location. If a timely objection is filed with the AAA, the AAA shall have the power to determine the location, and its decision shall be final and binding. After the appointment of the arbitrator, the arbitrator shall resolve all disputes regarding the location of the hearing.

10. Date and Time of Hearing

The arbitrator shall have the authority to set the date and time of the hearing in consultation with the parties.

11. Qualifications to Serve as Arbitrator and Rights of Parties to Disqualify Arbitrator

(a) Standards of Experience and Neutrality

  (1) Arbitrators serving under these rules shall be experienced in the field of employment law.

  (2) Arbitrators serving under these rules shall have no personal or financial interest in the results of the proceedings in which they are appointed and shall have no relation to the underlying dispute or to the parties or their counsel that may create an appearance of bias.

  (3) The roster of available arbitrators will be established on a nondiscriminatory basis, diverse by gender, ethnicity, background, and qualifications.

  (4) The Association may, upon request of a party or upon its own initiative, supplement the list of proposed arbitrators in disputes arising out of individually negotiated employment contracts with persons from the regular Commercial Roster, to allow the Association to respond to the particular needs of the dispute. In multi-arbitrator disputes, at least one of the arbitrators shall be experienced in the field of employment law.

(b) Standards of Disclosure by Arbitrator

Prior to accepting appointment, the prospective arbitrator shall disclose all information that might be relevant to the standards of neutrality set forth in this Section, including, but not limited to, service as a neutral in any past or pending case involving any of the parties, or that may prevent a prompt hearing.

(c) Disqualification for Failure to Meet Standards of Experience and Neutrality

An arbitrator may be disqualified in two ways:

  (1) No later than ten (10) days after the appointment of the arbitrator, all parties jointly may challenge the qualifications of an arbitrator by communicating their objection to the AAA in writing. Upon receipt of a joint objection, the arbitrator shall be replaced.

  (2) Any party may challenge the qualifications of an arbitrator by communicating its objection to the AAA in writing. Upon receipt of the objection, the AAA either shall replace the arbitrator or communicate the objection to the other parties. If any party believes that the objection does not merit disqualification of the arbitrator, the party shall so communicate to the AAA and to the other parties within ten (10) days of the receipt of the objection from the AAA. Upon objection of a party to the service of an arbitrator, the AAA shall determine whether the arbitrator should be disqualified and shall inform the parties of its decision, which shall be conclusive.

12. Number and Appointment of Neutral Arbitrators

(a) If the parties do not specify the number of arbitrators, the dispute shall be heard and determined by one arbitrator. If the parties cannot agree upon the number of arbitrators, the AAA shall have the authority to determine the number of arbitrators.

(b) If the parties have not appointed an arbitrator and have not provided any method of appointment, the arbitrator shall be appointed in the following manner:

(1) Immediately after it receives the Demand, the AAA shall mail simultaneously to each party a letter containing an identical list of the names of all arbitrators who are members of the regional Employment Dispute Resolution Roster. To the extent possible, the AAA will provide the names of the parties or their representatives in recent cases decided by the listed arbitrators.

(2) Each party shall have ten (10) days from the date of the letter in which to select the name of a mutually acceptable arbitrator to hear and determine their dispute. If the parties cannot agree upon a mutually acceptable arbitrator, they shall so notify the AAA. Within ten (10) days of the receipt of that notice, the AAA shall send the parties a shorter list of arbitrators who are members of the regional Employment Dispute Resolution Roster. Each party shall have ten (10) days from the date of the letter containing the revised list to strike any names objected to, number the remaining names in order of preference, and return the list to the AAA. If a party does not return the list within the time specified, all of the listed persons shall be deemed acceptable to that party.

(3) The AAA shall invite the acceptance of the arbitrator whom both parties have selected as mutually acceptable or, in the case of resort to the ranking procedure, the arbitrator who has received the highest rating in the order of preference that the parties have specified.

(4) If the parties fail to agree on any of the persons whom the AAA submits for consideration, or if mutually acceptable arbitrators are unable to act, or if for any other reason the appointment cannot be made from the list of persons whom the AAA submits for consideration, the AAA shall have the power to make the appointment from among other members of the Roster without the submission of additional lists.

13. Vacancies

If for any reason an arbitrator is unable to perform the duties of the office, the AAA may, on proof satisfactory to it, declare the office vacant. The vacancy shall be filled in accordance with applicable provisions of these Rules.

In the event of a vacancy in a panel of neutral arbitrators after the hearings have commenced, the remaining arbitrator or arbitrators may continue with the hearing and determination of the controversy, unless the parties agree otherwise.

14. Representation

Any party may be represented by counsel or by any other person whom the party designates. For parties without representation, the AAA will, upon request, provide reference to institutions which might offer assistance. A party who intends to be represented shall notify the other party and the AAA of the name and address of the representative at least ten (10) days prior to the date set for the hearing or conference at which that person is first to appear. If a representative files a Demand or an Answer, the obligation to give notice of representative status is deemed satisfied.

15. Attendance at Hearings

The arbitrator shall have the authority to exclude witnesses, other than a party, from the hearing during the testimony of any other witness. The arbitrator also shall have the authority to decide whether any person who is not a witness may attend the hearing.

16. Confidentiality of Hearings

The arbitrator shall maintain the confidentiality of the arbitration and shall have the authority to make appropriate rulings to safeguard that confidentiality, unless the parties agree otherwise or the law provides to the contrary.

17. Postponements

The arbitrator: (1) may postpone any hearing upon the request of a party for good cause shown, (2) must postpone any hearing upon the mutual agreement of the parties, and (3) may postpone any hearing on his or her own initiative.

18. Oaths

Before proceeding with the first hearing, each arbitrator may take an oath of office and, if required by law, shall do so. The arbitrator may require witnesses to testify under oath administered by any duly qualified person and, if it is required by law or requested by any party, shall do so.

19. Majority Decision

All decisions and awards of the arbitrators must be by a majority, unless the unanimous decision of all arbitrators is expressly required by the arbitration agreement or by law.

20. Order of Proceedings and Communication with Arbitrators

A hearing shall be opened by: (1) filing the oath of the arbitrator, where required; (2) recording the date, time, and place of the hearing; (3) recording the presence of the arbitrator, the parties, and their representatives, if any; and (4) receiving into the record the Demand and the Answer, if any. The arbitrator may, at the beginning of the hearing, ask for statements clarifying the issues involved.

The parties shall bear the same burdens of proof and burdens of producing evidence as would apply if their claims and counterclaims had been brought in court.

Witnesses for each party shall submit to direct and cross-examination as approved by the arbitrator. With the exception of the rules regarding the allocation of the burdens of proof and going forward with the evidence, the arbitrator has the authority to set the rules for the conduct of the proceedings and shall exercise that authority to afford a full and equal opportunity to all parties to present any evidence that the arbitrator deems material and relevant to the resolution of the dispute.

Documentary and other forms of physical evidence, when offered by either party, may be received in evidence by the arbitrator.

The names and addresses of all witnesses and a description of the exhibits in the order received shall be made a part of the record.

There shall be no ex parte communication with the arbitrator, unless the parties and the arbitrator agree to the contrary in advance of the communication.

21. Arbitration in the Absence of a Party or Representative

Unless the law provides to the contrary, the arbitration may proceed in the absence of any party or representative who, after due notice, fails to be present or fails to obtain a postponement. An award shall not be based solely on the default of a party. The arbitrator shall require the party who is in attendance to present such evidence as the arbitrator may require for the making of the award.

22. Evidence

The parties may offer such evidence as is relevant and material to the dispute and shall produce such evidence as the arbitrator deems necessary to an understanding and determination of the dispute. An arbitrator or other person authorized by law to subpoena witnesses or documents may do so upon the request of any party or independently.

The arbitrator shall be the judge of the relevance and materiality of the evidence offered, and conformity to legal rules of evidence shall not be necessary. The arbitrator may in his or her discretion direct the order of proof, bifurcate proceedings, exclude cumulative or irrelevant testimony or other evidence, and direct the parties to focus their presentations on issues the decision of which could dispose of all or part of the case. All evidence shall be taken in the presence of all of the arbitrators and all of the parties, except where any party is absent, in default, or has waived the right to be present.

23. Evidence by Affidavit or Declaration and Post-Hearing Filing of Documents or Other Evidence

The arbitrator may receive and consider the evidence of witnesses by affidavit but shall give it only such weight as the arbitrator deems it entitled to after consideration of any objection made to its admission.

If the parties agree or the arbitrator directs that documents or other evidence may be submitted to the arbitrator after the hearing, the documents or other evidence shall be filed with the AAA for transmission to the arbitrator, unless the parties agree to a different method of distribution. All parties shall be afforded an opportunity to examine such documents or other evidence and to lodge appropriate objections, if any.

24. Inspection or Investigation

An arbitrator finding it necessary to make an inspection or investigation in connection with the arbitration shall direct the AAA to so advise the parties. The arbitrator shall set the date and time, and the AAA shall notify the parties. Any party who so desires may be present during the inspection or investigation. In the event that one or all parties are not present during the inspection or investigation, the arbitrator shall make an oral or written report to the parties and afford them an opportunity to comment.

25. Interim Measures

At the request of any party, the arbitrator may take whatever interim measures he or she deems necessary with respect to the dispute, including measures for the conservation of property.

Such interim measures may be taken in the form of an interim award, and the arbitrator may require security for the costs of such measures.

26. Closing of Hearing

The arbitrator shall specifically inquire of all parties whether they have any further proofs to offer or witnesses to be heard. Upon receiving negative replies or if satisfied that the record is complete, the arbitrator shall declare the hearing closed.

If briefs are to be filed, the hearing shall be declared closed as of the final date set by the arbitrator for the receipt of briefs. If documents are to be filed as provided in Section 23 and the date set for their receipt is later than that set for the receipt of briefs, the later date shall be the date of closing the hearing. The time limit within which the arbitrator is required to make the award shall commence to run, in the absence of other agreements by the parties, upon closing of the hearing.

27. Reopening of Hearing

The hearing may be reopened by the arbitrator upon the arbitrator's initiative, or upon application of a party for cause shown, at any time before the award is made.

If reopening the hearing would prevent the making of the award within the specific time agreed on by the parties in the contract(s) out of which the controversy has arisen, the matter may not be reopened, unless the parties agree on an extension of time. When no specific date is fixed in the contract, the arbitrator may reopen the hearing and shall have thirty (30) days from the closing of the reopened hearing within which to make an award.

28. Waiver of Oral Hearing

The parties may provide, by written agreement, for the waiver of oral hearings in any case. If the parties are unable to agree as to the procedure, the AAA shall specify a fair and equitable procedure.

29. Waiver of Objection/Lack of Compliance with These Rules

Any party who proceeds with the arbitration after knowledge that any provision or requirement of these rules has not been complied with, and who fails to state objections thereto in writing, shall be deemed to have waived the right to object.

30. Extensions of Time

The parties may modify any period of time by mutual agreement. The AAA or the arbitrator may for good cause extend any period of time established by these Rules, except the time for making the award. The AAA shall notify the parties of any extension.

31. Serving of Notice

Each party shall be deemed to have consented that any papers, notices, or process necessary or proper for the initiation or continuation of an arbitration under these Rules; for any court actions in connection therewith; or for the entry of judgment on an award made under these procedures may be served on a party by mail addressed to the party or its representative at the last known address or by personal service, in or outside the state where the arbitration is to be held.

The AAA and the parties may also use facsimile transmission, telex, telegram, or other written forms of electronic communication to give the notices required by these Rules.

32. The Award

(a) The award shall be made promptly by the arbitrator and, unless otherwise agreed by the parties or specified by law, no later than thirty (30) days from the date of closing of the hearing or, if oral hearings have been waived, from the date of the AAA's transmittal of the final statements and proofs to the arbitrator.

(b) The award shall be in writing and shall be signed by a majority of the arbitrators and shall provide the written reasons for the award, unless the parties agree otherwise. It shall be executed in the manner required by law.

(c) The arbitrator may grant any remedy or relief that the arbitrator deems just and equitable, including any remedy or relief that would have been available to the parties had the matter been heard in court. The arbitrator shall, in the award, assess arbitration fees, expenses, and compensation as provided in Sections 36, 37, and 38 in favor of any party and, in the event any administrative fees or expenses are due the AAA, in favor of the AAA.

(d) The arbitrator shall have the authority to provide for the reimbursement of representative's fees, in whole or in part, as part of the remedy, in accordance with applicable law.

(e) If the parties settle their dispute during the course of the arbitration, the arbitrator may set forth the terms of the settlement in a consent award.

(f) The parties shall accept as legal delivery of the award the placing of the award or a true copy thereof in the mail, addressed to a party or its representative at the last known address, personal service of the award, or the filing of the award in any manner that may be required by law.

(g) The arbitrator's award shall be final and binding. Judicial review shall be limited, as provided by law.

33. Modification of Award

Within twenty (20) days after the transmittal of an award, any party, upon notice to the other parties, may request the arbitrator to correct any clerical, typographical, technical, or computational errors in the award. The arbitrator is not empowered to redetermine the merits of any claim already decided.

The other parties shall be given ten (10) days to respond to the request. The arbitrator shall dispose of the request within twenty (20) days after transmittal by the AAA to the arbitrator of the request and any response thereto.

If applicable law requires a different procedural time frame, that procedure shall be followed.

34. Release of Documents

The AAA shall, upon the written request of a party, furnish to the party, at that party's expense, certified copies of any papers in the AAA's case file that may be required in judicial proceedings relating to the arbitration.

35. Judicial Proceedings and Exclusion of Liability

(a) No judicial proceeding by a party relating to the subject matter of the arbitration shall be deemed a waiver of the party's right to arbitrate.

(b) Neither the AAA nor any arbitrator in a proceeding under these rules is or shall be considered a necessary or proper party in judicial proceedings relating to the arbitration.

(c) Parties to these procedures shall be deemed to have consented that judgment upon the arbitration award may be entered in any federal or state court having jurisdiction.

(d) Neither the AAA nor any arbitrator shall be liable to any party for any act or omission in connection with any arbitration conducted under these procedures.

36. Administrative Fees

As a not-for-profit organization, the AAA shall prescribe filing and other administrative fees to compensate it for the cost of providing administrative services. The AAA administrative fee schedule in effect at the time the demand for arbitration or submission agreement is received shall be applicable. The filing fee shall be advanced by the initiating party or parties, subject to final apportionment by the arbitrator in the award.

The AAA may, in the event of extreme hardship on any party, defer or reduce the administrative fees.

37. Expenses

Unless otherwise agreed by the parties, the expenses of witnesses for either side shall be borne by the party producing such witnesses. All expenses of the arbitration, including required travel and other expenses of the arbitrator, AAA representatives, and any witness and the costs relating to any proof produced at the direction of the arbitrator, shall be borne equally by the parties, unless they agree otherwise or unless the arbitrator directs otherwise in the award.

38. Neutral Arbitrator's Fees

Arbitrators shall charge a rate consistent with the arbitrator's stated rate of compensation. If there is disagreement concerning the terms of compensation, an appropriate rate shall be established with the arbitrator by the AAA and confirmed to the parties.

Any arrangement for the compensation of a neutral arbitrator shall be made through the AAA and not directly between the parties and the arbitrator. Payment of the arbitrator's fees and expenses shall be made by the AAA from the fees and moneys collected by the AAA from the parties for this purpose.

39. Deposits

The AAA may require the parties to deposit in advance of any hearings such sums of money as it deems necessary to cover the expenses of the arbitration, including the arbitrator's fee, if any, and shall render an accounting to the parties and return any unexpended balance at the conclusion of the case.

40. Interpretation and Application of Rules

The arbitrator shall interpret and apply these rules as they relate to the arbitrator's powers and duties. When there is more than one arbitrator and a difference arises among them concerning the meaning or application of these Rules, it shall be resolved by a majority vote. If that is not possible, either an arbitrator or a party may refer the question to the AAA for final decision. All other procedures shall be interpreted and applied by the AAA.

EMPLOYMENT MEDIATION RULES

1. Agreement of the Parties

Whenever, by provision in an employment dispute resolution program or by separate submission, the parties have provided for mediation or conciliation of existing or future disputes under the auspices of the American Arbitration Association (hereinafter AAA) or under these rules, they shall be deemed to have made these rules, as amended and in effect as of the date of the submission of the dispute, a part of their agreement.

2. Initiation of Mediation

Any party to an employment dispute may initiate mediation by filing with the AAA a submission to mediation or a written request for mediation pursuant to these rules, together with the applicable administrative fee.

3. Request for Mediation

A request for mediation shall contain a brief statement of the nature of the dispute and the names, addresses, and telephone numbers of all parties to the dispute and those who will represent them, if any, in the mediation. The initiating party shall simultaneously file two copies of the request with the AAA and one copy with every other party to the dispute.

4. Appointment of Mediator

Upon receipt of a request for mediation, the AAA will appoint a qualified mediator to serve. Normally, a single mediator will be appointed, unless the parties agree otherwise or the AAA determines otherwise. If the agreement of the parties names a mediator or specifies a method of appointing a mediator, that designation or method shall be followed.

5. Qualifications of Mediator

No person shall serve as a mediator in any dispute in which that person has any financial or personal interest in the result of the mediation, except by the written consent of all parties. Prior to accepting an appointment, the prospective mediator shall disclose any circumstance likely to create a presumption of bias or prevent a prompt meeting with the parties. Upon receipt of such information, the AAA shall either replace the mediator or immediately communicate the information to the parties for their comments. In the event that the parties disagree as to whether the mediator shall serve, the AAA will appoint another mediator. The AAA is authorized to appoint another mediator, if the appointed mediator is unable to serve promptly.

6. Vacancies

If any mediator shall become unwilling or unable to serve, the AAA will appoint another mediator, unless the parties agree otherwise.

7. Representation

Any party may be represented by a person of the party's choice. The names and addresses of such persons shall be communicated in writing to all parties and to the AAA.

8. Date, Time, and Place of Mediation

The mediator shall fix the date and the time of each mediation session. The mediation shall be held at the appropriate regional office of the AAA, or at any other convenient location agreeable to the mediator and the parties, as the mediator shall determine.

9. Identification of Matters in Dispute

At least ten (10) days prior to the first scheduled mediation session, each party shall provide the mediator with a brief memorandum setting forth its position with regard to the issues that need to be resolved. At the discretion of the mediator, such memoranda may be mutually exchanged by the parties.

At the first session, the parties will be expected to produce all information reasonably required by the mediator to understand the issues presented. The mediator may require any party to supplement such information.

10. Authority of Mediator

The mediator does not have the authority to impose a settlement on the parties but will attempt to help them reach a satisfactory resolution of their dispute. The mediator is authorized to conduct joint and separate meetings with the parties and to make oral and written recommendations for settlement.

Whenever necessary, the mediator may also obtain expert advice concerning technical aspects of the dispute, provided that the parties agree and assume the expenses of obtaining such advice. Arrangements for obtaining such advice shall be made by the mediator or the parties, as the mediator shall determine.

The mediator is authorized to end the mediation whenever, in the judgment of the mediator, further efforts at mediation would not contribute to a resolution of the dispute between the parties.

11. Privacy

Mediation sessions are private. The parties and their representatives may attend mediation sessions. Other persons may attend only with the permission of the parties and with the consent of the mediator.

12. Confidentiality

Confidential information disclosed to a mediator by the parties or by witnesses in the course of the mediation shall not be divulged by the mediator. All records, reports, or other documents received by a mediator while serving in that capacity shall be confidential. The mediator shall not be compelled to divulge such records or to testify in regard to the mediation in any adversary proceeding or judicial forum.

The parties shall maintain the confidentiality of the mediation and shall not rely on, or introduce as evidence in any arbitral, judicial, or other proceeding:

(a) Views expressed or suggestions made by another party with respect to a possible settlement of the dispute;

(b) Admissions made by another party in the course of the mediation proceedings;

(c) Proposals made or views expressed by the mediator; or

(d) The fact that another party had or had not indicated willingness to accept a proposal for settlement made by the mediator.

13. No Stenographic Record

There shall be no stenographic record of the mediation process.

14. Termination of Mediation

The mediation shall be terminated:

(a) By the execution of a settlement agreement by the parties;

(b) By a written declaration of the mediator to the effect that further efforts at mediation are no longer worthwhile; or

(c) By a written declaration of a party or parties to the effect that the mediation proceedings are terminated.

15. Exclusion of Liability

Neither the AAA nor any mediator is a necessary party in judicial proceedings relating to the mediation.

Neither the AAA nor any mediator shall be liable to any party for any act or omission in connection with any mediation conducted under these rules.

16. Interpretation and Application of Rules

The mediator shall interpret and apply these rules insofar as they relate to the mediator's duties and responsibilities. All other rules shall be interpreted and applied by the AAA.

17. Expenses

The expenses of witnesses for either side shall be paid by the party producing such witnesses. All other expenses of the mediation, including required traveling and other expenses of the mediator and representatives of the AAA and the expenses of any witness and the cost of any proofs or expert advice produced at the direct request of the mediator, shall be borne equally by the parties, unless they agree otherwise.

Source: Reprinted with permission of the American Arbitration Association.

Appendix G

AMERICAN ARBITRATION ASSOCIATION INTERNATIONAL ARBITRATION RULES

INTRODUCTION

The world business community uses arbitration to resolve commercial disputes arising in the global marketplace. Supportive laws are in place. The New York Convention of 1958 has been widely adopted, providing a favorable legislative climate. Arbitration clauses are enforced. International commercial arbitration awards are recognized by national courts in most parts of the world, even more than foreign court judgments. Arbitration institutions have been established in many countries to administer international cases. Many have entered into cooperative arrangements with the American Arbitration Association. These International Arbitration Rules have been developed to encourage greater use of such services. By providing for arbitration under these rules, parties can avoid the uncertainty of having to petition a local court to resolve procedural impasses. These rules are intended to provide effective arbitration services to world business through the use of administered arbitration. Parties can arbitrate future disputes under these rules by inserting the following clause into their contracts:

INTERNATIONAL ARBITRATION RULES

Article 1

1. Where parties have agreed in writing to arbitrate disputes under these International Arbitration Rules, the arbitration shall take place in accordance with their provisions, as in effect at the date of commencement of the arbitration, subject to whatever modifications the parties may adopt in writing.
2. These rules govern the arbitration, except that, where any such rule is in conflict with any provision of the law applicable to the arbitration from which the parties cannot derogate, that provision shall prevail.
3. These rules specify the duties and responsibilities of the administrator, the American Arbitration Association. The administrator may provide services through its own facilities or through the facilities of arbitral institutions with whom it has agreements of cooperation.

I. Commencing the Arbitration

Notice of Arbitration and Statement of Claim

Article 2

1. The party initiating arbitration (claimant) shall give written notice of arbitration to the administrator and to the party or parties against whom a claim is being made (respondent[s]).
2. Arbitral proceedings shall be deemed to commence on the date on which the administrator receives the notice of arbitration.
3. The notice of arbitration shall include the following:
   a. a demand that the dispute be referred to arbitration;
   b. the names and addresses of the parties;
   c. a reference to the arbitration clause or agreement that is invoked;
   d. a reference to any contract out of or in relation to which the dispute arises;
   e. a description of the claim and an indication of the facts supporting it;
   f. the relief or remedy sought and the amount claimed; and
   g. proposals as to the number of arbitrators, the place of arbitration, and the language(s) of the arbitration.
4. Upon receipt of the notice of arbitration, the administrator shall communicate with all parties with respect to the arbitration and shall acknowledge the commencement of the arbitration.

Statement of Defense and Counterclaim

Article 3

1. Within 30 days after the commencement of the arbitration, a respondent shall submit a written statement of defense, responding to the issues raised in the notice of arbitration, to the claimant and any other parties, and to the administrator.

2. At the time a respondent submits its statement of defense, a respondent may make counterclaims or assert setoffs as to any claim covered by the agreement to arbitrate, as to which the claimant shall within 30 days submit a written statement of defense to the respondent and any other parties and to the administrator.

3. A respondent shall respond to the administrator, the claimant, and other parties within 30 days after the commencement of the arbitration as to any proposals the claimant may have made as to the number of arbitrators, the place of the arbitration, or the language(s) of the arbitration, except to the extent that the parties have previously agreed as to these matters.

4. The arbitral tribunal, or the administrator if the arbitral tribunal has not yet been formed, may extend any of the time limits established in this article if it considers such an extension justified.

Amendments to Claims

Article 4

During the arbitral proceedings, any party may amend or supplement its claim, counterclaim, or defense, unless the tribunal considers it inappropriate to allow such amendment or supplement because of the party's delay in making it, prejudice to the other parties or any other circumstances. A party may not amend or supplement a claim or counterclaim if the amendment or supplement would fall outside the scope of the agreement to arbitrate.

II. The Tribunal

Number of Arbitrators

Article 5

If the parties have not agreed on the number of arbitrators, one arbitrator shall be appointed, unless the administrator determines in its discretion that three arbitrators are appropriate because of the large size, complexity, or other circumstances of the case.

Appointment of Arbitrators

Article 6

1. The parties may mutually agree upon any procedure for appointing arbitrators and shall inform the administrator as to such procedure.

2. The parties may mutually designate arbitrators, with or without the assistance of the administrator. When such designations are made, the parties shall notify the administrator so that notice of the appointment can be communicated to the arbitrators, together with a copy of these rules.

3. If within 45 days after the commencement of the arbitration, all of the parties have not mutually agreed on a procedure for appointing the arbitrator(s) or have not mutually agreed on the designation of the arbitrator(s), the administrator shall, at the written request of any party, appoint the arbitrator(s) and designate the presiding arbitrator. If all of the parties have mutually agreed upon a procedure for appointing the arbitrator(s) but all appointments have not been made within the time limits provided in that procedure, the administrator shall, at the written request of any party, perform all functions provided for in that procedure that remain to be performed.

4. In making such appointments, the administrator, after inviting consultation with the parties, shall endeavor to select suitable arbitrators. At the request of any party or on its own initiative, the administrator may appoint nationals of a country other than that of any of the parties.

5. Unless the parties have agreed otherwise no later than 45 days after the commencement of the arbitration, if the notice of arbitration names two or more claimants or two or more respondents, the administrator shall appoint all the arbitrators.

Challenge of Arbitrators

Article 7

1. Arbitrators acting under these rules shall be impartial and independent. Prior to accepting appointment, a prospective arbitrator shall disclose to the administrator any circumstance likely to give rise to justifiable doubts as to the arbitrator's impartiality or independence. If, at any stage during the arbitration, new circumstances arise that may give rise to such doubts, an arbitrator shall promptly disclose such circumstances to the parties and to the administrator. Upon receipt of such information from an arbitrator or a party, the administrator shall communicate it to the other parties and to the tribunal.

2. No party or anyone acting on its behalf shall have any ex parte communication relating to the case with any arbitrator, or with any candidate for appointment as party-appointed arbitrator except to advise the candidate of the general nature of the controversy and of the anticipated proceedings and to discuss the candidate's qualifications, availability, or independence in relation to the parties, or to discuss the suitability of candidates for selection as a third arbitrator where the parties or party-designated arbitrators are to participate in that selection. No party or anyone acting on its behalf shall have any ex parte communication relating to the case with any candidate for presiding arbitrator.

Article 8

1. A party may challenge any arbitrator whenever circumstances exist that give rise to justifiable doubts as to the arbitrator's impartiality or independence. A party wishing to challenge an arbitrator shall send notice of the challenge to the administrator within 15 days after being notified of the appointment of the arbitrator or within 15 days after the circumstances giving rise to the challenge become known to that party.

2. The challenge shall state in writing the reasons for the challenge.

3. Upon receipt of such a challenge, the administrator shall notify the other parties of the challenge. When an arbitrator has been challenged by one party, the other party or parties may agree to the acceptance of the challenge and, if there is agreement, the arbitrator shall withdraw. The challenged arbitrator may also withdraw from office in the absence of such agreement. In neither case does withdrawal imply acceptance of the validity of the grounds for the challenge.

Article 9

If the other party or parties do not agree to the challenge or the challenged arbitrator does not withdraw, the administrator in its sole discretion shall make the decision on the challenge.

Replacement of an Arbitrator

Article 10

If an arbitrator withdraws after a challenge, or the administrator sustains the challenge, or the administrator determines that there are sufficient reasons to accept the resignation of an arbitrator, or an arbitrator dies, a substitute arbitrator shall be appointed pursuant to the provisions of Article 6, unless the parties otherwise agree.

Article 11

1. If an arbitrator on a three-person tribunal fails to participate in the arbitration for reasons other than those identified in Article 10, the two other arbitrators shall have the power in their sole discretion to continue the arbitration and to make any decision, ruling, or award, notwithstanding the failure of the third arbitrator to participate. In determining whether to continue the arbitration or to render any decision, ruling, or award without the participation of an arbitrator, the two other arbitrators shall take into account the stage of the arbitration, the reason, if any, expressed by the third arbitrator for such nonparticipation, and such other matters as they consider appropriate in the circumstances of the case. In the event that the two other arbitrators determine not to continue the arbitration without the participation of the third arbitrator, the administrator on proof satisfactory to

it shall declare the office vacant, and a substitute arbitrator shall be appointed pursuant to the provisions of Article 6, unless the parties otherwise agree.

2. If a substitute arbitrator is appointed under either Article 10 or Article 11, the tribunal shall determine at its sole discretion whether all or part of any prior hearings shall be repeated.

III. General Conditions

Representation

Article 12

Any party may be represented in the arbitration. The names, addresses, and telephone numbers of representatives shall be communicated in writing to the other parties and to the administrator. Once the tribunal has been established, the parties or their representatives may communicate in writing directly with the tribunal.

Place of Arbitration

Article 13

1. If the parties disagree as to the place of arbitration, the administrator may initially determine the place of arbitration, subject to the power of the tribunal to determine finally the place of arbitration within 60 days after its constitution. All such determinations shall be made having regard for the contentions of the parties and the circumstances of the arbitration.

2. The tribunal may hold conferences, hear witnesses, or inspect property or documents at any place it deems appropriate. The parties shall be given sufficient written notice to enable them to be present at any such proceedings.

Language

Article 14

If the parties have not agreed otherwise, the language(s) of the arbitration shall be that of the documents containing the arbitration agreement, subject to the power of the tribunal to determine otherwise based upon the contentions of the parties and the circumstances of the arbitration. The tribunal may order that any documents delivered in another language shall be accompanied by a translation into the language(s) of the arbitration.

Pleas as to Jurisdiction

Article 15

1. The tribunal shall have the power to rule on its own jurisdiction, including any objections with respect to the existence, scope, or validity of the arbitration agreement.

2. The tribunal shall have the power to determine the existence or validity of a contract of which an arbitration clause forms a part. Such an arbitration clause shall be treated as an agreement independent of the other terms of the contract. A decision by the tribunal that the contract is null and void shall not for that reason alone render invalid the arbitration clause.

3. A party must object to the jurisdiction of the tribunal or to the arbitrability of a claim or counterclaim no later than the filing of the statement of defense, as provided in Article 3, to the claim or counterclaim that gives rise to the objection. The tribunal may rule on such objections as a preliminary matter or as part of the final award.

Conduct of the Arbitration

Article 16

1. Subject to these rules, the tribunal may conduct the arbitration in whatever manner it considers appropriate, provided that the parties are treated with equality and that each party has the right to be heard and is given a fair opportunity to present its case.

2. The tribunal, exercising its discretion, shall conduct the proceedings with a view to expediting the resolution of the dispute. It may conduct a preparatory conference with the parties for the purpose of organizing, scheduling, and agreeing to procedures to expedite the subsequent proceedings.

3. The tribunal may in its discretion direct the order of proof, bifurcate proceedings, exclude cumulative or irrelevant testimony or other evidence, and direct the parties to focus their presentations on issues the decision of which could dispose of all or part of the case.

4. Documents or information supplied to the tribunal by one party shall at the same time be communicated by that party to the other party or parties.

Further Written Statements

Article 17

1. The tribunal may decide whether the parties shall present any written statements in addition to statements of claims and counterclaims and statements of defense, and it shall fix the periods of time for submitting any such statements.

2. The periods of time fixed by the tribunal for the communication of such written statements should not exceed 45 days. However, the tribunal may extend such time limits if it considers such an extension justified.

Notices

Article 18

1. Unless otherwise agreed by the parties or ordered by the tribunal, all notices, statements, and written communications may be served on a party by air mail,

air courier, facsimile transmission, telex, telegram, or other written forms of electronic communication addressed to the party or its representative at its last known address or by personal service.

2. For the purpose of calculating a period of time under these rules, such period shall begin to run on the day following the day when a notice, statement, or written communication is received. If the last day of such period is an official holiday at the place received, the period is extended until the first business day which follows. Official holidays occurring during the running of the period of time are included in calculating the period.

Evidence

Article 19

1. Each party shall have the burden of proving the facts relied on to support its claim or defense.

2. The tribunal may order a party to deliver to the tribunal and to the other parties a summary of the documents and other evidence which that party intends to present in support of its claim, counterclaim, or defense.

3. At any time during the proceedings, the tribunal may order parties to produce other documents, exhibits, or other evidence it deems necessary or appropriate.

Hearings

Article 20

1. The tribunal shall give the parties at least 30 days' advance notice of the date, time, and place of the initial oral hearing. The tribunal shall give reasonable notice of subsequent hearings.

2. At least 15 days before the hearings, each party shall give the tribunal and the other parties the names and addresses of any witnesses it intends to present, the subject of their testimony, and the languages in which such witnesses will give their testimony.

3. At the request of the tribunal or pursuant to mutual agreement of the parties, the administrator shall make arrangements for the interpretation of oral testimony or for a record of the hearing.

4. Hearings are private, unless the parties agree otherwise or the law provides to the contrary. The tribunal may require any witness or witnesses to retire during the testimony of other witnesses. The tribunal may determine the manner in which witnesses are examined.

5. Evidence of witnesses may also be presented in the form of written statements signed by them.

6. The tribunal shall determine the admissibility, relevance, materiality, and weight of the evidence offered by any party. The tribunal shall take into account appli-

cable principles of legal privilege, such as those involving the confidentiality of communications between a lawyer and client.

Interim Measures of Protection

Article 21

1. At the request of any party, the tribunal may take whatever interim measures it deems necessary, including injunctive relief and measures for the protection or conservation of property.
2. Such interim measures may be taken in the form of an interim award, and the tribunal may require security for the costs of such measures.
3. A request for interim measures addressed by a party to a judicial authority shall not be deemed incompatible with the agreement to arbitrate or a waiver of the right to arbitrate.
4. The tribunal may in its discretion apportion costs associated with applications for interim relief in any interim award or in the final award.

Experts

Article 22

1. The tribunal may appoint one or more independent experts to report to it, in writing, on specific issues designated by the tribunal and communicated to the parties.
2. The parties shall provide such an expert with any relevant information or produce for inspection any relevant documents or goods that the expert may require. Any dispute between a party and the expert as to the relevance of the requested information or goods shall be referred to the tribunal for decision.
3. Upon receipt of an expert's report, the tribunal shall send a copy of the report to all parties, who shall be given an opportunity to express, in writing, their opinion on the report. A party may examine any document on which the expert has relied in such a report.
4. At the request of any party, the parties shall be given an opportunity to question the expert at a hearing. At this hearing, parties may present expert witnesses to testify on the points at issue.

Default

Article 23

1. If a party fails to file a statement of defense within the time established by the tribunal without showing sufficient cause for such failure, as determined by the tribunal, the tribunal may proceed with the arbitration.

2. If a party, duly notified under these rules, fails to appear at a hearing without showing sufficient cause for such failure, as determined by the tribunal, the tribunal may proceed with the arbitration.

3. If a party, duly invited to produce evidence, fails to do so within the time established by the tribunal without showing sufficient cause for such failure, as determined by the tribunal, the tribunal may make the award on the evidence before it.

Closure of Hearing

Article 24

1. After asking the parties if they have any further testimony or evidentiary submissions and upon receiving negative replies or if satisfied that the record is complete, the tribunal may declare the hearings closed.

2. The tribunal in its discretion, on its own motion, or upon application of a party, may reopen the hearings at any time before the award is made.

Waiver of Rules

Article 25

A party who knows that any provision of the rules or requirement under the rules has not been complied with, but proceeds with the arbitration without promptly stating an objection in writing thereto, shall be deemed to have waived the right to object.

Awards, Decisions, and Rulings

Article 26

1. When there is more than one arbitrator, any award, decision, or ruling of the arbitral tribunal shall be made by a majority of the arbitrators. If any arbitrator fails to sign the award, it shall be accompanied by a statement of the reason for the absence of such signature.

2. When the parties or the tribunal so authorize, decisions or rulings on questions of procedure may be made by the presiding arbitrator, subject to revision by the tribunal.

Form and Effect of the Award

Article 27

1. Awards shall be made in writing, promptly by the tribunal, and shall be final and binding on the parties. The parties undertake to carry out any such award without delay.

2. The tribunal shall state the reasons upon which the award is based, unless the parties have agreed that no reasons need be given.

3. The award shall contain the date and the place where the award was made, which shall be the place designated pursuant to Article 13.

4. An award may be made public only with the consent of all parties or as required by law.

5. Copies of the award shall be communicated to the parties by the administrator.

6. If the arbitration law of the country where the award is made requires the award to be filed or registered, the tribunal shall comply with such requirement.

7. In addition to making a final award, the tribunal may make interim, interlocutory, or partial orders and awards.

Applicable Laws and Remedies

Article 28

1. The tribunal shall apply the substantive law(s) or rules of law designated by the parties as applicable to the dispute. Failing such a designation by the parties, the tribunal shall apply such law(s) or rules of law as it determines to be appropriate.

2. In arbitrations involving the application of contracts, the tribunal shall decide in accordance with the terms of the contract and shall take into account usages of the trade applicable to the contract.

3. The tribunal shall not decide as amiable compositeur or ex aequo et bono, unless the parties have expressly authorized it to do so.

4. A monetary award shall be in the currency or currencies of the contract unless the tribunal considers another currency more appropriate, and the tribunal may award such pre-award and post-award interest, simple or compound, as it considers appropriate, taking into consideration the contract and applicable law.

5. Unless the parties agree otherwise, the parties expressly waive and forego any right to punitive, exemplary, or similar damages, unless a statute requires that compensatory damages be increased in a specified manner. This provision shall not apply to any award of arbitration costs to a party to compensate for dilatory or bad-faith conduct in the arbitration.

Settlement or Other Reasons for Termination

Article 29

1. If the parties settle the dispute before an award is made, the tribunal shall terminate the arbitration and, if requested by all parties, may record the settlement in the form of an award on agreed terms. The tribunal is not obliged to give reasons for such an award.

2. If the continuation of the proceedings becomes unnecessary or impossible for any other reason, the tribunal shall inform the parties of its intention to terminate the proceedings. The tribunal shall thereafter issue an order terminating the arbitration, unless a party raises justifiable grounds for objection.

Interpretation or Correction of the Award

Article 30

1. Within 30 days after the receipt of an award, any party, with notice to the other parties, may request the tribunal to interpret the award or correct any clerical, typographical, or computation errors or make an additional award as to claims presented but omitted from the award.
2. If the tribunal considers such a request justified, after considering the contentions of the parties, it shall comply with such a request within 30 days after the request.

Costs

Article 31

The tribunal shall fix the costs of arbitration in its award. The tribunal may apportion such costs among the parties if it determines that such apportionment is reasonable, taking into account the circumstances of the case. Such costs may include:

a. the fees and expenses of the arbitrators;
b. the costs of assistance required by the tribunal, including its experts;
c. the fees and expenses of the administrator;
d. the reasonable costs for legal representation of a successful party; and
e. any such costs incurred in connection with an application for interim or emergency relief pursuant to Article 21.

Compensation of Arbitrators

Article 32

Arbitrators shall be compensated based upon their amount of service, taking into account their stated rate of compensation and the size and complexity of the case. The administrator shall arrange an appropriate daily or hourly rate, based on such considerations, with the parties and with each of the arbitrators as soon as practicable after the commencement of the arbitration. If the parties fail to agree on the terms of compensation, the administrator shall establish an appropriate rate and communicate it in writing to the parties.

Deposit of Costs

Article 33

1. When claims are filed, the administrator may request the filing party to deposit appropriate amounts, as an advance for the costs referred to in Article 31, paragraphs (a), (b), and (c).
2. During the course of the arbitral proceedings, the tribunal may request supplementary deposits from the parties.
3. If the deposits requested are not paid in full within 30 days after the receipt of the request, the administrator shall so inform the parties, in order that one or the other of them may make the required payment. If such payments are not made, the tribunal may order the suspension or termination of the proceedings.
4. After the award has been made, the administrator shall render an accounting to the parties of the deposits received and return any unexpended balance to the parties.

Confidentiality

Article 34

Confidential information disclosed during the proceedings by the parties or by witnesses shall not be divulged by an arbitrator or by the administrator. Unless otherwise agreed by the parties or required by applicable law, the members of the tribunal and the administrator shall keep confidential all matters relating to the arbitration or the award.

Exclusion of Liability

Article 35

The members of the tribunal and the administrator shall not be liable to any party for any act or omission in connection with any arbitration conducted under these rules, except that they may be liable for the consequences of conscious and deliberate wrongdoing.

Interpretation of Rules

Article 36

The tribunal shall interpret and apply these rules insofar as they relate to its powers and duties.

The administrator shall interpret and apply all other rules.

Source: Reprinted with permission of the American Arbitration Association.

Appendix H

CPR CORPORATE POLICY STATEMENT
on
ALTERNATIVES TO LITIGATION©

COMPANY

We recognize that for many disputes there is a less expensive, more effective method of resolution than the traditional lawsuit. Alternative dispute resolution (ADR) procedures involve collaborative techniques which can often spare businesses the high costs of litigation.

In recognition of the foregoing, we subscribe to the following statements of principle on behalf of our company and its domestic subsidiaries.

In the event of a business dispute between our company and another company which has made or will then make a similar statement, we are prepared to explore with that other party resolution of the dispute through negotiation or ADR techniques before pursuing full scale litigation. If either party believes that the dispute is not suitable for ADR techniques, or if such techniques do not produce results satisfactory to the disputants, either party may proceed with litigation.

CHIEF EXECUTIVE OFFICER

CHIEF LEGAL OFFICER

DATE

Our major operating subsidiaries are

Source: © 1998, CPR Institute for Dispute Resolution, New York, NY. Reprinted with permission. The CPR Institute for Dispute Resolution is a nonprofit initiative of 500 general counsel of major corporations, leading law firms, and prominent legal academics in support of alternatives to litigation. CPR develops new methods to resolve business and public disputes by alternative dispute resolution (ADR).

More than 4,000 operating companies have committed to the Corporate Policy Statement on Alternatives to Litigation©. The CPR Corporate Pledge obliges subscribing companies to seriously explore negotiation, mediation or other ADR processes in conflicts arising with other signatories before pursuing full-scale litigation. The list of companies subscribing on behalf of themselves and their major operating subsidiaries is available on the CPR Web site (www.cpradr.org).

CPR Institute for Dispute Resolution
366 Madison Avenue, New York, NY 10017 Tel (212) 949-6490
Fax (212) 949-8859 Internet: www.cpradr.org

Appendix I

CPR LAW FIRM POLICY STATEMENT
on
ALTERNATIVES TO LITIGATION

_____
FIRM
_____
ADDRESS
_____
CITY, STATE, ZIP
_____
TELEPHONE

We recognize that for many disputes there may be methods more effective for resolution than traditional litigation. Alternative dispute resolution (ADR) procedures—used in conjunction with litigation or independently—can significantly reduce the costs and burdens of litigation and result in solutions not available in court.

In recognition of the foregoing, we subscribe to the following statements of principle on behalf of our firm.

First, appropriate lawyers in our firm will be knowledgeable about ADR.

Second, where appropriate, the responsible attorney will discuss with the client the availability of ADR procedures so the client can make an informed choice concerning resolution of the dispute.

_____
PARTNER EXECUTING ON BEHALF OF FIRM (signature)
_____
PARTNER'S NAME (please print or type)
_____
DATE

Source: © 1998, CPR Institute for Dispute Resolution, New York, NY. Reprinted with permission. The CPR Institute for Dispute Resolution is a nonprofit initiative of 500 general counsel of major corporations, leading law firms, and prominent legal academics in support of alternatives to litigation. CPR develops new methods to resolve business and public disputes by alternative dispute resolution (ADR).

More than 1,500 law firms have signed the CPR Law Firm Policy Statement on Alternatives to Litigation©, including 400 of the nation's 500 largest firms. The Law Firm Pledge obliges subscribing firms to assure that appropriate lawyers are knowledgeable about ADR and to discuss the availability of ADR with clients. The full list of subscribers is available on the CPR Web site (www.cpradr.org).

CPR Institute for Dispute Resolution
366 Madison Avenue, New York, NY 10017 Tel (212) 949-6490
Fax (212) 949-8859 Internet: www.cpradr.org

INDEX

A

Ad hoc arbitration, 237
Ad hoc proceeding, 161
Adhesion contracts, 299
Adjudicative processes, 30–31
  arbitration, 30
  mediation–arbitration, 30
  private judging, 30–31
ADR adjudicatory mechanisms, 155
ADR. *See* Alternative dispute
  resolution
Adversarial, common law model, 4
Advisory or mock jury, 127
Advisory verdict, 134
Agreement to mediate, 98
Alternative dispute resolution
  advantages, 31–34
    cost, 31
    flexibility, 33
    internationalization, 33–34
    privacy, 32–33
    productive outcomes, 32
    timeliness, 31
  defined, 28
  disadvantages, 34–54
    enforcement concerns, 50–54
    procedural concerns, 34–42
    public policy issues, 42–50
  ethical concerns arising from use of,
    324–29
  lawyers views of, 105
  processes, 29–31
    adjudicative, 30–31
    party–driven, 29–30
Appeal, 7
Arbitral panel, selection of, 72–76
Arbitration Act of 1888, 200
Arbitration award, 173, 178
Arbitration Center of the World
  Intellectual Property Organization
  (WIPO), 240
Arbitration, 30
  and mediation compared, 106
  court-annexed, 188–94

defined, historical development of,
  157–61
employment, 201–11
grievance, 212–13
grievance or rights, 218–27
hearing, 177–78
interest, 212–13
labor, 200–01
remedies, 173
within monetary limits, 318
Arbitrator, selection of, 172–76
Authority to settle, 98

B

Baseball arbitration, 214
"Best case" presentations, 145
Business ADR, future trends in,
  333–35
Business dispute resolution systems,
  overview of, 296–97

C

Canons, 173
Case of first impression, 102
Caucus, 99
China International Economic and
  Trade Commission (CIETAC), 239
Choice of process memorandum, 311
Choice-of-forum clause, 234
Choice-of-law clause, 234
Civil justice expense and delay
  reduction plan, 133
Civil Justice Reform Act, 91
Civil litigation systems, 4–6
Closure, 100
Code of ethics for arbitrators in
  commercial disputes, 344–53
  Canon I, 345–46
  Canon II, 346–48
  Canon III, 343
  Canon IV, 348–49
  Canon V, 349–50
  Canon VI, 350
  Canon VII, 351–53

Coerced participation, 324
Coercion, 80
Collaborative model, 63
Commercial Arbitration and Mediation
  Centre for the Americas (CAMCA),
  259
Commercial arbitration, vs. private
  judging, 275–80
Commercial dealings, 247
Common law, 333
Comparability groups, 214
Competitive negotiation training, 64
Competitive-compromise model, 63
Conditional summary jury trial, 143
Confidences, 111
Conflict of interest, 82, 97
Contract private judge, defined,
  266, 267–70
Court-annexed arbitration, 188–94
Court-annexed minitrial, 143
Court-supervised judging, temporary
  judges, 270
Court-supervised private judging, 270
Cross-cultural negotiation, 83–84

D

Delaware ADR program, 95–96
Demand form for arbitration, sample,
  165
Direct negotiation, vs. other ADR, 62
Disclosure, 174
Discovery, 7, 317
Dispute Review Board, 319
Domestic arbitration, distinctions
  between international commercial
  and, 253–59
Due process, 35, 280–84

E

Employee contracts and handbooks,
  298
Employment arbitration, 201–11
Environmental ADR, 116
Equal protection, 35, 284–88
Evaluative mediation, 97

429

External dispute resolution policies, 310–16
  role of customers, 311–16
  role of insurer, 311
  role of outside counsel, 310–11
External disputes, 28, 310

F

Facilitated negotiation, 99
Facilitative mediation, 97
Facilitative mediation conference, steps in, 101
Facilitator, 111
Fast-track arbitration, 240
Federal Arbitration Act (FAA), 158
Federal Mediation and Conciliation Service, 90
Federal Rule of Evidence, 408, 67
Federal Rules of Civil Procedure, 91, 271
Federal Service Labor-Management Relations Statute, 213
Final offer selection, 214
First Amendment, 289
Forms
  demand for arbitration, 166
  juror questionnaire, 135
  jury verdict, 137
  submission agreement, 163–64
  submission for dispute resolution, 166
  voluntary labor arbitration rules, 202
Frivolous lawsuit, 12

G

Grievance and interest arbitration, 212–13
Grievance or rights arbitration
  defined, 212
  overview of, 218–27
Grounds for appeal under the FAA, 179–80

H

High-low arbitration, 173
Hong Kong International Arbitration Centre (HKIAC), 239

I

Impartiality, 111
Impression management, 74
Individual employment contract

exclusion, 201
Information exchange, 145
Inquisitorial, civil law model, 4
Institutional arbitration, defined, 238
Institutionalizing dispute resolution, future trends in ADR, 329–33
Interest and grievance arbitration, 212–13
Interest arbitration
  defined, 212
  overview of, 213–18
Internal dispute resolution policies, 298–310
Internal disputes, 28, 298
Internal union administration, 213
International administering organizations, summary of, 238–40
International arbitration
  sample clauses for, 235
  summary checklist, 237
International Chamber of Commerce (ICC), 238
International commercial arbitration, 234
  distinctions between domestic and, 253–59
International commercial disputes, national litigation vs. arbitration, 234–52
  concerns about neutrality, 234–40
  dealing with multiple lawsuits, 240–43
  enforceability of arbitration clauses and awards, 244–53
International Court of Arbitration (ICC Court), 238
International negotiation, 83–84
Israeli-Palestinian Peace Process, 72

J

Judgment of acquiescence, 146
Juror questionnaire, sample, 135
Jury verdict form, sample, 137
Just cause cases, 222

K

Knowing and voluntary waiver, 300

L

Labor arbitration, 200–01
Labor Management Relations Act of 1947, 90
Legal reforms

attorneys, 23
  damages, 22
  party rights, 23
  procedure, 23
Legitimacy, 76
Liability crisis, 8
Licensing and regulation of ADR professionals, 334
Litigation
  civil systems, 4–6
  impact on business, 8–22
  legal reforms, 22–24
  stages of lawsuit and use of ADR, 6–8
London Court of International Arbitration (LCIA), 239

M

Management prerogative or rights, 213
Mandatory court-annexed ADR programs, 333
Mandatory mediation, 117–21
Med-arb, 161
Mediation, 29
  advantages, 93–94
  and arbitration compared, 106
  attorneys use of, 334–35
  disadvantages, 95–96
  forms of, 96–97
  historical development of, 90–93
  introduction to, 93–96
  mandatory, 117–21
  overview of, 97–101
  selecting cases appropriate for, 101–06
Mediation-arbitration, 30
Mediator opening statement, 98
Mediator
  model standards for conduct of, 338–44
  roles and ethics of, 110–16
  selection of, 106–10
Memorandum of Agreement, 122
Minitrial, 29
  advantages, 147–48
    expertise of neutral advisor, 148
    maintenance of business relationship, 148
    party control over the process, 147–48
  birth of, 146–47
  compared to summary jury trial, 150

components of, 143–47
　"best case" presentations, 145
　information exchange, 145
　initiation of procedure, 144
　limited discovery, 144
　selection of neutral advisor,
　　144–45
　settlement discussions with
　　neutral advisor, 145–47
defined, 143
disadvantages, 148–49
　credibility of witnesses, 149
　need for courtís legal
　　interpretation, 149
　unequal bargaining power
　　between disputants, 149
overview of, 143
Misrepresentation, 77
Mock or advisory jury, 127
Model standards of conduct for
　mediators, 338–44
Modifying an arbitration award, 179

N

National Franchise Mediation
　Program, 303
National Labor Relations Act (NLRA),
　201
National Labor Relations Board
　(NLRB), 201
National Mediation Board (NMB),
　200
National Railroad Adjustment Board
　(NRAB), 200
Negotiating, with uncooperative
　parties, 74–76
Negotiation ethics, 77–83
Negotiation models, 63–65
　collaborative, 63
　comparing, 65
　competitive-compromise, 63
Negotiation practice, skills-oriented
　overview, 70–74
Negotiation, 29, 62
　ADR trends in, 84
　defined, 62–63
　effect of representation in, 65–66
　evaluating the outcome, 76–77
　international and cross-cultural,
　　83–84
　relationship to the legal process,
　　66–69
Neutral advisor, 144

New York Convention, 244
Noncontingent, 77
Nondomestic award, 244
Nonfiling and nonassistance
　covenants, 324

O

Ombudsman, 304
Order of appointment, 270
Order of general reference, party
　agreement on request for, 272
Order of reference, 271
Outcome-determinative, 188

P

Panama or Inter-American
　Convention, 250
Party opening statements, 99
Party-driven processes, 29–30
　mediation, 29
　minitrial, 29
　negotiation, 29
　summary jury trial, 30
Plenary review, 277
Post-award actions, 179
Predispute arbitration agreement
　(PDAA), 162
Predispute contract clauses
　defined, 311
　from the American Arbitration
　　Association, 318–22
Pre-hearing preparation, 177
Preliminary hearing, 177
Pre-SJT conference, 134
Presumption of arbitrability, 169
Pretrial stage, 7
Principle of competence-competence,
　254
Private arbitration, compared to
　private judging, 276
Private judging, 30–31
　compared to private arbitration, 276
　constitutional concerns, 280–89
　　due process, 280–84
　　equal protection, 284–88
　defined, 265
　overview of, 266–67
　vs. commercial arbitration, 275–80
Privilege, 304
Pro se, 177
Procedural arbitrability, 164
Procedural order, 146
Professional conduct, 334

Public access　42

Q

Quasi-judicial immunity, 108
Question-and-answer session, 136

R

Railway Labor Act of 1920 (RLA),
　200
Reciprocity, 247
Referee, 270
Referee's report, 271
Reference statutes, 266
Referenced-mandated judging, 270–75
　general or special references,
　　271–75
　referees or special masters, 270–71
Religious law systems, 6
Rent-a-judge, 266
Rent-a-jury, 270
Representation, 65
Rules by reference, 62

S

Self-help remedies, 200
Settlement talks, 136
SJT. *See* Summary jury trial
Special master, 271
Special reference, 272
Submission agreement, 162
　sample, 163–64
Submission form for dispute
　resolution, sample, 166
Substantive arbitrability, 164
Summary jury trial (SJT), 30
　advantages, 136–41
　　confidentiality of proceedings
　　　and documents, 137–40
　　empowerment of businesspeople,
　　　141
　　psychological benefits, 141
　　respect for jury process, 141
　　savings in time and costs, 136–37
　compared to minitrial, 150
　components of, 127–36
　　hearing, 134–36
　　pre-SJT conference, 134
　　screening cases, 127–34
　　selection of jurors, 134
　　settlement talks, 136
　defined, 125
　development of, 126–27
　disadvantages

constitutional concerns, 142–43
lack of precedential value, 142
mixed results on time and cost
    benefits, 141–42
predictive value, 142
Summary presentations, 127

T

Temporary judges, 270
Terms of reference, 238
The Judicial Improvements Act of
    1990, 133
Title VII claims, 300

Trial, 7
Trial de novo, 188

U

UNCITRAL Arbitration Rules, 236
UNCITRAL Model Law, 236
Uniform Arbitration Act, 158

V

Vacating the arbitration award, 179
Voluntary arbitration
    advantages, 183–86
    aspects of, 161–83

agreement to arbitrate, 162–72
arbitration hearing, 177–78
arbitration or arbitral award, 178
defined, 161
determining procedures, 161–62
disadvantages, 186–87
post-award actions, 179–83
pre-hearing preparation, 177
selection of arbitrator or arbitral
    panel, 172–76
Voluntary labor arbitration rules,
    sample, 202
Voluntary petition, 270

CASE INDEX

Aetna Life Ins. Co. v. The Superior Court of San Diego County, 273–75

Babcock v. Northwest Memorial Hospital, 9–11

Bank of America National v. Hotel Rittenhouse, 42–49

Borden, Inc. v. Meiji Milk Products Co., Ltd., 255–57

Carman v. McDonnell Douglas Corporation, 306–09

Celulosa Del Pacifico S.A. v. A. Ahlstrom Corporation, 248–50

Cincinnati Gas and Electric Company v. General Electric Company, 138–40

City and County of Denver v. The District Court in and for the City and County of Denver, 331–33

Collins v. Blue Cross Blue Shield of Michigan, 181–82

Commonwealth Coatings Corp. v. Continental Casualty Co., 174–76

D.R., By His Parents and v. East Brunswick Bd. of Education, 50–54

Damon v. Sun Company, Inc., 78–80

Degaetano v. Smith Barney, Inc., 169–72

Dworkin-Cosell Interair Courier Services, Inc., et al. v. Avraham, 245–47

E.E.O.C. v. Astra USA, Inc., 325–29

Federal Reserve Bank of Minneapolis v. Carey-Canada, Inc., 129

Ferlito v. Johnson & Johnson Products, Inc., 12–14

G. Heileman Brewing Company v. Joseph Oat Corporation, 117–21

Gibson v. Neighborhood Health Clinics, 299–303

Haworth, Inc. v. Steelcase, Inc., 16–21

Hill v. Gateway 2000, Inc., 312–15

Honeywell Protection Services v. Tandem Telecommunications, Inc., 192–93

In re Goodman Beverage Company, Inc., and Teamsters Local 571, 225–27

In re Monroe Manufacturing, Inc. and Union of Needletrades, Industrial & Textile Employees, Local 2638, 223–25

In re NLO, Inc., 131–33

In re Waterloo Community School District and American Federation of State, County, & Municipal Employees (AFSCME) Council 61, Local 2749, 214–18

J & C Dyeing, Inc., v. Drakon, Inc., 167–68

Jerome S. Wagshal v. Mark W. Foster, 107–10

Kientzy v. McDonnell Douglas Corporation, 304–06

OíNeil v. Hilton Head Hospital, 203–04

Old Republic Ins. Co. v. St. Paul Fire & Marine Ins. Co., 277–80

Poly Software International, Inc., et al. v. Yu Su, Datamost Corporation, et al., 112–16

Productos Mercantiles E Industriales, S.A. v. Faberge USA, Inc., 251–53

Prudential v. Lai, 206–08

Rhea v. Massey-Ferguson, Inc., 41

Richardson v. Sport Shinko (Waikiki Corporation), 189–91

Ronald H. Howlett v. Holiday Inns, Inc., 80–82

Root v. Honorable Floyd Schenk, 282–83

San-Dar Associates v. Adams, 194

Sauk County v. Grede Foundries, Inc. and Teel Plastics, Inc. v. William Beard, et al., 103–04

Scherk v. Alberto-Culver Co., 241–43

Schwarzkopf Technologies Corporation v. Ingersoll Cutting Tool Company, 92–93

Securities Industry Assín v. Connolly, 159–61

Sheng V. Starkey Laboratories, Inc., 68–69

Solorzano v. The Superior Court of Los Angeles County, 285–88

State Farm Mutual Automobile Insurance Company v. Broadnax, et al., 36–40

United Paperworkers International Union, AFL-CIO v. Misco, Inc., 219–21